TEACHER THINKING IN CULTURAL CONTEXTS

SUNY Series, The Social Context of Education
Christine E. Sleeter, editor

TEACHER THINKING IN CULTURAL CONTEXTS

edited by

Francisco A. Ríos

State University of New York Press

Published by
State University of New York Press, Albany

© 1996 State University of New York

For information, address State University of New York
Press, State University Plaza, Albany, N.Y. 12246

Production by Dana Foote
Marketing by Fran Keneston

Library of Congress Cataloging-in-Publication Data

Teacher thinking in cultural contexts / edited by Francisco A. Rios.
   p.   cm. — (SUNY series, social context of education)
   Includes bibliographical references and index
ISBN 0–7914–2881–8 (hardcover : alk. paper). — ISBN 0–7914–2882–6
   (pbk. : alk. paper)
   1. Teacher-student relationships—United States. 2. Multicultural
education—United States. 3. Teachers—United States—Attitudes.
4. Teaching—United States—Sociological aspects. 5. Educational
anthropology—United States. I. Rios, Francisco, 1956–
   II. Series.
            LB1033.T26   1996
371.1'023—dc20   95–51310
                                                        CIP

10 9 8 7 6 5 4 3 1

CONTENTS

Part III
Thinking about How to Change Thinking

PREFACE

As a student in graduate school, I struggled with finding my place in academia. On the one hand was my interest and enthusiasm for psychology applied to education. I looked forward to seeing the next semester's class schedule in educational and cognitive psychology and wondered how I could possibly fit into my schedule all the classes I wanted to take. On the other hand was my passionate interest in issues of student diversity and knowledge of the overwhelming disparity in academic achievement experienced by students of color in comparison to their mainstream counterparts.

As I began those classes in educational and cognitive psychology, I noticed a "void" of discussion about student diversity. This was usually all right because my professors often let me tailor assignments to fit my interest in cultural and linguistic diversity. I was dismayed, however, when one professor who told me (perhaps he was playing the "devil's advocate") that issues of student diversity "complicate" the establishment of models of cognition. It then struck me that the field of educational and cognitive psychology might be advancing models of cognition that could be used to further define ethnic minority communities as deficient. I became determined to ensure that such "hegemonic" models of cognition would not be established, regardless of how much it "complicated" our work.

I became further committed to bridging the gap between the fields of educational and cognitive psychology and issues addressed in multicultural education. In a way these bridges resembled (though certainly on a different level) the bridges most scholars of color have had to build as they strive to be successful in academia while simultaneously maintaining a commitment to advancing the agendas critical to our communities. Perhaps this text is one tangible example of the kinds of bridges that need to be constructed.

This project could not be possible without the hard work and commitment of many individuals. First, I want to thank the people who have contributed to this book. Though they come from different communities and universities, I know that they are all committed to advancing the academic standing of students of color.

I would also like to thank Christine Sleeter for her encouragement and insight in the earliest phases of the development of this text. When I told her about my idea, she pushed me to make it become a reality and opened doors to assist me in making that happen. I know that I (and other contributors to this text) have been affected by her scholarly work and her supportive manner when relating to other scholars. Most importantly, she introduced me to Priscilla Ross at SUNY Press—an introduction for which I am most grateful.

I would also like to thank my colleagues at California State University—San Marcos for helping to create a climate in which people are rewarded for thinking in ways that build bridges. Of note is my continual appreciation for my colleagues in multicultural and bilingual education (Castaneda, Spencer-Green, Whitehorse, and Ulanoff) and in the middle-level teacher education cohort (Christopher, McDaniel, and Stowell). Thanks are also extended to Dean Lilly for his support, insight, and commitment to doing things differently.

Finally, I wish to thank my wife Deb and my children Zekial and Natalia for their enduring love, their undying support, and their life-affirming joy.

Francisco A. Ríos
February, 1994

INTRODUCTION

Francisco A. Ríos

The population of the United States is becoming increasingly multicultural. In education, students of color make up 40 percent of the students in U.S. schools (Garcia, 1994). Since 1981, the majority of students in public, central city schools have been African American and/or Hispanic (U.S. Department of Education, National Center for Education Statistics, 1993a). With this increase in students of color in schools is documentation showing that students are treated differently, and that the cultural background of the student is often a reason for this differential treatment (Cazden, 1986; Jackson & Corsca, 1974; Morine-Dershimer, 1985; Sadker & Sadker, 1985). For example, Sadker and Sadker (1985) found that teachers tend to interact with, call on, praise, and intellectually challenge white, male, middle-class students most and reprimand black, male students most. Morine-Dershimer (1985) found that minority students' contributions to discussions received less attention when compared with those of majority students. Unfortunately, the research in this area has so far been limited to behavioral indices, with a minimal attempt made to understand why (that is, to uncover the underlying thinking processes) teachers treat students of color differently. Only after understanding teachers' cognitive processes and products can we more fully answer the question Cazden (1986 p. 447) asks: "Is this helpful individualization or detrimental bias?"

Of equal importance is documentation showing that the number of teachers of color is substantially small: 13 percent of all teachers are nonwhite (U.S. Department of Education, National Center for Education Statistics, 1993b). One fear resulting from this disparity is that Euro-American[1] teachers will not reflectively and critically question the social, political, historical, or cultural tradition of their own educational experience and will thereby replay the "hidden" curriculum taught to them, which might serve to "colonize the mind" of these students of color. The hidden curriculum, Eisner (1985) suggests, includes messages about individual students (for example, in using more wait time, the teacher expects the student to come to the right answer and thus sees the student as capable), about how students relate to each other and authority figures (in allowing students a say in the classroom rules, the teacher expects students to participate actively in a climate of democratic decision making), and about the society in general (in portraying Mexican-Americans only as farm workers, no matter how positively, the teacher implies that farm work is their only "place"). Thus the failure to think through fully the social, cultural, and political implications of teaching in cultural contexts will undoubtedly ensure that opportunities for the advancement of students of color will continue to shrink.

With the increase in students of color, then, comes a corresponding need to understand teachers' cognitive processes and products with respect to the culturally diverse classroom. The purpose of this book is to shed light on current research on teacher thinking in cultural contexts and to identify promising practices in teacher education that take the most salient contextual variables into account. The purpose of this chapter will be to provide a brief overview of the nature of teacher thinking and its relationship to cultural contexts. In explicating the schism between traditional (positivist) approaches to teacher thinking and the need to understand that thinking in a cultural context, it will summarize an alternative research paradigm (interpretive) that serves to bridge this gap between thinking and context in the following chapters. Finally, before highlighting the chapter contributions, this chapter will detail the critical questions that are the focus of this volume.

TEACHER THINKING: AN OVERVIEW

An expanding body of research has focused attention on teacher cognition.[2] This research breaks from the dominant behavioristic paradigm of understanding teaching (such as the process-product orientations of Brophy & Good, 1974) by attending to the mental processes of teachers as a potential influence on their activity in classrooms (Jackson, 1968; Macmillan & Garrison, 1984). This move is informed by and parallels advances in cognitive psychology. Cognitive psychology rests on our knowledge of how information is processed (transformed, reduced, elaborated, stored, recovered, and used) (Neisser, 1967). From this, three interrelated principles of learning have emerged that guide work in the area of cognitive psychology:

> First, learning is a process of knowledge *construction*, not of knowledge recording or absorption. Second, knowledge is *knowledge-dependent;* people use current knowledge to construct new knowledge. Third, learning is highly tuned to the *situation* in which it takes place (Resnick, 1989, p. 1).

With this new move toward exploring cognitive processes comes interest in understanding the *origins* of teachers' actions as well as their consequences. This interest rests on the assumption that teachers are thoughtful practitioners not unlike other professionals (doctors, lawyers, architects, etc.) (Argyis & Schon, 1975; Schon, 1983; Shulman, 1986). Thus scholarship in this area suggests that teachers' cognition (beliefs, theories, and knowledge) play a powerful role in their behavior. The connection between teacher thinking and action, mediated by how one interprets what one sees, is of critical importance (Argyis and Schon, 1975; Borko, Cone, Russo, & Shavelson, 1975; Clark & Peterson, 1986; Mandl & Huber, 1982; Wittrock, 1987). For example, Leinhardt and Greeno (1986) suggest that because teaching is such a complex and demanding task, mechanisms for processing information and making rapid-fire decisions become the hallmark of effective teaching. Thus teachers' thinking serves as an "attention selection" device as well as a mechanism for chunking information for later recall and use. The belief, then, is that teacher thinking guides what teachers pay attention to and remember; this, in turn, triggers "routines of action," habitual ways of acting in the classroom (Calderhead, 1983; Kaplan, 1964; Lavely, Berger, Bullock, Follman, Kromrey, & Sawilowsky, 1986; Leinhardt & Greeno, 1986).

In contrast, this connection between teacher thinking and action has been questioned. For example, Morine-Dershimer (1979) found a degree of incongruity between belief and action in the classroom. Indeed, many factors outside of the teacher's control work to constrain behavior in ways that make for incongruity between thought and action (Duffy, 1977). Pearson (1985) advanced the notion that although some specific beliefs were incongruous with classroom action, the bulk of those beliefs (and especially the most critical beliefs) were congruent with action. He concluded by suggesting that teacher thinking is hierarchically structured, with certain beliefs, points of knowledge, and theories being more salient (and congruous) with action. Likewise, Tabachnick and Zeichner (1986) advance the notion that teachers move toward greater consistency between thought and action over time (either by changing thought or by changing action). Perhaps Munby (1984) was most accurate in suggesting that teacher thinking (beliefs and principles, specifically) is a significant part of a teacher's *context* for making choices in behavior.

One attempt to resolve the thought-to-action debate has been to focus on teachers' practical knowledge (beliefs, habits, and knowledge) that helps them to do their job. It is time bound, situation specific, personally compelling, and oriented toward action. As Elbaz (1981) explains it, teacher knowledge is held in relationship to practice and shapes practice.

A second characteristic of teacher cognition is that it is multidimensional (Calderhead, 1983; Elbaz, 1981; Leinhardt, 1990; Peterson, 1988; Shulman, 1987). Generally, it includes an individual's beliefs (see, for example, Pajares, 1992) and knowledge (with several kinds of knowledge of special interest, including discipline content, curriculum content, pedagogical content, and knowledge itself; Shulman, 1987). Other approaches linked to understanding the "what" of teacher thinking include the schema theory approach, the practical argument approach, and the concept-mapping approach. Alternately, instead of focusing on content (*the epistemological stream*, Solas, 1992), some researchers have chosen to conduct their research on the processes of thinking (*the psychological stream;* Solas, 1992), including how teachers plan (preactive and postactive), how teachers make decisions in the course of interaction (Clark & Peterson, 1986), and how teachers develop implicit theories (Clark, 1985; Copa, 1984; Kelly, 1955). Consistent with this latter stream is research linked to the reflection-in-action approach.

Another characteristic of teacher cognition is that it is not static; rather, it is fluid and dynamic (Anderson-Levitt, 1984; Schon, 1983). It is continually affected by contextual constraints and opportunities (Clark & Peterson, 1986) as well as by student actions. As teachers act on their thoughts, they are continually receiving feedback from their students (and/or colleagues). This feedback establishes a loop that provides valuable information and that has the potential to affect their thinking.

Although teacher cognition is located in the individual's psyche (such as in beliefs, values, biases, prejudices, and generalizations drawn from personal experience, "rules of thumb," etc.; Clark, 1988), it is critical to recognize the socializing power of the culture of teaching on one's thinking (Feiman-Nemser & Floden, 1986; Zeichner & Gore, 1990). Briefly, research in this areas suggests that there exists a shared "teaching" culture and that this culture of teaching imposes beliefs about appropriate ways of acting on the job. When most individuals share these beliefs, they become norms of actions (expected ways of interacting).

Teachers' thinking is shaped by the culture of teaching through a complex and extended process of socialization. Stephens (1967), for example, argues that all individuals have a degree of spontaneous primitive pedagogical tendencies that have evolutionary and survival value. Wright and Tuska (1968) provide a psychoanalytic explanation that suggests that the teacher-student relationship is a replica of the parent-child relationship with all its implications. Yet the most powerful force on teacher socialization before formal training is the thousands of hours each individual spends watching teachers in action throughout her or his educational experience, in what Lortie (1975) calls an "apprenticeship of observation." Additional socialization factors include the kind of university or college the preservice teacher attends, what courses she takes (general, subject matter specialty, and education course work), the student teaching experience, the classroom environment, and finally, how the teacher herself actively construes the meaning of these socializing demands and her response to them.

Even though scholars have begun to describe the characteristics of teacher cognition, fewer scholars have advanced a theoretical structure of teacher cognition. Of note then is the model advanced by Clark and Peterson (1986). In 1988, Porter and Brophy expanded the model to show more clearly the complex, multidimensional nature of teacher cognition (see the figure below). In this model, background, classroom, and external factors influence teachers' knowledge, planning, and routines for instruction. Teachers' knowledge, planning, and routines influence how teachers teach. This instructional activity influences the students' responses to that activity (which is influenced, in turn, by their

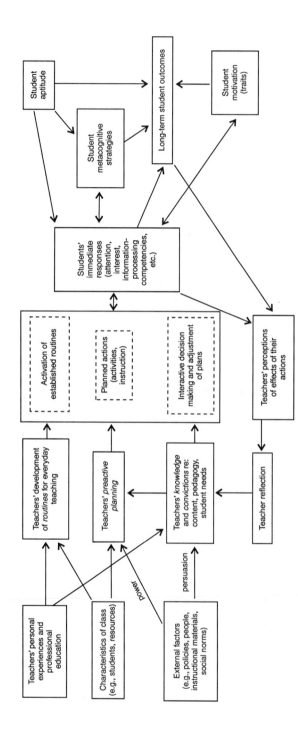

Porter and Brophy's Model of Factors Influencing Teachers' Instruction in Particular Contexts (from *Educational Leadership*, 45[8], p. 76; used with permission.)

aptitude, motivation, and metacognitive strategies) as well as potentially having a long-term effect on student outcomes. This model also demonstrates how teachers modify their instruction *when they reflect* on students' reactions (and outcomes), thus leading to potential changes in the teachers' own knowledge and future instructional actions.

Although this model is an attempt to describe a hidden process (teacher thought), it is not without limitations. One difficulty with the Porter and Brophy model is that it assumes that the individual is equally aware of and equally influenced by the characteristics in each "box" (for example, by the characteristics of the class, personal and professional experiences, external factors of the school, etc.) of the model.

A second difficulty is that it assumes that individuals are rational and logical when it comes to interpreting events and identifying a course of action. What's lacking in their model is the role of affect, prejudice, bias, desires, needs, self-serving tendencies, and so forth. For example, one must consider all the logic and reasoning used to undertake preservice and inservice training that takes place around preparing teachers to teach in culturally and linguistically responsive ways; it often comes up short because of the "resistance" to thinking about teaching in more inclusive ways. This resistance is not always rational, but it is very real. All these elements (affect, resistance, prejudices, etc.) are as critical to the sense making and decision making that take place in teaching as are those elements Porter and Brophy identify. Thus, beyond searching for scholarship that seeks to understand teacher thinking in context, we must also search to capture the greater complexity of teacher thinking that goes beyond rational sense making.

A final limitation of this model is that it focuses exclusively on the dynamic interaction between teacher, student, and curriculum. What is missing is contextualizing this dynamic in the school, community, and nation-state with an eye on the sociocultural and sociopolitical context.

In sum, our understanding of teacher cognition is continually expanding (for a more complete literature review, see chapter 1). We are aware of some of the elements that make up teacher cognition and are aware of the interdependency of cognition and action. We know that teacher thinking affects teacher action, which in turn affects teacher thinking. For the most part, what is missing in the research base on teacher cognition is the connection between teacher thinking and issues raised by our expanding interest in questions of diversity. Thus, even when teacher thinking is made explicit, the context in which this thinking exists in usually not the subject of specific discussion.

THE CULTURAL CONTEXT[3]

Without a doubt, the context in which teachers operate has a salient effect on how they think. Indeed, any competent professional needs to be aware of the particular contextual variables that pertain to a specific setting (Montero-Sieburth, 1989). Historically, however, mainstream educational researchers exploring teacher cognition have ignored contextual variables such as the students' cultural background or the degree to which changes in the curriculum influence their thinking (Shulman, 1986). "Good teaching" is what is advanced if educational problems are to be alleviated irrespective of the environment. Contextual variables may be ignored because they provide researchers with greater power to generalize findings across contexts and to describe teacher thinking in nearly universal terms. The negative result, however, is an inability to document teachers' thinking in specific contexts. A concomitant inability is demonstrating opportunities for reconstructing knowledge that take that thinking into account. What is needed, according to Montero-Sieburth (1989), is:

> viewing . . . teachers' implicit and explicit knowledge not in a vacuum but in relation to students, to the curriculum, and, most importantly, to the culture of the school and its socioeconomic, family, community, societal and institutional structures. Understanding how urban teachers' knowledge becomes enhanced or constrained by oppositional institutional and instructional contexts is central to the processes of producing, distributing, and regenerating that knowledge. (p. 342)

Indeed, a teacher's knowledge is socially constructed; accordingly, a teacher will automatically shape subject matter to account for ethnic or economic factors that influence or are held to influence students (Elbaz, 1981).

Without doubt, there is an increasing need for ways of thinking about issues of diversity with greater "cognitive sophistication." Simply putting teachers in situations that require them to think about issues of diversity is important but not sufficient for fostering this sophistication. For example, McDaniel, McDaniel, and McDaniel (1988) found that relying on experience alone was not sufficient because the need exists for a "cognitive modality" in learning that emphasizes abstract thinking, scientific and logical reasoning, and sense making of experience. This conclusion was further supported by a review of the literature on interventions designed to affect the thinking of preservice and inservice teachers with respect to issues of diversity (Grant & Secada, 1990). Among their findings are the following:

1. Programs that combine academic training with exposure to different ethnic groups (via fieldwork) were most effective for changing attitudes and improving teaching over those with just fieldwork or just academic training.
2. Based on the individual's thinking, different interventions may be required.

One particular approach to looking at what this cognitive sophistication may mean in terms of teacher thinking comes by way of the expert-novice research paradigm (see, for example, Artiles, this volume; Chi, Glaser & Rees, 1982; Larkin, McDermott, Simon, & Simon, 1980; Voss, Greene, Post, & Penner, 1983). Basically, this research approach attempts to understand differences between experts and novices in thinking and behaving. Based on this literature, we would expect that the most expert teachers might do the following:

1. Make more accurate inferences than novices.
2. Hierarchically structure knowledge so that there are greater connections among concepts.
3. Focus more on implicit states and conditions rather than explicit, surface features of the context.

Lavely et al. (1986) would add that expert teachers will have more knowledge than their novice counterparts. Therefore, we can assume that teacher experts who understand and account for the cultural context in their thinking will be more knowledgeable about student diversity and multicultural education, see beyond the surface-level features of the classroom environment, and see the connections between the teacher-student relationship and the broader social and institutional structures. These all help teachers achieve greater inferential power.

THINKING ACROSS INTERDISCIPLINARY LINES: SEARCHING FOR NEW QUESTIONS

The intent of this book, then, is to explore the relatively recent scholarship which attempts to pay attention to teacher cognition (content and/or processes) as it is developed and influenced by variables of race, ethnicity, and culture or by the movement toward a multicultural curriculum in classroom and school settings as they are understood from broader sociocultural, sociolingual, and/or sociopolitical perspectives. Fortunately, this task is made considerably easier by advances in other disciplines such as anthropology, sociolinguistics, and sociology as they have been applied by those who are cognitive psychologists and curriculum and instruction specialists. The result has been a move away from the positivist research paradigm and toward the interpretive paradigm (Erickson, 1986; Shulman, 1986).

On the surface level, the differences in these research paradigms are obvious. For example, the positivist research tradition applies quantitative methodologies via the cataloging of observable features of the classroom (such as teacher behavior exemplified in the amount of wait time provided students after being questioned) as they correlate with some quantitative measure of student academic achievement (such as scores on an achievement test). Classic to this approach is process-product research (for a comprehensive review, see Good & Brophy, 1986). On the other hand, the interpretive paradigm applies largely qualitative ethnographic techniques to get "thick critical descriptions" of classrooms (such as field notes carefully documenting what happens in a particular setting). Consideration is given to the context (schools and communities) and to "the intuitive sense of relevant research questions and of conclusions which emerge by induction" (Erickson, 1986, p. 139), such as analytically reflecting on those field notes and reporting conclusions using the field note descriptions as a source for demonstrating *plausibility*.

Since research paradigms are driven by the goals they seek to attain, it becomes evident that these two approaches have differing objectives. The positivist approach is *etic* (it assumes all human beings are all alike; Sue & Padilla, 1986) as it searches for *laws* about teaching, learning, and so forth (Shulman, 1986). It is, in short, a research paradigm in search of answers. The interpretive research approach is *emic* (it assumes human beings are all different according to culture; Sue & Padilla, 1986) as it searches for the *meanings* constructed by participants as they seek to make sense of what they encounter in classrooms (Shulman, 1986). The result, for the interpretive researcher, is not to search for answers but rather to search for a source of criticism and the generation of new questions.

Since the reader may not be familiar with the interpretive research approach, since the interpretive approach is open-ended enough to capture more fully the complexity of teacher thinking, *and* since nearly all of the studies reported in this volume follow it and thus require some background knowledge (schemata) for understanding them, a brief description about the belief system upon which the interpretive paradigm rests is in order.

Central to the interpretivist perspective is the belief (a) that classrooms are socially and culturally organized environments, (b) that teaching is mediated by the sense the learner *and* teacher make of the social context of the classroom situation (since, it is argued, this is the level at which the "hidden" curriculum plays itself out), (c) that events occurring at any system level (such as ability group, classroom, school, community) must be seen at the next higher and next lower system levels, (d) that the thoughts, attitudes, perceptions, and so on of the participants are a critical source of data because personal meanings are the focal point of inquiry, and (e) that a critical focus has to be on the specific difficulties encountered by those who are relatively powerless in educational contexts, such as ethnic minority students (for a comprehensive review, see Erickson, 1986; Shulman, 1986).

As an example of the power the interpretive paradigm has to reshape the way we think about teaching and learning, consider the influence that sociolinguistic researchers have had on our understanding of why students of color have failed to attain parity in levels of academic achievement with Euro-American students. Earlier presage-product research found a correlation between ethnicity and academic achievement. The result was that explanations focused on genetic and/or cultural deficiency. As sociolinguists began to observe in classrooms to understand the dynamics of communication interactions between students of color and their nonminority teachers, and compared those to the communication interaction styles they observed in the home and community context of those minority students, it became evident that there were

considerably different patterns of interaction taking place between the school and the home and community. These differing
patterns of interaction caused misunderstandings between
teachers and their students, with a concomitant result being negative attitudes about the "other." As teachers were retrained to
communicate in ways that resembled the communication patterns of their students in their homes, student academic achievement increased (see Cazden, 1986, for a review of classroom
discourse research). Thus failure was not attributed to the "victim" but to the dynamic interaction of teachers and students in a
specific context.[4]

None of this is to suggest that the interpretive paradigm is
faultless or that it should replace the positivist paradigm
(Erickson, 1986; Shulman, 1986). Indeed, the approach researchers may be best advised to take should be one of including
multiple perspectives, multiple research approaches, multiple
conceptions of problems, and multiple foci on events. A research
project is enhanced when the proper balance between qualitative
and quantitative, emic and etic, search for laws and search for
meaning, and so forth, can be attained.

CRITICAL SCIENCE: BEYOND THE POSITIVIST
AND INTERPRETIVE PARADIGM

While it is essential to understand the philosophical and methodological frameworks that dominate educational research, it is
equally essential to ask: for what purpose do we do this work?
Indeed, some do such work for the tangible personal benefits it
may bring (e.g. tenure and promotion). More hopefully, some do
such work because they are interested in uncovering the laws
(causes and effects) of teaching and learning which, when uncovered, can be generalized to other situations for the improvement of all situations (such as attempts positivism). Some do such
work because they wish to uncover, in its entire complexity, the
meanings people make and the purposes they pursue which,
when uncovered, can provide context specific improvements as
well as an appreciation for complexity (such as attempts inter-
pretivism).

More recently, attention has been paid to the "critical science"
paradigm of educational research (see, for example, McCutcheon
& Jung, 1990). Inspired by the work of Freire (1968), it has as its

underlying intent (goals and purposes) uncovering those laws, meanings and/or purposes that support educational practices aimed at social and educational equity and the reduction of cultural hegemony. It is, at its core, focused on understanding the "oppressed" and on minimizing the difficulties experienced by those who are powerless.

In this vein, then, research would include the study of phenomena with an eye on the broader social and economic context. In doing this, it is possible to understand why schools are effective for some (the "haves") and ineffective for others (the "have nots"). Thus it is posited that schools are inherently structured unfairly so that there remains a subordinated unskilled labor pool to be exploited and/or a permanent underclass (caste) of people (Ogbu & Matute-Bianchi, 1986). These purposes are rarely made explicit since the "system" works more effectively by providing an illusion of fairness. Thus attention is given to those unintended actions in the support of oppression as enacted by those who are blind to ways in which they oppress.

Beyond understanding the (unjust) status quo, it also seeks to understand how academic achievement and student behavior in school is influenced by feelings of injustice and powerlessness (Cummins, 1986) when students and their caregivers come to understand their oppressed condition. It is through reflection, and then action (which Freire, 1968, termed *conscientizacão*) aimed at understanding, naming, and dismantling oppressive conditions that schooling becomes meaningful and lives come to be filled with hope (Freire, 1994).

It should be noted that a critical science framework can be applied to either positivist or interpretivist research (since either can be undertaken for purposes of social justice). It is, thus, not mutually exclusive. More immediately, understanding this purpose (and the critical science paradigm) will help readers better comprehend the intention and interpretation of the works that appear in this volume.

TEACHER THINKING IN CULTURAL CONTEXT: OVERVIEW OF THIS VOLUME

The aim of this volume is to uncover some of the meanings teachers construct of students who are different from themselves, the meanings teachers make of a more inclusive curriculum and instruction embodied in multicultural education, and the ways in which the meanings individuals bring to teaching can be reconstructed (if at all possible). It asks the following questions:

1. In what way do teachers make sense of students who are different from themselves? How do students being "at risk," the students' ethnicity, or classroom events influenced by student ethnicity and gender influence the sense teachers make? What sense do student teachers make of these dimensions when confronted directly with these for the first time during their student teaching fieldwork?

2. In what ways do teachers make sense of multicultural education, especially as it interacts with a specific approach to curriculum, a specific approach to school reform, or as a result of a state's mandate for teaching in a particular way?

3. In what ways is it possible (if at all) to reconstruct teachers' understandings of what it means to teach in cultural contexts? Would it make a difference if instruction addressed their concerns, employed a "constructivist" approach during preservice education, focused on the teacher-student relationship as a major dimension of learning, or created a community of learners concerned about addressing the needs of ethnic minority students?

Before exploring these questions, this volume begins by offering a critique of the way in which research in the area of teacher cognition has ignored the connection with the constraints and challenges of teaching in one specific context—the urban context. Through his review of the literature, Alfredo Artiles in chapter 1 points to provocative scholarship that is specific to the urban context. Importantly, he provides suggestions for how research in the area of teacher cognition might proceed in explicitly connecting cognition to context and the direction it might go if it has this focus. Of note is his call for the inclusion of sociocultural models in researching teachers' cognition in urban contexts.

This volume in broken into three parts. In part 1, the focus is on the sense teachers make of students who are different from themselves. In part 2, the focus is on the sense teachers make of curriculum and instruction embedded in multicultural education. In part 3, the focus is on the possibility of reconstructing teachers' thinking about either of these two dimensions of teaching.

Part I: How Teachers Understand Students Who Are Different from Themselves

Teachers' personal experiences and professional education are one dimension affecting their routines and knowledge (Porter & Brophy, 1988). Critical to this dimension as it relates to teaching in cultural contexts is the fact that both personal experiences and professional education are culturally conditioned. Thus the personal experiences of most teachers (who are typically female, Euro-American, and from middle-class backgrounds) and the professional education they have received (which historically and, in many places, currently focuses on "generic" students with nominal attention to student diversity) may be fundamentally at odds with the experiences their students from diverse backgrounds have had, the context of the urban, multicultural schools they might teach in, and what we know constitutes a culturally relevant curriculum (Ladson-Billings, 1992).

In any event, it seems evident that Euro-American teachers have a worldview not shared by teachers or students of color. Yet this worldview plays a fundamental role in the sense the teacher makes of students, instruction, curriculum, community, and so forth in the limited context of the classroom. Equally important, teachers often do not tune into the worldview of their students nor see their work in the larger sociocultural, sociopolitical context of schools. The net result is that many teachers continue to use "deficit" models to explain minority student failure.

To begin this section, Martha Montero-Sieburth in chapter 2 explores the worldview of teachers by focusing on education professionals' knowledge base concerning a school's policies and practices for responding to Latino students who are "at risk." In this regard, her interest is in the "epistemological stream" of teachers' thinking as described earlier. In her chapter, Montero-Sieburth points out that many teachers, counselors, and administrators do not see the specific cultural background of the students (they're all Latinos) and have difficulty identifying the implications of their background for being at risk. For those teachers, however, who have knowledge of and commitment to their students' communities, beliefs and understanding of this interplay become increasingly more sophisticated, as do the approaches they might use for resolving difficulties these students experience.

In chapter 3, Clara New provides a case study of the connection between teachers' thinking and a specific group of students: African-American male students in urban schools. New focuses her chapter on what the teachers in her study were perceiving and thinking during moments when decision making was important. New's approach is consistent with the "psychological stream" of teachers' thinking. She advances the notion that thinking about students also requires considering implicit theories that explain student achievement, issues of cultural identity, teachers' conceptions of diversity and differential treatment, and their locus of control for success when working with African-American male students. These theories, she argues, are connected to how teachers plan and act in the classroom. African-American students, responding to teacher expectations communicated in action, respond with oppositional behavior. New's chapter ends by exploring the important role of teacher education programs to help teachers in training to uncover these implicit theories and resultant expectations about students so that they do not become "perceptually blind" about students of color.

In chapter 4, Maureen Gillette focuses on student teachers who have never experienced a school made up of an African-American majority. Her work explores the thinking of seven student teachers as they contemplate their students and the resultant curriculum and instructional practices affected by their thinking. Thus Gillette is employing the "practical argument" approach to understanding student teacher thinking. How they acted, in turn, influenced their overall feeling of success or failure in this context. In identifying "resisters, rethinkers, and culturally-relevant" student teachers, Gillette explores differences which result over issues such as the student teacher's locus of control, the foci of planning curriculum, the degree of openness to self-reflection, and theories of diversity. The hope is that by identifying these factors we can help student teachers overcome "dysconscious racism."

In chapter 5, I explore the connection between knowledge and acting embedded in teachers' "principles of practice" in this study of teachers in an urban, multicultural high school. Like Gillette, I focus is on the "practical argument" of teachers' thinking. I identify ways in which these principles constitute implicit theories and serve as a framework for responding to issues of student motivation, student personal difficulties, and challenges to instruction by students from diverse cultural and linguistic groups. Of note are those principles of practice left out: principles focused on diversity and focused on ways to promote student academic achievement.

Part II: How Teachers Understand Curriculum and
Instruction Embedded in Multicultural Education

As suggested earlier, a second element in education impacted by our ethnically diverse society is expanded interest in the curricular and instructional implications associated with multicultural education. Shulman (1986) suggests that one of the most serious faults of the interpretive paradigm is its lack of focus on the "substance" of classroom life: on the explicit curriculum and subject matter being explored. Indeed, in the teaching-learning context, there are two agendas being negotiated. Besides the social and interactional curricula there exists the curricular agenda with its focus on the knowledge, skills, and attitudes explicitly being taught. McDiarmid (1991) suggests that it is critical for teachers in multicultural contexts to consider the I-Thou-It triangle, including the sense teachers make of the curriculum (the "it"), the sense students make of the curriculum, and the reciprocal sense making that teachers and students advance of each other.

James Banks (1993) has most prominently begun to address the question of what knowledge is critical to know and teach in a multicultural, democratic society: personal and cultural knowledge, popular knowledge, mainstream academic knowledge, transformative academic knowledge, and school knowledge. Of central importance is that discussion about cultural contexts include the curriculum.

In chapter 6, Dawn Abt-Perkins discusses student ethnicity as it interacts with a teacher's knowledge of multicultural education and a specific strategy for teaching (writer's workshop). Taking the "epistemological stream" to teacher thinking, Abt-Perkins identifies both past (personal biographies, social identities, etc.) and present influences on a teacher's interpretation of content as it relates to specific students from diverse backgrounds and how the teacher "negotiates" these differences. Abt-Perkins also demonstrates how teachers' *stories* can be used to uncover teachers' knowledge about the cultural context.

In chapter 7, Mary Lynn Hamilton describes a school that is attempting to reform itself so that students feel empowered (via increasing statements to them promoting self-esteem and self-responsibility). An additional element of this empowerment is the inclusion of a multicultural curricula. Hamilton is aiming to explore the connection between reform efforts and multicultural education to how teachers think. Thus she is interested in the "epistemological stream" of teachers thinking. Hamilton points out that the latter element did not significantly change the way teachers' thought, taught, or communicated in symbols. Thus teachers are more effectively *persuaded* to reconceptualize how they think about some aspects of schooling and not about others. Hamilton advances some notions about this differentiation for "persuading" teachers to change their thinking.

For their part, Carmen Montecinos and Deborah Tidwell, in chapter 8, use a cross-case analysis of two secondary language arts teachers who expressed a commitment to multicultural education. Montecinos and Tidwell show how teachers' responses to state-mandated standards for *infusing* teaching with a multicultural, nonsexist curriculum represent an interweaving of the multiple sources of knowledge that inform practice. They suggest that the diversity in approaches to multicultural education described in the literature can be traced to the level of commitment to the standards; prior knowledge, especially of multicultural education; beliefs about instruction in a specific content area; and personal biographies. Drawing from an information-processing model of thinking, they suggest that when language arts teachers are asked to incorporate multicultural teaching practices into their instructional repertoire, they will adapt those practices to make them fit with their existing understandings about schooling (in general) and reading processes (in particular).

Part III: How, If at All, Teachers' Thinking Can Be Constructed and Reconstructed

The question of how we might change teachers' worldviews is a weighty one. Much attention has been paid to this issue (see, for example, Grant & Secada, 1990), though Haberman (1991) questions whether we can provide any kind of experiences or teacher preparation that can significantly alter the way these teachers think. If one takes the latter view, then the only alternative is to be more selective about those we let in to the profession (such as, only those who share the students' worldview or who are sensitive enough to understand it). Yet changing the selection criteria for those entering the profession may be a considerable challenge itself, since many of the characteristics associated with teaching effectiveness in contexts of significant diversity are difficult to quantify (flexibility, critical self-examination, etc.). Another challenge would be to change the structure of schooling so that individuals are socialized into teaching with a worldview compatible with teaching students from diverse backgrounds.

The last four chapters focus on specific strategies for constructing and reconstructing teachers' thinking about issues of diversity. In chapter 9, Patricia Marshall explores the connection between teachers' personal experiences and professional education as it affects "concerns" these teachers have about teaching in multicultural classroom contexts. These concerns make up part of teachers' "epistemological" considerations. She points out that these concerns are hierarchically structured and are directly related to the differences (absence of synchronization) between the personal and cultural experiences of teachers and their students from diverse backgrounds. Marshall explores her construction of the "Multicultural Education Concerns Survey" and the preliminary findings of certain concerns: familial and group knowledge, strategies and techniques, interpersonal competence, and school bureaucracy. She then applies this construction to the developmental stage differences between novice and experienced teachers. Marshall argues that after the concerns teachers have at different developmental levels are identified, professional education experiences can be constructed to effectively meet those specific concerns.

In chapter 10, Teresita Aguilar and Cathy Pohan propose using a constructivist approach to the multicultural curriculum, since this approach, they argue, challenges teacher candidates' attitudes and beliefs toward issues of cultural diversity and social inequities. In doing so, they explore the connection between salient personal experiences and provocative professional education for changing teachers' thinking. They provide a vision and framework for teacher preparation programs, addressing the role of knowledge acquisition, attitudinal and belief changes, *and* cultural experiences intended to transform monocultural teacher candidates into multicultural educators. They are, in short, hoping that reflection-in-action will facilitate this transformation.

In chapter 11, the focus moves toward seeing the valuable role of the *relationship* between students and their teachers (in this instance, student teachers) embedded within the context of the student diversity as it impacts Euro-American preservice teachers in changing their thinking about issues of diversity. Linda Valli discusses the initial perceptions these student teachers held and how being placed in a context of significant student diversity created concern for issues that had not existed previously. In doing this, Valli points out how beginning teachers' beliefs about issues of diversity are impacted by actual experience. Of note is the transformation of their thinking about teaching in cross-cultural contexts and the critical role of personal relations and the value of diversity to that transformation.

Marilynne Boyle-Baise and Judith Washburn, in chapter 12, describe their attempt at using coalition building as a means to sustain change in teachers' thinking. In this sense, they located external elements (namely, leadership and support from others equally committed to issues of diversity) as they connect to teacher thinking (specifically to a vision for diversity and a sense of self-efficacy) for creating teacher-activists committed to responding to diversity. Using a case study of six active members of a grass-roots coalition that was developed to support the professional development of teachers with regard to multicultural education, they focus on the collective thinking of the teachers as they reflect on the work related to their involvement in the coalition. Of note in their chapter is the use of research methods that result in a cognitive map of the collective (cultural) thinking of this group of teachers.

The last chapter of this book, by David Whitehorse, highlights several key themes evident in the preceding chapters. He then describes how these themes extend existing models of thinking in ways that make them more comprehensive. Finally, he offers additional questions and challenges raised as a result of the work described herein and suggests some implications of those questions with respect to teachers' values, to the sense they make in the classroom, and to teaching practice.

MOVING FORWARD

As you press forward into the pages of this volume, it is hoped that you will see yourself or that which you intend to study reflected in here. Perhaps you may recall your first significant contact with students who were ethnically and linguistically different from yourself. Perhaps you will think about the ways in which you have attempted to make courses address teaching that is culturally or linguistically responsive. Perhaps you will reflect on teachers who taught with either a monocultural or multicultural perspective. Perhaps your interest rests not in the concepts laid out by these scholars as much as by the methods used for uncovering teacher thinking while remaining sensitive to the cultural context. In any event, it is hoped that this volume will allow you to connect your own experience or interests to that described in these chapters.

Consistent with an inquiry and interpretivist approach to understanding teacher thinking, this book is less about "answers" and more about the generation of additional questions. It is not about finding some universally effective strategies for teaching students from diverse backgrounds or for teaching with a multicultural perspective. Indeed, Cochran-Smith (1993) argues that it is antithetical to the concept of diversity itself, since teachers are asked to remain sensitive to the particular nuances of the student population, the school, and the community. Thus the reader is encouraged to allow for a variety of perceptions (often conflicting) among the chapters and between the writers. Keeping this in mind will help you to remain open to the ideas and methods presented in this volume.

There are other questions which we do not confront in this volume yet which beckon our consideration. Here are just a few questions that this book does not even attempt to ask:

1. What sense do teachers make of other aspects of the cultural context? For example, how do teachers think about socioeconomic differences, learning and handicapping differences, and so forth? How do teachers think about students who are Native American or Asian-American? How does the students' grade level make a difference in how teachers think about the cultural context? How do these factors *interact* to affect the way a teacher thinks?

2. What other elements of the context are left aside that affect how a teacher thinks about diversity? How does the teacher's ethnicity fit into the meaning made of a cultural context? What roles do school policy, discipline plans, school improvement plans, and so on have that either negatively or positively impact the way teachers think about diversity?

Although these questions remain unanswered, this book sets forth an important advance in the area of teaching and learning (generally) and teacher cognition (specifically). When the specific elements and contexts of interest in teacher cognition are identified, the picture of what and how teachers think, while not complete, certainly comes into greater focus. Likewise, these questions become points of departure for current and future investigation.

It is pivotal that educators and researchers begin to illuminate the ways in which teachers make sense of their increasingly diverse students and the call for a more inclusive curriculum that is sensitive to the specific contexts in which that sense making is taking place. We intend this volume to be a means by which the discussion about teacher thinking in cultural contexts, already begun, can be sustained and furthered.

TEACHER THINKING IN URBAN SCHOOLS
The Need for a Contextualized Research Agenda[1]

Alfredo J. Artiles

Education has undergone revolutionary changes in recent years. Conceptual refinement and increasing sophistication of the methodological arsenal available to educational researchers have enhanced the breadth and depth of the academic conversation in education. In this vein, two of the most visible ongoing discussions in education are the plight of minority students in urban schools and the role of teacher thinking in teaching and learning processes.

First, the increasing diversity of this country's population augments the pressure exerted on educators to serve all students equitably and efficiently. This pressure is further complicated by the nefarious school outcomes exhibited by ethnically or linguistically diverse students who typically come from low-income households. Interestingly—because of historical, socioeconomic, and political factors—this diverse population represents the bulk of students that attend urban schools. To make things worse, there is increasing evidence that educational processes and outcomes in urban schools tend to be constrained and negatively impacted by many variables (Kozol, 1991; Natriello, Pallas, & McDill, 1990; Wilson, 1987).[2] Meager financial and material resources, teacher burnout, overpopulated classes, and escalating violence in the surrounding communities do not make urban schools the most pleasant places to learn or work.

Regarding the study of teacher cognitions, educators today are more interested in assessing mediating variables during teaching and learning processes. The role of metacognition, strategy use, beliefs, and decision-making processes in learning are important notions in this paradigm. From this perspective, it is assumed that just as teachers orchestrate the instructional process in the classroom, students also engage in intricate cognitive processes that enable them to receive, process, transform, appropriate, and use knowledge (Leinhardt & Putnam, 1987). It is thus acknowledged that complex cognitive mechanisms underlie instruction and learning.

Although discussions in both camps have evolved considerably, I contend that researchers in the two areas are not informing or conversing with one another. That is, researchers concerned with urban education have not followed the strides made by investigators in the realm of teacher thought processes. Conversely, educators that scrutinize teacher thinking have failed to factor in the role of distinct contexts (e.g., urban versus suburban settings) in these cognitive processes. In this vein, Hodapp and Dykens's (1994) assessment of the two cultures of behavioral research in a related field summarizes my point: "Researchers have worked in virtual isolation one from another. Each side has worked in its own research tradition, with its own disciplines, journals, and bodies of knowledge. This lack of knowledge about the findings or concerns of the other culture has resulted in each side losing much, including a mutual and 'cross-cultural' sharing in the excitement of recent advances and discoveries" (p. 684).

Hence, the fundamental thesis of this chapter is that we need to start crossing the cultural borders that divide the study of urban education and the cognitive paradigm of learning and instruction to enhance our insights about the educational processes and outcomes of minority students. The goal of this manuscript is to delineate a research agenda on teacher thinking that is sensitive to the context of urban schools. For this purpose, I present a brief critical review of the literature on teacher thinking and identify major gaps in this research. Next, I make the case for the inclusion of contextual variables in the study of teacher thinking by highlighting aspects from the knowledge base on urban schools. Finally, I delineate an interdisciplinary research agenda on teacher thought processes in urban schools that is grounded in a sociocultural theory of development and learning.

RESEARCH ON TEACHER THINKING:
A CRITICAL APPRAISAL

It was not until 1976 that a significant number of studies on teacher cognitions started to appear in the literature (Clark & Peterson, 1986). In this paradigm, teaching is conceptualized as a cognitive task. For example, teachers have to keep track of the plan they have prepared for the lesson, maintain a certain pace for the delivery of information, check for students' understanding, interpret and process students' responses and/or questions, and assess whether the intended objectives are being achieved. Teachers certainly have numerous issues in mind and constantly respond to immediate and simultaneous stimuli.

Clark and Peterson (1986) propose a conceptual framework to explain the intricate relationship between teacher cognitions and actions. The paradigm has two encompassing areas: (a) teachers' thought processes and (b) teachers' actions and their observable effects (e.g., teacher and pupil classroom behavior, student achievement). Teacher thought processes and actions are seen as bounded by opportunities and constraints. Furthermore, the two domains are seen as interconnected, and thus as influencing or interacting with each other. That is, teachers' thoughts incite teachers' actions and vice versa.

Although researchers have proposed conceptual frameworks to understand how specific and isolated areas of teacher thinking (e.g., attributions, decision making) influence classroom instruction, Clark and Peterson's paradigm represents one of the few comprehensive models crafted to explain teacher thought processes as a major area of educational inquiry (see also Porter & Brophy, 1988). However, I contend that this comprehensive model be reformulated so that it includes crucial elements related to the contexts of classroom and instruction. For instance, teacher thoughts and actions are also heavily influenced by the physical setting, by the social world of the classroom, and by classroom discourse patterns. Moreover, variables in the school environment and in the participants' (i.e., students' and teachers') histories also shape teacher thought processes. In short, I contend that a more holistic framework of teacher thought processes must be proposed and tested empirically. Before I discuss the need for such a framework in greater detail, I present an overview of research on teacher thinking.

Although four major research programs in teacher thinking have been developed (schema theory, reflection-in-action, pedagogical content knowledge, practical arguments), I summarize the literature in this field by constructs or areas investigated. Some of the most commonly studied areas are teacher beliefs and theories, teacher interactive thoughts and decision making, and novice and expert teachers.

With respect to teacher theories and beliefs, studies in this area can be classified into two broad groups: teacher implicit theories and teacher attributions.

Teacher Implicit Theories and Beliefs

Nowadays, most researchers acknowledge that the study of theories and beliefs in teachers is central to an understanding of the complexity of teachers' knowledge. In fact, it has been argued that "teacher thinking may be guided by a personally held system of beliefs, values and principles" (Isenberg, 1990, p. 324). Carter (1990) defines implicit theories as "conceptions of the personal values, beliefs, and principles that seemed to guide action" (p. 300). Likewise, Harvey (1986) defines a belief system as "a set of conceptual representations which signify to its holder a reality or given state of affairs of sufficient validity, truth and/or trustworthiness to warrant reliance upon it as a guide to personal thought and action" (cited in Richardson, Anders, Tidwell, & Lloyd, 1991, p. 562). In addition, research on theories and beliefs attempts to explore teachers' propositional or practical knowledge. Practical knowledge is defined as "the knowledge teachers have of classroom situations and the practical dilemmas they face in carrying out purposeful action in these settings" (Carter, 1990, p. 299). The major purpose of this line of inquiry is to unveil the contexts and points of reference that teachers use in perceiving and processing information (Clark & Peterson, 1986).

Carter (1990) points out that most of the research on teacher knowledge to date has been concerned with the cognitive processes of teachers rather than with the substance of teachers' knowledge. In addition, Pajares (1992) contends that a fundamental problem in this line of inquiry is determined, to a large extent, by the nebulous nature of the construct. He argues that "beliefs are seldom clearly defined in studies or used explicitly as a conceptual tool, but the chosen and perhaps most artificial distinction between belief and knowledge is common to most definitions: Belief is based on evaluation and judgment; knowledge is based on objective fact" (p. 313). To elucidate the artificial distinction made between knowledge and beliefs, Pajares asserts:

> What may be missing from these conceptualizations is the element that cognitive knowledge, however envisioned, must also have its own affective and evaluative component. The conception of knowledge as somehow purer than belief and closer to the truth or falsity of a thing requires a mechanistic outlook not easily digested. What truth, what knowledge, can exist in the absence of judgment or evaluation? But, sifting cognition from affect, and vice versa, seems destined to this sort of fence straddling. (p. 310)

In conclusion, the bulk of research on teacher beliefs has been descriptive and primarily concerned with content. The ways in which beliefs are structurally organized in teachers' explanations has been a major focus of this research program and has produced a voluminous inventory of teacher beliefs on myriad topics. With few exceptions (e.g., Nespor, 1987), most researchers in this area have neglected the development of a conceptual framework of teacher beliefs and have limited their work merely to describing and listing the beliefs teachers hold about diverse aspects. We are only starting to use more dynamic notions of teacher beliefs and beginning to include contextual variables in this area of inquiry. For example, research on teacher knowledge is perhaps one of the most vibrant and promising areas of work in this camp (see Fenstermacher, 1994, for a thorough review of this research). I shall discuss a few of these new developments in the final section of this chapter.

Teacher Attributions

Weiner (1992) explains that attributional theorists see human beings as "scientists, seeking to understand the world around them and themselves and using naive statistical techniques and principles of covariation to reach their conclusions" (p. 860). Others have suggested that teacher attributions provide significant insights into our understanding of how teacher expectancies affect student achievement (Cooper, 1985; Cooper & Tom, 1984; Peterson & Barger, 1985; Weiner, 1986).

Hunter and Barker (1987) contend that people typically impute success and failure to any of four factors: ability, effort, task difficulty, and luck. In turn, three dimensions of causality have been identified: locus (internal/external), stability (unstable/stable), and controllability (controllable/not controllable). Locus (location of a cause) is related to pride and self-esteem. For instance, individuals with an internal locus will enhance their self-esteem after success and vice versa. Stability is linked to expectancy of success. That is, if success is attributed to a stable cause (such as aptitude), similar outcomes will be anticipated in future endeavors. Finally, controllability has a bearing on affective reactions such as anger, shame, pity, and guilt. Depending on the perceived control of the cause, a person may experience any of these emotions. For example, pity or sympathy could be expressed to a student who fails as the result of an uncontrollable cause (such as ability) (Weiner, 1992).

Furthermore, the emotional and behavioral reactions produced by the controllability dimension also may function as attributional cues which sometimes can have a paradoxical effect. Graham (1990) asserts that "this unintended communication of attributional information appears to be particularly likely when the teacher wishes to protect the self-esteem of the failure-prone student" (p.18). From this perspective, Graham argues that presumably "positive" teacher behaviors can sometimes be read as low-ability cues. Examples of these behaviors are pity following failure, praise following success at easy tasks, and help when it is not requested (Graham, 1990).

Moreover, researchers have identified two sources of bias in the study of attribution. Weiner (1992) refers to them as the "hedonic bias" and the "actor-observer perspective difference." The former refers to the principle by which people attribute success to themselves and failure to others. The actor-observer perspective difference is seen when the "actors ascribe their outcomes to the situational factor in their visual field, whereas observers ascribe outcomes to the actor, who is their focus of attention" (Weiner, 1992, p. 861).

Furthermore, the role of culture appears to be a relevant consideration in the study of the consequences of attributions. Rodríguez and Tollefson (1987), for instance, asked 155 elementary teachers in Costa Rica to report their expectancies of success for two hypothetical low-achieving students. One student performed poorly because of low ability (an internal stable uncontrollable factor) and the other because of little effort (an internal, unstable, controllable factor). Rodríguez and Tollefson (1987) contend that, unlike teachers in the United States, Costa Rican teachers are more willing to aid students who have better prospects for future success. A major conclusion drawn from the study is that the stability/expectancy of success connection (i.e., low effort versus low ability) may be less affected by cultural factors, whereas the notions of evaluating, helping, and liking may be more permeable to the influence of culture (see also Clark & Artiles, 1994).

In conclusion, research on teacher attributions has made significant conributions to the education and psychology fields. It should be noted, however, that research on attributions has tended to neglect its connections with several contextual variables. For instance, it is important to develop more studies that look at the link between teacher attributions and teacher behaviors during instruction. Likewise, the connection between teacher attributions and other areas of teacher thinking (e.g., teacher theories and/or decision-making processes) has been overlooked. Lastly, the relationship between teacher attributions and other relevant variables must be included in this line of research. Examples of these variables include teachers' levels of experience (Artiles, 1992), the perception of the performance history of the student (Rolison & Medway, 1985), and students' race (Wiley & Eskilson, 1978), social class (Clark & Peterson, 1986), and gender (Fennema, Peterson, Carpenter, & Lubinski, 1990).

Teacher Decision Making and Interactive Thoughts

In this field of study attention has focused on the five following areas (Borko & Shavelson, 1990; Clark & Peterson, 1986): (a) the definition and frequency of interactive decisions (e.g., teachers make an interactive decision every two minutes), (b) the content of interactive thoughts (e.g., content most frequently includes the learner, instructional procedures and strategies, subject matter, and instructional objectives) (Armour-Thomas, 1989), (c) the consideration of alternative courses of action (Peterson & Clark, 1978; Shavelson & Stern, 1981), (d) the antecedents of interactive decisions (e.g., judgments about the environment, the teacher's cognitive or affective states, or the appropriateness of a particular teaching strategy), and (e) the relation between teacher effectiveness and interactive decision making.

Regarding the latter type of studies, Clark and Peterson (1986) conclude that effective teachers possess cognitive skills that are lacking in ineffective ones. These skills include rapid judgment, "chunking" or transformation (the "ability to group discrete events into larger units," p. 279), and differentiation or selectivity (the ability to "discriminate among units in terms of their immediate and long-term significance," p. 279).

In sum, studies on teacher decision making have focused, for the most part, on the topography of these processes (e.g., frequency, content, antecedents). Most of these studies have been based on a functional analysis of behavior in which acts are seen as contingent upon their antecedents and consequences. Once again, contextual variables (teacher level of experience, urban versus suburban settings, subject matter, diversity of students) have been blatantly ignored.

Studies of Expert and Novice Teachers

Research studies in disciplines outside of the education field have shown that there are significant differences in the ways that expert and novices think, know, and act (Borko, Bellamy, & Sanders, 1992). Hence, educational researchers have increasingly turned their attention to the study of experts' and novices' ways of teaching and knowing (Berliner, 1987; Borko & Livingston, 1989; Borko & Shavelson, 1990).

The identification of distinctive cognitive and behavioral characteristics in novice and expert teachers might ultimately enable researchers and teacher educators to model and prepare educators to use the thinking skills and behaviors of expert teachers that prove to have a greater impact on pupil achievement. Presumably, it will also allow researchers to understand the developmental changes that a novice teacher experiences in her or his evolution to become an expert teacher and how expertise is acquired from experience (Carter, 1990).

It should be noted that there is no consensus yet as to how to define the "expert teacher" (Lampert & Clark, 1990) (for this reason, investigators sometimes use the notion of "experienced" teacher). Borko et al. (1992), for example, used teacher center coordinators' nominations and Berliner's (1987) model of pedagogical expertise (novice, advanced beginner, competent, proficient, and expert) to identify expert teachers. In contrast, Swanson, O'Connor, and Cooney (1990) identified expert teachers according to years of experience (at least ten years), level of education (at least a master's degree), nomination by the school principal, and selection as a mentor teacher within the California Public School System.

Thus far, research on expert and novice differences suggests that (a) expert teachers have more mature schemata (elaborate, interconnected, and accessible knowledge structures) and their schemata about "students" differ significantly from those of novices (Borko & Livingston, 1989; Clark & Peterson, 1986; Needels, 1991); (b) expert teachers appear to be more aware of what takes place in classrooms and direct their attention to the work system in the classroom (they quickly judge visual images of classroom scenes in terms of how well students are performing) (Carter, 1990); (c) experienced teachers have abundant routines to organize and manage instruction (Carter, Sabers, Cushing, Pinnegar, & Berliner, 1987); (d) expert teachers process information linked to management activities in terms of what they consider typical or atypical in classroom events and recall more precisely classroom incidents (Carter, 1990) (e.g., experienced teachers recall vividly the progress or difficulties of the "collective student" at particular important points during a lesson) (Bromme, 1987);[3] (e) experienced teachers have deeper knowledge of their students and make more use of this knowledge in interacting with their students; and (f) experienced teachers are more aware of and showed more flexibility about changing plans in accordance with contextual demands.

Critique of Research on Teacher Thinking

Despite the increasing popularity of the research paradigm on teacher thinking, investigators have criticized it on several grounds. Kagan (1990), for instance, purports that "research on teacher cognitions may be too vague or ambiguous to promote its use" (p. 420). Kagan identifies four problems with this line of research, namely, (a) the construct is nebulous, (b) one must infer teacher cognitions because they cannot be assessed directly, (c) the methods used to tap teacher cognitions are time consuming, and (d) it is difficult to draw comparisons against an assumed "ideal" profile of teacher thinking.

Similarly, Shulman (1986) identifies two major problems in this research paradigm. First, he asserts that researchers have scrutinized teacher thinking on a narrow range of teaching activities.

Furthermore, many of the issues investigated have "little practical or theoretical interest" (p. 24). Second, the study of teacher cognitions has been divorced from the new exciting developments in the investigation of pupil cognitions.

In addition, Kagan (1990) questions the "ecological validity" of this research program by asking, "Are teachers' performances on a particular tool or task related to their classroom behaviors or to valued student outcomes?" (p. 422). Investigators have tested this empirical question and found that the hypothesized link between teacher thoughts, behaviors, and/or pupil responses to instruction is tenable (Artiles, Mostert, & Tankersley, 1994; Richardson et al., 1991). On the other hand, researchers have reported conflicting evidence regarding the connection between teacher thinking and behaviors (see the introduction), and the debate is far from being resolved.

Another criticism advanced in this volume is that this line of research has attempted to identify and study discrete areas of teacher thinking without taking into account the role of context. That is, researchers have tried to understand how isolated cognitive constructs (beliefs, decision-making processes, attributions) work in teachers' minds without looking at the potential mediating impact of variables such as school setting (urban or suburban), gender, socioeconomic status, ethinicity, or classroom discourse processes.

Furthermore, investigators have seldom scrutinized multiple areas of teacher thinking within a single study. For instance, very little is known about the link between teacher attributions and teacher decision-making processes, or between teacher self-efficacy beliefs and theories of students' learning. Examination of multiple areas of teacher thinking in different contexts would allow researchers to gain insight into the complex and dynamic cognitive life of teachers. From this perspective, inquiry on teacher cognitions would not aspire to prescribe thinking processes for effective teaching. Rather, this paradigm would provide an overarching set of theoretical principles that would allow us to understand complex cognitive processes in the context of the socially negotiated world of the classroom.

In addition, researchers have designed studies on interactive teacher thinking as if it were a unidirectional phenomenon. In other words, the teacher has been used as the critical unit of analysis as if his or her thoughts were isolated and impermeable entities. By using the teacher as the unit of analysis, they have disregarded the very interactional nature of these thought processes. I argue that the teacher-pupil dyad might be a more suitable unit of analysis because it will place the interactive thought processes of teachers in the context in which they naturally occur.

In conclusion, although research on teacher cognitions has become more popular in educational research, the meaningfulness and usefulness of its contributions have been questioned in recent years (Floden & Klinzing, 1990; Kagan, 1990; Lampert & Clark, 1990; Shulman, 1986). To a great extent, the influence of the process-product paradigm is evident in the scope and methods used to tap teacher cognitions. On the other hand, exciting new developments in this area indicate that researchers are moving to a more contextualized view of teaching and instruction (see Marshall, 1992). I purport that research on teacher thought processes in urban contexts ought to be one of the new avenues to pursue in this field of study.

THE CONTEXT OF URBAN MULTICULTURAL SCHOOLS

Urban schools are complex contexts in which student diversity and school variables interact in complicated fashions. I argue that an understanding of urbanicity is necessary if we want to grasp the complex life of urban schools. For this reason, I discuss briefly the notion of urbanicity before presenting a synthesis of the literature on urban schools.

Urbanicity

The United States is becoming an urban nation. Ethnic diversity, poverty, overcrowdedness, high mobility, and scant resources compose the typical image of the urban gettho. Wilson (1987) has documented the historical trajectory of change in urban areas using a socioeconomic paradigm. He purports that economic opportunities, migration patterns, and demographic forces have segregated ethnic minorities in urban neighborhoods and deteriorated considerably their quality of life.

Nevertheless, the population in urban areas is characterized by its dramatic heterogeneity. Ornstein (1984) asserts that five major groups of people live in urban areas (above 500,000 inhabitants). First, there are the yuppies who stayed in the city for the social opportunities that cities offer. Second, there are the "ethnics, traditional, deeply religious, and family oriented (Ornstein, 1984, p.

482). Next are the increasing numbers of "economically trapped" groups, which are overwhelmingly white, though minority representation is increasing steadily in these groups (e.g., older people, blue- or white-collar people, young and middle-aged couples with low salaries of $20,000 to 35,000). Fourth are the recent immigrants from developing countries who feel alienated by legal, economic, educational, linguistic, and societal (e.g., prejudice, discrimination) constraints. Finally, there is the "structural poor." Because of familial and societal forces, this group lives in a self-perpetuating cycle of poverty that is inherited from one generation to the next. As documented elsewhere, blacks are overrepresented in this group (Wilson, 1987).

Gordon and Armour-Thomas (1992) contend that because of the unique composition of urban communities, we find a tension between congruency and incongruency.

> Just as there are diverse positions, there are conflicts of interest, that is, lack of congruency between the interests of one group and those of another. Talking about large, congested, and diverse populations requires talking about the lack of congruence among the many subgroups that make up these populations. Incongruence among the various elements of society, then, is a special characteristic of urbanicity, not because incongruence is unique to urban areas, but because the immediate contiguity highlights the contradictions. (p. 1461)

A direct consequence of this tension is a perennial pressure for change. Specifically, inhabitants of urban areas experience increasing pressure to learn to live with an incessant massive influx of people with disparate backgrounds. Life in urban areas also increases people's sense of anonimity, alienation, and lack of control over their own lives. Ironically, bureaucracy in urban communities not only expands constantly to preserve the system but also coerces the individual to conform. In short, urban life places individuals in a dialectical situation in which, on one hand, they are forced to change constantly, while at the same time they are impelled to conform to the system (Gordon & Armour-Thomas, 1992). Undoubtedly, this intricate configuration of forces has enormous consequences for urban schools.

Urban Schools: Processes and Outcomes

Ornstein (1984) reports that "in 1950, all but one of the nation's 25 largest city school systems had a White student majority. By 1980, all but two had a majority of minorities" (p. 478). Indeed, the diversity of the student population is a distinctive characteristic of urban schools. Unfortunately, educational indicators in most urban schools reflect a disastrous situation in terms of student achievement levels and school effectiveness.

The interplay between ineffective resource allocation and student diversity has been offered as an explanation for the low levels of student achievement in urban schools. It is argued that administrators and teachers ought to be cognizant of the impact that their resource allocation decisions have on diverse students' learning (Gordon & Armour Thomas, 1992; Winfield, Johnson, & Manning, 1993). "What makes the urban school context unique is the interaction of these administrative decisions with the kinds and amount of diversity represented in urban student populations. The differential impact on student learning outcomes is evidenced by the achievement gap between racial/ethnic groups" (Winfield et al., 1993).

The notion of the opportunity to learn plays a central role in explaining these differential patterns of achievement. The opportunity a student has to learn is determined by what teachers do in classrooms during instruction. Among other factors, the role of content coverage, content exposure, content emphasis, and the quality of instruction is typically examined to determine the opportunity to learn (Stevens, 1993). In this vein, it has been found that certain institutionalized school practices (e.g., special education placement, tracking) might augment the chances that low-ability minority students have for school failure. Unfortunately, a significant number of students that are thought to need special education services and low-track placement come from minority groups (Artiles & Trent, 1994; Oakes, 1992).

Finally, factors commonly listed as predisposing or precipitating forces for the low achievement of minority students in urban schools can be clustered around at least four domains, namely, (a) the teacher (e.g., teacher hiring, assignment, and attrition, stereotypical perceptions of student inadequacy, low standards of performance), (b) the student (e.g., deficits, lack of previous success in school), (c) the school and classroom milieu[4] (e.g., features of effective schools, negative peer pressure, ineffective instructional grouping, teaching conditions, inappropriate curriculum and instruction), and (d) the differences between school and home cultures (e.g., differences between parental and school norms) (Ornstein & Levine, 1989). Because of the focus of this volume, I will discuss briefly only the first domain.

Teachers in Urban Schools

Teachers and their labor in urban schools have been studied from at least two perspectives. The first looks at the work of teachers from an organizational and systemic perspective. Specifically, researchers attempt to assess the impact of urban schools' stressful environments on phenomena such as teacher recruitment and attrition, teacher effectiveness, and teacher efficacy. The second line of work looks at teachers' cognitive processes when working in urban classrooms (e.g., perceptions, beliefs). Although the second area is directly related to the study of instructional processes in urban schools, it tends to be oblivious to contextual variables. That is, this research has looked at the perceptions and beliefs of teachers as discrete and isolated entities.

Organizational and systemic perspectives. In this area of study, the work of teachers in urban schools is seen as a rather strenuous endeavor that is constrained or enhanced by organizational and/ or systemic forces. Lack of material and administrative support, huge cultural differences within the student population (e.g., ethnic backgrounds, socioeconomic status, place of residence), and an atmosphere of danger explain in part the high rate of teacher burnout and attrition in urban communities. In the same vein, Finn and Voelkl (1993) found that school size is a critical variable that explains the quality of student engagement. Specifically, the size of the school has a bearing on student absenteeism, classroom participation, and students' sense of environment supportiveness and warmth.

Pflaum and Abramson (1990) report that large urban school districts tend to have fewer qualified teachers (not fully certified, inexperienced). Haberman and Rickards (1990) reported that 50% of the nation's new teachers will leave the profession in the first six years; in urban schools it will take five years. In practice, this means that many students in urban schools will have several teachers during an academic year. Interestingly, Haberman and Rickards (1990) found that the reasons teachers offered for quitting schools *before* teaching and *after* working at an urban school are not quite the same. Specifically, teachers' perceptions of major problems in urban schools *before* teaching were ranked according to student factors (underachievement, discipline, cultural backgrounds) and family factors (lack of parental support). In contrast, *after* teaching at an urban school, even though teachers still ranked student factors as a major problem (discipline), they perceived that school variables were crucial problems (lack of administrative support, heavy workload).

Likewise, Maxwell (1993) found that urban teachers' "staying behaviors are a function of their sense of efficacy and the nature of staff relations in the school . . . It seems reasonable to conclude that as collegial and professional staff relations increase, teachers' sense of efficacy and perceptions that students are capable of learning might also increase - which enhances their propensity to stay" (p. 21).

The findings reported in this section indicate that recruitment and hiring of more minority teachers will not be enough to solve the staff problems of urban schools. Substantial transformations will have to be effected not only in the cultures of urban schools but also in teacher education programs to prepare, recruit, and retain a qualified and diverse cadre of educators in urban schools (Haberman, 1984; Trent, 1992).

Urban teachers' cognitions. Although still in its infancy, researchers have started to study the role of teacher thought processes in urban settings as an important mediating variable. In this vein, Farkas, Grobe, Sheehan, and Shuan (1990) tested a cultural resources/social interaction model of school achievement and found that teachers' grading practices are influenced by their perception of student noncognitive characteristics (e.g., perception of students' homework, class participation, effort, and organization). Farkas et al. concluded that "student work habits, as reported by teachers, determine coursework mastery and, net of such mastery, student grades . . . [these findings also call] for future attempts to deepen our understanding of the micro-processes underlying stratification outcomes by providing data on the way gatekeeper judgments are constructed from a myriad of day-to-day interactions" (p. 138).

In conclusion, exploratory inquiry and case studies looking at the role of teacher attributions, decision-making processes, teacher beliefs, teacher expectations, and teacher knowledge in urban classroom processes and outcomes have started to appear in the literature (Artiles, 1992; Montero-Sieburth, 1989; Ríos, 1993; Winfield et al., 1993). I argue that this line of work still needs to operationalize the role of context to offer substantive insights about the complexity of teaching and learning in urban settings. A discussion of this line of research will be presented in the last section of this chapter.

Critique of Research on Urban Multicultural Schools

A review of the literature shows that a number of factors and program features that produce significant gains in student academic achievement in urban schools have been identified. Unfortunately, most efforts in this domain are based on a production-function formula in which outcomes are a function of inputs. Once again, a sociocultural framework is needed to transcend the mechanistic conceptualization of urban school processes and outcomes.

It should be noted that the scope and sophistication of research designs in this area of work are far more thorough than in the models used in the research on teacher thinking. However, more longitudinal studies and inquiry into microanalyses of program processes are needed to document the stability of students' achievement gains. Furthermore, longitudinal designs will allow us to assess the differential effects of intervention packages on different groups of students. More importantly, although research on urban school processes and outcomes has included contextual variables, the study of mediating variables during instruction and learning is alarmingly absent. Given the rich and complicated configuration of social and cultural variables in urban schools, it is fundamental that inquiry on urban classrooms be developed from a sociocultural perspective. By doing this, we will contribute to both the refinement of the research agenda on teacher thinking and the enrichment of our understanding of urban processes and outcomes. For that purpose, I delineate this research agenda in the next section.

TEACHER THINKING IN URBAN MULTICULTURAL
SCHOOLS: THE NEED FOR A CONTEXTUALIZED
RESEARCH AGENDA

The preceding discussion has made evident the need to develop a contextualized research agenda on teacher thinking in urban schools. I argue that myriad variables in inner city schools interact to maintain the pervasive rate of school failure among minority students. Teachers and students bring into these classrooms rich backgrounds and previous experiences that shape instruction and learning. Thus there is an urgent need to include contextual and mediating variables (e.g., teacher thinking) in the study of urban school processes and outcomes.

Although the research program on urban schools has evolved considerably, many questions remain unanswered. For instance, what happens in urban classrooms so that some minority students fail and others succeed (Lee, Winfield, & Wilson, 1991; Winfield, 1991)? Why do certain school characteristics have a differential effect on teachers' and students' sense of efficacy? If danger has an enormous developmental impact on the lives of inner city children (Garbarino, Dubrow, Kostelny, & Pardo, 1992), how is that reflected in the cognitive processes of these students and their teachers during instruction?

I argue that a contextualized research agenda on teacher thinking might offer meaningful responses to these and other puzzling queries. I propose that such an agenda be grounded in a constructivist view of teacher thinking, which in turn will need to redefine student learning. Similarly, this new agenda should strive to benefit from the knowledge bases generated in related areas of inquiry. Finally, this contextualized research agenda will need to broaden the traditional methods used to tap cognitive processes to account for the complexity of the phenomena targeted for scrutiny.

A Sociocultural View of Teacher Thinking

A sociocultural view of children's development and learning has revolutionized the work of developmental psychologists, educators, and other professionals in allied disciplines. Investigators concerned with teacher education and teaching are starting to apply the works of Vygotsky (1978) in their deliberations and inquiry efforts (e.g., Colton & Sparks-Langer, 1993; Condon, Clyde, Kyle, & Hovda, 1993; Manning & Payne, 1993; Prawat,

1992; Tharp & Gallimore, 1988). However, the bulk of work using a sociocultural approach has been developed mostly with children and few attempts have been made to use it with adults such as teachers. The delineation of this framework as it applies to teacher thought processes intends to bridge this gap.

Perhaps the most distinctive characteristic of the sociocultural view of learning is the emphasis on the interdependence between cognitive processes and sociocultural activities. Individuals' cognitive processes are understood in the sociocultural context in which they occur. That is, the unit of analysis is not the individual's intrinsic psychological processes but the "individual-in-action within specific contexts" (Rueda & Moll, in press). It is further assumed that higher-order thinking is developed as a result of the apprentice's social interactions with capable others as he or she engages in meaningful activities. From this perspective, individuals' interpretations of events are as important as the cognitive processes used to construct meanings. As can be inferred, language mediates higher-order thinking because it is through the use of language in social interactions that individuals communicate, interpret, and construct meanings. However, other cultural artifacts or symbols can also mediate social interactions and people's sense making of events (e.g., literacy, mathematics).

In addition, higher-order thinking is self-regulated by the individual through the conscious realization of his or her own cognitive processes (i.e., metacognition). By engaging in these activities and processes, individuals eventually master and appropriate the cultural tools needed to learn in their own sociocultural context. In sum, "in describing the rudiments of a sociocultural approach, then, several key elements appear to stand out: the role of social interactions, the influence of culturally-based knowledge and practices, including the use of cultural technologies; the mediating role of signs and symbols, our cultural tools, as well as that of peers or more competent others; and finally, a focus on thinking as inseparable from social and cultural activities" (Rueda & Moll, in press).

Chandler (1992) summarizes the critical assumptions of the sociocultural theory as it applies to social interactions and work in classrooms. However, although context and knowledge construction are pivotal constructs in this framework, distinct thought processes are rarely alluded to in specific ways. This just reinforces the idea that teacher thinking processes ought to be understood as embedded in sociocultural contexts of joint activity. The assumptions are as follows:

Classrooms are communicative environments. The social world of classrooms is a fertile medium for numerous communication exchanges. In this context, communication helps teachers and students differentiate their roles, and in consequence, their relationships might be either symmetrical or asymmetrical (teachers might communicate differentially with distinct groups of students). Similarly, teachers and students make sense of classroom events from different perspectives, for each of them has personal experiences and frames of references that filter his or her perceptions. Finally, communicative participation patterns and exchanges have an impact on student achievement.

Contexts are constructed during interactions. Students and teachers relate to each other in specific contexts while at the same time they co-construct contexts during interactions. In addition, students and teachers interact and participate in class following a set of rules that is embedded (i.e., implicit) in social contexts. When teachers interact with students in activities, they develop participation structures that are contextualized by the cues that are constantly exchanged. These cues signal different meanings to the participants, and thus contribute to the ongoing unpackaging of instructional processes and outcomes. Consequently, behavior expectations are constructed as part of these interactions.

Meaning is context specific. As teachers and students interact, they send verbal and nonverbal cues that will be used to construct meaning. That is, meanings are determined by and extracted from observed sequences of behavior. From this perspective, meanings are mutually constructed according to the specificity of a situation. Paradoxically, this also indicates that meanings are constrained by contexts because of their situation-specific nature (all instances of a behavior are not equal).

Inferencing is required for conversational comprehension. Communication and participation during classroom work is of primary importance in understanding the constructivist paradigm. These processes are governed by rules learned in the sociocultural context of participants. Teachers and pupils have frames of reference that guide their participation, and these frames are developed over time. As can be expected, frame clashes occur because of the different perceptions and meanings constructed by teachers and students. Finally, the form and function of the participants' speech during conversations do not always match. This might result in discontinuities in the communication process of students and teachers, and ultimately in the accentuation of achievement differentials.

Teachers orchestrate different participation levels. Teachers orchestrate instruction by balancing the co-ocurring demands stemming from the academic curriculum and the participation system of the classroom. As teachers develop lessons, they keep in mind their preestablished goals while at the same time evaluating students' abilities and understandings by interpreting verbal and nonverbal cues. Finally, teacher goals and theories of pedagogy can be inferred from their verbal and nonverbal behaviors.

Students have an active role in knowledge construction. Pupils deal with numerous issues during classroom instruction that are simultaneous and immediate. They construct meanings and knowledge based on their previous experiences and on the sociocultural context of the classroom. For instance, students participate in disparate ways depending on their status in the peer culture and on the demands posed upon them by the teacher. Likewise, pupils are simultaneously part of the peer and teacher-student cultures. They also interpret academic and social events by observing teacher-student, student-student, and student-group interactions.

The implications of the sociocultural framework for the study of teacher cognitions are immense. From this new perspective, this line of inquiry will not be based on a linear model of thinking and action. The study of decision-making processes, for example, will not be limited to counting the number of decisions made by teachers, or to elucidating the content and antecedents of teacher decisions. Rather, decision-making processes ought to be understood in the context of social interactions which are overwhelmingly charged with meanings and situated in the context of negotiations within particular participation structures.

The complex context of an urban school, with its inherent characteristics, opportunities, and constraints, makes the urban school a suitable setting to be scrutinized through a sociocultural lens. Myriad cultures and subcultures, along with participants' communication styles, expectations, and frames of reference, make urban schools a natural laboratory for studying the role of mediating variables (such as thought processes) in instructional processes and outcomes. In particular, the study of knowledge construction as a pivotal element in the learning process ought to be a priority in this research agenda. Unfortunately, "while research on teachers' knowledge in general is plentiful, research that focuses specifically on teachers' knowledge in urban schools or on urban teaching is limited. Part of the reason for this is that the conclusions with regard to teachers' knowledge have not been differentiated between urban, suburban, rural, or semirural schools but instead have been described in universal terms" (Montero-Sieburth, 1989, p. 339).

To reiterate, the study of teacher thinking cannot consist of the assessment of unidirectional isolated phenomena. Instead, the scrutiny of teacher thoughts must include features of the context (e.g., characteristics of students, resources and constraints in the classroom, rules and assumptions of the classroom culture), and of the students themselves. That is, inquiry into teacher thought processes becomes the study of dyads, triads, and groups embedded in urban contexts.

Recent advances in the study of thinking processes (e.g., beliefs and knowledge) might be seen as precursors of the research that will be conducted within this new model. Indeed, research on teacher beliefs and knowledge will contribute to our understanding of, for example, the connection between teacher thinking and differential academic achievement patterns in urban schools, or of teacher referral and placement of at-risk students in compensatory and special education programs. In this vein, Winfield et al. (1993) report a study on the role of teacher beliefs about at-risk students in urban classrooms. By taking into consideration the intricacies of the urban context, they were able to elucidate how teachers' beliefs about at-risk students were intertwined with complex institutional constraints and practices such as special education referrals and tracking (see Montero-Sieburth, chapter 2).

Research on teacher development (i.e., expert and novice teachers) with its emphasis on constructs such as schemata and pedagogical content knowledge is also a promising area of study in this sociocultural model of teacher cognitions. In this realm, it is assumed that novice and expert teachers construct meanings and knowledge in different ways. From a constructivist perspective, "knowing is created rather than imparted or transferred, and teachers must understand how students construct and use their understandings . . . Since each student's knowing is a unique complex of constructions, the more a teacher understands about each student's understanding. . . , the more effective teaching is likely to be" (Cochran, DeRuiter, & King, 1993, p. 265).

Thus we might ask how novice and expert teachers construct their knowledge about culturally diverse students' understandings in urban settings. Moreover, if we consider that a significant number of novice teachers are assigned to urban schools, it seems that a sociocultural model of novice teacher thinking might contribute to our understanding of teacher development in urban settings. So far, such line of inquiry has not been pursued.

Similarly, the work on pupil thought processes (Weinstein, 1983; Wittrock, 1986) and its link with sociolinguistic studies of classroom discourse and social interactions (Cazden, 1986; Marshall & Weinstein, 1986; Morine-Dershimer, 1983, 1985) must be included in the study of teacher thinking in urban schools. As stated above, the experience of pupils should be incorporated in this paradigm if we want to understand fully the cognitive experience of teachers in constrained milieus. How does the convergence (or divergence) of teacher and student perceptions about classroom events shape the participation patterns during instruction? How do pupils influence teachers' understandings of pupil progress and difficulties during instruction? How do teachers make sense of pupils' understanding in different subject matters? How does teacher knowledge of subject matter influence knowledge co-construction with different students during instruction? Although some preliminary work has been conducted to address these questions (Artiles, 1992; Bromme, 1987; Leinhardt, Putnam, Stein, & Baxter, 1991; Peterson, Fennema, & Carpenter, 1991), a sociocultural framework of teacher thinking has not been used.

Developing a research program based on a sociocultural model of thinking, however, will not be easy. The difficulties inherent in moving toward a constructivism model of teaching for understanding have been discussed elsewhere (Prawat,1992; Talbert, McLaughlin, & Rowan, 1993). This should not prevent us, however, from working toward such a laudable goal. On the other hand, to embrace a sociocultural model of teaching and thinking would also require a reconceptualization of student learning. A brief discussion on this issue follows.

Enhancing the Notion of Learning

I argue that student learning should be defined from a broader perspective. First, we need to acknowledge that "learning is a tacit, elusive, and largely invisible act" (Weade, 1992, p. 88). Traditional definitions disregard the role of context as a dynamic and ever-changing influence on learning processes. These definitions also omit the role of students' biographies and cultural perspectives through which they make sense of content and events. Consistent with the constructivist view of teacher thinking presented in this chapter, learning "consists of building on what the learner brings to the situation and restructuring initial knowledge in widening and intersecting spirals of increasingly complex understanding. Because learners come with different background knowledge, experience, and interests, they make different connections in building their knowledge over time. Therefore, classrooms within this framework stimulate multiple opportunities for coming to understandings" (Marshall, 1992, p. 11).

Moreover, learning occurs within meaningful contexts and is a process that evolves over time. Conceptual change is crafted in students' minds as they revisit background knowledge and as basic assumptions are challenged by current events. From this perspective, then, learning and thinking occur simultaneously within sociocultural contexts—not only within individuals' minds. Teachers are also actively engaged in learning processes as they teach and experience exactly the same knowledge construction processes described above.

Hence, teaching, learning, and thinking simultaneously unpack in spatial and temporal planes. Consequently, an integrated theory of learning and instruction should frame research on teaching and thinking (Artiles & Aguirre-Munoz, in press; Shuell, 1993). That is, cognitive variables should be studied in the context of teaching practices. In this vein, this research "should look at learning processes as a conglomerate of cognitive, metacognitive, developmental, affective, and motivational variables that act simultaneously during the learning process" (Artiles & Aguirre-Munoz, in press). For instance, motivational beliefs (e.g., self-efficacy, values, goal orientations) and other contextual variables (e.g., subject matter, student/teacher characteristics, classroom resources) mediate conceptual change processes (Artiles & Aguirre-Muñoz, in press; Pintrich, Marx, & Boyle, 1993). Accordingly, "as teachers expand their knowledge of how children actively and often collaboratively construct their own knowledge, they modify their teaching practices" (Marshall, 1992, p. 13).

In sum, the task before us is not an easy one. Whether we see learning as knowledge construction, as teaching for understanding, or as conceptual change, we will have to devise original ways to grasp the complex multidimensionality of student and teacher thinking and learning processes. How do teachers and students make sense and construct knowledge in urban classrooms? As students and teachers co-construct meanings in urban classrooms, how do they mutually shape the decisions they make about each other? In what ways do the unique organizational features of urban schools interact with student and teacher beliefs about learning? How do teachers' understandings and knowledge of student learning evolve across settings, subject matters, and types of students (e.g., gender, ethnicity)? These and many other related queries could be addressed in this new research agenda.

Benefiting from Related Areas of Inquiry: Toward an Interdisciplinary Paradigm

I have argued thus far that a switch to a contextualized view of teacher cognitions must be comprehensive, and hence it should include a redefinition of teaching, thinking, and learning. I also propose that this change be accompanied by a perennial pursuit for an interdisciplinary knowledge base. For that purpose, researchers must work in collaboration with professionals in allied fields, or at least should maintain constant communication with colleagues in other areas of study so that this research agenda benefits from advances in other camps. Examples of several related areas of study that might offer meaningful contributions to the study of thinking processes in urban schools are included below.

Multicultural education. A renewed interest in human diversity has emerged in education (Banks, 1993; Cushner, McClelland, & Safford, 1992). The construct *multicultural education* has been used as an umbrella term that encompasses the efforts directed to promote and secure equality for culturally diverse students (in its broadest sense) in the educational system. I should note that there is considerable controversy about the different connotations ascribed to the term, though most theorists agree on the stated overarching goal of this construct.

Banks (1993) contends that the most important dimensions of multicultural education are content integration (e.g., infusion or transformation of multicultural content in curricula), knowledge construction (e.g., ownership of knowledge, sociopolitical nature of knowledge), prejudice reduction (e.g., improvement of human relations), equity pedagogy (e.g., use of instructional methods that promote academic achievement of culturally different students), and empowering school culture (e.g., transformation of school culture to promote equity of diverse students and empowerment of their cultural backgrounds). As a result of these foci, we have recently witnessed an increase in the number of scholarly and practice-oriented publications in mainstream educational journals. It should be noted, though, that the empirical evidence documenting the impact of efforts in this realm is rather scarce. Fortunately, educators are (just) starting to study the interplay between teacher cognitions and issues of diversity. For example, studies have been reported on the link between teacher beliefs and practices when teaching limited English-proficient students (Johnson, 1992), on the evaluation of teaching in multicultural contexts (Dwyer, 1993), on the link between teacher beliefs about multicultural education and attributions for classroom events (Ríos, 1993; Ross & Smith, 1992), on the implementation of action research in multicultural contexts (Cochran-Smith & Lytle, 1992), on the impact of multicultural education inservice training (Artiles, 1995; Chow & McClafferty, 1995; McDiarmid, 1992), and on teacher perceptions of ethnicity and gender in academic achievement (Avery & Walker, 1993). Indeed, this new line of empirical research will benefit investigators interested in teacher thinking in urban schools.

Effective teaching for disadvantaged students.[5] Efforts have been made to identify teaching strategies that increase the academic achievement of low-income students. Researchers working in this area typically identify a discrete variable or area of study and aim to assess the impact of this factor on student and school outcomes in urban settings (for exhaustive discussions on effective teaching for at-risk and disadvantaged students in urban schools, see also Brophy & Good, 1986; Levine & Ornstein, 1989; Levine, Levine, & Eubanks, 1985). An example of this research is the work based on an ecobehavioral paradigm developed by Charles Greenwood and his associates (Greenwood et al., 1992) at the Juniper Gardens Children's Project. They have found, for instance, that pupils' IQs or socioeconomic status were not related to academic achievement in urban classrooms (Greenwood et al., 1981). Instead, "opportunity to respond" was identified as a critical variable that differentiated effective from ineffective classrooms. Embedded in this notion is the idea that the types of responses elicited are as important as the response opportunities that are afforded to students. It will be interesting to add the cognitive and contextual dimensions discussed in this chapter to enhance this paradigm of teaching and learning.

Children's risk and resilience processes. Developmental psychologists have built a sound research program that looks at the complex interactions between the individual and the environment. This line of work aims to map out and predict the potential complex interactions between individual, familial, social, and school variables. Research in this area is based on a probabilistic model in which the chances a child has to exhibit negative or positive developmental outcomes are predicted (Pianta, 1990). The probabilities are enhanced or constrained depending on the presence or absence of factors and/or mechanisms that protect or place a child at risk for different outcomes (e.g., maladaptive behavior, school failure) (Keogh, 1992). In this vein, the presence of stressors and the vulnerability or competence a child has to deal with them are crucial processes in this field of study (Luthar & Zigler, 1991).

Educational researchers have turned their attention to this field and have started to study the mechanisms that protect—against all odds—many minority students in urban schools (Lee, Winfield, & Wilson, 1991; Winfield, 1991). We have not explored, however, the link between teacher and pupil thought processes and risk and protective factors. For instance, we might attempt to respond to the following empirical questions: What are the theories of teachers about at-riskness and what is the relationship between these theories and their planning practices and student expectancies? To what extent do teacher and student attributions interact to produce negative school outcomes as a function of the perceived controllability of student risk factors?

Achievement motivation. Exciting developments are occurring in this area of study. Examples are the refinement of a cognitive social learning theory to understand teachers' self-efficacy (Bandura, 1986, 1993), the interest in student self-competence and goal orientations (Ames, 1992; Blumenfeld, 1992), the importance of strategy use in problem solving (Greenfield, 1979), and the promotion of self-regulated learning (Meece, in press; Pintrich & De Groot, 1990; Pokay & Blumenfeld, 1990; Zimmerman, Bandura, & Martinez-Pons, 1992). Presumably, these motivational variables mediate teachers' instructional and evaluation styles and student academic performance. Interestingly, calls for a contextualization of research in this area of study have been manifested recently (Ames, 1992; Blumenfeld, 1992). Not surprisingly, however, few studies have looked at these variables in the contexts of urban schools, and even fewer studies have related them to the cognitive processes of minority students and urban teachers (Schultz, 1993).

Sociolinguistic studies. Research on classroom discourse using a sociocultural perspective might also offer meaningful contributions to the study of thought processes in urban classrooms (Gutierrez, 1993; Gutierrez, Kreuter, & Larson, in press). In this research tradition, language "involves context and provides context" (Duranti & Goodwin, 1992). To illustrate, Gutierrez (1993) scrutinized literacy activities of Latino students using a multidisciplinary theoretical framework (e.g., sociocultural and sociohistorical theories, language socialization theory, and cross-cultural research on development). She contends that "through [the] process of shaping and being shaped by activity within and across events of everyday life, children acquire both linguistic and sociocultural knowledge for what it means to be a member of a community and to act in socially appropriate ways" (p. 337).

Among other things, this model of inquiry will provide researchers interested in contextualized teacher thinking with tools and frames of reference to start disentangling the intricate embroidery formed by cultural context, social interactions, discourse patterns, knowledge exchange systems, and belief systems in urban classrooms.

Industrial anthropology. The work of anthropologists conducted in complex organizations and industries might also offer meaningful analytical tools to develop this new research agenda. For instance, Lytle (1992) argues that several notions used in industrial anthropology might assist educators in understanding the complexity of urban schools. These constructs include subcultures, myths and rituals, isomorphism (i.e., "tendency to design formal structures that adhere to the myths of the environment in order to promote success and survival," p. 119), highly elaborated institutional environments, legitimacy (i.e., "acting on collectively valued purposes in a proper and adequate manner and in accordance with accepted standards," p. 119), leadership, and artifacts, values, and basic assumptions.

Consequently, we might pose several questions from this perspective: What is the role of academic evaluation myths and rituals in teacher cognitions? How are they reflected in the cognitions of students? How does isomorphism contribute or interfere in the negotiations of meanings and conceptual change in urban classrooms?

Cross-cultural and comparative education. Studies of teachers' and students' thought processes in urban schools ought to be implemented in different cultures and nations. This exercise would allow educational researchers to assess the role of culture on these cognitive processes. By using a sociocultural model to study cognitions across cultures, we would gain significant insights about the cultural variations of meaning-making processes, theories of learning and deviance, attributions of success and failure, and so forth. Situated cognition, self-regulation, and competence might have completely different connotations in other cultures as well. By looking into other cultures' urban classrooms and by understanding such intricate processes, we will understand better our own urban school processes and outcomes.

Critical theory. Critical theory with its emphasis on constructs such as hegemony, power struggles, sociopolitical differentials, and empowerment might be a valuable framework for looking at thinking processes in urban schools (Kincheloe & Steinberg, 1993; McLaren, 1989). But what is the relevance of these notions for the ways teachers and students see their roles and strata in urban classrooms? To what extent do the students that attend urban schools use the notions of power and hegemony to interpret and think about their schooling experiences? These and many others questions are empirical questions that could be addressed in this new research agenda.

Broadening the Boundaries of Methods

Marshall (1992) contends that "theory and research methodology can constrain or enlighten what is observed and what can be concluded about classroom learning, the meaning of learning, and the consequences to individuals" (p. 3). That is why one of the most critical recommendations of this new agenda of inquiry is to reflect about the methods we have used to tap teacher cognitions, and to ponder whether the knowledge base in this domain has been enhanced or constrained by these methodologies. Further, we need to ask to what extent informants might provide us with distinct views, facets, or perspectives of the same thinking construct if we use different methodologies.

Hence we need to revamp the means we use to see classroom instruction, thought processes, and conceptual changes. For example, we need to look at the teacher-student-dyad-in-activity when examining interactive thinking processes. For the theoretical reasons offered in preceding sections, the use of this unit of analysis is justified. Furthermore, multiple foci (e.g., processes and outcomes) and eclectic research designs (e.g., quantitative and qualitative components) are more powerful means to address complex questions. In addition, original approaches such as autobiography and repertory grids (Artiles & Trent, 1990; Solas, 1992), storytelling and narratives (Carter, 1993), concept maps (Artiles, 1995; Chow & McClafferty, 1995; Morine-Dershimer et al., 1992); and others should be utilized in this new program of research. Finally, teachers and students should be involved in inquiry efforts to collect and analyze data on their own thought processes. Such participatory models will help strengthen the link between educational researchers and practitioners.

CONCLUSION

After reviewing the literature on teacher thinking and urban schools, I conclude that it is time to transcend atomistic linear models of inquiry in these fields. For that purpose, I propose that researchers in both camps cross the boundaries that separate their academic discourses. By doing this, researchers in urban education will start including the role of mediating variables (thought processes) when looking at classroom processes. In the same vein, research on teacher thinking will have more relevance for practice if we start disaggregating the setting in which thought processes occur (i.e., urban schools). From this perspective, the aim of teacher thinking studies will no longer be to scrutinize frozen frames of insular cognitive activity. Instead, thought processes will be construed as fluid, dynamic, malleable cognitive processes embedded in multidimensional contexts.

In order to achieve such a paradigmatic shift, I have suggested that a sociocultural view of teaching, learning, and thinking be embraced. As stated above, this conceptual platform will give prominence to the role of contexts when looking at urban classrooms and thinking processes. But just as we change the definition of teaching and thinking, I argue that the notion of learning be enhanced in accordance with the sociocultural model. Finally, I suggest we embark on an eclectic research agenda that strives to construct an interdisciplinary knowledge base and that perennially revises its conceptual and methodological foundations. This will enable us to recycle our own thinking about cognitions, teaching, and learning. Ultimately, I hope our efforts will contribute to reach those who seem unreachable, will invite thoughtfulness in those who seem apathetic, and will help confirm indisputably that human potential is not culturally determined.

THINKING ABOUT STUDENTS
FROM DIVERSE BACKGROUNDS

TEACHERS', ADMINISTRATORS', AND STAFF'S IMPLICIT THINKING ABOUT "AT-RISK" URBAN HIGH SCHOOL LATINO STUDENTS

Martha Montero-Sieburth

How do Latino students become identified and labeled by administrators, teachers, and staff as "problems" within schools? What criteria are used to determine their being "at risk"? Are Latino students who are identified as at risk perceived differently than other students? Once they are identified as being at risk, how does such thinking affect the relationship, the delivery of services, and teaching of such students?

These are the questions that I attempt to examine and report in this chapter, as part of a larger quantitative and qualitative study in a Boston urban high school during the 1989–1990 academic year which attempted to understand the schooling processes and practices affecting ninth- and tenth-grade Latino students.[1] Subsequent research with teachers and visits to their classrooms continued during 1990–1992.[2]

In the major study, four students in a ninth- and tenth-grade bilingual basic math class from Nicaragua, Puerto Rico (one U.S. born, another from the island), and El Salvador and four students in a ninth and tenth-grade mainstream civics class of Puerto Rican (three U. S. born and one from the island) backgrounds were shadowed, interviewed, and observed during the school year in their respective classes to ascertain what schooling processes and practices created at-risk conditions for them. The intent was to focus on in-school factors that contribute to students' decision for staying or leaving school rather than to focus on home and community conditions that are not within the school's control.

Although none of these students were identified as being at risk—having low achievement, retention in grade, behavior problems, substance abuse, unemployment, poor attendance, poverty, single-parent families, and low socioeconomic status (Pallas, Natriello, & McDill, 1989)–they nevertheless fit the description of the national dropout literature, which identifies factors such as "being poor, having limited English proficiency, and being Latino in the United States" as contributing to early school leaving (Steinberg, Blinde, & Chan, 1984). In that respect, these students were considered potentially at risk.

The case studies of their school life reflected the demands schooling placed on them to conform to codes, rules, and regulations and indicated how well they responded and negotiated between such demands and their own particular Puerto Rican, Nicaraguan, and Salvadoran backgrounds. The findings demonstrated that even when Latino students had been mainstreamed, spoke English well, and had every reason to succeed, other factors such as poor grades, extended absences, the lure of the workplace, difficult and escalating confrontations with the teacher, speaking Spanish in an English class, the use of basic discriminatory practices, and abuse at home contributed to their leaving school.[3] None of the eight students were known to have any disciplinary problems.

At the end of the academic year, five of the eight potential at-risk students had either dropped out or not passed their classes. Only three (two in the bilingual math and one in the mainstream civics class) completed the year and were promoted to the next grade. During 1990–1991, a student who had dropped out of the bilingual class came back twice as a serial dropout and left before the end of the year. Two of the mainstream civics class students did not return to school. Of the two who failed the previous year, one repeated bilingual math and the other civics. By 1991–1992, the two remaining students in the bilingual program continued in school. One was mainstreamed into all-English classes and the other continued to come to class while pregnant. The one student who had been promoted from the mainstream class was married in 1992 and was hoping to complete her senior year.

The findings of the major study provided schooling and practice-level analysis in uncovering the way students negotiate school life, rules, and regulations and their decisions to stay or leave. Yet another level of research analysis was needed to shed light on the perspectives and beliefs that teachers, administrators, and staff held about at-risk students in general, and particularly about at-risk Latino students. Missing was a description and explanation of the thinking structure and context that pervaded the school.

In this regard, finding out how bilingual and mainstream teachers, administrators, and staff thought about their roles and beliefs vis-à-vis at-risk students, and at-risk Latino students in particular, became important in determining the images, attitudes, and responses they had in treating these students. This type of thinking is conditioned by contextual and cultural variables, and in urban schools by the general "culture" of the school, which differs from the "cultures" of suburban, rural, private, and mono-cultural schools.

Urban schools, as I have argued elsewhere (Montero-Sieburth, 1989), have their own norms, rules, status markers, and boundaries of appropriate and inappropriate behaviors. Learning to use such knowledge means learning explicit ways of doing things, yet that knowledge base is often shaped by those in power. Since that knowledge is primarily accessible to those of the majority culture, learning how to decode what is expected and how to act determines how well students from underrepresented groups have access to the implicit knowledge (or out-of-awareness learning) of teachers, administrators, and staff (Montero-Sieburth, 1989; Ríos, 1993). The same type of analysis also pertains to the relationships between bilingual and mainstream teachers, especially if their knowledge base is experientially and culturally different from the mainstream dominant (Anglo) culture.

Uncovering the implicit level of thinking of administrators, teachers, and staff seemed an appropriate way to understand the context that influences at-risk Latino high school student's options and opportunities for schooling. To that end, thirty-two administrators, teachers, and staff who had direct contact with Latino students were interviewed. Each of the eight potential at-risk Latino students were also interviewed in depth. The data from their interviews provided the basis for developing individual case studies and vignettes of their experiences and are published elsewhere (see Montero-Sieburth, in press). By combining both interviews, one could draw a holistic picture of the types of thinking that prevailed at this school.

For the purpose of this chapter, the multilayered analysis of the thirty-two interviews with adults, their thematic codification, and direct verbatim extracts from the content are presented. Where pertinent, cross-checks by ethnic background, gender, and longevity of time in the school are highlighted.

CONTEXT

Situated in a white (97.3 percent) working-class neighborhood where over 60 percent of the residents live in public housing, the school in this study is one of many Boston public schools administered by a "High School Zone" superintendent. It serves students who do not attend exam schools or magnet schools[4]. This high school was specifically selected on the basis of nominations from state education officials for its mix of diverse students.

Well over 80 percent of the 1050 students in grades 9 to 12 are bussed in from diverse parts of the city in compliance with a 1974 desegregation order to maintain the racial and ethnic balance. The diversity of the student body is 18 percent white, 24 percent Latinos, 31 percent Black, 26 percent Asian with less than 1 percent Native American. Latinos are drawn primarily from a predominantly stable Puerto Rican community and an emerging Central and South American area.

From the total 245 Latino students (137 males and 108 females) enrolled in December of 1989, 139, or 57 percent, of the Latinos (13 percent of the student body) were in the bilingual program (86 males and 53 females),[5] and 106 (66 males and 40 females) attended the mainstream or "regular" program[6]. Of those Latinos in the bilingual program, the majority were from El Salvador (49), Colombia (29), and Puerto Rico (28); smaller numbers came from the Dominican Republic (13), Mexico (6), Honduras (5), Ecuador (3), Nicaragua (2), Guatemala (2), Costa Rica (1), and Peru (1).

The bilingual transitional program is aimed at providing native language instruction in Chinese and Spanish while introducing English as a Second Language (ESL) courses augmented with English subject classes until students can be fully mainstreamed into all-English classes. This process reportedly occurs within the first four years.

The bilingual teaching staff, including a director and assistant director, is mostly composed of 10 ESL, bilingual math, science, business, language arts, and history Spanish-speaking and

Chinese-speaking teachers. Except for the administrators and four teachers who are veteran staff at the school, most of the bilingual teachers, including a resource specialist and career counselor, are newcomers with less than three years' experience at the school.

Unlike other similar programs, the bilingual program, considered to be exemplary in the state, has one of the lower drop out rates for bilingual students. Close to 85 percent of its senior bilingual class reportedly go on to college, and many of the students, mostly those with Asian names, are honored with awards.

The mainstream program has a high concentration of over sixty certified teachers and administrators across all subject areas. Many have been in the Boston public schools for more than twenty-two years. Newcomer (less than three years' experience) teachers, administrators, and staff, however, are in the minority. In both programs, multiple grades in each subject area, such as math, science, and social studies, are taught to accommodate a range of student abilities. The total school personnel is about one hundred teachers, administrators, and staff.

METHODOLOGY

The negotiation of entry into the school in the fall paralleled the setting up of interviews. Once negotiation of classrooms for observations was under way, an hour-long interview schedule was set up with all of the bilingual and several mainstream teachers, administrators, and staff who were known to have frequent contact with Latino students through teaching, counseling, or support programs. The selection of those to be interviewed was based on names most frequently mentioned by the staff of teachers, administrators, and personnel and from observations conducted at faculty and after-school meetings.

A total of 32 administrators, teachers, and staff were interviewed by the researcher and two assistants. These included the principal, assistant principal, disciplinary officers (2), department heads (4), the director of the Bilingual Program, Spanish-speaking bilingual teachers (6), a Chinese-speaking bilingual teacher who taught ESL, ESL instructors (2), a bilingual counselor, mainstream teachers[7] in different subjects areas (9), a Compact Venture administrator, a resource specialist, a career counselor, a librarian, one of four police officers, and the school nurse[8]. Table 2.1 describes the gender, ethnicnity, and length at school of these individuals.

Table 2.1.

Interviewee (*N* = 32) Profile by Gender, Ethnicity, and Length at School

Gender	
Male	66%
Female	34%
Ethnicity	
African-American	19%
Chinese	6%
Latino	29%
White	53%
Length at School	
Veteran[a]	72%
Newcomer[b]	28%

[a]Veteran: more than three years' experience at this school; some have been at the school for more than twenty years, and one has been teaching for thirty-four years.

[b]Newcomer: less than three years' experience at this school; still adjusting to the system.

It should be noted that because the sample of interviewees in any given category as administrator, bilingual teacher, mainstream teacher, career counselor, and so on is small, generalizations from the data could not be made except in terms of aggregate number responses. When all or most of the Spanish-speaking bilingual teachers responded similarly or the Chinese-speaking bilingual teacher and administrator responded in the same way, statements in relation to ethnic perspectives were made.

In-depth interviews of the two teachers, Ms. B in the bilingual basic math class and Mr. M in the mainstream civics class, were additionally conducted to gather information on their educational backgrounds, pedagogical philosophies, and expectations for Latino students. All of the eight students of the primary study were given lengthy in-depth interviews. However, only two were given additional home interviews, since they were the only students available at the end of the third quarter.

The analysis of the in-depth interviews was based on the content and frequency of responses given by each interviewee on an 17 item one-hour semi-structured protocol. In each case, notes were taken for twelve interviewees and the remaining twenty interviewees were audiotaped. The notes and audiotaped interviews were transcribed and coded by the categories that emerged from the data. These categories were cross-referenced with other emergent data sets, and thematic relationships were established through focus group meetings of the researchers each month. The complete analysis, consisting of cross-tabulations of selected themes and emergent propositions was elaborated further and the theory behind teachers' thinking and implicit knowledge (Peterson, 1988; Montero-Sieburth, 1989; Ríos, 1993) was used to inform the findings.

To summarize, the initial interviews with staff, administrators, and teachers provided a composite of at-risk factors, some of which were pertinent to Latino students at this school. Some of the verbatim remarks compellingly highlighted their concerns. In addition, the in-depth interviews with the teachers directly involved with the eight students from each program gave further insights of their perspectives of Latino students. Finally, the observations within the school, coupled with classroom observations and informal and formal interviews with the eight potential at-risk Latinos, provided an ongoing account of the students' responses.

FINDINGS

The analysis of the perspectives of teachers, administrators, and staff regarding at-risk students in general, and of at-risk Latino students in particular, identifies issues that help address the following basic questions of this study.

What Criteria Are Used to Determine "At-Riskness"?

Definitions of "at-risk" students. The operational definitions for students at-risk for over 50 percent of the respondents concurred with the characteristics mentioned by the literature on at-risk students: one who is in danger of dropping out because of problems with attendance and discipline, is behind grade or skill level, has low grades, is a repeater, has low self-esteem and motivation, and is one who will "never make it."

The majority of the respondents associated the concept of "dropout" as part of being "at risk." Except for the Chinese-speaking and several of the Spanish-speaking bilingual teachers and newcomer teachers, all the rest mentioned discipline problems, low motivation, low self-esteem, poor reading levels, and poor attendance as markers of being at risk.

The Chinese-speaking and Spanish-speaking bilingual teachers and an African-American ESL teacher focused on the obstacles and challenges that students faced while in school and as they were assimilated into American culture. They emphasized "culture shock, pregnancy without having extended families, the fear of not feeling confident enough to go on to a university, being over age, being ambivalent, experiencing the pains of earning a living while going to school, and lacking English-language proficiency," as situations that seemed insurmountable to students yet could be overcome since they were not endemic to students nor failure.

The director of the Bilingual Program referred to "students who are on the verge of dropping out as being those who teachers and administrators need to concentrate on as at risk." She realized that "academic problems abound especially with students who come from the rural part of China or from war-torn countries of Central America." To help them gain a foothold in school, she identifies such students as "preliterate, or illiterate" and offers remedial work and after-school tutoring.

Range of conceptions for at-risk students. Interestingly, the definitions for being "at risk" ranged from out-of-school issues such a societal pressures, family, and neighborhood life to specific within-school factors. Some of the teachers and administrators viewed home and neighborhood life as reflecting student behavior in school. One regular classroom teacher commented that "all urban students are at risk." Another referred to "children who have children as being at risk." Yet another bilingual teacher commented, "In this society, we are all at risk." A resource teacher defined as "at risk" not only the students who have "a greater than average chance of dropping out before they finish . . . high school, but also have a greater than average chance of dropping out but still staying in high school on an emotional level, by not engaging themselves in what's happening in the school and becoming isolated."

The career counselor considered the "at-risk" label to refer to "virtually all kids in the public school system as well as the suburban schools in that criteria such as poor academic performance, behavioral problems, broken home environments are present." Unlike others, this counselor felt that "the school plays a larger part in not making the institution an attractive place to be particularly for students of difference or color."

For one mainstream teacher, "how well a student obeys the common rules of decency in a classroom . . . or how routinely the student performs the tasks and assignments given to him or her, what is their performance on an examination" are some of the basic indicators that need to be sought out for understanding why they may be academically at risk. In contrast, the school nurse viewed physical risk, suicide, and serious health problems as well as emotional and social problems as causes for students to be at risk.

Use of at-riskness to identify the pathology of the student and home. It is remarkable that except for two respondents, all respondents used "at-risk" definitions that attributed failure to the student. These were linked to either the students themselves—their inability to value education, to know how to read, write, or express themselves—or to conditions at home. Some of the responses implicitly blamed the students for being at risk, while others blamed "the problems of the school and society as a consequence of the breakdown of the family." One of the mainstream teachers characterized the students as "having troubles because they choose to have troubles. They choose not to come to school. The same kid could pass, . . . they're lazy." Only two respondents mentioned the possibility that the school does not challenge the student and offers an inadequate curriculum.

Notably, the "at-risk" label at this school may not apply to students who are at risk but who may also have difficulties that the school is unaware of or inadvertently ignores. Students are not often identified as being at risk unless there is reason to suspect abuse. One of the focal students of the major study who stopped coming to school before the end of the year kept appearing on the school roster even though a social worker had filed a complaint of abuse form.

It is clear that the term *at risk* provokes different responses from teachers, administrators, and staff. However, the definitions are eschewed, with a focus on either the students or on the obstacles and hardships immigrant students face. Furthermore, the conceptualization of "at risk" has both out-of-school explanations that include the home, community, and family contexts and within-school explanations of academic and social behaviors.

What Identification Procedures Are Used?

The school's identification of at-risk students. The consensus of over half (47 percent) of the respondents was that although the use of the "at-risk" label allows school personnel to recognize individual students needing help, its use does not necessarily help or hinder that process. Many of the interviewees wondered if the students knew they were at risk or whether the label was even used in the school. In fact, one of the case managers considered the term to be "a good catch phrase for funding. It can be helpful if it enables the system to focus programs on a certain population and to help them (such as clustering); the problem is that kids don't necessarily know they're clustered."[9] Another commented that the meaning of "at risk" has become diluted because of the numbers of at-risk kids.

The usefulness of the "at-risk" label and how it might influence adult expectations of students, as it already had at the school, was questioned by some of the personnel at this school. Its usage was found to be not useful by one-fourth (25 percent) of the respondents, and another one-fifth (19 percent) suggested that the label carried negative connotations. A smaller number of respondents (9 percent) mentioned that they did not like the label and felt it should not be applied. For those not liking or wanting to use the label, remarks ranged from "actually digging up the students who are 'at risk' on your own without prejudging them" to "not using the label of 'at risk' at all since teachers do not want to be told what someone else thinks about a student," and once labeled, "the student would think, 'I'm stupid, I'll never make it.'"

Thus it is clear that although the majority of the teachers, administrators, and staff see the importance of identifying students in order to help them, they realize that simply labeling such students as "at risk" is detrimental. Instead they prefer to discuss potential at-risk students by flagging them early on and finding "the cause in order that something can be done." Thus identifying at-risk students is viewed as being more of a preventive measure than as a crisis outcome. Moreover, several of the Spanish-speaking bilingual teachers, namely, the special education, math, and language arts teachers, viewed the use of *at risk* as limited and not appropriate within the school.

Two of the respondents pointed out that when *at risk* is used simply as a label, it can do more harm than good by creating negative expectations, with "students acting as labeled" and "not offering the necessary response if the student is not vocal nor demanding of attention." The philosophy of one of the mainstream teachers was that "everybody is at risk, but some students so labeled will get the attention which is denied another group of students, hence it is not democratic."

Uncertainty about school procedures for dealing with at-risk students. The ambiguous use of the term *at risk* was compounded by the uncertainty expressed by more than half (59 percent) of the respondents over how the school identifies such students. Although there was some speculation on possible processes, more than one-third (38 percent) cited referrals from either the school (teacher, guidance counselor, nurse, etc.) or outside sources (parents, community agencies, etc.). Others cited commonplace factors such as grades, behavior, attendance, and test scores as ways to identify at-risk students.

Even though the school identifies and diagnoses at-risk students, there were no set procedures nor prescriptions set forth to help them. Furthermore, when students are known to be at risk, such information is not necessarily shared with teachers. It appears that school personnel are left to on their own to deal with at-risk students as they see fit. This suggests that the issue of at-risk students is not directly addressed by the school as a unit but is made the individual responsibility of teachers and counselors and specific programs.[10]

What Are the Perceptions about At-Risk Latinos?

School identification of at-risk Latino students. One-fourth (25 percent) of the respondents identified the same reasons for Latino students as for any other group of at-risk students, and close to half (50 percent) mentioned attendance and/or behavior characteristics as generally being associated with at-risk Latino students.

A sixth (16 percent) mentioned work as contributing to at-risk behaviors. Although "full-time jobs and five days of school don't mix," the reality for Latino students was different from that of mainstream students. According to the Spanish-speaking bilingual teachers, their students were more likely to work overtime. Some worked twenty-six hours a week, exceeding the fifteen hours the school considers appropriate. Ms. B asked:

> Can you blame the students if options such as working, even for five dollars an hour for full-time work, are presented to them? You are talking about kids who are illegal. They're concerned about being protected. They want money. They have families to support. They have their mother in El Salvador who's starving to death. They don't care. They lie. They say, I'm 21. Who's gonna ask them.

About a tenth (9 percent) mentioned "lack of support from the family," especially when "education is not valued, and where poor family conditions (single-parent homes, poverty, etc.) add to their plight."

Bad grades was another issue. However, it needs to be questioned, especially when dealing with immigrant students who do not know English yet and have come with school learning skills that are different from those of an urban high school. Students may receive bad grades for different reasons. The same at-risk indicator (bad grades in this case) as applied to two different students does not necessarily infer the same underlying causal factor.

A notion that was not addressed by any of the respondents except by the bilingual teachers, the resource teacher, and the career counselor was the lack of community-to-home connections since students are bussed in and out of this school. Students don't have an opportunity to know their school community. The resource teacher acknowledged:

> If a child is going to a school that's outside of the community, then there is no link between the community and the school on a physical basis; if I can't see the school when I look outside my window and know that my child is there, then the school is this entity that isn't part of the community.

The career counselor commiserated as well: "How can you get any kind of feeling of community here when these kids have no time to congregate other than seeing each other in the halls?"

Dealing with at-risk Latino students. There was very little consensus and widespread variation over the ways to deal with at-risk Latino students, or over approaches used with other at-risk students that might be effective with Latinos.[11] Half of the interviewees (49 percent) said that, discounting the needs of language and culture, at-risk Latino students could be dealt with in the same way as any other at-risk students. The influence of ethnicity as well as cultural and linguistic differences, including space, comfort, or living conditions, did not seem to be viewed as salient. This indicates a lack of awareness of the influence of sociocultural nuances and behaviors for individual students.

Similarly, illiteracy in English and Spanish, which would have a bearing on being at risk was only mentioned by one respondent. Surely this is a significant issue that was not fully explored in relation to being "at risk" at this school. A student with limited skills in any language is at a clear disadvantage as a learner in a competitive high school setting.[12]

One of the Spanish-speaking bilingual teachers stated, "While drug use affects all students and places them 'at risk,'" for Latinos, it is "being immigrants, unstable, having an inadequate curriculum, having to work at night, and having home environments which are not supportive." Another bilingual teacher stressed "family structure, economic stability, poor knowledge of English and their status as immigrants" as factors contributing to their being at risk.

An important result of these responses is the implication that all at-risk students are perceived as the same, since they become at risk for the same reasons. Yet their sameness erodes when they become "problems." At that point distinctions in terms of ethnicity, language, and expectations come into play.

Comparisons between and within ethnic groups. Distinctions between ethnic groups also give rise to within-group comparisons. The observations of the resource specialist who worked mostly with the Chinese-speaking and Spanish-speaking bilingual teachers are a case in point:

> The Chinese students perceive the Latino students as being more aggressive, talkative. The Chinese teachers look at the Latino students and they say, "those Latino students, all they like to do is sing and dance. You can't get them to stay after school to get tutored with English, but you sure can get them to stay after school if they're going to have a party and sing and dance." All I know is that the Chinese are perceived to be the best in everything.

This same teacher noticed that Latinos appear to be more integrated than Asian students, and to have more positive interaction with mainstream students who seem to respect them, since she hears less negative talk about Latinos. She found American students attempting to imitate Chinese student speech in the halls, but did not observe them attempting to do the same or sound like Latinos. Similarly, the career counselor observed that Latino students seem to assimilate more than the Asian students because "their cultural temperament seems to be less reserved and a little bit more outgoing than the more reserved Far East traditions of the Asian students." Yet this same integration between Latinos and Anglos does not seem to occur with blacks. The career counselor reported:

> There are certain kids which will choose to come here because of the great programs being offered such as the bilingual program. Those kids which tend to be Spanish-speaking or Chinese have created their own community here. Black kids don't feel invested in this place at all or very little. It's a stifling, unenergizing, unstimulating environment.

During a school field trip in which teachers selected those students they most enjoyed to go on the trip, no blacks were on the bus even though there were about thirty Chinese students and fifteen to twenty Latino students. For one of the staff, this situation characterizes a mindset that he believes works like this: "White kids we understand, even if they are bad kids. Chinese kids are marvelous because they are better than white kids. They have assimilated to white culture, they do even better then we do. They are polite, hospitable, hard working, gracious and respectful." This comparison between the "model minority" Asian students, African-Americans, and Latinos sets the stage for stereotyping to occur. Yet the more subtle within-group comparisons are equally as harmful.

Intragroup differences among Latinos surfaced in the descriptions provided by several mainstream classroom teachers and even by one Spanish-speaking bilingual teacher who as a Puerto Rican had never dealt with Central and South American students before. She felt that because "a lot of these [Latino] students are illegal, they need to be given more opportunities to assimilate."

Puerto Ricans as a whole were characterized by a few mainstream teachers as "having a very low self-image and seeming lazy, reflecting attitudes of I don't care" in their lack of work or in not thinking twice about "going back to Puerto Rico for a week or two weeks and missing school." In contrast, South Americans were considered to be "more respectful, more afraid of authority and willing to work with you." One of the teachers regarded Colombians, Ecuadorians, Costa Ricans, Venezuelans, and Hondurans as being more in line with his expectations than Puerto Ricans. He commented: "I find a much higher failure rate among the Latinos from Puerto Rico than I do from any other parts of North America."

Interestingly, only one of the mainstream teachers challenged the practice of grouping Latino students together as one. He believed that "they are as different as night and day," yet he shared the assumption that

> there is a stronger motivation toward education from the Central American Boston sector than from the Puerto Rican sector. Part of the reason for this is the schooling of Central·Americans tends to be strict with corporal punishment being part of it. There is respect for an elder that is not coincidental with the Puerto Rican students, which are American basically. They have been brought up in a Spanish-speaking American education system, whereas the South and Central American kids have a different background.

Yet he attributed those differences to the neighborhoods from which these students came, particularly because one of the neighborhoods was primarily Puerto Rican and the other Central American. Only the resource teacher recognized that the issues among all of the Latino students were different; she insisted that "they are not a racial group, but it's like totally different cultures."

Another perception that only a few bilingual and mainstream teachers contested was the belief that Latino students were passive and uninterested about their schoolwork. As one mainstream teacher noted, contrary to this perception, Latino students were outspoken without needing to have others speak for them: "They speak out and don't go to the faculty, they go right to the headmaster or the representative on the Faculty Senate."

What Responses Are Employed to Prevent At-Risk School and Home Conditions?

Addressing the needs of at-risk students. Confusion among some personnel as to how the school actually addresses the needs of at-risk students was evident in about one third (31 percent) of the respondents. One stated that there are no set rules or procedures for addressing at-risk students; and another stated that teachers deal with at-risk students as they see fit. About a sixth (16 percent) of the respondents referred to the various support services (guidance counselors, tutoring programs, and the Special Education Department) as the school's way of addressing the needs of at-risk students.

Another third (34 percent) mentioned contacting the parents of at-risk students. The fact that not all of the respondents mentioned this does not necessarily mean that the school does not contact the parents of all of its at-risk students. Several school personnel seemed unsure of the school's procedures regarding the handling of at-risk students; therefore, even if the school routinely contacts parents in such cases, some school personnel might be unaware of this practice. The interviews indicate that contacting parents even for absences is a daily task undertaken by teachers. As noted by one interviewee, "the school can only control the student when he or she is in school."

Evaluating the at-risk condition of each individual student through a battery of tests, procedures, or assessments is another issue of concern. About one sixth (16 percent) of the respondents included evaluating the student as part of the process for addressing the at-risk condition. Judging from the interviewees' responses, there does not appear to be such a clearly defined process for handling at-risk students in the school's departments, except for Special Education and the Bilingual Program.[13]

School prevention of at-risk conditions. Many interviewees mentioned ways in which the school can contribute to preventing at-risk conditions. They listed ideas that ranged from making the students feel good about themselves to how the high school can provide opportunities for student success, enhance students' self-esteem and motivation, acknowledge student concerns, make students feel they are accepted as part of the school, show the students that the teachers care about them, and treat the students like adults. Sports, the arts, and vocational education were greatly emphasized as ways in which students could be challenged by quite a few of the mainstream teachers. The Spanish-speaking bilingual teachers stressed playing soccer, cultural activities, and clubs as affecting Latino students' sense of teamwork.

One mainstream administrator stressed the need for "more vocational programs. . . . A lot of kids aren't academically talented. Not everybody's cut out for strictly academics. They get frustrated and they quit school." This same mainstream administrator emphasized the need to break down professional prejudice so that being a mechanic, a farmer, or a bus driver was not viewed negatively, but with pride. Although this interviewee may have assumed that not everyone is "cut out" for academics, she or he has overlooked the converse of this statement: Academic programs are not designed to motivate all learners. Another interviewee commented, "They're more at home in a hands-on-type environment rather than schoolwork. . . . I think more vocational/industrial arts programs—not just for Hispanics, any immigrant . . . " Although these examples were stated as aims, they lacked specificity and remained ambiguous.

One mainstream teacher remarked, in referring to the upcoming voucher system that allows inner city students to choose a suburban school, "It's not the schools, it's the kids in the schools. It's the building that creates the student? No, it's the student that creates the building. Even if you transfer all of these kids, they're not going to behave differently."

Among the three respondents who mentioned culture, one suggested that the school should attempt to make Latinos aware of the contributions of their culture to the United States; another mentioned recognizing cultural differences in designing the curriculum, in staff development, and in teaching personnel about Latino cultures; and a third recommended infusing the mainstream curriculum with items relevant to Latino culture. Interestingly, two were Spanish-speaking bilingual teachers and the other was the career counselor.

In addressing the issue of the relevance of curriculum in reducing at-risk conditions, it is noteworthy that well over half (55 percent) of those who answered were Chinese-speaking bilingual and Spanish-speaking bilingual teachers, along with one African-American ESL teacher. None of the white teachers or administrators except for the career counselor and resource teacher made any mention of this. Furthermore, close to half (45 percent) of the combined Chinese-speaking and Spanish-speaking bilingual respondents mentioned self-esteem and motivation as being related to success, whereas none of the whites did, and over a third (36 percent) of the Chinese-speaking and Spanish-speaking bilingual teachers and an African-American ESL teacher mentioned making the Latino students feel accepted. None of the white teachers, except for a career counselor and a resource specialist, mentioned this. Conversely, none of the Chinese-speaking and Spanish-speaking teachers or the ESL African-American teacher mentioned increasing vocational education programs, whereas close to one-fifth (22 percent) of the white respondents mentioned this.

Other responses that were made to reflect characteristics of an effective program for at-risk Latino students included "lowering the student-teacher ratio, involving parents in their children's education, using peer learning strategies in the classroom, and ongoing assessment of curriculum and staff development for cultural relevance." In this regard, the notion of high expectations was raised by one of the mainstream teachers:

> If you provide them with consistency in the classroom, they know what they can expect when they come into my class. They know what I expect of them. They know that I give them respect, and I demand respect in return. . . . I treat them fair, and I expect fairness in return. And I have very little discipline problems because of that.

Two individual responses are worth mentioning. One respondent stated that "students should be mainstreamed as quickly as possible"; the other affirmed that the bilingual program creates at-risk conditions by "separating students from others and by keeping them for a long time in the program." His thesis was that "students naturally fall back on their language that they feel more comfortable with, and not much stress is made on them to use the other language; therefore by not feeling comfortable using English they are not able to engage in their classes." Clearly in this last case, knowledge of the state-mandated bilingual law, which requires that classes be set up for students numbering more than twenty with a bilingual teacher and with extension beyond the basic three years with parents' approval, is not known.

Finally, one-fifth (20 percent) of the mainstream and bilingual teacher mentioned the need for a full-time bilingual counselor and a bilingual attendance officer as critical in creating an outreach to the community and in maintaining communication between the school and families. One interviewee commented, "They [policymakers] don't listen to teachers, but they might listen to community demands."

School responses to the problems of at-risk Latino students. The bilingual program was viewed as being far more effective than the mainstream program in helping at-risk Latino students by one-third (34 percent) of the respondents. Close to one-fifth (19 percent) cited bilingual teachers and the bilingual counselor as positive elements because of their involvement with the students, because of their knowledge of Latino cultures, and because they provided positive role models for the students.

However, one respondent stated that there was too much Spanish used in the bilingual program and that English writing skills were especially lacking. For many of the interviewees, the general consensus was that the Latino students stayed in the bilingual program too long, even though the exit rates into mainstream programs show the contrary.

One of the interviewees reported that some Latino parents had requested that their children continue in the bilingual program beyond the third year but were denied such a request. Another commented that other parents wanted their children to learn English quickly and therefore pushed for mainstreaming as soon as possible. The pressure that the bilingual program has for showing that it does not keep students, especially beyond three years, seems to influence the decisions being made by the administration in placing students. This suggests that the school does not necessarily dissuade parents from placing their children in the mainstream program instead of the bilingual program unless there are evident language difficulties.

What goes on within the bilingual program appears to be a mystery for many of the mainstream teachers, who do not know how it functions or what its internal policies are, except that it promotes bilingual students into all-English classes. For the bilingual teachers, the bilingual program represents the basic funnel through which all incoming immigrants and high numbers of U.S.-born Latino students, irrespective of their academic backgrounds, are placed in order to learn English or to receive special education classes. They are, by and large, the brokers of the system for the linguistically different student.

One Spanish-speaking teacher complained about the special education classes he had: "Only 2 to 4 percent of these students should be here, 20 percent of those present don't belong here, they are simply dumped here because of language problems."

With respect to the mainstream program, the lack of staff dealing with at-risk students was mentioned by two respondents, and the fact that the mainstream staff was not bilingual, which makes communication difficult, was mentioned by one.

It should be noted that none of the intervention programs available for at-risk students, such as Compact Ventures, have personnel who speak Spanish; thus counseling and information sharing takes place only in English, limiting the access of potential at-risk Latino students who are most in need of services. Seeing mainstream Latino students return to their Spanish-speaking bilingual teachers years after they have left the bilingual program comes, then, as no surprise. As several bilingual teachers echoed, "They feel out of place in the mainstream program."

The role of home and community in preventing at-risk conditions. Among those home and community factors that are important in preventing at-risk conditions for Latino students, one-third (34 percent) of the respondents mentioned parental involvement and support; one-fourth (25 percent) mentioned the value of education in the everyday life of the student, both in the home and in the community; and one-sixth (16 percent) mentioned "the home environment with two parents, a safe neighborhood, a quiet place to study, and structure and discipline" as essential to student engagement and retention. About one-fifth (20 percent) of the respondents stated that community activities play a role by keeping students involved in positive pursuits under controlled conditions (i.e., by "keeping them off the streets").

Activities to be and not to be undertaken by the school in dealing with Latino students. Activities that should be taken on by outside agencies, rather than the school, include the following: psychological and psychiatric counseling, medical services, and drug and alcohol abuse counseling, cited by one-fourth (25 percent) of the respondents, and immigration and other legal issues cited by few. The idea that the school should be the only source of support was questioned at least by one administrator, who stated, "City kids in public school generally don't get the support to go one step beyond. Somebody has to be a role model, some community agency has to reinforce it. It's not only us, it's the community, the parent, the church—a four-sided attack."

The fact that over a third (34 percent) of the respondents indicated that they are not sure what activities the school should not undertake or who should undertake them suggests that the school itself needs to be well aware of the resources in the community that provide these services.

Activities between Latinos and other ethnic groups. Over one-third (34 percent) of the respondents mentioned school activities in which Latino students participate and associate with other Latinos and members of other ethnic groups as being (a) elective, mainstream, or ESL classes; (b) sports, cited by close to one-sixth (16 percent); (c) free lunch, cited by another one-fourth (16 percent); (d) the Spanish Club and social events such as Mother's Day, also cited by at least one-sixteenth (6 percent); and (e) ROTC, mentioned by one respondent.

However, when specifically asked about special programs for Latinos, the Spanish Club was mentioned by over one-third (33 percent) of the respondents even though it is open to all. Apparently, only Latino students (99 percent) and particularly Central and South American students choose to participate. Close to one-fourth (22 percent) of the respondents mentioned the bilingual program as being targeted for Latinos. Some noted, though, that the Chinese students also have a bilingual program; therefore, the Spanish bilingual program is not unique. About one-third (30 percent) stated that they were unaware of any special programs for Latinos.

Sports activities for Latinos were particularly emphasized, both as a team builder of confidence, and because sports demand that students be academically qualified to participate; hence they demand responsibility. One department chair stipulated that if students "are treated as adults, are made to feel good about themselves, and can get into programs such as dance, drama, sports, beyond strictly academics, then students can have opportunities for success."

Altough the Spanish dance program was viewed as positive by a few of the respondents, one mainstream teacher pointed out the following:

> Given an absentee rate that is unacceptable for Latinos, the fact that they are pulled out of class for rehearsals hurts their academic opportunities. The Latinos seem to be very excitable when they are going to perform or have a dance. The excitement itself makes it hard to settle them down and get the work done. Then to be pulled out of a class. . . . "

The regularity with which extracurricular activities (such as the Spanish Club, sports, arts, or vocational education) serve as the socializing and assimilating avenues for Latino students implies that making room for the students' own cultural and social activities only takes place outside the classroom. Opportunities to legitimatize the students own cultural backgrounds within the classrooms and halls of the school are not commonly found.

Identifying those who speak on behalf of Latino students. In identifying the advocates for Latino students, two-thirds (55 percent) identified Latino and one-third (34 percent) identified non-Hispanic staff. It is important to note the ways in which these non-Latinos and Latinos interact with each other. Close to three-fourths (70 percent) mentioned the Spanish Bilingual Counselor (Ms. T), and close to a half (40 percent) mentioned a bilingual teacher (Ms. L), who was involved in the major study, as the primary advocates for the Latino students. Ms. L was referred to by one of the mainstream teachers "as a pied piper of a sort." However, this teacher cautioned that "when the Latino kids leave school, there won't be nobody in the corner named Ms. L to take care of them." Ms. L's protection of Latino students was looked upon with suspicion by several mainstream teachers, who felt her to be "overprotective, especially if she does not push them to mix."

Firsthand observation of the interactions of these two individuals with students supports the general opinion of the school personnel that they are critical to Latino students. Their dedication and caring were evident not only through counseling but also in times of need. Ms. L actually fed, clothed, and lodged several of the immigrant students as they sought housing or needed help in getting settled. She paid to take them on skating trips in order to show them that "someone cares." Both teachers addressed the Latino students affectionately in Spanish, using a motherlike register such as "mi amor, mi hijo/mi hija," and were usually the first to intervene when the students needed to communicate with non-Spanish-speaking school personnel. Several school personnel, such as the principal and assistant principal, noted that the relationship between these two individuals and some of the Latino students was akin to that of parent and child.

In fact, some of the Latino students continue to return to the bilingual program teachers even after being mainstreamed in all-English classes because they feel out of place having left the program. Ms. T and Ms. B as well as Mr. M recognize this as the students' need for advice, help, understanding, and moral support through listening. Some students even cut classes in order to speak to them.

To summarize the findings, several issues warrant attention:

1. *The use of "at-risk" labels by personnel is ambiguous and varied.* Although identifying at-risk students is generally viewed as positive, the actual process of identifying such students is ambiguous and not clearly defined by school policies. Instead such identification occurs arbitrarily on a teacher-by-teacher basis or by the accountability measures of specific programs, such as special education or bilingual education.

2. *A schoolwide policy for identifying at-risk students is lacking.* Unless difficulties are uncovered beyond an individual basis, students may end up being inadvertently ignored. Hence those who are most visible and vocal may receive the attention that is overlooked in other cases.

3. *Except for bilingual education and special education, no known processes or procedures exist to help students identified as at-risk.* Each teacher or administrator deals discreetly with such students as she or he sees fit. This implies that, given the daily grind of schooling, uncovering who is at risk demands time and energy that cannot be expended under a normal teaching load.

4. *At-risk students are explained in terms of the pathology of their family and home.* Since students are held accountable for their success and failure, the student and his or her family are to blame if they are viewed as being at risk. In some cases, it is the student who is regarded as the problem, irresponsible in meeting the demands of learning. Hence the school does not fail the student, instead the student makes a conscious decision to fail.

5. *At-risk Latino students are assessed and treated like any other at-risk student.* While issues of language and culture may be discounted in assessing at-risk Latino students, other matters, such as degree of acculturation, living conditions, and adjustment, to school environment, are not accounted for.

6. *Traditional family support, school involvement, and community networks are used as a basis to explain template for at-risk Latinos.* The fact that traditional family systems, parent involvement, and community membership are viewed as the ideal when assessing at-risk Latinos implies that their absence is causally linked to failure. School personnel think that today's students are like those they were exposed to twenty years ago; they dismiss the nature of today's multiethnic student body and the impact of Latino immigrants and migrants in schools.

7. *Uncertainty exists over who is responsible for providing help to at-risk students and whether agencies are more adequate than schools.* There is an uncertainty about who is to provide help to at-risk students and the belief that outside agency services can do a better job than schools; this suggests both fear of not having the appropriate resources but also the belief that these are issues out of the control of the school.

DISCUSSION

Clearly the analysis of the interviews presents a complex picture of the perspectives and thinking that mainstream and bilingual administrators, teachers, and staff alike have of at-risk students, and particularly at-risk Latino students. Such perspectives are embedded within the institutional or deep structure of schooling—the scheduling, curriculum orientation, and tracking (Tye, 1987)—but also within the traditional patterns of teaching and managing that have prevailed in the school. Both affect the delivery of services provided to at-risk students and to at-risk Latinos. Hence, it is important to understand the influence of power and culture, language, ethnicity, and newcomer and veteran status as contextual parameters of schools.

Power in the Cultural Context

The fact that the school is top-heavy, with underrepresented students, a majority of white teaching staff, a small, ethnically mixed administration, and separate bilingual and mainstream programs, suggests that the school is very much run in the image of those who are numerically strong and have the power. The institutional power base is centered in the majority or mainstream culture. Anderson (1984, p. 8) states that "the knowledge a person already possesses is the principal determiner of what a person can come to know. Knowledge, in turn, is conditioned by culture. Therefore a person's culture is a principal determiner of what he or she can come to know." Thus what emerges for a knowledge base in this school are generalized beliefs of some administrators, teachers, and staff about at-risk students and at-risk Latino students that are colored by their cultural assumptions and knowledge of these students. To the extent that they know the culture of these students and incorporate these students' experiences into their management and teaching repertoires, administrators, teachers, and staff in this school appear to rely on the more traditional cultural patterns of teaching and administering that have worked for them for the past twenty years in dealing with Latino students.

Not knowing the neighborhoods where these students come from, nor many of the issues they face within the neighborhoods or the streets, the administration as well as teachers act upon the knowledge that they *can* control within the schools. Thus their concerns are not necessarily about knowing the students as much as about knowing what to concretely do to keep them in school. As the career counselor pointed out:

> If you walk by the classes you will see a good number of kids totally tuned out, sleeping, not looking. There are people here who have been teaching for 30 years and whose ideas which worked 30 years ago are not working well now. They believe that since the ideas worked well 30 years ago they should continue to work well, therefore its the student's fault and not the teacher's.

Knowing about the student's culture is viewed as an exercise that is either extracurricular (during celebrations, festivals, or schoolwide activities, as in a dance class) or is the prerogative of a teacher's class.

These generalizations hold up when Latinos are considered in monolithic and homogeneous terms as one single culture and language. But as the teachers and administrators encounter unexplainable behaviors and attitudes that they cannot control in the variety of Latinos whom they teach, explanations about the differences between and among each group take on different flavors. For example, when comparisons between Latino groups were made by several of the mainstream teachers, qualifiers such as the communities they came from in the city, the degree of Americanization and assimilation they have experienced, and whether they are Puerto Rican or Central American became distinctive criteria for judging the engagement of the groups in school.

Language and Color Blindness

The unfolding of a belief system held, by and large, by the veteran mainstream administrators and teachers vis-à-vis at-risk Latino students was not based on any single knowledge base about such students, but rather on the generalized knowledge of all students; hence the uniqueness of the student's immigrant, migrant, rural, suburban, Spanish-speaking, or English-speaking experiences may not even be considered. With the exception of some of the bilingual teachers who are involved on a day-to-day basis with bilingual students, particularly immigrant Latinos, and the resultant obstacles they confront, the criteria that are used to identify at-risk Latinos by the school and most administrators and teachers are the same criteria used for any other student. Thus color blindness and language to a lesser degree seem to operate as a mechanism for not acknowledging differences in these students' ability to academically and socially perform within the school.

The career counselor, disciplinary officers, bilingual counselor, and one specific bilingual teacher provided a different sense of student needs than did many of the other teachers or administrators. The proximity or distance to the student's life seemed to determine the type and degree of intervention that could be accomplished. Ms. B responded by meeting basic food needs, clothing, visits to the doctors, and so on. One of the disciplinary officers, who is African-American, responded to the Latino students, as with other ethnic students, by trial and error: "There comes a point when you just keep trying what you think will work."

These beliefs imply that there are universal ways in which all adolescents can be treated, and all students can be sanctioned and condoned by the same set of rules and requirements. It also assumes that all students entering high school start on the same footing. Yet the outcomes of the at-risk Latino bilingual and mainstream students during 1989–1991 would suggest that most did not "fit" these general set of expectations.

Ethnicity

Another assumption that pervades the knowledge base of teachers, administrators, and staff is the belief that teachers of the same ethnic group will be able to engage such students because they are of the same language group and culture. Here again, the more context-specific understanding that there are varied differences between and among Spanish-speaking Latino teachers and students is often not understood. Being of the same ethnic or language group does not naturally guarantee such linkages. Social class, degree of ruralness, urbanness, and acculturation may prove to create greater differences. In fact, the Italian Spanish-speaking and the U.S.-born Puerto Rican bilingual teachers who grew up in New York City without ever being in Puerto Rico may operate more out of their own experiences, mores, and knowledge and less out of the Latino ethnicity that they are purported to share as bilingual teachers.

Particularly striking were the explicit differences between Puerto Rican and Central American students that were identified mainly by mainstream teachers. The selection of certain behaviors and cultural values for each of these groups suggests implicit thinking in terms of a "pecking order" for Latino students by which preferential likes and dislikes are manifested according to whether students acquiesce to the teacher's demands and follow the rules. When incidents occur at the school and it is known that Latinos are involved, Puerto Ricans are most commonly identified and blamed as the perpetrators, a situation that creates embarrassment and resentment among Puerto Ricans and friction with other Latinos.

Veteran and Newcomer Status

The newcomer teachers and staff appeared to express different concerns than the mainstream teachers over at-risk Latino students. This may well be due to their being neophytes and finding themselves in similar roles and the fact they have extended contact with these students. The nurse explained how she had to overcome judging Latino parents' physical spanking of their children as being the same as committing physical abuse. The librarian explained how she was frustrated when she saw Latino students reading more magazines than books even though she encouraged them to learn how to use the library productively for their classes.[14] She also found that keeping silent in libraries was an unexpected request for some the Latino students. The police officer acknowledged that each student needs to be approached differently, including Latinos. Thus he disciplines students by helping them out, and when he can't find a solution, he resorts to referrals. His own involvement with students has led him to believe that "for some kids, the school is more a home than home."

Some of the newcomer staff dealing with counseling and resources questioned their own need for sensitivity about confronting basic biases about students. They also articulated ways in which the school may be at-risk in being separated from the home and community environments of the students. Their insights were challenging given the more veteran milieu of the school.

Policy and Classroom Implications

This study has implications for schools and classrooms about acknowledging the different contexts in which schooling and engagement and disengagement of students occur. More importantly, the findings stress the importance of understanding the effects of context-specific thinking on underrepresented students. Given the example of this schools' administrators, teachers, and staff and how they think about at-risk students, including at-risk Latinos, it is first important to understand that such thinking emanates from a primarily white schooling infrastructure that address the needs of underrepresented students with generation differences. This is not to say that the school is unable to meet the needs of these students, but it does mean that more context-specific knowledge about these students and their backgrounds, culture, and language is needed. These students are not simply the students of the bilingual program and teachers, but are the responsibility of the total school.

Second, it is clear that a paradigm shift needs to occur from viewing urban schools as solely inner city schools directed only at serving "poor and disadvantaged youth" to schools in urban contexts whose culture is capable of supporting and adapting to the needs of a diverse group of students.

Third, schools need students to teach, yet students need to be welcomed in schools. As one teacher stated, "It is not what the school offers, but the kind of support that is found therein" that will attract students. Changing the perspective from students as liabilities to assets may also help change the perspective of students from disadvantaged to students who have valuable funds of knowledge. This also implies needing to understand the context-specific issues of Latino students. Not all mainstream students are the same, and not all Latinos are the same, nor are their combined experiences one and the same. Moreover, what is perceived of Latino students in less than favorable ways may also be perceived of the faculty who serve them. One of the bilingual teachers commented how important it is "to overcome the negative picture of the statistics with belief that Latinos are here today, gone tomorrow and when they reach eighth grade, they can't graduate and teachers are also viewed as not being able to do anything." Hence it is important to know how to legitimize the role of Spanish-speaking faculty within a framework of other faculty and administrators.

Fourth, integrated schools need to integrate their policies and classrooms; that is, students should be encouraged through adequate curriculum and instructional materials as well as teaching to interact with each other in problem-solving, thinking, and deciphering new ideas. Hence, using dual-language classes where students are exposed to differences and similarities on an equal base may help break down the symbolic yet real barriers experienced by students and teachers.

Fifth, schools need to develop procedures for identifying issues or concerns of students through appropriate channels and services. Having Spanish-speaking counselors allows for the kind of communication needed; but by the same token, becoming aware of the local needs beyond the community is also important if less than adversarial roles are to be developed. This urban school's context appears to be distant to Latino parents and students. With bussing as the only means by which Latinos come to school, the alternatives are limited. Fostering after-school tutoring, peer tutoring across ethnic lines, and particularly parent training in ESL may help these communities be recreated. As the career counselor summarized:

> Latino groups in Boston are screaming out—recognize us—deal with us—we have problems—but the reason we have problems is because you never look at them. The hostility of the community to people of color and to

> people of difference is felt. If it weren't for assigned
> bussing, I don't see anyone wanting to come to this
> school outside of the kids who live in the immediate
> vicinity and possibly the bilingual kids.

Given the national concerns for dropout rates ranging from 40 to 70 percent across urban centers[15] and the expansion of the Latino population as a whole,[16] potential at-risk Latinos may continue to inflate such numbers unless there is some serious consideration given to the types of contexts in which students learn. If teachers, administrators, and staff are to go beyond colorblind policies and practices, they will need to recognize that Latino students *are* distinct from other students, that the traditional methods of teaching and managing may not be revelant today and that understanding Latinos in their own right requires accepting their cultural and linguistic backgrounds as a starting point for dialogue. Making the implicit thinking of faculty and administrators explicit may help challenge outdated perspectives and practices.

TEACHER THINKING AND PERCEPTIONS OF AFRICAN-AMERICAN MALE ACHIEVEMENT IN THE CLASSROOM

Clara A. New

The essential need to investigate factors that contribute to the success or in-school demise of African-American males in school settings is evidenced by the increasing proliferation of local and national forums that address this issue. Given the noticeable absence of teachers of color in teacher preparation programs and in urban classrooms during the past decade, that query has elicited varied responses, the most provocative of which appears to be that African-American males are best able to teach African-American males in public schools (Greathouse & Sparling, 1993; Leake & Leake, 1992). Additionally, the disproportionate ratio of females, primarily white females, teaching in elementary schools has prompted discussion regarding the overwhelming feminization of education in K–8 grades, and the possible impact on practices employed to guide males' adjustment through the early childhood years from kindergarten through the third grade.

Reasons for the ensuing interest in teachers' thinking and perceptions of, and expectations for, the academic achievement of African-American males include the phenomenal rate of retentions, suspensions, expulsions, withdrawals, and academic failures experienced by students of color, particularly African-American males; the glaring disparity in exceptional and alternative program placements for African-American males; and the

Table 3.1.

Rates of Suspension Data from the National Coalition of Advocates for Students

Group	Percent
African-American Students	9.07[a]
Hispanic-American Students	4.45
Native-American Students	4.10
White Students	4.05
Asian-American Students	2.29

[a]The rate of suspension for this group was more than twice that of other groups.

Source: J. Williams, Reducing the disproportionately high frequency of disciplinary actions against minority students: An assessment-based policy approach, *Equity and Excellence, 24* (2), 31–37, 1990.

concomitant pathological social conditions that exist within and outside school environments that severely curtail resources and options for African-American male attainment. For example, data released in 1990 by the National Coalition of Advocates for Students illustrate the dilemma public schools must confront if educational access for African-American males is to be equitable (Table 3.1).

Research literature poses a multitude of hypotheses in the attempt to identify likely influences on achievement. A plethora of data exist related to family income, parental achievement, familial support for school achievement, self-perception, self-esteem, self-concept, school climate, administrative style, school structure, and curriculum (Anderson, 1989; Eagle, 1989; Johnson, 1990; Sizemore, 1987; Tempes, 1987). The knowledge bases for teacher perceptions, for teacher expectations, and for examining teacher thinking are expanding. Reports on teacher thinking when working with students from culturally diverse backgrounds will likely increase as populations of color become the majority in schools across the nation. Considering the alterations in the framework of education and the shifting demographic trends, the need to help preservice and inservice teachers more explicitly critique their thinking in multicultural contexts, and to examine the result on the achievement of males of color, is imperative (Koehler, 1988; Ogbu, 1990).

More far-reaching information is needed to increase and sustain the meangingful quality and kinds of education provided in urban schools. This chapter will present case studies that describe teacher thinking and behavior with males of color in diverse classrooms in urban school settings. Authenic excerpts from the case studies provide descriptive content for subsequent discussion about teacher perception and thinking in regard to student achievement, and how teacher thinking differs with different students. Finally, the role of teacher preparation programs in perpetuating or altering preservice teachers' notions about males of color will be explored.

PERSPECTIVES SET FORTH

A substantial number of research investigations found in the literature appear to have emanated from the notions of cultural deprivation that were widely accepted with minimal empirical substantiation during the early 1960s, and which continue to persist. Explanations set forth to facilitate understanding of academic failure for African-American students purport to be the inability to learn, the lack of intrinsic motivation, low socioeconomic status, the absence of parental interest and support, and hyperactive, aggressive behavior, as well as disrespect and disdain for the values of education. Many audiences, both public and private, perceive these factors as being primary contributors to the failure that numerous African-American students encounter in urban classrooms. Which factor or factors yield the strongest impact is not explicit in the literature. These theoretical perspectives posit the African-American culture as monolithic and one whose legacy produces flaws in the personality of its youth (Washington, 1989). Succinctly stated, there appears to be something inherently inferior and amiss with students who exhibit the aforementioned characteristics.

Yet schools, teaching, and learning are complex concepts. More complex explanations are found in other viewpoints that emphasize differences in learning styles, perceptions, and the use of multicultural curriculum as a vehicle to lessen prejudice and racism based on culture, social class, race, gender, religion, language, exceptionality, and age (Banks, 1989, 1991; Bennett, 1990; Hale-Benson, 1982; Hilliard, 1982, 1989; Shade, 1991; Sleeter, 1991; Sleeter & Grant, 1988). Less prominent in number and attention are studies that explore possible differences in the perceptions that African-American students have of themselves and their attainment versus teacher-held perceptions of the same (Allen, 1985; Kraft, 1991; Tracey & Sedlacek, 1985). Unfortunately, first-hand observations in university classes and urban classrooms provide ample evidence that the concept of deficiency in intellect tends to hold sway with a sizeable segment of experienced and preteachers, with their perceptions and expectations and perhaps their thinking being manifested in ways unknown to them, but rather subtly perceived by students of color. The perceptions tend to be negative and the expectations minimal.

TEACHER COMMUNICATION AND EXPECTATIONS

School districts across the nation have made attempts to address the advances in technology, bolster and create new instructional methods, and involve parents in more meaningful ways. How to assist teachers in becoming more precise in evaluating their roles as leaders and learners in the classroom has received attention in the literature for several decades, with an increasing emphasis on the association between teacher perceptions and expectations and educational outcomes (Good & Brophy, 1986). The extent to which teachers are able to identify their positions in the educational equation appears to have critical impact on their ability to accurately monitor other aspects of the educational process in classrooms, particularly in urban settings. Past and recent data on teacher perceptions and expectations also provide a valuable source for making current observations.

Babad, Bernieri, and Rosenthal (1991), in their investigation of sensitivity to the verbal and nonverbal communication of teachers, used five groups of judges ranging from fourth graders to experienced teachers to rate brief videotaped samples of teacher behavior as the teachers spoke with and about students for whom they held high or low expectations. Students were not shown in the videotapes. Judges rated the unseen student more positively when the teachers in the video were involved with a high-expectancy student than when they were involved with low-expectancy students; thus an expectancy detection effect was found (demonstrating the deductibility of teachers' expectancy-related behavior). Similar to teachers in this study, some teachers found in present-day schools may exhibit behaviors that they are unable to recognize or accurately analyze after the fact. Additionally, the context in which teacher and culturally diverse student behaviors occur may be difficult for teachers to describe.

Rist's (1970) ethnographic study of African American children in an inner city kindergarten class recorded the teacher's differential treatment of students based on her perceptions of their socio-economic status and her expectations for their academic success. Early assignment of students to ability groups—occurring on the eighth day—were maintained through the second grade. Students in the highest-ability group received more attention from the teacher, achieved greater academic success, and exhibited more acceptable behavior. The self-fulfilling prophecy is borne out when uncounted numbers of teachers conclude that students cannot learn, that they lack intellectual acumen.

Good and Brophy (1991), too, have provided vigorous debate regarding the distinctions between induced expectations and naturally formed teacher expectations that are created before actual involvement with students occurs, or at least quite early in the semester when firsthand information is minimal. In the latter instance, one study showed that although the reading test scores of two groups of middle school students did not differ, those boys whose teachers believed and expected them to perform as well as girls in the study achieved higher scores than did boys whose teachers expected them to attain lower scores than those earned by girls (Parlardy, 1969). Good and Brophy (1991) surmise that teacher expectations beget behaviors that are differentiated according to the student, who then perceives a message about the teacher's expectations for behavior and performance. Consistent communication of teacher behavior which may be contrary to students' perceptions of self, but which are passively received, will likely affect students' overall well-being and achievement in the classroom as well as teacher-student interaction. Teachers' low or high expectations, according to Good and Brophy, are then reinforced as students accept the expectations without provocation, thus completing the self-fulfilling prophecy.

Ornstein and Levine (1989) allege that teachers who doubt students' potential to acquire knowledge are less likely to expend the effort required to help students make gains in academic performance. An insidious cycle of low teacher expectations, and low student achievement resulting from the influence of teachers' low expectations, is perpetuated, creating ever-expanding, captured populations of poor and African-American males in urban school districts. The ultimate dispensation for a large percentage of these populations is special or alternative education programs if they persist in school. When teachers experience continual, intense frustration in classrooms, the probability for accepting low standards of performance increases.

Students recognize differential treatment that may be based on teachers' perceptions of their inabilities. Bell (1985) postulates that maturity in African-American children is accompanied by experiences and discernment of the many culturally imposed hostilities of American society. A "Definition of Reality" resulting from this process encourages the children to believe that they can continue to anticipate powerlessness, low caste, and discrimination against them from a white society. Adaptation to this Definition of Reality culminates in African-American children devoting less energy and time to schoolwork by the time they reach early adolescence. In addition, Bell observed that the avoidance of intellectual competition is rooted in fear, and it complicates African-American males' efforts to remain in school.

Residing in and attending school in a comparatively affluent community may not provide sufficient mediation between teachers' negative perceptions, low expectations, a modified caste system, and achievement for African-American students, as was demonstrated by Smith's (1987) research. More importantly, Alexander, Entwistle and Thompson (1987) found that teacher-expectancy effects intimate that teachers' perceptions of minority students' potential formed in the initial grades tend to emanate from superficial and inappropriate cues of style, such as dress, behavior, and language.

Excerpts from two case studies conducted by the author are presented in this chapter. Data from two kindergarten classrooms, located in adjacent cities, were gathered during five and one-half full-day instructional periods along with pre- and postconferences with each cooperating teacher to verify their comments for teacher and student outcomes, and to discuss unique methods to be employed to achieve stated objectives. Their statements were then read back to them to permit modification where needed. Postconferences were conducted using these same statements as they applied to male students in the case studies presented in this chapter. Data were analyzed to note trends identified in teacher-student and teacher-interviewer communication, namely: (1) teacher communication regarding the context in which tasks were to be completed; (2) teacher communication regarding differentiated student response to task; (3) teacher communication regarding responsibility for student learning and effective instruction in the classroom context; and (4) teacher communication regarding equity versus similarity of treatment in the classroom context.

CASE STUDY 1

Howard Elementary School is located in a middle-class, white community in a southwestern city containing more than 400,000 residents. Howard's student population is primarily white, with less than 10 percent being from families of color. One kindergarten classroom serves the needs of almost sixty students equally distributed in the morning and afternoon sessions. Three African-American children and two children of Hispanic origin attend the afternoon session.

Students arrive for the afternoon session, immediately remove their coats and jackets, and approach a large, painted circle; some sit on shapes painted on the floor while others sit in previously assigned places inside or on the line of the circle. A question-answer period which follows two movies generates minimal student participation. The teacher directs the students to disperse to various interest centers, reminding them that they are to complete assigned tasks before moving to activities they prefer (also prescribed).

A white male student approaches the teacher and stands approximately two and one-half feet away from her; he speaks but it is not possible to understand what he is saying.

Teacher: What did you say—I can't hear you? (She smiles and beckons him toward her in friendly fashion. He does not move.)

Student: Where are the puzzles that were on the shelf yes—?

Teacher: I can't hear or understand what you are saying, come closer so that I can.
(She repeats the same gesture and steps toward him with her hand extended. The student takes a step backward and to the side; she quickly moves directly in front of him, puts her hand on his shoulder, bends down to face him, smiles and pats his shoulder as he squirms away from her hand.)

Student: Can I play with the puzzles that were on the shelf by your desk?
They were there now they're gone. I want to . . .

Teacher: The puzzles are not on that shelf anymore. Tomorrow they will be in a special new place just for reading. You will not be able to do anything but read when you come to this shelf. Tomorrow—.

Student: But I am looking for the puzzles. I finished the work and I want the—.

(The teacher takes his hand, walks to a reading shelf, places a two-page story in his hands, and tells him to sit in the chair and look at the story. He does not protest; he looks very sad, as though he might cry. The teacher smiles.)

Teacher: See if you can read some of the words. (She walks away. A white female student looking for something to do notices the boy in the chair and goes to him)

W Female: Do you want to play or do you have to read?

W Male: I don't know—

(He picks up the two-sheet story from his lap, starts to rise from the chair then quickly sits down as he spies the teacher watching him from the Math center table.)

Teacher: (Walking toward white male student.) I know how much you like to look at pictures and figure out the words. Do it! (Turns back to look at a lone African-American male sitting at the math center table and speaks to him.) Oh, My! Here is another excellent reader and writer. What have we here, Jason?

(Jason sits with his head cradled in both hands looking at the worksheet of laminated cupcakes with candy chips. He scribbles over previously determined answers. A white female student returns to the math table and bends over the table to peer at Jason's worksheet. The teacher walks rapidly to Jason's chair and gently pushes the white female toward the Home center area. She [student] looks up at the teacher, then at Jason, and slowly walks away.)

W Female: (Over her shoulder.) I'll be waiting for you over here.

Teacher: (To Jason.) Shall I get that wonderful story you wrote yesterday and let you read it for Mrs. X (aide)?

(Jason does not reply. Getting the story from her desk, the teacher returns to Jason's side and pushes his math worksheet toward the middle of the table. Jason attempts to hold on to a corner of the paper; the teacher removes his hand and puts an arm around his shoulder. He lowers his head to the table.)

Jason: (Voice quakes.) I missed my play time. Everybody's playing but me. I want—(voice is muffled.)

Teacher: I bet you can really read this exciting story with no help. Show Mrs. X how well you can make up your own story and write it, too!

(She smiles, places the written story in front of Jason, takes his stiff middle finger, and indicates that he is to point to the words as he reads. He is silent and she prompts him.)

Teacher: The title of your story is . . . (She pulls his rigid hand along the page as she speaks.)

Jason: I don't remember—that's the name for all the stories and . . . the funny fox and the sunny. (Stops and looks at the teacher.)

Teacher: That's right, the sunny day. (Points to the first word on the following line and forms her lips to make an O.) Oh, Jason, you know this letter's sound. (She hugs him, he speaks inaudibly.) That's right, you wrote this story—a wonderful story. (Points to the next line—there are eight—and smiles.)

During a postconference, the teacher characterized the white male student's behavior as being momentarily indecisive, thus requiring less directed effort on her part. She stressed his willingness to sit in the chair and read. The teacher stated that the white male's responses, generally, gave evidence of his immaturity. She categorized Jason's behavior as being "stubborn and passively aggressive" because of his probable home environment and lesser ability in academic endeavors. The teacher deduced that Jason was determined to have his own way, that he lacked respect for significant authority; she predicted failure in subsequent grades unless she was able to alter his behavior, and expressed doubt about his being able to complete elementary school satisfactorily. Jason was "not really unhappy, he was just acting out" to get attention, and his low frustration level was due to attention deficit. She thought that her task was to eliminate his unacceptable behavior by imposing her will over him at all times.

The teacher was unable to draw any parallels between the males' responses to her direct verbal and nonverbal behaviors. Neither student demonstrated the ability to read; in fact, both overtly tried to avoid involvement with reading tasks as they pleaded to do things that were more meaningful and interesting to them. She compared Jason's resistance to pointing to words in his story with the white male's compliance as he sat in the chair and read, and she identified this incident as proof for her prediction of Jason's failure in academic pursuits. She was confident that she treated both male students equitably, that the differences in their responses (differences that she perceived) were the result of events beyond her control and responsibility in the classroom.

CASE STUDY 2

Harry attends kindergarten at a large, inner city elementary school located in a moderate- to low-income neighborhood. Though the majority of students are white, students from African-American, Hispanic, and Asian backgrounds also attend this school in representative numbers. Surrounding neighborhoods would be classified as blue-collar working class. Fifty percent of the students in Harry's class are students of color, with equal numbers of males and females.

The classroom is highly structured. Students quietly enter, hang up their wraps, take their name cards from a small table and place them in a box, and immediately sit on the floor in front of the teacher. Harry is the last student to arrive. He retrieves his name card, counts the remaining cards, then turns and starts to count the children sitting on the floor. Some students count aloud with him.

Teacher: Hurry, Harry! We don't need you to count, it's not your turn today, you have two days to wait.
(Harry continues to silently count, pointing at students as he slowly approaches the group. He sits in back of the group, keeping considerable distance from the nearest child. The teacher reads a lengthy story, gives directions about three phonics worksheets they will complete, and goes to the board to demonstrate correct letter formation. Harry alternately stares toward an adjacent corner of the room, sings softly to himself, counts on his fingers, and uses them to draw numbers and letters on the floor. Each change in his routine provokes a pointed stare from the teacher. He stops momentarily, covers his face, then completes the cycle of counting or writing.)
Teacher: If everyone was listening, you know what to do. Go to your tables. Your worksheets are there for you. Get started! Harry, your sheets are on the table by the window.
(Harry remains on the floor and watches the teacher as she speaks to the teacher aide. Her whispers are audible.)
Teacher: (To aide.) Just ignore him, he can't listen. He does not belong in school, I told Mr. X the first week . . . just don't let

him draw on the worksheets. (To Harry.) Go to your work right now! (Smiles.)

(Harry slowly rises, meanders past three tables, stops to look at examples on the chalkboard and other students' work. The teacher is watching Harry.)

Harry: Ms. (teacher), she (student) is doing it wrong . . . she . . .

Teacher: Go to your work and mind your own business. Hurry!

Harry: She made the wrong letter for dog (starts to giggle) . . . B for bog (giggles louder), B for bog, B . . .

Teacher: Get to your work right now! This is your last chance.

(At his table, Harry looks at each sheet, picks up his pencil, and prints his name on each paper. He spreads the worksheets on the table, looks at the pictures and quietly mouths the beginning sounds of names that belong with each picture. He does not write anything; he just looks at pictures and murmurs the sounds over and over. As the teacher and aide move to the front of the room, he quickly turns one worksheet over and begins to draw an elaborate picture of a car. He does not see the teacher reappear until she is standing in back of his chair.)

Teacher: Let me see your work. This is not drawing time for you while the others are working. (Reaches over his head to take the sheet he has drawn on, turns it over, crumples it up, and gives him another.)

You have to do just as much work as the other students do. Now get busy or you will be late going home today.

(Harry writes his name at the top of the sheet and initiates the previous routine. He identifies each beginning sound correctly.)

Teacher: Stop talking like that, please; you are disturbing others. This is quiet work. If you had listened on the floor . . . (Another student raises his hand for help; the teacher watches Harry over her shoulder as she helps a white male.) Write, Harry, write, write, write!

Harry: I did, I'm through with this stuff . . . B is for bog. (Starts to laugh loudly.)

Teacher: That's enough. (Rushes to Harry's table, snatches all of the worksheets, crumples them, and puts them in the wastebasket.)

(Harry begins to bump his head on the table slowly, increasing the pressure with each blow to the table. The teacher stands, stares, shakes her head at him while some of the students begin to laugh, and others shout at him to stop before he hurts himself. The aide moves to Harry's table and forcibly removes him to the cloakroom.)

The teacher shared her thinking about Harry during the lunch period. Harry, a foster child, lived with his grandmother after being in three foster homes. The teacher stated that there must be something wrong with Harry, since nobody wanted him. He obviously had a speech disorder which interfered with the level and quality of oral participation that she expected from students in her kindergarten classes. She said that kindergarten students should not be engaging in monologues, but rather have developed the sophistication to think quietly without disturbing others. Harry's persistent murmurings were evidence of his "hostile" behavior toward her authority, as well as factual indications of his inability to follow simple directions. He simply could not comprehend the meaning of "quiet," probably because he came from a disordered and dysfunctional environment having only a grandmother. She thought that his grandmother encouraged Harry's unstructured, unacceptable behavior because she was always bragging about his beautiful artwork at home that she exhibited on walls and in scrapbooks. The teacher said that she did not allow Harry to share the scrapbook during Show and Tell because she did not want other children to think of Harry as special. According to the grandmother, Harry enjoyed other children, but was not unhappy being alone. His observations about the content of his works provided meaningful conversation at home. The teacher could not reconcile her demand that Harry write more and draw less with the grandmother's pride in his growing collection. Harry talked about school when he brought pictures home; otherwise, he shared little about classroom events. The teacher thought that Harry needed to be evaluated for special education, that his home environment nurtured his intellectual deficiency, and that her efforts to help him change were futile. When asked whether there were other students that she considered to be "slow" learners, she replied that the boys, generally, were below par; their written work was far below what she expected in her classes, but Harry appeared retarded. His intermittent laughing at the student who wrote "B" for the beginning sound of dog was offered as evidence of his exceptional needs. This type of behavior was the most unacceptable to her. When asked if she could repeat anything he murmured, the teacher was unable to, and assigned all of this behavior to the "retarded" category. None of it made sense to her in the context of the classroom.

TOWARD A SYSTEM OF EQUITY FOR AFRICAN-AMERICAN MALES

Those African-American males who do assert themselves, even when punishment results, are often exhibiting psychological health and interest in school. According to Bennett and Harris (1982), confused, acting-out behaviors may very well be the result of conflict in opposing levels of personal and school efficacy. A majority of teachers from the eleven schools in their study felt that problems of prejudice were exaggerated, expressed disapproval for the civil rights movement, and perceived white students to be intellectually superior and more socially astute than African-American students in the sample. It is not unlikely for some students of color to openly question and critique teacher behavior, particularly when they detect a covert trend of negative expectations. Classroom discourse may become highly charged, understandably so, where white teachers who are unsure of their own comprehension about race tend to feel threatened when African-American males are vociferous. Not being certain of the degree to which African-American male students might challenge how they understand various aspects of race, and to avert potential threat, such teachers resort to punishment as the first defense.

With significantly few exceptions, African-American males come to the school setting liking themselves and anxious to explore and conquer academic tasks. They do not bemoan their social status, race, gender, patterns of discourse, or place of residence (Bridges, 1986), barring traumatic circumstances. Given equitable opportunity, they eloquently display a notable degree of personal efficacy in the classroom and on the playground. The transition to a position of learned helplessness varies in length of time and scope. Some African-American males may begin to display nonconforming (according to teacher definition) behavior during the kindergarten year, whereas others persist beyond the third grade. Thereafter, many face multiple retentions, suspensions, and/or outright expulsion because teachers are in great need of knowledge, skills, and the expertise to perform objective assessment of, first, their thinking and perceptions, and second, their expectations for African-American male achievement.

Successful African-American students have shown a great tendency to persist because of positive perceptions of self to accomplish (Steward & Jackson, 1989). When teachers are unable to convert their instructional goals into efficient strategies that facilitate learning for African-American students, the outcomes for students from diverse cultures are quite different, and too frequently, dismal (Marrett, 1985).

It is abundantly clear that African-American males and other males of color cannot continue to do what is expected of them in low-achieving, urban classrooms (Hammond & Howard, 1986). Likewise, teachers' thinking, perceptions, and expectations must be acknowledged in nonjudgmental fashion if incongruent, discomforting behavior is to be modified inside and outside the class setting. Many teachers can and must be assisted in learning to more accurately monitor classroom milieu and their behavior, for it is hardly conceivable that African-American males actively seek frustration, rejection, and failure. Compelling data exist to imply that students' attitudes and achievement are influenced by teacher behavior. Furthermore, teacher behavior may be driven by teacher thinking, perceptions and expectations through verbal and nonverbal behavior that encourages or discourages student learning. Classrooms seldom, if ever, remain static, and teachers do make a difference. The literature does not support the premise that students do not want to learn. It does provide extensive evidence of researchers' efforts to discover teacher thinking, perceptions, and behaviors that may contribute to or interfere with students' academic achievement. The effects of teacher thinking, perceptions, and expectations on the attainment of African-American males merits extensive attention.

Teacher expectations may cause African-American males—regardless of grade level—to appear inept, especially when teachers are perceptually blind, and their definitions of multifaceted constructs such as learning, motivation, and achievement become so narrowly delineated that they observe only a singular dimension of the concept. They do not recognize what they are observing, nor are they cognizant of ways to utilize antecedent behaviors that may be culturally bound and that serve as excellent reinforcers for learning in the classroom. It is exceedingly difficult, if not impossible, for such teachers to translate instructional plans into vehicles of thinking that benefit students who do not fit the norms of compliance.

Commonalities in thinking and behavior were expressed by the teachers in the aforementioned case studies:

1. They were unable to identify any relationship between what they were thinking, their decision to act, and student behavior. In Case 1, the teacher was unable to see similarities between the resistance behaviors of the white male and Jason, that is, the white male attempting to physically allude her and Jason's holding on to the math worksheet and refusing to let her guide his finger. Each teacher thought that the students should have intuitively understood how everything worked every day without any explanation of the teacher's behavior. For any student to respond in a fashion that questioned teacher behavior was totally unacceptable.

2. They viewed the students' behavior as totally inappropriate, with minimal consideration given to the context within which the students' behavior occurred. When asked if their planning demanded consideration of student response, all thought every student should be able to respond with minimal discomfort. Harry (Case 1) could count, write, and identify the beginning sounds of words, as well as note any inaccuracies, though his teacher was unable to distinguish these learning behaviors. Both teachers attributed student behavior to factors beyond their control in the classroom, and accepted no responsibility for what occurred, except to state that the students behaved in expected ways.

3. The teachers saw little or no hope for future attainment. In Cases 1 and 2, the teachers consistently reiterated the fact (as they saw it) that modification of the males' behavior was the primary focus of their efforts. Both stressed the students' lack of compliance to their demands—stated or implied—as a source of continued bother and nuisance. Jason (Case 1) was directed to "read," and Harry was instructed to "write." The males' responses were casually dismissed by the teacher.

4. Both teachers thought that the African-American male students were deficient in some manner while revealing miniscule comprehension of their behavior. Each teacher perceived the males' responses to the tasks as generalized reflections of

intellectual deficiency, such as the inability to understand directions (Cases 1 and 2) different from the norm. When asked whether Harry's monologues (Case 2) were pertinent to the task at hand and typical of children in egocentric stages, the teacher stated that Harry was retarded, because, in her experiences, most persons so categorized talked to themselves, and were not to be taken seriously. Direct intervention (e.g., removing Harry physically) was seen as the most effective way to deal with Harry's "mumbling" and Jason's "stubbornness" (e.g., forcing him to point at words).

5. The teachers discussed the students in individualistic terms, but they evaluated their behavior collectively, thinking it aberrant, and stemming from sources beyond the classroom. Each teacher in Cases 1 and 2 ascribed student responses to poor home environment, passive-aggressive, hostile attitude toward authority, and inadequate preparation for an intellectual setting. When asked to identify specific examples of overt hostility toward authority, the replies of both were specific to group membership, such as "Children who come from one-parent homes," "Most of the children who live in Jason's area are from families on welfare," "It's too bad that all children like Harry [Case 2] cannot be in a special preschool program," and so on. Harry's teacher thought that his inclination to draw stemmed from his intent to not do as much work as other students, rather than his interest in pursuing a unique avenue of expression that effectively communicated his understanding of the world around him. The teacher in Case 1 thought that the white male student had simply followed her suggestion, citing previous examples of what she deemed to be indecisive behavior. She was able to recall specific reasons for referring him to specific activities.

6. Both teachers saw their responses to the male students as being the same as that given to all other students. Having the choice to respond differently was not considered; in order for the male students to meet teacher expectations, the teachers thought

that the children had to respond the way they did. Each teacher expressed minimal expectation for the males' achievement unless their behavior was altered. In Case 2, the teacher audibly admonished the aide to "ignore Harry . . . don't let him draw . . . he does not belong in school." Each teacher thought that conformity in response to tasks and teacher instruction guaranteed equal treatment for all students; thus each strove to enforce—and to reinforce—conformity in student response, regardless of task. Lack of conformity was not a viable alternative in any of the classrooms, because the teachers felt that even the smallest deviation bred contempt for authority and undermined the teacher's status as the instructional leader. Each teacher used *equal* and *equitable* interchangeably.

CONCLUSION

Teacher preparation programs must become prime focal points of initiation for individuals to experience awareness of their thinking, perceptions, and expectations for the achievement of all students, especially African-American males and other males of color. Efforts must be redoubled to revise, reorder, and delete curriculum content across disciplines which perpetuates and enhances ignorance and stereotypes. A rigorous, intentionally pervasive multicultural approach to learning and teaching that functionally challenges intolerance, ineptness, and racism is also requisite for teacher education faculty and staff.

The necessity for preservice teachers to experience in urban classrooms what is being challenged and examined in university courses cannot be overemphasized. Though reports on preservice teacher pools have occasionally mentioned white middle-class persons as constituting the largest segment in teacher preparation programs, the phenomenon of the shrinking middle class has relegated a growing number to a lower economic and living status, making representation from one-parent, female heads-of-households more common. Whereas these once moderately affluent, suburban individuals were isolated from persons of color, they are now being thrust into urban settings to support themselves and their children. Also, preservice teachers who have resided in comparatively segregated communities within urban centers, like their suburban counterparts, and who lack direct experiences with persons from diverse cultures, are returning to higher education institutions in record numbers. Both of these preservice teacher populations should be placed in realistic urban settings that provide the experiences essential for self-reflection and evaluation of their thinking, perceptions, and expectations for the academic achievement of students of color, or the tendency toward perceptual blindness will be reinforced. Helping preservice teachers identify, examine, and challenge thinking that hinders student learning and teaching should commence with the first education field experience, and provide a dominant measure for assessment of potential ability for teaching.

It is difficult to discuss and examine what one cannot conceptualize. Likewise, it is self-defeating (and therefore difficult) to discuss one's limitations and biases; questioning then becomes moot. Teacher preparation programs must become repositories of questioning, as opposed to computer files of pat-answer responses, with urban-based field experiences occupying a prominent place in the preteaching portfolio if future teachers are to meet with success in urban classrooms. Equitable, quality education of African-American males and other males of color demands such a commitment from teacher education institutions.

Although the teacher-student interactions described here involve African-American males in kindergarten contexts, the conclusions reached may have far-reaching implications for how some teachers tend to perceive, think about, and repond to the classroom behavior of male students who are culturally different. The following suggestions are posed to inspire further exploration of teacher thinking and perception in the classroom context:

1. Further investigation of teacher thinking, focusing specifically on working with culturally diverse males in early childhood, is strongly recommended. Differences in learning styles and socialization practices are manifest when males of color enter organized teaching-learning settings, and teacher thinking about differences are made evident to children at the onset.
2. A greatly expanded sample of beginning and experienced teachers will provide another means of comparison of teacher thinking about the behavior of culturally diverse males in the classroom context.

3. Explication of some of the sources in teacher preparation programs that reinforce inequitable thinking about the academic attainment of males of color in classroom contexts is greatly needed to improve the ability of teacher education faculties to prepare preservice teachers to understand the ways children think.

RESISTANCE AND RETHINKING
White Student Teachers in Predominately African-American Schools

Maureen D. Gillette

The student teaching practicum is considered the capstone experience of any teacher preparation program. It is awaited with excitement and trepidation by preservice teachers because it is seen as the final test of their ability to become professionals. Failure is rare; however, "success" in the student teaching semester is often defined in terms of maintenance of the status quo. This is problematic, because there is much evidence that poor and non-White students continue to be undereducated in the "status quo" schools of our country. For example, Comer (1988) has pointed out that children in urban areas are often found to be two academic years behind the national average. Additionally, as many of 50 percent of them will drop out of school before receiving a high school diploma. There is also increasing evidence to suggest that low academic performance among poor children and children of color is not limited to urban areas (Zeichner, 1989). All of these facts are not surprising when research has indicated that teachers have not been effectively prepared to work with nonWhite groups, with the poor, or in multicultural and bilingual settings (Bennett, Okinaka, & Xiao-Yang, 1988; Grant & Koskela, 1986).

Much has been written about the rapidly changing student demographics and the consistency of the teacher population. Recent statistics indicate that, by the year 2035, 50 percent of the population under eighteen will be children of color (Tamayo-Lott, 1993). Statistics also indicate that the current teacher population is approximately 90 percent White, with no significant changes in this percentage for the forseeable future (Grant & Secada, 1990). A majority of the current and prospective teaching population come from rural or suburban areas, can be described as monolingual (English only) and female, and generally have little knowledge about or understanding of those who are different from themselves (Irvine, 1992; Zimpher & Ashburn, 1992).

The way that schools operate today (the textbooks, the instructional practices, the policies) is not substantially different from the student teachers' own school experience (Goodlad, 1984). Children who do not conform to the teacher's view of "normal" are often distinguished as "different" based on skin color, language, physical ability, academic achievement, socioeconomic status, or a combination of these factors. Teachers then address the needs of students who do not fit their conceptions of "normal" from a deficiency perspective. King (1991) uses the term *dysconscious racism* to describe the unexamined practices, beliefs, and attitudes of teachers who maintain, without question, the status quo. Since many preservice teachers enter the profession unfamiliar with children whose background and experiences are different from their own, they often bring a skewed or distorted way of thinking about people unlike themselves. Support and assistance in reconceptualizing their perspectives is critical if they are to break with dysconsciousness. Unfortunately, when the school policies and procedures are dominated by mainstream practices, beliefs, and assumptions, the student teaching semester usually flows easily because the student teacher is accustomed to and quickly becomes a part of the mainstream operation of the classroom. When White student teachers are placed in schools and classrooms where the staff and student population is predominantly White, or even racially mixed, the dominant mode of operation is usually that of mainstream schooling and student teachers assume a cultural compatibility between themselves, the students, the cooperating teacher, and the routines of everyday life in schools (Grant & Sleeter, 1986). The cultural nuances and unspoken understandings, the management and discipline techniques, and the "rules" for communicating with parents are taken for granted.

In contrast, when White student teachers enter a school populated by students of color, such as the one that will be described in this chapter, it is usually their first extended experience as a minority group member with no substantive cultural knowledge about the majority group. The uncomfortable feelings that begin to emerge are exacerbated if the principal and many of the teachers are people of color. This means that, for the student teachers, a person of color is in a position of ultimate authority in the school and, for many, a person of color is in a direct evaluatory position over them. The manner in which student teachers conceptualize and react to this situation, as well as their knowledge base, attitudes, and beliefs about the school, the children, their parents, and the community, affect their subsequent actions in the classroom. For example, if a student teacher is unfamiliar with or afraid of the community, he or she is unlikely to enrich the curriculum by including community members in the classroom or planning activities that foster student involvement in the community.

This chapter explores the experiences of seven White student teachers as they negotiate the final rite of passage in their professional career in a school where the culture, experiences, and lived reality of the student population are dramatically different from their own. They entered the school almost totally unprepared in their liberal arts background and their professional sequence to deal with diversity.

This chapter begins with a brief description of the students and the school setting, where at least eight weeks of the student teaching semester were completed. A discussion of the student teachers' experiences is placed in a framework that describes how their thinking about the students affected their professional decisions about curriculum, instructional practices, the parents, and, ultimately, the degree of "success" they experienced as student teachers. The final section poses some difficult questions about the necessary work that must be done if student teachers are to overcome their "dysconscious" state and learn to become "culturally relevant" (Ladson-Billings, 1991).

THE STUDENT TEACHERS

Seven White student teachers, two males and five females, completed at least one 8-week student teaching session during the 1992–1993 school year at an elementary school whose student population is 99 percent African-American. Three students were in their early thirties, and the remaining four were between twenty-three and twenty-eight years of age. All of the students were single; one was the mother of two elementary school-aged children. Two of the students, one male and one female, were graduate students participating in an alternative route program leading to elementary teaching certification. One had an undergraduate degree in sociology and the other in marketing. Five were traditional undergraduates.

These student were quite similar to the national profile of the current and prospective teacher population. Four grew up in rural or suburban areas. The three that grew up in an urban environment lived in predominantly White sections of their city, two in areas inhabited by specific groups of people with whom they had an ethnic affiliation, Jewish-Americans and Greek-Americans. Both of these students were fluent in the language spoken by members of their ethnic communities, Hebrew and Greek. All of the students reported being generally unfamiliar with African-American history, culture, and current issues of importance to the local African-American community. They all reported being unfamiliar with curriculum materials that had African-American themes, such as trade books by African-American authors and resource material on important and famous African-Americans.

Five of the student teachers had completed a thirty-hour pres-tudent teaching practicum at Park Elementary. All reported positive experiences, but only one of the seven students requested a student teaching placement at Park. One requested *not* to be placed at Park, and the five others requested a placement in a suburban school or at a city school where the student population was almost exclusively White.[1]

THE ELEMENTARY SCHOOL

Park Elementary School[2] has a student population of 850 students, approximately 99 percent of whom are African-American. The remaining 1 percent are children from a variety of ethnic backgrounds. Many of the children at Park come from families that were described by the principal as the working poor. Park is located in an area of low-income housing projects, row house rental units, and small, single-family homes. Most of the parents in the area work at jobs that pay at or slightly above minimum wage. Several streets in the area have a reputation for drug trafficking and occasional violence. The entire community is somewhat isolated from the rest of town by expressways and major thoroughfares that make access somewhat treacherous.

Several aspects of the Park environment are immediately different from the personal school experiences of the White student teachers who completed their preservice training there. The school is an open concept building constructed in the early seventies. There are no permanent walls between classrooms, and although the teachers have constructed their own walled-in space with bookshelves and carrels, individual classroom activities are easily audible in the surrounding areas. Grade levels are grouped in pods, and the school is a maze of ramps and stairways. It it easy to lose one's way if one is unfamiliar with the building.

The walls and ceilings of the school are painted in bright, primary colors. Walls and window spaces are covered with posters and pictures of African-American people. Each morning the children read announcements and say the Pledge of Allegiance. Following the Pledge, a tape is played of the children's choir singing "My Country 'Tis of Thee" in a soulful cadence.

Many of the children have names that are unfamiliar to the student teachers. They look over their class lists in surprise, and it usually takes much longer to learn to pronounce and spell the students' names than it would if they were in a predominantly White school. The support staff (classroom aides, parent volunteers, custodians, food-service workers) are predominantly African-American.

There are free or reduced-cost breakfast and lunch programs. The notion that children pay for their meals on a sliding scale and that some receive free meals came as a surprise to some of the student teachers. There are after-school and weekend programs at the school and nearby YMCA. Many of these are sports related, but several programs address topics that are of interest to the community, such as African-American history and hair braiding.

NEGOTIATING THE STUDENT TEACHING SEMESTER

The manner in which each of the student teachers negotiated the student teaching semester was different. Many factors influenced their strategies and behaviors: the degree to which they were committed to becoming effective teachers for the students at Park, the degree to which they wanted or needed a positive letter of recommendation from their supervisor and their cooperating teachers for their credential file, the degree to which they saw themselves as teachers and as teachers of students unlike themselves, and the degree to which they were willing to become self-reflective or self-critical. On the one hand, some students defined "passing" the student teaching semester at Park as "getting through it" or meeting the formal requirements set forth by their college and their cooperating teachers. Other students looked upon the formal requirements of student teaching as minimal and only tangentially related to effective teaching at Park. They understood the informal rite of passage as not necessarily related to meeting official college requirements but as becoming good teachers for the African-American children at Park. This notion was reinforced in a way that related to the practical needs of the students teachers, their future job prospects, by some cooperating teachers, who repeatedly stated, "If you can make it here [at Park], you can make it anywhere."

All of the students experienced a degree of what the cooperating teachers refer to as "culture shock" based upon the "dysconscious" way in which they entered the building. The manner in which they dealt with this culture shock—their status as minorities and the differences between the students, the cooperating teachers, and themselves, and the differences in their preconceived notions about how schools and students should be—has provided data that can serve to explain their experiences.

Data Collection and Analysis

Several types of data were analyzed in order to connect the student teachers' attitudes, beliefs, and knowledge base about the children to their actions in the classroom and their views of their role as teachers in the Park setting: notes from the ongoing meetings between the college supervisor[3] and the student teachers, scripted notes from weekly lesson observations, the official evaluation forms completed by the college supervisor and the cooperating teacher, and notes on informal conversations with the children and the cooperating teachers. Additionally, the student teachers were required to complete an action research project in which the intent was for them to critically examine an aspect of ctheir teaching.[4] These projects required the student teachers to make explicit their rationales for classroom action in discussion and through written analysis of the work. In conjunction with this, the students were required to audiotape and videotape themselves and write a two-page analysis of their teaching as related to their personal goals. The action research projects and the verbal and written statements provided the most salient data on the student teachers' thinking about their own practice.

Data analysis consisted of close scrutiny of the notes and written documents for trends or patterns in which the beliefs of the students could be clearly connected to subsequent classroom action or, in some cases, inaction. As a result of the analysis, the seven student teachers could be separated into three categories: the "resisters," the "rethinkers," and one student whose approach to teaching had many of the characteristics of what Ladson-Billings (1991) has termed "culturally relevant teaching." This student was characterized as a "culturally sensitive" teacher. Each is described below.

The "Resister"

"Resisters" are students who resisted becoming critically conscious of their own beliefs, attitudes, and stereotypes about the children at Park. They would never overtly admit to holding negative views about the students and their parents, but such views were evident in their conversations and writings. They resisted accepting any responsibility for their teaching problems and were unable or unwilling to see connections between their actions and the children's learning. They also resisted assignments and requirements that fostered more reflective and self-analytic approaches to examining their teaching practice. In short, resisters never moved beyond the "culture shock" stage and rebuffed any attempts to assist them in negotiating the student teaching experience in a manner that would supportively disrupt their "dysconscious" state. A common theme that emerged in formal and informal discussions with these two students was a concern for themselves: "What am I getting out of this experience?" Several characteristics describe Ben and Sue, the two students who were placed in this category.

1. *The resisters entered the semester with notions about the children and their parents that reflected a deficiency orientation. They clung tenaciously to these throughout their student teaching experience.*

Both Ben and Sue completed a thirty-hour prestudent teaching practicum at Park and reported positive interactions with the children. At the end of this experience they wrote the following in response to the debriefing question "What is the most important thing that you learned from your experience at Park?"

> I learned that students in an innercity school must not
> be prejudged. They struck me as bright, educated, and

committed students. Not what I expected to find. Students are students regardless of their parents' SES. (Ben)

I learned that you should not let a stereotype get in your way and dampen your experiences. I totally enjoyed Park. (Sue)

Despite these stated "conversions," the resisters clung to deficiency notions, often in the face of more contradictory evidence. Rather than change their way of thinking, they often rationalized the evidence in a way that fit their conceptions of the students. For example, if the students behaved appropriately and achieved academically, the resisters would state that the children were "having a good day." If the same students behaved inappropriately or did not do well on an assignment, the resisters would shrug such phenomena off as typical from "these kids." A "good day" was seen as the exception, and their teacher expectations were formed accordingly.

Throughout the semester, Ben and Sue interpreted the words and actions of the students in ways that reinforced their existing, stereotypic beliefs despite continuous examples of alternative interpretations provided by the supervisor and the cooperating teacher. For example, the student teachers were required to accompany their class to art, music, and physical education at least once and to take objective observation notes. Following a set of three observations the students were to write a one-page analysis of what they learned by observing their class with other teachers. Both Ben and Sue turned in observation notes that were consistent with their own beliefs and were hardly objective. For example, Ben's observation sheets from each class contained the words *disruptive* and *disrespectful* numerous times without any concrete incidents that substantiated these evaluatory terms. He then concluded in the analysis, "These kids don't obey or respect anyone, including each other, so how am I supposed to get them to respect me?"

Evidence that the deficiency orientation that these two student teachers brought to Park remained unchanged is illustrated in two discussions that occurred at the end of the semester. During an informal conversation between the student teachers and their supervisor over lunch one day, the supervisor related an interaction that had occurred on a nationally syndicated morning television show between the female host and guest Spike Lee. Lee was being questioned about the filming of *Malcolm X* when the host noted that he had been filming on location in Egypt and in Africa. Lee did a slow burn and very politely said, "Well, I'm sure you realize that Egypt is *in* Africa." Sue replied that she hated Spike Lee because all he does is stir up controversy with the movies he makes. Another student teacher, Gina, stated that Sue's type of thinking was exactly the problem. She further noted that we were all taught inaccurate information in school, so it is important to speak up when things like this occur. She continued to say that African-American contributions have been hidden and that all people, especially white people, really need to know these things. She finished her reply by stating that she wouldn't let something like that pass and was glad to hear that Spike Lee did not. Sue responded, "These kids don't need to learn about controversy. They need to just learn how to do their regular schoolwork."

Ben's "lead" week of student teaching, the week when he was solely responsible for planning, designing, and implementing curricular and instructional practices, was a disaster. He had written academic progress reports for the students to take home, and they promptly tore them up and threw them away in front of him. When the college supervisor came, the floor was littered with spit balls and the students openly displayed their empty pen shafts as shooters. Ben was beside himself. He related the punishments he doled out during the week as the supervisor listened. She then asked him to describe his attempts to discuss the students' behavior and progress with their parents. Ben related that he had not talked to any parents in the previous seven weeks, despite the supervisor's emphasis on the need for the student teachers to develop a "parents as partners" approach. When questioned about this, Ben replied, "I assume that if I call the parents of these children I will find the same bad attitude about school as is evident in their children."

2. Resisters saw their role as curriculum designers and their choices in instructional methodology apart from the learners.

Ben and Sue began an eight-week student teaching session, in sixth and second grade, respectively, by slowly assuming teaching duties subject by subject. Both taught traditional subject matter in traditional ways. Their practices could be described as teacher centered, and were dominated by the use of textbooks and worksheets despite the fact that their cooperating teachers encouraged them to experiment with curriculum development and instructional strategies. Two examples are illustrative.

Ben planned a lesson around a magazine that arrived weekly for the students. He selected an article on strip-mining in national forests that he believed the students would find interesting. He divided the class into two groups and assigned the task of reading the article and preparing either a "pro" or "con" argument related to strip-mining. He told the class that at the end of twenty minutes of preparation time there would be a class debate. The class began to work in groups but soon lost interest and began to talk about other topics among themselves. The debate did not meet Ben's expectations and he was frustrated with the students. In a postobservation conference, he told his supervisor that his lesson goal was to interest the students in current events. The supervisor noted that there were seven articles in the magazine, all dealing with current events. Ben stated that *he* thought the article on strip-mining was important for the students to read. The supervisor attempted to engage Ben in alternative ways to structure the lesson to meet his goals, such as student self-selection of articles followed by a grouping technique whereby students who selected the same article were grouped to discuss their views and present their findings to the class. Ben noted that the lesson "fell apart" because students did not know how to work together and it was the end of the day, so they were "antsy." He insisted that the article should have been of importance to the students because they will inherit the environmental decisions that are being made now.

Sue had observed that another student teacher was doing a teaching unit on Africa and was experiencing quite a bit of success. Her colleague's cooperating teacher was bragging in the teacher's room that the unit was exceptional. Sue decided to do a unit on Africa as well. Sue knew little about Africa, yet, borrowing her colleague's materials, she began her unit. Her work was fraught with inaccuracies and stereotypes. For example, she told the children that Swahili was the language of Africa and she did not distinguish between different African countries or geographic areas. She did not attempt to locate material or human resources to assist her, nor did she inquire about the second graders' knowledge base concerning Africa. By the end of two weeks, the children and the student teacher were confused. The cooperating teacher and the supervisor were frustrated as Sue lamented that this unit "worked" for her colleague but could not understand why it did not work for her.

3. *Resisters placed the primary responsibility for the success or failure of a lesson on the students. They viewed their role (teacher) as secondary.*

Ben and Sue experienced numerous difficulties in the student teaching semester. Each had problems with classroom management, discipline, design of curriculum, and implementation of instructional strategies. These types of problems inevitably led to unsuccessful lessons, lessons in which student learning is minimal and disruptions abound. Each time this occurred, both Ben and Sue looked outside themselves for solutions. For example, Ben videotaped a lesson on grammar that he adopted from the English textbook. He never moved from the front of the room during the forty-minute lesson. The video clearly showed the students at the back of the room engaged in various activites, none of which were related to the lesson. Several females were reading novels under their desks and several males were folding paper. Ben initially pronounced this lesson "effective" after viewing the video because the students were not disruptive. Since he has given no assignment, he had no information about student learning. When the supervisor raised the issue of the students in the rear of the room, Ben stated that they should have known not to be reading or folding paper and it was their responsibility to pay attention.

Sue blamed her problems in getting the second graders to pay attention on the fact that the students worked at tables rather than at desks. Following a discussion with the cooperating teacher, Sue was given permission to bring in desks and arrange them in a manner that she felt would assist her in gaining the students' attention. Sue experimented with four different desk and table arrangements over the course of seven weeks and concluded that, no matter what the desk arrangement, there were problems. Her action research report contained a litany of student offenses (e.g., talking too much, copying, getting up out of their seats) which she related to the desk arrangement. She never connected her role as a classroom manager and designer of instruction to the students' behavior.

Both of these student teachers subverted efforts at regular three-way conferences with their cooperating teacher when they began experiencing difficulty. Each requested, on several occasions, that the cooperating teacher not be present, and Sue purposefully arranged postobservation conferences at times when her cooperating teacher was not available despite the supervisor's insistence that she be present. This made it easier to place the blame for ill-planned lessons and problems with student behavior on the practices of their cooperating teacher or on things over which they had no control, such as the home lives of the children.

Both student teachers had to be forced to complete the required audio- and videotaped self-analysis and action research project. Both resisted discussions that connected student achievement to their teaching practices. Neither read the supervisor's observation notes prior to postobservation conferences. These scripted notes of the lesson, given to the student without evaluative comments, were designed to foster the ability of student teachers to identify trends and patterns in their own teaching that affected the success or failure of their goals. When Ben and Sue finally did complete these requirements, they did not analyze their teaching but pronounced their lessons as effective if the students were not disruptive.

4. *The resisters experienced some degree of success when the school or classroom environment was more "culturally compatible."*

It would be tempting to assume that Ben and Sue were simply weak teachers who would have experienced difficulties and displayed resistance in any teaching situation, but this was not the case. These two student teachers did not fail the semester because each had one acceptable eight-week experience. It is interesting to note the differences between the two sessions.

Ben, the Jewish-American male, completed his first eight weeks of student teaching in a private, Jewish day school. He was experienced with this population of children because he had done much volunteer work at the local temple. At the day school, Ben taught children who were predominantly like himself, experienced few behavioral problems, and often spent extra hours after school working with the students. He was supervised by another faculty member, who reported that his performance was exceptional. Ten observation reports from the first eight weeks contained the word *excellent* eleven times, the word *good* nine times, and a variety of positive descriptors such as *great, super, outstanding,* and *terrific.* Thus, the first eight weeks left him in a position to receive excellent letters of recommendation from his cooperating teacher and supervisor and to pass the semester barring any extreme breach of rules or requirements.

Ben's rite of passage through the final eight weeks at Park become an exercise in "getting through it." Often he would state that he didn't know why he had to be at Park when he had already done a prestudent teaching experience there. He stated, on numerous occasions, that he did not see what *he* had to gain from the experience. At the final three-way conference, the college supervisor has given Ben a rating of "fair," the second lowest descriptor. The cooperating teacher, who regularly and vocally complained about Ben, rated his overall performance as "very good," the second highest descriptor. Ben also rated himself as "very good." When the cooperating teacher was asked why he gave such a high rating to a student whom he did not consider to be a good teacher, the cooperating teacher stated, "Hey, I don't get much for this and I'm not going to rock the boat. If the supervisor flunks him, then I have to get involved. I don't need that kind of conflict."

Sue passed for another reason. Her eight weeks in the second grade were characterized by an overemphasis on control and an absence of learning. Her cooperating teacher and the supervisor gave her poor ratings. Prior to the second eight-week session, Sue was told by her supervisor that she was not going to pass the student teaching semester unless there was extensive evidence that she was willing to connect the curriculum to the academic needs and personal interests of the children. This meant that she had to find out the students' interests and abilities and use them to teach.

There was one main difference between Sue's two eight-week sessions at Park. Her first cooperating teacher was an African-American woman with whom Sue insisted she could not get along. She viewed her teaching as "too structured" for "these kids" and continually subverted efforts to have the three-way conferences. Sue never was able to see, nor did she understand, the underlying relationship between the cooperating teacher and the children. She continually lamented that she did not understand why the students behaved for the cooperating teacher and not for her. For the second eight weeks, Sue was placed in the fifth grade with a White cooperating teacher. This factor seemed to make all the difference to Sue's willingness to try. She often noted that she could relate to her new cooperating teacher much better despite the fact that in the beginning of the session this teacher expressed some of the same concerns about Sue's teaching as did the African-American cooperating teacher. Sue was willing to have regular three-way conferences and she moved slightly away from teacher-controlled activities, designing lessons based on the students' interests. She experimented with hands-on activities in all subject areas. For example, she designed math story problems based on the children's interests outside of school such as their favorite foods and recording artists. She brought in menus from local restaurants and brochures from the mall. She could hardly keep up with the story problems as the students' enthusiasm grew. Soon she had them developing story problems on their own.

Working with a White cooperating teacher, and under threat of failure in an enterprise that almost no one fails, Sue did what she had to do to pass student teaching. She did gain some positive insights about effective teaching methods, but this occurred at the end of her preservice training. It took much work and a culturally compatible cooperating teacher for her to even begin to adjust her view of the children and her teaching practices.

The Rethinkers

Four student teachers were categorized as having potential for success in urban schools. Despite their "status quo" views of schooling and their "deficiency" orientation toward the students and their parents, these students were willing to modify their positions based on information that contradicted their views, constructive critique of their work, and support for changing their actions. They saw a connection between the students and themselves. Whereas the "resisters" focused on themselves, the rethinkers understood that their success as a teacher was defined, in large part, by the degree of academic and personal growth experienced by the students. The passage of these student teachers through the semester was characterized by a continuum of internal (within themselves) and external (with the supervisor or the cooperating teacher) arguments in which competing viewpoints related to educational issues arose (e.g., the students' academic performance and behavior, parental involvement). They openly discussed their dilemmas and were willing to listen to opinions that differed from their own. They thought about alternative perspectives on an ongoing basis and would often tell their supervisor or cooperating teacher days after a conversation that they had rethought a belief, perspective, or interpretation. Their rethinking would then be evident as they all began to move toward practices that placed the learner at the center of instruction.

1. *The rethinkers also entered Park with a "deficiency orientation" in their view of children and their parents. They were willing to "rethink" these orientations, and often able to reconceptualize them, as new evidence presented itself.*

Three of the four students in the "rethinker" category openly admitted holding negative stereotypes about the students at Park and of the community surrounding the school. The fourth asked *not* to be placed there for the student teaching semester. Many of these fears came from their parents, who they reported were worried that their son or daughter was student teaching in a "bad part of town." Two of the students in this group were placed in sixth grade, one was placed in fifth grade, and one in first grade.

Two of the "rethinkers" did a prestudent teaching practicum at Park. Each wrote undocumented false statements in the debriefing forms. For example, both wrote that the majority of the children came from single-parent homes and that the parents were not employed outside of the home. One student noted that he would consider teaching at Park, but the "mental ability and the socioeconomic lifestyle" of the population would make it very challenging. The other two students in this group completed their prestudent teaching practica in suburban schools with predominantly white student populations.

Despite these initial notions, each "rethinker" quickly built a positive rapport with the children and often noted that the skills and knowledge base of the students exceeded their expectations. These student teachers participated in parent-teacher conferences in conjunction with their cooperating teachers. They were surprised to discover the extent to which the parents cared about their students' progress. As a result, this group of student teachers reported not being afraid to contact parents through written notes, phone calls, and school conferences and did so on numerous occasions.

Self-evaluation statements, written at the end of the semester, indicate that their perspectives were decidedly more positive:

S1. I had a good rapport with the students [in sixth grade]. It took me a while to gain their respect but I think I did.

S2. I have really enjoyed Park, it was a great experience. The sixth graders were fun to teach because they were so knowledgeable.

S3. I have learned the philosophy "teaching for success."

S4. I've learned to get the students involved as much as possible . . . I tried to use cooperative grouping and vary my instruction. . . . I would have preferred to stay sixteen weeks.

No claim is made here that the student teachers' orientations toward diversity were permanently altered, but unlike the resisters, the rethinkers did not "blame the victim" for their limitations as student teachers. Their statements indicate that they see themselves and their actions as tied to students' success.

2. The rethinkers saw their role as curriculum designers and their choices for instructional practices as linked to the children.

All four students had a relatively strong content background, as evidenced by their above-average grade point averages, the accuracy of their lessons, and their ability to connect content to the lives of the children. Each was impeccably prepared for his or her lessons with a well-thought-out plan and a willingness to be flexible.

There are several examples of successful curricular efforts. Steve, a sixth-grade student teacher with a biology concentration at the college, initially told his supervisor that the students at Park were not able to do "hands-on" science because they did not know how to behave and did not have an adequate scientific knowledge base. After much discussion between the student teacher, the supervisor, and the cooperating teacher, Steve designed a "hands-on" experiment that excited the students. He was surprised at their enthusiasm and knowledge. Soon he was directing weekly experiments and teaching the students how to write lab reports using the rigorous methodology of his college biology courses.

Another sixth grade student teacher, Sara, was frustrated by her attempts to have the students use a process approach to writing stories on an assigned topic. The students did not want to write nor did they want to edit and publish their work. Sara rethought her goals and tried anew, this time having the students write autobiographies. Sara instituted "large group share" sessions in which students voluntarily read portions of their stories aloud. Sara videotaped these sessions to assess the degree to which the students were paying attention to and being respectful of their classmates. As their rough drafts grew longer and longer, Sara began teaching the rules of grammar and punctuation in systematic minilessons. The unit lasted three weeks, and the autobiographies were published and displayed for members of the State Board of Education, who visited Park.

A third student teacher researched and redesigned a health unit on substance awareness and abuse when she discovered in her initiating activity that the students already knew the material she had initially planned to cover. She solicited input from them regarding what they wanted to know, redesigned her unit so that both her goals and the students' goals were addressed, and incorporated reading, writing, and math activities into her hands-on lessons. She constructed her individual lessons so that they built on students' personal knowledge. Another student teacher in this group developed personalized, easy-to-understand data collection sheets in a first-grade classroom to track students' progress in reading and math skills. She shared this information with the parents as a more effective means of helping them understand their child's strengths and weaknesses.

3. Rethinkers viewed the responsibility for the success or failure of a lesson as being split equally between the children and the teacher.

All four "rethinkers" were willing to be self-reflective. They regularly audio- or videotaped themselves as required and were able to clearly see or hear themselves in a way that challenged their initial beliefs that the problem areas in their teaching were all the fault of someone or something else. All three stated that they viewed the supervisor and the cooperating teacher as partners in helping them become better teachers. They were accommodating in arranging three-way conferences to ensure positive interactions between the student teaching triad. All of the rethinkers attempted to connect the curriculum to the students, to use ongoing, authentic assessment techniques, and to maintain high student expectations for achievement and behavior.

The rethinkers each had difficult periods in their rite of passage. Individually, they overcame problems similar to the two "resisters." For example, one female had difficulty adjusting to what she considered to be the strict nature of her African-American cooperating teacher, yet she was open to observation and a continual barrage of alternative interpretations of the teacher's behavior. In week five of the eight-week term, the student teacher admitted that perhaps it was *she* who was uptight about the teacher. By observing and questioning, she had discovered *why* the cooperating teacher took various courses of action. This led to new understandings for the student teacher.

4. *Rethinkers recognized the limitations of their experience and stated that they would not begin their career in a school populated by students of color.*

Three student teachers stated that they learned more than they ever thought they would during their short stay at Park, and they were humbled by the amount of self-examination and commitment necessary to ensure that Park's student population got an excellent education. None of these students wanted to begin their teaching career at a school like Park, although each expressed a desire to teach in an urban area after gaining teaching experience in an environment where that was more culturally compatible. One member of this group continued on to graduate school to become a bilingual teacher. She stated that she needed much more information about diversity before she entered the elementary classroom as a full-time teacher.

Toward a Culturally Relevant Teacher

Ladson-Billings (1991) describes "culturally relevant" teachers as teachers who

> see teaching as an art as opposed to a science with prescriptive steps to be learned and demonstrated, who see themselves as a part of the communities in which they teach and see their role as giving something back to the community. They believe that success is possible for each and every student and a part of that success is helping students make connections between themselves and their community, national, ethnic, and global identities. They believe that black students as a cultural group have special strengths to be explored

and utilized in the classroom. . . , they understand that the way social interaction takes place in the classroom is important to student success. . . , they believe that knowledge is continuously recreated, recycled, and shared. They take a critical view of the knowledge and content and demonstrate a passion about what they teach. Through the content, which often is related to students' lives, they help students develop the knowledge base or skills, to build a bridge or scaffolding and often accompany the student across to new and more difficult ideas, concepts and skills (pp. 13–114).

One student teacher, Gina, evidenced many of these characteristics. A novice teacher is very much in the process of "becoming"; thus the student described here will be referred to as a "culturally sensitive" student teacher.

1. *The culturally sensitive teacher entered the student teaching semester with a "culture-rich" orientation toward the children and their parents.*

Gina was an honor student and a single mother of two elementary schoolchildren. Although she had little experience with people unlike herself, she began the semester with a positive outlook on her placement site. The first student teacher–college supervisor meeting occurred after the group of student teachers had been in a student teaching orientation for three hours. The supervisor stated that they were probably overwhelmed and asked if they had any immediate questions or concerns. Gina immediately asked, "Why are you supervising at Park?" The supervisor replied that she had requested supervision at Park because she believed that many good things were going on there despite that fact that outsiders and the media promoted a negative view of the school and the community. She showed the student teachers her collection of books and resources by and about African-Americans. She stated that they were welcome to borrow any materials that might be helpful to their work. Gina stated, "Well, I'm glad you want to be there because I wouldn't want to work with you if you didn't." She alone stayed after the meeting and browsed through the office shelves, leaving with a tote bag full of books and materials.

Gina was open-minded about the students and their parents. She viewed students as having potential rather than pathology. In the beginning of the term she stated,

> When I found I was assigned to Park I saw it as a good thing. Going in there I had a keen interest in learning more about African-American culture. I saw it a great opportunity for me to grow. . . . I wanted to make my teaching in some way specific to the population I was teaching. I mean they are kids just like any other kids but I was very interested in reading them books and using materials that would have meaning to them and their lives.

In the second week she began referring to the students as "my kids" in the loving and respectful manner of her cooperating teacher. Interestingly, no other student teacher ever used this term.

Gina began regular contact with the parents in the beginning of the semester. She maintained this contact throughout the term. She attended cultural events at the school and in the community, noting to her supervisor that it took a while before she got used to the idea that she was one of only a few White people at some events. She purchased books and materials relevant to teaching African-American children so that she could begin a personal collection.

2. The culturally sensitive teacher saw her role as curriculum developer and her choices in curriculum design in relation to the children.

Gina was willing and able to make the curriculum and the instructional practices relevant to the students from the first day she set foot in her second-grade classroom. She researched and utilized outside materials and people to enhance her lessons, connecting the content to the children. Gina sometimes built lessons around the traditional textbooks her cooperating teacher required, but even then found ways to make them personalized for the children. She utilized information she had garnered about the students' activities outside of school as a means for building new vocabulary or math problems.

The example that best exemplifies Gina's commitment to culturally relevant teaching is the teaching unit she designed on Africa. Although much of what happens at Park is "Africentric," Black History Month is a time of celebration and parental involvement. Mrs. Patterson told Gina in mid-January that she would be responsible for the Black History Month activities. Gina developed an interdisciplinary teaching unit on Africa with the following rationale:

> February is Black History Month and the students at Park Elementary are learning about the important contributions that African-Americans have made and continue to make to our society. In addition to learning about Black Americans in the United States, it is important that the students learn about the countries and people of Africa because it is the original homeland of Africans in America. The students should know where Africa is, about the many countries that make up the continent of Africa, and about the cultures of the people of Africa. As the students continue to learn about the people, places, languages, art, and music of Africa, they will gain insight into their ancestry and heritage and become increasingly proud of it.

Gina focused on West Africa and the Swahili language. She completely dispensed with standard textbooks for three weeks and taught reading, writing, math, and social studies through the lens of West Africa. She connected her lessons to the skills normally covered by the texts in math and reading. All of the activities incorporated art and music. Gina centered her initial lessons around the following books: *The Drums Speak: The Story of Kofi A Boy of West Africa, Moja Means One: The Swahili Counting Book; and Jambo Means Hello.* Numerous other books were displayed, and the excitement and enthusiasm of the children were evident in the frequency with which they read these books during "choice" time. Gina brought in guest speakers, including the school principal, who had recently visited West Africa, and a Tanzanian student from the college who taught the students a new list of Swahili words as they begged for more. The culminating activity, a Swahili rap song written by the cooperating teacher, was performed at the all-school convocation at the end of February.

3. *The culturally sensitive teacher assumed* primary *responsibility for the success or failure of a lesson.*

Gina designed an action research project over the course of the student teaching semester that shifted focus but was tied to her notions that, as a teacher, she was responsible for the academic and personal growth of the students. Her initial question was "How can I use active learning to help students to meaningfully learn the same material they would otherwise learn by rote methods?"

As Gina gradually took responsibility for different areas of the curriculum, she incorporated new ideas for student involvement. She introduced games and manipulatives in mathematics, interactive (teacher-student) journals for spelling and reading work, "hands-on" experiments in science, and the student-centered activities that were described above.

Introducing and recording the results of each new technique led Gina to new discoveries about herself as a teacher. She refocused her question in the second eight-week session when she was placed in a fourth-grade classroom. She explained;

> By the end of my first week in fourth grade, I could see that I was going to have classroom management challenges that I had not encountered in second grade. There were several students who overtly refused to comply with the cooperating teacher's requests, who engaged in disruptive, attention-getting behaviors, who could become angry and hostile with seemingly no provocation, and who could not stop themselves once involved in heated verbal exchanges. I also witnessed three fights. When I approached one boy and tried to talk to him, he said, "Get out of my face, man." At this point, I was very concerned about what techniques I could use that would be effective with this group of students. Even though I knew I had only seven weeks with them, it was important to me to try to foster a mutual positive regard by emphasizing caring, trust, and respect. I wanted my students to know that I cared about them, that I believed in them, and that each one was an important member of the class. I did not to rely on coercive control . . . I felt that I owed it to myself and to them to focus on a *process* and *style* of

management that would be geared toward a long-range goal of self-discipline. My key question is, What kinds of classroom management strategies and interpersonal skills could I use which would encourage my students to be responsible for their own behaviors?

Gina was frustrated on many days, but she never blamed the students, their parents, or external factors for lessons that did not go as she had planned. Although she recognized that outside factors (e.g., a fight on the way to school) affected what occurred in the classroom, she continually focused on herself as the key to teaching success.

4. *The culturally sensitive teacher expressed a desire to continue to teach in a school populated by students of color.*

At the end of the semester, Gina stated that she would like to continue to teach in a school populated by students of color because she found diversity exciting. She stated, "When I was younger I appreciated people who were the same as me, with the same kind of values, attitudes, lifestyles. Now that bores me to a degree. I try to seek out people who are different from me. They have something to teach me." Gina is currently employed in an urban school populated by a very diverse student body and is in her third successful year of teaching.

DISCUSSION

The information presented in this paper is preliminary and limited because it is based on the experiences of seven White students, but several summarizing statements can be made. First, it is clear that most student teachers enter a school where the students' background and experiences are different from their own with preconceived notions, many of them inaccurate and negative, about those "others" with whom they will work. This is not a new finding (see, for example, Paine, 1988; Weinstein, 1989) but one that must be addressed with a greater fervor than has heretofore been evidenced. Second, consistent with the work of Ladson-Billings (1991), becoming a "culturally relevant" teacher for the African-American children at Park did not depend on skin color but on commitment, open-mindedness, and a propensity for critical reflection on one's work. Third, limited exposure to unfamiliar knowledge, people, and environments is insufficient to affect any significant change in student teachers' perspectives and practices. Although many teacher educators advocate placing prospective teachers in field placements populated by diverse students, this should not occur for the first time during the student teaching semester. The student teaching semester is a difficult one for all prospective teachers. They are under pressure to excel in order to obtain a positive evaluation and letter of recommendation while occupying the lowest status position in a school. The experience of the resisters raised ethical questions about the impact on children of color and children in urban schools when student teachers with deficiency orientations are placed in their classrooms.

It is incumbent upon teacher educators, whose clientele is and will remain predominantly White, to undertake several simultaneous courses of action. First, efforts must be made to assess prospective teachers' orientations toward diversity early in teacher education programs. Comprehensive course work and field experiences must be designed in a way that breaks the myths, stereotypes, and inaccuracies that students hold about people who are different from themselves. Second, teacher educators must continue to develop recruitment and support programs that encourage people of color to enter the teaching profession. A diverse student body promotes the acceptance and affirmation of multiple ways of learning about all aspects of teaching.

Third, institutions of teacher preparation must recruit and support diverse faculty to train prospective teachers. Faculties in schools of education across the country are demographically similar to the teaching population, predominantly White, monolingual, and unfamiliar with diversity (Grant, in press; Haberman, 1987). This situation serves to perpetuate the status quo in teacher preparation and in our schools.

Fourth, mainstream research on teacher thinking, as summarized by Clark and Peterson (1986), does not include attention to diversity. White student teachers who complete their rite of passage in a school like Park need assistance and support if they are to change their inappropriate notions about children unlike themselves and to implement culturally relevant teaching strategies. The "rethinkers" clearly illustrated this point. Additionally, we need more information about how "culturally sensitive" teachers acquired their perspectives and about effective strategies for assisting them in becoming increasingly successful teachers. Teacher educators must commit to developing a comprehensive research agenda regarding teacher thinking about diversity and its connection to classroom action if, as Montero-Sieburth (1989) notes, "urban schools are to do more than just survive" and predominantly White students are to begin to understand and affirm people who are different from themselves.

Finally, teacher educators must collaborate with school districts, community agencies, and community institutions to more closely connect the work of their respective institutions. The barriers that prevent student teachers from becoming excellent teachers for all children, that prevent teacher educators from preparing teachers who have the knowledge, skills, and dispositions to educate all children, and that prevent professionals at the school level from assisting in that endeavor are real. They are personal, institutional, and ingrained in the very fabric of the status quo as it operates in us and through us. Asa Hilliard (1991) has noted that the type of restructuring necessary to significantly alter the status quo is more than technical and logistical. We need what he terms *deep restructuring,* referring to the reconceptualization of status quo theories, philosophies, and conceptions about children, schools, and the educational process. Although each constituency noted above may have a different primary clientele, our common interest is ultimately what is best for our children.

TEACHERS' PRINCIPLES OF PRACTICE FOR TEACHING IN MULTICULTURAL CLASSROOMS[1]

Francisco A. Ríos

Two major issues seem to pervade much of recent educational scholarship; the first is the shift in demographics toward nonwhite majorities (Hernandez, 1989), and the second is the decreasing academic performance of students of color (Humphreys, 1988). In their review of theories advanced to explain this failure, Sue and Padilla (1986) identify four central perspectives. They include (a) contextual interaction explanations, (b) deficiency or deprivation explanations, (c) interpersonal or institutional racism, and (d) the cultural "mismatch" between the school and the student's home culture.

The most recent explanation advanced is called the "contextual interaction" theory (Cortes, 1986). This theory suggests that minority students fail because of the unfortunate interaction of many variables, such as student background, school factors, social factors, and factors associated with teaching. Thus the contextual interaction approach looks for the combination of factors operating that negatively affect any individual or group of individuals within a specific context.

One contextual variable of interest is the role of the teacher's behavior as she or he interacts with students of color. As suggested earlier (introduction, this volume), students of color are treated differently, yet the basis for this differential treatment is unknown. Thus the purpose of this study is to identify specific aspects of teachers' thinking that guide their behavior during typical yet significant activity in multicultural classrooms.

TEACHERS' THEORIES: AN OVERVIEW

Professional competence entails the development of personal theories of action (Argyis & Schon, 1975; Schon, 1983). These theories of action involve subjective representations of experience and tacit rules for behavior. That is, they help explain what is happening now and how the practitioner will behave. These theories are "working hypotheses" and are called "personal constructs" in the language of the psychology of personal constructs (Kelly, 1955). The practitioner tests these hypotheses for validity through action; they are reinforced or modified based on the feedback the practitioner receives. Thus constructs develop in the course of action (Vallacher & Wegner, 1985; cited in Salmon & Lehrer, 1989). Teacher theories are practical, according to Copa (1984), because they arise from "dealing with specific problems with individual people in particular contexts" (p. 15).

The research in the area of teacher theorizing rests on several assumptions that are rarely articulated (Ríos, 1992). Of importance here is the assumption that the interaction between a teacher and his or her students is paramount. That is, the quality and quantity of interactions that students have with their teacher are perhaps *the most* critical factors affecting academic achievement (U.S. Commission on Civil Rights, 1973).

A second assumption is that teachers are theory makers. This assumption is informed by research in the cognitive sciences. As Clark (1985) describes it, "The teacher of 1985 is a constructivist who continually builds, elaborates and tests his or her personal theory of the world." Copa (1984) characterizes these theories as "schema by which teachers made sense and acted upon aspects of their classrooms." People are theory builders because theories help to simplify complex situations.

Personal theories of action operate like hypotheses to be tested. Anderson-Levitt (1984), for example, found that many theories that teachers hold about individual students are malleable. Indeed, teacher theories are developed, refined, and challenged by how students act. There is, however, a strong tendency for teachers to confirm their theories via selective attention, as predicted by schema theory.[2]

One goal of the research in the area is to attempt to make those implicit (or only partially articulated) theories explicit (Marcelo, 1987). Thus researchers have taken an interest in how these theories are built, what they consist of, how they are structured, and how they impact behavior. For example, one area of research has focused on how teachers' theories affect the attributions that teachers make of student behavior (Darly & Fazio, 1980; Peterson & Barger, 1984). Additionally, research has focused on the theories of one specific curriculum and subject area (reading) (Duffy, 1977), on the teacher's role (Janesick, 1977), on the curriculum (Olson, 1981), on the role of evaluation (Marcelo, 1987), on varying instructional strategies (specifically about "open" education; see Bussis, Chittenden, & Amarel, 1976), on individual teacher differences in theories held (Bussis et al., 1976; Munby, 1983), on theories of students (Bussis et al., 1976), on the teacher's role and responsibilities (Olson, 1981), and on theories of teacher-student interaction (Conners, 1978; Marland, 1977).

One novel approach to this research area has been Elbaz's (1981) attempt to understand the structure of a teacher's knowledge base.[3] She asserts an active relationship between teacher knowledge and the world of practice. Teacher knowledge is used to express purpose, to give meaning to experience, to resolve tension between interpersonal and institutional demands, and to accommodate to classroom practices. Elbaz suggests that teachers' knowledge consists of four categories: content knowledge (subject matter, curriculum, instruction, and social milieu), orientations (novel ways of thinking), cognitive style, and structures. These structures are organized on three levels (moving from specific to general) consisting of rules of practice (heuristics for behavior), principles of practice (implicit theories that explain "why" things happen), and images (visions of how teaching should be).

Elbaz's work is critical in that it identifies the connection between practice (via strategies teachers' employ) and implicit theories (via principles of practice). Carter (1990) concurs that implicit theories involve principles that seem to guide action as well as conceptions of personal values and beliefs. In short, both Elbaz and Carter suggest that principles of practice are a critical, but not exclusive, part of the content and process of teachers' implicit theories.

Of particular interest has been the work of Conners (1978) and Marland (1977) in that, using stimulated recall, they focus on teachers' principles of practice. Marland found that five principles of practice guided elementary schoolteachers, and Conners found

FRANCISCO A. RÍOS

Table 5.1.

Review of Principles of Practice Identified by Marland (1977) and Conners (1978)

Marland (1977)
1. *Compensation*—discriminating in favor of shy, introverted, low-ability, and "culturally-impoverished" students
2. *Strategic leniency*—ignoring behavior infractions by students who the teacher feels need special attention
3. *Power sharing*—using an informal power structure to influence students
4. *Progressive checking*—periodically checking student progress, identifying problems, and providing encouragement
5. *Suppressing emotions*—consciously displaying little emotion in hope that students will suppress their emotions also

Conners (1978)
"Overarching" Principles
1. *Suppressing* emotions
2. *Teacher authenticity*—presenting oneself as honest, sincere, open, and fallible
3. *Self-monitoring*—remaining aware of one's behavior and potential effects on students
Pedagogical Principles
1. *Cognitive linking*—maintaining that new information should be explicitly linked to past knowledge and experience
2. *Integration*—providing practice of skills so that they might transfer across contexts
3. *Closure*—summarizing, reviewing, and tying together main points at the end of a lesson
4. *General involvement*—pushing all students to participate in class activities
5. *Equality of treatment*—providing fair and consistent treatment to each student

three "overarching" principles and five principles related to pedagogy (Table 5.1).

One obvious limitation of these two studies is that they focused exclusively on elementary schoolteachers. In work at a junior high school, Munby (1983) was unable to find a similarity among the fourteen teachers interviewed with respect to their implicit theories; he found, for example, that teachers even in the same grade level and same subject area held distinctly different theories. One way to limit this variation is to specify the aspect of teaching of interest (i.e., evaluation of students) or to specify exactly the classroom context (Garcia, 1987). Thus researchers need to continue looking at teachers' theories across a wider variety of grade, subject, and social contexts.

THE MULTICULTURAL CLASSROOM

The context in which teachers operate is a salient factor affecting how they think. Any competent teacher needs to be aware of the particular contextual variables that are important in that setting (Montero-Sieburth, 1989). The need exists, then, to look at teacher thinking in multicultural contexts; the aim of this paper is to uncover teachers' thinking about students of color in multicultural contexts.

The overriding concern that teachers have in planning and interactive decision making has to do with the students (McNair, 1978–1979; Semmel, 1977; Taylor, 1970). Teachers' treatment of their students is in large part a product of the theories teachers hold of students generally and the theories teachers hold of each specific student (Anderson-Levitt, 1984; Calderhead, 1983). For example, Calderhead argues that teachers have four kinds of knowledge related to students: (a) knowledge about pupils in general (based on stereotypes), (b) general knowledge about particular students, (c) specific knowledge about students, and (d) routines for dealing with student difficulties. In her qualitative ethnographic study, Anderson-Levitt (1984) noted that teachers' thoughts of students contain a heavy evaluative component, that the cues used by the teacher to evaluate were ambiguous, that other students' reactions to the individual student were an important source of information the teacher used to confirm or deny her theories, and that students tend to conform to the teacher's theory of them.

To date, very little has been done to investigate the theories teachers hold of students of color (though Marland [1977] suggests some forms of "compensation" for those who are culturally deprived). In a study done by Wiley and Eskilson (1978), race was a factor in determining external versus internal causes of attributions of success and failure, with the behavior of African-American students rated as more external and Euro-American student behavior rated as more internal. Cooper, Baron, and Lowe (1975) found that the effect of race was mediated by socioeconomic status.

Rist (1970) suggested that a student's social class influences a teacher's expectations, resulting in differential treatment and a self-fulfilling prophecy. In his study, he postulated that the teacher has an "ideal" image of a successful student; the teacher expects success of those students who fit the ideal. The initial "expectation" of failure for some students snowballed into a rigid castelike system in the schools that is reinforced throughout a student's school experience. This is made possible, in part, by student poor performance resulting from differential treatment and by informal discussions in the school among teachers. Also, students assumed to be "unsuccessful" were exposed to more control-oriented behavior, leading to greater discontent and therefore the need for even greater control.

Since Rist (1970) was working in a segregated (African-American) school, he identified factors that separated the "success" from "failure" students as socioeconomic (dress, physical appearance, condition of the student's hair, etc.) without considering that race was also a factor (even though he noted that skin color and linguistic ability were factors considered). Rist speculated that this process of differential treatment may be attributed to the teacher's role as an agent for society to ensure a permanent "underclass" of workers or may simply be a mechanism the teacher employs to differentiate and separate those who "can be saved" from those who can't. These speculations were never directly confirmed.

The only study of a teacher's specific theories relative to student gender and race did not begin as a study of such (Stanic & Reyes, 1986). Using a case study, Stanic and Reyes found a teacher deliberately engaging in differential treatment toward his students as a function of gender and race. The teacher was critical of an African-American male student's academic efforts, suggesting he was in danger of falling into the "black athlete syndrome." By contrast, the teacher was more encouraging and gave more latitude to a Euro-American male student. With an African-American female student, he was more social in his orientation but less interactive academically, whereas the opposite was true in his interactions with a Euro-American female student.

The study described here is driven by the following research question of interest: For situations involving personal, instructional, and discipline issues, can teacher's implicit theories (via their principles of practice) of the multicultural classroom be identified by their responses to analogous situations of that classroom?

THE THEORETICAL AND METHODOLOGICAL BASE

Clark and Peterson (1986) describe approaches used to identify teachers' theories (thinking aloud, simulated recall, etc.). One approach, the repertory grid technique, is a provocative, useful approach and is based on a solid theoretical framework. Importantly, it has been used in a variety of educational research contexts, including those with teacher thinking as a specific focus (Solas, 1992).

George Kelly proposed a psychology of personal constructs. Kelly (1955) argued that all people are like scientists whose ultimate aim is to control and predict the future; they develop theories, test hypotheses, weigh the evidence, and reformulate (if need be) existing theories. The goal of theorizing, according to Kelly, is twofold: to help make sense of the world, and to help efficiently predict future events. The anticipatory nature of these theories and the idea that theories help make sense of the world is compatible with the constructivist principle advanced in the cognitive sciences (Mancuso & Shaw, 1988).

The psychology of personal constructs rests on one postulate. The postulate states that "a person's processes are psychologically channelized by the ways in which he anticipates events" (Kelly, 1955, p. 46). This means that the naturally active psychological processes that comprise our personality are shaped and directed into customary patterns, by the ways and means in which we reach out to the future through the window of the past (Ewan, 1984).

From this postulate and the corollaries that followed, Kelly devised the repertory grid technique (likened to a structured interview) to get at an individual's construct system. In brief, the technique involves the identification (or elicitation) of elements of interest. These elements may be people, situations, and so forth. The elements must be within the range of convenience of the constructs of interest and must represent the pool from which they are drawn (Fransella & Bannister, 1977). Constructs are elicited (usually) by asking the individual to identify the similarity and/or difference between a triad of the elements (or via dyads of the elements, laddering, constructing pyramids, etc.—see Fransella & Bannister, 1977). The researcher should now have a matrix of elements by constructs. In the typical case, the individual then is asked to rate each construct's application to each element. From this, a quantitative analysis of the ratings can be made to reveal patterns of association. Afterward, statistical analysis (such as cluster analysis, factor analysis, multidimensional scaling, etc.) can be applied to reveal distances among the constructs.

Using "scenes" in conjunction with repertory grid techniques is one approach used to understand a professional's implicit theories. For example, Salmon and Lehrer (1991) constructed a variety of scenes, manipulating specific variables within each scene (child behavior, teacher thinking about that behavior, etc.). On the basis of previous research studies by Chi, Glaser, and Rees (1982) which established that initial problem identification greatly influences strategy selection, Salmon and Lehrer found that two school psychology consultants differed with respect to how they organized the scenes (i.e., which variables served as the organizing device) in ways consistent with their approach to practice. Other studies have replicated the findings of differences observed between experts and novices in other disciplines (Salmon & Lehrer, 1991).

THE CURRENT STUDY

Subjects

The subjects chosen for this study came from a pool of interested (paid volunteer) teachers at a high school on the south side of an urban city in the upper Midwest. I gave all interested teachers a preliminary survey card. From a group of forty-two, I chose sixteen candidates. The teachers chosen were my best effort to get a representative sample (equal number) of teachers based on gender and subject matter (social science and language arts). Subject matter was a criterion for teacher inclusion, since Sleeter (1989) found that teachers from these disciplines tend to incorporate multicultural issues into the curriculum and to adapt instruction more than teachers in math and science. I assured all participants complete confidentiality.

Procedures

I conducted all further research on an individual basis, and each interview was taperecorded. Each teacher was interviewed twice, for no more than ninety minutes each time.

Interview 1. In the first phase of this interview, I obtained a biographical sketch of the teacher. This yielded valuable information about the teacher's experiences as well as helped establish rapport between the interviewer and interviewee. The second phase began when I showed the teacher twelve scenes (randomized to minimize any placement effect) that described a teacher-student issue. As discussed earlier, scenes were used because constructs develop in the course of action (Vallacher & Wegner, 1985, cited in Salmon & Lehrer, 1989). I developed the scenes to examine typical and significant issues teachers face in the classroom.[4] Four of these scenes were related to discipline issues, four to personal (student) issues, and four to academic issues[5] (though several of these scenes overlap categories). The teacher read a scene, and then described what she or he thought the "cause(s)" of the issue were and what strategies she or he would use to deal with this issue. After paraphrasing these responses to the teacher's satisfaction, I wrote them into the row on a rating grid matrix.

The last phase began by having the teacher rate (on a scale of 1 to 5, with 5 being "very important" and 1 being "not important at all") the importance of each of the strategies she or he identified for each scene.

I conducted this first interview with all teachers before I conducted any of the second interviews. Before the second interview, I employed a proximity matrix (Euclidean Distance) to establish a measure of association between each rating in the matrix for every teacher. These measures were fitted to an additive cluster model (Additive Similarity) of analysis to suggest the general clusters used by each teacher (Sattath & Tversky, 1977; see Aldenderfer & Blashfield, 1984, for a comprehensive discussion of cluster analysis techniques).

Interview 2. After initial introductory comments, the second interview involved showing the teacher the cluster analysis (tree diagram) of her or his strategies identified in Interview 1. I asked the teacher to identify the "principle of practice" behind each cluster.

Finally, I asked the teacher a variety of questions designed to get at definitions of terms and issues related to multicultural education. The answers to these questions shed additional light on the teacher's perspective of multicultural education.

Analysis

I analyzed information about the teachers' theories with respect to academic, personal, and discipline issues as well as information about the salience of these ideas to student characteristics. The analysis was descriptive in nature. In particular, details of the city, community, school, and teachers were collected. As Delpit (1988) described it, "It seems impossible to create a model for the good teacher without taking issues of culture and community context into account" (p. 285). Then I listed the strategies these teachers identified along with resulting principles of practice.

RESULTS

The Context

Two key observations stand out about this context. First, the setting for this study is multicultural with respect to ethnicity. The city's racial population is made up of Euro-Americans (60 percent), African-Americans (29 percent), Hispanics (6 percent), Asian-Americans (2 percent), and Native Americans (1 percent). Yet the racial makeup of the student population at the school was 42 percent Hispanic, 25 percent Euro-American, 25 percent African-American, 5 percent Asian-American, and 3 percent Native American. Thus, for individuals to work successfully in this area, it is important that they come to terms with their ethnic background and the ethnic backgrounds of others. This is as true for Euro-Americans, who represent the largest group of people in the city, as it is for other minority groups. Unfortunately, the city is also highly segregated along ethnic lines, so that one need not leave the enclave of one's own ethnic community. This changes, however, when one moves from the community and into the school system.

The second observation is that the target school is struggling with issues of academic achievement. The school is battling a high dropout rate, low test scores, and low grade point averages. The knowledge of this low academic achievement, periodically made public in community newspapers, may itself exacerbate the problem by decreasing student, parent, and teacher expectations and contributing to a negative self-fulfilling prophecy. The men and women who teach at this school are aware of these difficulties and persist in the face of these academic challenges. Thus any results must be understood in light of these academic shortcomings.

Descriptive Profile of the Teachers

I chose 16 male (*n* = 7) and female (*n* = 9) teachers of social science (*n* = 7) and language arts (*n* = 9) disciplines. One teacher is Puerto Rican, one is African-American, and the other 14 are Euro-American (Table 5.2). Most had positive high school experiences, and all attended segregated schools. Almost all of these teachers spent their full professional experience in urban contexts.

Interestingly, these teachers had very similar conceptions of multicultural education based on the approaches described by Sleeter and Grant (1988). By consensus, they were able to identify the dominant conception of multicultural education for 15 of the 16 teachers after reading the transcripts of the interviews, which focused on multicultural issues (C. Sleeter & C. Grant, personal communication, July, 1991). The largest group (*n* = 9) conceived of multicultural education as human relations (seeking to promote unity and harmony among ethnic groups). The next highest group (*n* = 4) were those taking the business-as-usual approach. They classified one teacher as conceiving of multicultural education as "teaching the culturally different." All three of these approaches are distinct but are on the "lower" end of the scale with respect to multicultural education. One teacher, however, was at the opposite end, seeing it as education that is multicultural and social reconstructionist. One teacher could not be classified. Sleeter (personal communication, August, 1991) concluded that these teachers (with the one exception) were strikingly similar with respect to conceptions of multicultural education.

These similarities are consistent with the findings reviewed elsewhere (Montero-Sieburth, 1989; Schon, 1983; Zeichner & Gore, 1990). For example, Montero-Sieburth (1989) suggests that "what goes on in the classroom, as a factor of the urban teachers' implicit and explicit knowledge, is significantly related to the structure of schooling" (p. 344). These similarities might be a product of coincidence, a product of social and cultural forces that have shaped these teachers' perspective, or a product of similarity in the teachers' personality. The similarity in conception of multicultural education also might be explained by the fact that the teachers based their knowledge on personal experience and not on academic training (with the one notable exception). Thus it seems that personal experience by itself does not expand one's

Table 5.2.

Individual Teacher Profiles

TN[a]	GDR[b]	SM[c]	YRS[d]	YRS-T[e]	TOT[f]	CME[g]
1	F	LA	0	11	11	HR
2	F	SS	7	11	18	HR
3	F	LA	10.5	0.5	11	CD
4	F	LA	13	13	26	HR
5	F	LA	2	11	13	HR
6	M	LA	2	18	20	HR
7	M	SS	4	26	30	BU
8	F	LA	1	23	24	UN
9	F	LA	2	16	18	BU
10	M	SS	2	30	32	BU
11	M	LA	1.5	0.5	2	HR
12	M	LA/SS	5	10	15	HR
13	F	SS	0.5	3.5	4	SR
14	M	SS	7	11	18	HR
15	M	SS	11	7	18	HR
16	F	SS	12	6	18	BU

[a]TN = teacher number.

[b]GDR = gender.

[c]SM = subject matter: LA, language arts; SS, social science

[d]YRS = years of teaching not at target school.

[e]YRS-T = years of teaching at target schools.

[f]TOT = total teaching years.

[g]CME = conception of multicultural education: HR, human relations; CD, culturally different; BU, business as usual; UN, unspecified; SR, social reconstructionist.

vision of multicultural education beyond a certain point, supporting the review of the literature made by Grant and Secada (1990).

One final observation about the teachers profiled is notable. The teachers made twenty different remarks when given the *general* prompt to provide reactions to their students; half of the remarks were negative and only four were positive. Ten of the sixteen teachers mentioned the ethnic diversity of the school; six of them said that the students were apathetic; and five said the students were academically ill prepared. Three of the teachers said they liked the students; two teachers said the students were excellent. Only one teacher said the students wanted to learn. It was hard not to notice that these teachers were demoralized. Only one of sixteen said the students wanted to learn, and only four of the sixteen said the students can learn. The implication for teacher expectations and negative self-fulfilling prophecies may be troublesome. However, this observation must be tempered by knowledge that these interviews took place at the end of a school year, when many teachers feel "burnt out."

Principles of Practice

Recall that the question guiding this study focused on identifying the principles of practice for situations involving personal, instructional, or discipline issues via their responses to classroom scenes. When presented with the twelve classroom scenes, the teachers discussed a variety of distinct strategies (98) that they would employ, with an average of 18 strategies discussed per teacher (Table 5.3). Undoubtedly, this number would have been greater except that I asked the teachers to discuss only their two primary strategies. Notwithstanding this variation, each teacher grouped her or his strategies into either three of four principles of practice that guided the use of those strategies.

There was considerable overlap in the principles described by the sixteen teachers. A naive rater was employed to look at all 58 of the teachers' principles and to construct a summary sheet grouping principles that were similar. This rater and I put the same 42 (out of 58) principles into five groups, with 88 percent agreement as to group placement for those 42. Interestingly, this rater and I had exactly the same descriptive headings for each of the five groups. For all 58 principles, we had 83 percent agreement on group placement.

Each of these top five principles will now be described and are summarized in Table 5.4. Before beginning, it must be emphasized that these principles of practice are important only for the types of issues described in the scenes. Thus they may not be relevant or appropriate with respect to issues of student evaluation (grading) or curriculum.

The principle of practice that dominated (in terms of number of teachers describing it) is the principle of student control. This supports the study of Hoy and Rees (1977), who found that student control was a primary issue for most teachers. Recall, however, Rist's (1970) argument that student control also leads to decreased academic performance. C. Grant (personal communication, December, 1991) questions whether student misbehavior or poor instruction and an inadequate curriculum are implicated. This principle has many possible meanings that can only be understood through a more comprehensive study of the school.

Table 5.3.

Teacher Strategies and Number of Teachers Using Them (in parentheses) in Order of Frequency of Response

1. Work with a school professional (16)
2. Get student help through a community agency (15)
3. Have the student explain his or her behavior (12)
4. Make the student feel valued by praising her or him (12)
5. Send the student to an administrator (10)
6. Make the student abide by the rules (9)
7. Find alternative ways to do the assignment (9)
8. Get the student into a support-group (8)
9. Allow the student to choose an option of interest (8)
10. Use other students as a resource (8)
11. Talk about the issue with the class (7)
12. Ask the student to consider the consequences (7)
13. Call the student's parents (7)
14. Ignore the issue (6)
15. Give student the teacher's perspective/feelings/advice (6)
16. Get the student more involved in the class (6)
17. Get the student involved in a small group task (6)
18. Work one on one with the student (6)
19. Honor the student's request (5)
20. Talk with the student (5)
21. Change the student's schedule; put the student into a "specialty" class (5)
22. Ask the student to stop the behavior; tell him or her it's unacceptable (4)
23. Have the student talk about her or his experiences in class (4)
24. Have the student tested for a disability problem (4)
25. Encourage the student to speak with his or her parents (4)
26. Tell the student that she or he has a problem and the teacher knows (4)
27. Have the teacher, student, and/or administrator work to resolve the issue (4)
28. Get the student to expand her or his interests and school requirements (3)
29. Create positive experiences for the student (3)
30. Get a curriculum the student could relate to (3)
31. Encourage the student to get involved in some outside activity (3)
32. Encourage the student to talk honestly with the teacher (3)
33. Teach the student how to tolerate other students' behavior (3)
34. Listen to the student (3)
35. Encourage the student to get help (3)
36. Get the student to propose a solution (3)
37. The teacher withdraws (gracefully) the request (2)
38. Talk with the student to offer support/comfort/acceptance (2)
39. Encourage the student to be a leader, not follower (2)
40. Try to be the student's friend (2)
41. Encourage the student to think about the future (2)
42. Talk with other teachers to help resolve the issue (2)
43. Stop the student's privileges (2)
44. Let the student know he or she doesn't have to do anything (2)
45. Give the student a written assignment (2)
46. Let the student know she or he will not fail (2)
47. Share the teacher's experiences and weaknesses with the student (2)
48. Don't single the student out (2)
49. Ask the student if she or he wants help (2)

Table 5.3. Continued

50. Encourage the student to speak with someone (2)
51. Find alternative ways to praise the student's achievement (2)
52. Find someone to go with the student to talk to the parents (2)
53. Move the student's seat (2)
54. Tell the student not to take the incident personally (2)
55. Encourage the student to do her or his best (2)
56. Maintain the student's sense of dignity (2)
57. Look at the student's school file (1)
58. Let the student know she or he is not alone (1)
59. Offer to work with the student outside of class (1)
60. Explain that it's the school (not teacher's) policy (1)
61. Talk with the other students in the class (1)
62. Bring in a speaker (1)
63. Maintain the student's confidences (1)
64. Let the student know she or he needs more help than the teacher can provide (1)
65. Put the student into another school (1)
66. Emphasize the value of the student's participation (1)
67. Make the student apologize to the class and teacher (1)
68. Contact the student's other teachers (1)
69. Talk with the student about her or his responsibilities (1)
70. Continue to work with the student (1)
71. Watch the student for evidence of inappropriate behavior (1)
72. Show the student her or his errors, without reprimands (1)
73. Use humor (1)
74. Tell the student that it's the teacher's problem (1)
75. Ask student to accept the teacher's authority (1)
76. Give the student less work (1)
77. Let the parents know that they can talk to the teacher (1)
78. Call the police (1)
79. Get the student to talk with the teacher about his or her feelings (1)
80. Slowly mainstream the student into regular classes (1)
81. Find out if the student is in danger (1)
82. Provide the student with a positive role model (1)
83. Be an advocate for the student (1)
84. Tell the class those behaviors aren't acceptable (1)
85. Take action only if the problem persists (1)
86. Encourage the parent to find a solution (1)
87. Encourage the student to learn and practice English (1)
88. Teach the student social skills (1)
89. Get the student involved in teacher-interested activities (1)
90. Bring the parents in to get involved in the issue (1)
91. Talk about cultural differences with the class (1)
92. Ask the student if outside activities hinder schoolwork (1)
93. Ask the student what his or her weaknesses are (1)
94. Work with the student on her or his weaknesses (1)
95. Get the student to empathize with other students (1)
96. Tell the student that his or her friends won't see the behavior negatively (1)
97. Ask the student about his or her interests (1)
98. Remove the student from the class (1)

Table 5.4.

Principles of Practice with Number and Proportion of Teachers
Endorsing Each Principle

Principle	Number Endorsing	Proportion (%)
Controlling student behavior	12	75.0
Using outside resources	10	62.5
Problem solving	8	50.0
Treating students as individuals	7	44.0
Building a positive environment	6	37.5
Promoting student responsibility	4	25.0
Building student esteem	3	19.0
Promoting teacher-student relations	2	12.5
Promoting student involvement	2	12.5
English language proficiency	1	6.0
Using alternative teaching strategies	1	6.0
Using curriculum for student issues	1	6.0
Providing options for learning	1	6.0

The second most discussed principle of practice is the principle of using outside resources. One interpretation of the origin of this principle is that the problems these teachers face are so intense and the demands are so high that they make the use of outside resources inevitable. Montero-Sieburth (1989) points out that teachers in urban, multicultural contexts need to have access to subject matter knowledge, pedagogical knowledge, and "social work" knowledge because they are asked to expand their instructional repertoires to include counseling skills, assessment methods, dropout prevention techniques, and so on. One way to attain this "social work" knowledge base is to work with those community resources who have that base. Alternately, this principle might be a product of teaching in an environment where the student's cultural background is different from that of the teacher. Because the teacher does not come from the same ethnic community (in almost all cases described here), it is to the teacher's advantage to fall back upon members of the school and local community as a means of extending the teacher's own professional competence.

The third principle, problem solving, is most heavily influenced by the type of scenes presented to the teachers. Most teachers saw these scenes as "problems" to be solved. Of interest, many of these teachers see "problems" as opportunities to teach problem-solving strategies.

The fourth principle is the principle of treating students as individuals. To be sure, students do share a common ethnic background. But so much variation exists within any one ethnic group (for example, with respect to assimilation, language competence, etc.) that individual treatment is more pertinent.

The final principle moves the teacher toward forging a positive learning environment. Ultimately, teachers want students to feel comfortable learning and to be successful in that environment.

Contrary to what Lortie (1975) has said, only two teachers discussed the principle of positive teacher-student relations. Lortie also suggested that teachers generally didn't want to work with others, a result contradicted by this study. Note that all sixteen teachers identified working with a school professional as a strategy to be employed (see Table 5.3). Perhaps this could be because the scenes called for this kind of cooperative action, or perhaps teachers today see getting help as "okay" and not necessarily an indication of incompetence. It may be related to the culture of this particular school. Teaching students whose cultural background is different from the teachers' also may induce teachers to rely more on "community" resources.

The findings of Marland (1977), with respect to the principles of practice, are only marginally reproduced. The teachers did not discuss *suppressing emotions* or *strategic leniency*. Indirectly they did discuss *compensation* (through the principle of individual treatment), *power sharing* (through the principle of using outside resources), and *progressive checking* (through the principle of problem solving). Differences with Marland's work may be a result of differences in grade level, classroom "scene," or methodology. They also might be explained by the fact that I strove to maintain the teachers' "voice" through their actual words; Marland inferred these principles from teachers' comments.

However, the findings described here do overlap more directly with those of Conners (1978). Altthough teachers did not show *suppressing emotions* or *closure* as principles, indirectly they showed *teacher authenticity* (through the principle of positive teacher-student relations), *self-monitoring* (through the principle of student control), *cognitive linking* (through the principle of building a positive, reinforcing learning environment), *integration* (through the principle of student control and the principle of problem solving), and *equality of treatment* (through the principle of student control). Directly, the principle of *general involvement* was replicated here by the principle of student involvement. Again, it is crucial to keep in mind that these principles of practice are only appropriate to the kinds of issues presented to the teachers. Different issues would have elicited different principles.

Importantly, we also learn from what principles are left out. None of the principles identified focus on academic achievement, even though many of the teachers noted the schools' academic achievement difficulties and several of the scenes focused on academic achievement as an issue. This may be a product of low teacher expectations where control, not academic achievement, is the overriding concern. Thus, rather than focusing on academic achievement as a principle, these teachers focus on discipline, affective considerations, and so on.

None of the principles described by the teacher are explicitly linked with how teachers think about culture, race, ethnicity, or language, even though most of the scenes made the race and gender of the student explicit. Several factors may explain this omission, including the heavy focus on "business-as-usual" and "human relations" approaches to multicultural education that dominate at this school. Both of these approaches aim to minimize differences between students and to connect to students on an individual level. Alternately, it may be a product of the teachers' comfort level in discussing (generally and with me specifically) issues of race and ethnicity; at worst, it may be that these teachers are uncomfortable thinking about race and ethnicity. Finally, this omission may be a product of the research methods employed.

In sum, I identified five major principles of practice, representing over 90 strategies, that these teachers employed for dealing with the types of scenes I've presented. Since several of these principles had not been discussed directly in previous research, I assert that these principles also are a product of the specific context in which these teachers work (grade levels, student composition, etc.). Though the contextual factors that account for these principles cannot be definitively deduced, the context is multicultural, and the scenes contained information about the students' ethnic background to suggest that it is a contributing element.

DISCUSSION

This study had a central question as its focus. Can the implicit theories (through principles of practice) of teachers who teach in multicultural classrooms be identified using classroom scenes? The answer seems affirmative, since 93 strategies were elicited covering ten principles of practice. It seems that by directing the teachers to discuss a specific range of issues (not simply providing a general prompt) we can gain more insight into those common conceptions that teachers hold. Yet it is difficult to say with certainty which of those principles are a product of the multicultural school environment.

This study has some important limitations. Though I felt comfortable with the scenes because they were teacher produced, since I took time to validate their application to this school setting, and since I received more comments by the teachers on their being real than on their being not real, the scenes still needed to be constructed more carefully. A common concern was that the scene did not represent a culturally conditioned issue (for example, the pregnant student could have been of any ethnic background). This limitation could be overcome by using observations of critical scenes in the target school.

Also, the use of scenes, although productive and easy, may have limitations when compared to more direct approaches such as classroom observation, teacher presentation of a classroom problem, or the use of videotaped segments of classroom acts. Using the scene approach in conjunction with direct observation may be best.

It is essential to keep in mind that these results have only a limited "range of convenience" with respect to the issues I have discussed. We learn little about curriculum issues, evaluation issues, and so on. Additionally, only when expanding the breadth of the issues presented as discipline, student personal, and instructional issues can more complete generalizations about teacher thinking with respect to these three issue types become possible. I consider these limitations and caveats important because they serve as jumping-off points for future studies.

The implications of this study for education are three fold. First, the notion that teachers are actively processing information and making thoughtful decisions is verified. Teachers might not think through the specific strategies that they use but they are guided by a few principles of practice from which these strategies spring. The next question is to find out which of these principles of practice are sound and, if possible, which can be taught in teacher training programs. Second, teachers need to be helped to make explicit those theories which guide their instruction. Reflective teaching

(Schon, 1987) may have the power of helping teachers to identify that which is often hidden. Finally, we have to be attuned as much to what teachers access in their thinking as what they don't access.

CONCLUSION

Exploring teacher thinking and the implicit theories they hold is an important step in knowing about teaching and teachers. Exploring teacher thinking in specific contexts is now required. The more we know about teaching and teachers in specific contexts, the more effective we will be in positively influencing the education process and in changing unproductive teacher thinking. It is my hope that this study extends the knowledge about teacher thinking in the multicultural school context, an extension made urgent by changing demographics and educational inequalities. More importantly, I hope this study continues the "great conversation" among education professionals with respect to teaching and learning.

THINKING ABOUT A MULTICULTURAL CURRICULUM AND INSTRUCTION

TEACHING WRITING IN A MULTICULTURAL CLASSROOM
Students and Teacher as Storytellers

Dawn Abt-Perkins

There is a paucity of studies, complete with descriptions of teaching contexts, that investigate how teachers come to understand and struggle to enact either the teacher education discourses on writing process theory or multicultural instruction. Much of the literature on writing process instruction and multicultural education foregrounds discussions of students and their development by investigating the effects of various instructional contexts and methods. The teacher—her or his experiences, beliefs, and social, cultural, and institutional identities—fades into the background. My study is an attempt to foreground the writing teacher herself in discussions about writing instruction and teaching in a multicultural society. As researchers, reformers, and teacher educators, we need to better understand who writing teachers are and what they bring to such initiatives as creating a writing workshop[1] based on writing process theory for culturally diverse writers. This interpretivist study should contribute to our knowledge of what Delpit (1988) calls the "variety of meanings available" (p. 385) for writing process pedagogy for diverse learners.

HOW IS TEACHER KNOWLEDGE ABOUT CULTURE, LITERACY, AND DIVERSITY OF STUDENTS DEVELOPED?

Shulman (1986), in his review of research on teaching, calls for turning the researcher's lens on the sources of teacher knowledge as we study the cultural implications of classroom life. He believes that unless interpretive research moves beyond documenting cultural mismatches between teacher and student communicative behaviors, it will not be able to do any more than portray the teacher as "the oppressor or the tool of oppression" and the "minority youngster as helpless victim" (p.22). Shulman challenges researchers to understand the "reasons why teachers' behaviors make sense to them" (p.22).

I propose that teachers develop a set of beliefs about learners, their role as educators in a democratic and multicultural society, and their obligations toward literacy education within and through the social communities in which they live and work. From this web of influences, teachers interpret theories that drive their practices. To understand teachers, we must see their words and practices in the context of socialization theory.

Zeichner, Tabachnick, and Densmore (1987) consider three levels of the socialization process in the development of teaching knowledge: the interactive level of the classroom, wherein the students influence teachers' perceptions of what it means to teach; the institutional level, wherein colleagues, administrators, and parents influence teachers' conceptions of their work; and the cultural level, wherein societal positions about education and the distribution of knowledge are mediated through the structures and processes of the school culture. In pointing to the interaction of these three dimensions of socialization, they emphasize that institutional control mechanisms alone cannot explain why teachers believe what they do or choose to act in certain ways. This work opens the door to the possibility that a broader variety of social and cultural influences, both within and outside the school culture that are contained in present teaching contexts as well as in past personal experiences could be brought to bear in on the analysis of a teacher's knowledge. This work also suggests that teacher socialization and knowledge development may be best understood as a process of interpretation of institutional demands and school cultural norms (see also the introduction to this volume).

Bakhtin (1981), a literary theorist, along with social interactionist psychologists such as Mead (1934) and Vygotsky (1978), foregrounds the study of discourse—patterned ways of speaking and acting that are appropriate within certain social communities—as a way to understand how people come to believe and act as they do. As a person makes choices about what to say and how to act, she or he is interpreting the institutionalized ways of being that are part of all social contexts and are part of language itself.

Bakhtin argues that dialogue is central to the process of development of one's identities within the social relationships that influence one's life. Bakhtin (1981) highlights the struggle of interpreting personal meanings within socially accepted and conventionalized discourses. Words are shared within certain social contexts and conditions. These conditions become part of the words themselves. He theorizes that the individual "accentuates" or gives personal meaning to the conventions, authority relations, and political positions inherent in the words that we share with others. In doing so, Bakhtin proposes that the individual negotiates between two basic forms of discourses—authoritative and internally persuasive. Bakhtin sees the language of authoritative discourse as demanding allegiance and full acceptance. Internally persuasive discourses are tentative, questioning, and open to various interpretive possibilities. And these voices "are not self-sufficient; they are aware of and mutually reflect one another" (Bakhtin, 1986, p. 91). The dynamic tension between these two forms of discourse is what makes changes in thinking and action possible. To Bakhtin, how the individual negotiates this tension between discourses is the essence of the identity formation process, what he calls the "utterance." To understand how and why teachers act in the ways that they do, it is essential to take into account the discursive landscape created within the various contexts that shape teachers' practices.

Based on Bakhtin's theories, I propose that learning to teach in new ways is a negotiation and interpretation process of the social communities, the "conversations" through which teachers gain their identities. New discourses of teaching—such as writing process instruction and multicultural teaching—challenge more conventionalized or "authoritative" discourses of teaching. I view the teacher as engaged in a struggle of interpretation of these new discourses within the traditions of teaching and learning that are already a part of a teacher's identity. The teacher—as he or she encounters new theories and practices—is engaged in a kind of conversation rather than a conversion process. Teachers must negotiate who they are—within their biographical, cultural, and institutional contexts—as they interpret who the new theories and practices suggest that they become. I suggest, along with Britzman

DAWN ABT-PERKINS

(1992) and Nespor and Barylske (1991), that we replace transformational views of teacher change and growth with notions of
crafting a self or interpreting an identity. This complexity must be
recognized in teachers who are struggling to learn to teach and be
teachers in new ways.

THE ROLE OF STORY IN TEACHER KNOWLEDGE STUDIES

When teachers talk about their practices, when they give language to their interpretation of the discourses shaping their work,
they do so in the form of stories. I propose teaching stories are at
the site of "utterance." Stories are positioned, "accentuated"
(Bakhtin, 1981) discourses encountered in social interactions.
Like McIntyre (1984), I believe that stories are the articulation of a
cultural self, a narrative ordering of "one of more of a selection of
culturally-ordered possibilities," for "the story of my life is always
embedded in the story of those communities from which I derive
my identity" (p.221).

I suggest that teaching stories are the site of construction of a
teacher's identity, the site of "utterance" to use Bakhtin's term. The
tensions among the discourses of teaching that are experienced by
teachers are found in the stories they tell. Elbaz (1990), in fact,
sets out a research agenda for teacher thinking that centralizes
story as form and method:

> The story is not that which links teacher thought and
> action, for thought and action are not seen as separate
> domains to begin with. Rather, the story is the very
> stuff of teaching, the landscape within which we live as
> teachers and researchers, and within which the work of
> teachers can be seen as making sense. This constitutes
> an important conceptual shift in the way that teacher
> thinking can be conceived and studied, and it is also
> (in my opinion) the direction in which the field should
> be heading. (p.32)

I focus on one teacher's stories as they position her within her
relationships to her past and present teaching identities. I take up
the project shared by Britzman (1992) of "tracing the word," by
tracing the stories of this teacher to the set of social meanings that
make the stories possible and the conflicts within her stories
understandable.

METHOD

Participants and Setting

Laura Mack[2] is a white,[3] middle-class woman with over twenty years' experience as a middle school language arts teacher. She has taught seventh grade at the same school—Market Street School—for nearly her entire career. The school where she teaches has undergone major shifts in the racial and socioeconomic composition of its student body. It is currently one of the most ethnically, linguistically, and socioeconomically diverse schools in the district.

Laura has recently completed a master's degree in language arts instruction at a local state university. Through her course work, she read the current literature on writing process theory and writing workshop approaches to instruction. Her reading of the literature and her exposure to multicultural education through staff development inservices at her school led Laura to change her writing program into a workshop program. She came to believe that a workshop approach was the best way to address the needs of the diverse student population whom she teaches.

I argue that Laura shares some common ground with many teachers of writing today. As the student population continues to diversify in terms of ethnicity and social class, white, middle-class females (the majority of the teaching population) search for ways to respond to students with whom they do not share much social experience. They read what the educational theorists have to say about the best approaches (in the case of writing instruction, Atwell's [1987] book, *In the Middle: Writing, Reading and Learning with Adolescents,* and the workshop approach it describes, has been promoted as an effective and culturally sensitive middle school model) and work to apply these instructional principles in their classrooms.

Data Collection

Through participant observation (e.g., talks between classes, working side by side with Laura and her students, attending faculty meetings, etc.), I collected information—stories, lesson plans, students' work, and her responses—that helped me understand her interactions with students, colleagues, administrators, and parents. In the classroom, I took on the role of teacher's aide

(Hart, 1982), which is somewhere between coteacher and detached observer. From this orientation, I examined the ways that Laura constructed her classroom environment and relationships with student writers as I took direction from her related to instructional activities. Most of the information from Laura comes from ethnographic interviews following the basic principles outlined by Spradley (1979). The research purposes of these interviews were twofold: (1) to create an opportunity for Laura to discover meanings for her practice, and (2) to elicit rich descriptions of her experiences in order to explore multiple dimensions to her practices. I conducted several structured interviews to collect biographical information.

Data collection began in August of 1992, when I conducted the first biographical career-history interview and collected documents describing the school and the community. I conducted interviews and participant observations for entire school days for a three-week period at the beginning of the school year. From this data, Laura and I decided in which of her writing classes I would continue to be a participant observer. I observed at least one writing class a day for a minimum of three days a week for the remainder of the semester and conducted other interviews as needed.

Narrative Analysis as a Window into Teacher Knowledge

The stories that Laura told throughout the semester to describe her practice provided the structure for the final analysis. All data, then, were analyzed in conjunction with Laura's stories through a process that has been described by Labov and Fanshel (1977, p.49) as "expansion," or the bringing together of all the information that will help in understanding the production, interpretation, and sequencing of her stories. I was not interested in categorizing the types of narratives or in conducting an in-depth analysis of the narrative structures of the interview data. Rather, I was interested in the ways in which narrative was a part of a teacher's theorizing about her practice. In other words, Laura's stories were not coded or cut apart to illustrate themes; rather my intent, as a writer of this research narrative, was to provide a context in which the stories Laura told could be understood.

Laura took into account who she believed her students to be when reading the stories that they wrote. In other words, she was narrating stories of her students' lives in order to understand their texts and their needs as writers. In reflecting on her students and their lives, Laura believed that she was taking into account students' cultural experiences. Culture, to Laura, was an aspect of the individual differences among students that must be understood and respected. She thought about how individual students interpreted (1) the culture of the classroom when considering their relationship to her and to their peers, (2) their family and home cultural experiences, and (3) macrocultural relationships regarding race, class, and gender. In interpreting what and how and why students wrote, Laura considered these three levels of cultural experience and their expression within her students' texts. From this understanding, my first research question evolved into "In what ways does Laura take into account students' cultural experiences in her interactions with individual students?"

I started to read the stories that Laura told me about her background as a student, her life as a wife and mother, and her career history within the context of trying to understand why she created certain stories of her students' lives and texts. From a narrative perspective, my questions began to shift from "What stories of students does Laura tell to guide her instruction?" to "What stories of students' lives are possible for Laura to tell?"

I also started to listen differently to the stories I heard from her colleagues and to the conversations she had with parents and her fellow teachers. Again, I was interested in how others in her teaching setting either supported or conflicted with Laura's stories of students' lives. Given my sociocultural perspective on teacher development, I was guided by a third research question, "What was it about Laura's experiences, social relationships, and cultural positions that supported these narratives about her students and their texts?" What started out as a study of a teacher and her beliefs evolved into a study of the variety of contexts and relationships that create a web of possible ways for Laura to understand students' lives and to make sense of her teaching practice.

Laura's Stories of Tina and Bridget

The case studies I present focus on how Laura makes decisions about the student writers in her class who come from backgrounds that are different from Laura's in terms of ethnicity and social class. Tina and Bridget are African-American girls from low-income backgrounds. The two students respond very differently to the workshop and to Laura's instruction.

In the school as a whole, these students were on the "at-risk" lists. In other words, they were considered to be problem cases, students to watch out for, to take special notice of. Laura did exactly that. These students were the subject of many conversations Laura had throughout the semester—conversations with school counselors, nurses, academic specialists, teaching colleagues, and me. Laura was deeply concerned about these students and struggled to reach them in ways she believed to be beneficial to their academic success as writers and as students in the school culture. Tina and Bridget were talked about in casual conversations between secretaries and teachers in the main office, over the teachers' lounge lunch table, and in official meetings between staff members as students who needed to be "saved." Staff members believed that they both had "potential" but that they could be "lost" at any time.

Through the two cases that I present in this section, I hope to capture Laura's storymaking—her intents, her actions, and reflections as she struggles to piece together her own stories of these students and their lives to guide her practice. These are living stories—without neat and tidy conclusions. With each new interaction between Laura and these students, their peers, and their families, Laura revises her story of who these students are as writers and amends her practices accordingly. The cases focus on the three sources of information that influence Laura's "storying" of these students' lives as writers and as students: (1) their classroom interactions, (2) information provided through school officials and contact with parents about students' home lives, and (3) the texts that they produced in class. Although each case has its unique features, the information that Laura takes into account comes from these three sources.

The Story of Tina: The Problem of Being a Second Mother

Tina's mom attended the open house held in the second week of school. Throughout the rest of the semester, Laura referred to what she learned from her interaction with Tina's mother at this conference:

> "I believe we have already met. Weren't you a student here a few years ago?" Laura asks.
> "More than a few years ago. Feels like a couple of lives ago. That was such a terrible time in my life. I'd

just as soon forget it ever happened. I was such a mess until I was about seventeen. I was so confused and scared. You see our mama moved us here in the middle of the night. We had to get out of Houston. There were a couple of killings involved and we had to leave there quick. I had never lived in a neighborhood with all white people before. It was definitely a culture shock you could say."

Laura just nodded and smiled and let Tina's mom tell her story.

"There were a lot of crazy things going on in my family. But we were told not to tell the white man anything because he may break up the family and put us all into foster homes. So, as much as the people here wanted to help, family counseling was out of the question. And my mother had no support system. We were here all alone. There were so many family secrets bottled up inside of me. It made me a very hyper kid and I was in no way prepared to be in school.

"But we are here to talk about Tina. Tina has written many books at home. There are filled notebooks all over the house. I'd like to buy her a trunk to put them all in so that we don't have to trip over them. I write too. I write when I am angry or frustrated and then I reread them to reflect on my feelings," Tina's mother continued.

"Well, you are modeling everything we are teaching this year. So I guess our job is done," Laura interrupts with a laugh.

"We draw life maps together—Tina and me. I tell her that the only way that you can get through the short term is to have a plan and believe in yourself. As a black woman in this society, you need to always be thinking ahead. People can tell you they aren't racist, but it is in the system. I've taught my daughter the meaning of the words *support network, racist institutions, problem solving, life plan, conflict resolution*. These words aren't just words to Tina, they have meaning."

Tina's mother concludes her part of the conversation by saying, "I hope we are both successful this year. To work with kids, to work in the helping professions like we do, you need to trace your own values, know where they come from and be ready to change the values that are no longer reasonable. Sometimes we need to change who we are. It is a constant fight." (9/9/92)

After the conferences, on our way out to our cars, Laura talked about how glad she was that Tina's mother was getting her life together. Laura also talked about how we needed to "nurture Tina's enthusiasm for writing from home to school" (9/9/92).

A week later, Laura explained one of Tina's classroom responses through an analysis of Tina's relationship with her mother. Although this interaction occurred during social studies, it is significant here because it marks the beginning of a new classroom writing pattern for Tina:

> It is the day after Columbus Day. Yesterday, Laura had asked the students to read a *Scope* magazine special insert on Columbus. The piece gives some basic facts about Columbus and the current controversy surrounding his place in history. Part of the reading the students are assigned is an insert of a series of short interviews of students from diverse backgrounds that point out different perspectives on the Columbus legacy.
>
> Laura begins the discussion by asking students to comment on what they remember from the interview insert on Columbus.
>
> Jason, a white boy, begins, "The opinion of the Native American boy made me mad. He was claiming that whites came and polluted the land and that we are responsible for pollution."
>
> Laura responds, "What bothers you about this statement? What are you getting at?"
>
> Jason follows up his earlier comment "that Whites are being judged this way. We did a lot of good for the Native Americans and their lifestyle too. They wouldn't have lived as good a lifestyle had Columbus never have come."
>
> Laura clarifies, "You mean what bothered you was the racism evident in the opinion, judging all people by the pigment of their skin and lumping all white together like that is wrong. Not all white people caused these problems after all."

Tina turns in her seat to face Jason and bursts into the dialogue, "This boy who said this has probably experienced more racism than you have. You have no idea how his people were treated for generations."

Laura interjects, "Now Tina, Jason has a right to his opinion. Remember these are just opinions. Anyone else?"

Laura continues the discussion by calling on students who have their hands raised.

After the discussion, Laura starts a video and pulls Tina aside to talk about how she needs to manage her outbursts in class. Laura wants her to do well this year and she doesn't want Tina putting herself at risk of getting into trouble by not listening and respecting others' opinions.

Tina returns to her desk and writes in her notebook nonstop throughout the entire video. She fills almost an entire notebook by the time the video is over. When I ask Tina what she is writing, she replies, "A story, but not for this class." (10/13/92)

This pattern of writing "stories, but not for class" continued throughout the rest of the semester. Laura viewed this extra writing as Tina's way of "letting off steam. She probably learned to do this at home because her mother is so volatile" (10/12/92). "She needs an outlet for her emotions because she has a difficult time communicating with her explosive, strong-willed, and articulate mother. She probably finds her intimidating. I think Tina is envious of Sheila because Sheila's mother is more softspoken and more malleable" (10/21/92). Laura does not try to discuss with Tina the reasons she is doing this writing because she feels that Tina is a "bit too rebellious" at the moment to be able to discuss this (10/13/92).

During a writing conference, Tina told me that she liked to write at home more than she did in the writing workshop because she preferred to write about other people rather than herself. She told me that the longest story she had ever written was forty-five pages long. I told Tina that I would like to read some of her "at home" stories. The next day she brought in a twenty-page single-spaced handwritten story with my name written at the top. Throughout the rest of the semester, Tina brought in various stories to share with me. She also continued to write these stories in class the way that she did the day of the Columbus lesson. She wrote when she was supposed to be doing something else.

I interviewed Tina about the first story she chose to share with me. The story was about a teenage, white, upper-middle-class girl named Breanna who tried to help her friend, who lived in a foster home, reunite with her mother. When I shared the story with Laura, we were both struck by the explicit ways in which Tina constructed the characters to be white and middle-classed. Laura believed that this was a form of "fantasizing" (10/23/92). It was my suggestion to interview Tina to find out more about the story. Laura was willing to read the interview and sit down to engage in an interview/conversation about it afterward. Of course, I obtained permission from Tina to share all of this with Laura before I did so. I wanted to know in what ways Laura would interpret this information in her construction of her story of Tina as a writer and as a student in her class.

I share part of the transcript of the interview with Tina here because it sets the context for Laura's comments:

Me: The part of the story I liked the best was the part about Rachelle.

Tina: It was more interesting. The rest is very normal stuff—like brothers and teasing and stuff like that. I don't have any brothers, so. . . . I don't know where I got that part about Rachelle from. Maybe it was from watching tv.

Me: Which tv shows do you think become part of your stories?

Tina: I don't know. Maybe it was a movie. I can't really remember but . . . but on tv all of the families are so perfect. Like the Cosby's are just so . . . they always have enough money to pay five kids way through college and not a lot of people can do that. At least, that I know of. I like to watch the Cosby's but sometimes it makes me mad because it is so perfect. I watch *Roseanne*, *A Different World*, and *Beverly Hills 90210*.

Me: What do you think about those in comparison to the Cosby's—like *Roseanne*?

Tina: Real stuff happens [on *Roseanne*]. Like the power goes out if they don't have enough money. And they fight. And they do make up at the end, but they don't do it like the Cosby's and stop and hug each other. In my family we don't hug each other—like I don't hug my sister. I just say "sorry" [with her arms folded].

Me: There's a lot of things that come into your writing then. What you watch on tv, relationships with your family, with your friends.

Tina: I don't like just perfect families. There has to be at least one problem.

Me: Why did you choose a dentist for a dad and a mom who is a librarian in your story?

Tina: I wanted them to be middle-class. I wanted them to have some money but not a lot of money. Just average.

Me: But Rachelle [Breanne's friend] is not from an average family, is she?

Tina: She has foster parents. Her foster parents are the same as Breanne's [middle class]. Her mom, though, is like really poor. She has to take in day care.

Me: Is that something you have experienced with people you know?

Tina: I probably heard it from one of my mom's friends. I don't know if they do day care, but that just came into my mind because she had this baby. My friend Carrie's older sister's friend has foster parents. That's where I got that from. And my mom had to live in a foster home for a while. (10/22/92)

Laura made the following comments after reading through the interview:

Me: What did you find helpful in this interview to you as a teacher?

Laura: I was just reading the part about the power going out and not having enough money. She sees that and has experienced that every day. She knows that. She sees herself and sees that she is limited as far as wardrobe, etc., and she sees that as such a handicap because that is part of her cultural statement.

The other thing that is so interesting is how she creates these white characters. As I look at her mother who has gone through so much in her life and has struggled so hard to gain a perspective, the reality is that when you have strained so hard—as the mother is trying to do probably— that it makes whites almost more attractive. I'm wondering if the mother hasn't pushed so hard that at times Tina is saying wouldn't it be nice sometimes not to have to worry so much about being black. Wouldn't it be easier to just be white and relax and enjoy the fact that there is no pressure on you. I wonder if the whiteness of this story isn't that— just erase the tensions. Relax. Enjoy money. Enjoy the lack of bigotry and racism.

Toward the end of the semester, Laura was having real problems communicating with Tina. She was concerned about developing a congenial working relationship with Tina. Tina seemed to be rejecting Laura's suggestions and not listening to her comments on her stories. At this time, I interviewed each of the students about what they were writing about, where they were getting their ideas, what critique they seemed to value, and how they felt about the choices they were being offered in the workshop. I shared each of the interviews with Laura and asked her to "think aloud" into a tape recorder so that I could have her reactions based on what she read in the interview transcriptions. One of the students, Sheila, mentioned in her interview having her parents read and respond to her writing at home. Tina, on the other hand, did not mention sharing her writing with her mother. Based on this, Laura constructed the following interpretation of the source of her problems with Tina:

> It is interesting how much sharing has gone on in Sheila's home. They have much more of a positive relationship with school [than does Tina and her mom]— the way they talk about stories and writing and so on whereas Tina mentions nothing. Yet I know her mother came in and said that there were notebooks filled with writing all over the place at home. But she never really said that she read Tina's work. So I think that maybe that is a key to how Tina feels about an adult editor. She hasn't experienced any positive effects of critique, constructive criticism. I don't believe that Tina is getting all that much nurturing at home. Tina is getting old enough where she is starting to question her mother's version of things and this is causing some problems. (1/26/93)

Home life, and, in particular, relationships with parents, seemed to play a role in Laura's interpretation of how students responded to her comments on their writing, to critique in general, and to the structure of the workshop.

The Story of Bridget: Making School A Comfortable
Place to Be

It is early on a Tuesday morning in the second week of school. Laura, her teaching partner, school counselors, home-school coordinator, the school nurse, and other school staff are all seated on old couches and overstuffed chairs.

Laura walks up to the blackboard and writes a list of students' names from her and Kurt's team. Bridget is one of the names.

Laura starts the meeting by telling what she already knows about Bridget's family from teaching her brother last year.

"We know that she is from a transient home. She wore some clothes I gave her the second day of school. Money has to be tight. We understand about the family situation from last year. But her absenteeism is of real concern. We need to know what is happening with Bridget. Have there been changes in the home?

The same counselor asks, "Who is dealing with the family? Who is at home now?"

No one responds for a moment. Laura eventually responds, "I know there was a stepfather in the house last year."

"That could be good or bad. I'm not sure what their relationship is like or how his leaving affects Bridget, her brother or her mom," states the home-school coordinator.

"Bridget is an above-average student. Given that she has bounced around so much in her school career, she has a lot of skills she has managed to pick up. This could be a swing year for her. We may lose her if we are not careful. She was in school the first two weeks, but she has missed two days a week since. The honeymoon period is over and we may have just lost her," Laura concludes.

One of the counselors responds, "We may need a home visit to find out what is going on."

The home-school coordinator agrees to do a home visit soon. (9/21/92)

On the second day of the writing workshop activities (Bridget was absent the first day), Laura read some examples of personal experience stories students had written the day before. Laura pointed out the imagery and use of detail that brought the stories to life. About two minutes into this twenty-minute minilesson, Bridget picked up her pencil and wrote without stopping. When Laura asked for volunteers to share their story beginnings, Bridget's hand shot up and she read:

"November 6, 1991. On a Wednesday at six o'clock in the morning, there was a phone call. It was my uncle, and from the sound of his voice, I could tell something was wrong. My grandmother had gone into the hospital the Friday before because she was throwing up blood.

"I asked him, 'Is it grandmother?'"

"He said, 'Yes, she's dead.'"

"I couldn't say anything. I was shocked.

"After a minute or two, he said, 'Her funeral is Saturday. It's going to be all right. I'll see you later.'"

"The next Friday we went to review her body. When I saw her, I froze. I couldn't even cry. I just stood there. She looked so bad, bare, and blank. I remember turning around looking at my mother. She was on her knees crying. I wanted to hug and comfort her, but I couldn't. I just couldn't move.

"The next day at the funeral, I finally let it all out. I cried so hard, my head was hurting. After the funeral, I would stop crying for a few minutes and start crying again. My life hasn't been the same. I miss looking at her in the morning and hearing her voice. I loved her so much. I wish I could have told her that."

The class is silent for a moment.

Then Laura says, "I felt that we could all understand her relationship with her grandmother from the details she used. She was shocked at how hard and cold she looked. This is obviously not the grandmother she knew."

"Yeah. Frozen, too," adds Hal.

"Frozen, like her life had just stopped. I'll read mine but it is dumb compared to Bridget's." Laura continues the lesson by reading a short story about a near accident she had on her way to school one morning. (9/22/92)

Laura was very pleased with Bridget's story. The combination of her expression of emotion and level of detail impressed Laura. Bridget had no trouble seeking or accepting critique from teachers. In the class writing survey, when she was asked, "How do people learn to write?" Bridget responded, "by going to my teacher and asking her to teach me the basics of writing." Laura worked easily with Bridget. Laura found that Bridget "had little trouble coming up with ideas for writing projects. She needs little motivation. She just jumps on stories" (12/15/92).

Laura was concerned about supporting Bridget's needs as a person. Laura continued to be concerned about Bridget even after she was placed in foster care for truancy and running away from home. She continued to bring Bridget's name up in weekly meetings with school counselors and support staff. She felt that the support personnel in the school believed that their job was done once Bridget was placed in a good foster home. They didn't believe that further monitoring of the situation was necessary as Laura did (1/4/93). Laura believed, in responding to Bridget's writing, that she should encourage her to express her feelings so that "writing could be an outlet for her" (1/4/93). Part of Laura's concern was related to the information that she received through the stories Bridget was writing in the workshop. In a story about an electrical fire that happened at her shelter home, Bridget wrote:

> I've been moved from place to place, ever since I was five years old. First, I was living with my mother. Second, I was staying with my grandmother for a while. Again I was with my mother. But after a while, I was sent to a shelter home. I was there for three weeks. It was going good for me at the shelter. I really liked it . . .
>
> Now I'm in a foster home. The lady is very nice and we get along very well. And I hope that I will not have to be moved anymore. But I have a feeling that I will be moved in the next couple of months. (12/20/92)

Laura's concerns about the instability of Bridget's living situation were heightened in early January. Bridget had gone home over the holidays to visit her mother. Her mother had sold all of Bridget's clothes for drug money. Laura took Bridget to the local mall and bought her a few things—underwear, socks, jeans—and gave her a coat and some other clothes her children had out-grown. "I can't imagine a mother selling a child's only winter coat" (1/4/93). Laura was concerned that Bridget would feel indebted to her and that this would affect their relationship as teacher and student in school (1/6/93). Laura believed that her responsibility as a teacher was "not to get involved in these kid's lives, to go to their homes and talk to their families and so forth. We (as teachers) can only keep the school climate comfortable. We could cause more trouble if we try to do more" (12/15/92). But Laura wanted Bridget to come to school. Bridget needed to have clothes in order to feel comfortable in school. So Laura felt that this was within her responsibility as a teacher.

Laura continued to gather as much information as she could to keep apprised of what was happening in Bridget's home life and to support her in ways that would keep her coming to school and to the workshop. "A lot will depend on who is there to support her now that it looks like her mother is cutting her ties altogether" (1/6/93). When Bridget showed up in school the morning of the following class day, Laura and Kurt, her teaching team partner, found Bridget in the hallway, wrapped their arms around her, and told her that "we are your mother and father and we can't keep giving you good grades if you skip school." She said, "Wow, I'm getting good grades?! I'm sorry," and she smiled. Laura told me that "we just had to let her know that we really needed her to come to school and we expected her to be here. And that we were pulling for her" (1/20/93). Laura felt that she was making some real pro-gress in keeping Bridget involved in school.

After I stopped my visits to Laura's class, Laura and I continued our conversations about Bridget over the phone and during occa-sional lunch visits. Well into the second semester, Bridget was still living with her foster mother, who was, Laura said, "giving her the nurturing that she needs and can't get from her own mother right now" (3/25/93).

In this section, I portrayed some of the specific struggles Laura encountered in her teaching of writing in a racially and socially diverse community. Whereas Laura believed in being a nurturing facilitator of students and their writing, her students responded differently to her nurturing because of their life experiences and because of their needs as writers. Laura believed that it was impor-tant to take into account the child's home and family life when considering her development as a writer in school. Whereas

Bridget seemed to respond warmly to Laura's overtures to help her as a writer and as a student, Tina responded with suspicion and aggression. Laura attributed differences between the girls' responses to her to the different adult relationships Tina and Bridget experienced in their lives. Laura believed that Tina and her mother had a strained and difficult relationship in which adults were perceived as tyrannical authority figures to be treated with suspicion. In contrast, Bridget had a nurturing relationship both with her grandmother and with her new foster mother.

Laura recognized that the texts Bridget and Tina produced were marked by class, race, and gender. Yet she struggled between maintaining this cultural perspective and using psychological principles to explain their classroom behaviors and choices as writers. She wondered if Tina was trying to "escape" her world of poverty and the limitations of her responsibilities at home and if Bridget needed an "outlet" for her frustration over an insecure home situation. She was always concerned about students' psychological "readiness" for certain experiences.

The cases of Bridget and Tina are stories about storytelling. Laura created stories of Bridget and Tina's lives based on the discourses, myths, and "grand narratives" (Geertz, 1983) embedded in her sociocultural experiences. In the following sections, I explore how Laura's experiences both within and outside of school culture help us understand the narratives she constructed of Tina's and Bridget's lives.

LAURA'S BIOGRAPHY

In order to understand the stories Laura creates of her students, we must understand better who Laura is and what experiences she brings to her role as teacher and storyteller. I portray my understandings of how Laura's life as a daughter, mother, and teacher shaped the ways that she viewed her responsibilities in her work.

Growing Up

> When I grew up in this neighborhood, it was more of a community. There wasn't the diversity that there is now. Where I lived was the Norwegian-based community. We knew everybody. I felt very safe. I think that is one of the things that has changed. It was not

fearful to be out. If you had to babysit and walk home at night, the people you babysat for would just stand out on their front porch and watch you go home. That seems so far removed from the experiences my students now have in this neighborhood.

We had problems. But not to the degree that there is today. Today's problems—the violence, the drugs— were not part of my world growing up. Most of the houses around were family dwellings. There wasn't the transient population that there is now.

So I think today I teach a child who doesn't have as secure a situation as I did. Also, the homes are different. My students frequently come from single-parent homes. Most of my students have moved at some point in their lives. I never moved. A child today has to become acclimated to the idea that he or she may be here today and might not be here tomorrow. And even if they don't move, their friends do. (9/21/92)

That isn't to say that my home life was perfect by any means. I can relate in some ways to my students because I grew up with an alcoholic father. I know how this affected my life as a student. We were encouraged in those days to keep quiet about family matters at school. Things have really changed in that regard. Now we are encouraged to understand students and their family situations. This took some getting used to.

I had to learn that my students do not share my values or my perspective on situations—especially discipline situations—because my students and I do not share family backgrounds. I used to make comments like "What would your mother say if she saw you doing that?" I know that I would have been horrified if my parents thought I had behaved poorly. This just isn't always true for my students today. (9/8/92)

The Lessons of Motherhood

Laura felt that her life as a young person in the community did not provide a useful framework for understanding the lives, homes, and parental relationships of her students today. She often referred, however, to her life as a mother in helping her understand her students' responses to her. She also believed that motherhood helped her put students' behaviors "within the context of the course of their lives" (9/21/92). "You have to experience being with children sometimes 24 hours a day to understand why kids behave the way they do. Otherwise it is pretty difficult to see them for an hour or two and try to put that into context with their whole lives" (9/21/92). Throughout the semester, Laura told stories about her son or daughter embedded within stories that she told about her students and their behaviors, families, and texts. Her mothering stories then provided a framework for her to make sense of her students and their lives and perspectives on her in the workshop context.

Learning to Teach

Laura was originally trained as a geography and history teacher. Early in her career, she was assigned both language arts and geography classes. She later completed a master's degree in language arts education. Her master's thesis (completed in 1990) was about how she planned to implement a writing and reading workshop approach. She began to experiment with a workshop concept shortly after its completion. Laura concluded her thesis by citing the reasons that she believed the workshop approach would be effective with her students:

> Students will need time to write about common human experiences and needs. They need to be encouraged to look at their own lives and how people have influenced them and how their own culture influences their thoughts and actions.
>
> Mike Rose (1989) speaks metaphorically about education being one culture embracing another. He compares two embraces (p.225). "Education can be a desperate smothering embrace, an embrace that denies the need of the other. But education can also be an encouraging, communal embrace—at its best an invitation, an opening." The workshop approach to learning attempts to meet the challenge of education by creating both social and cognitive means to develop abilities. Through the process of writing, meaningful communication, and positive interaction with others, the child's confidence and understanding will grow. I hope that my curriculum provides that encouraging communal embrace. (8/90)

In our interviews, I asked Laura to point to any educational experiences both within the university setting or in inservice staff development opportunities provided by the school district that may have shaped her writing instruction. Laura pointed to two particular courses that she took in her master's degree work that had an impact on how she viewed her curriculum:

> One of the most important courses I took was the writing project. It was really stimulating to me because you have a lot of ideas that you are given. You listen to new things that are happening out there. This was the first time that I became aware that people were truly breaking away and trying new things. This was in 1986. People said it was a lot of work, but they felt their efforts were paying off for kids. I was very excited and I incorporated a lot of those ideas right away.
>
> Another course I took that hit me particularly hard with the multicultural situation and the alternative lifestyles that I deal with was a course on teaching writing to diverse learners. You deal with these things as a teacher but nobody seemed willing to deal with these topics in education courses I had taken previously.
>
> This course pointed out to me the differences between the families portrayed on tv and in the media—the all-American family—and the families of my students. It hit me again when I was watching the Republican national convention on tv last night. Here was Bush on stage with his large extended family and all of the rhetoric about American values. All I could think about was how my students would have watched this production. How they might say that my family isn't like this. In fact, my mom's a homosexual or I haven't seen my dad in a long time, but when I do, he is with a different woman or my brother is in jail and he is sixteen. And you have a child asking, "Who am I?" "Am I really a loser?" "What am I doing here?" (8/20/92)

Laura recognized that her teaching was shaped in particular ways by the setting in which she taught, and she prided herself in being flexible enough to respond to the different expectations of the school community and the school administration over the years. When she spoke of her career and her development as a teacher, she did so within the context of changes that have occurred in the history of the school:

> In 1966, when I began teaching, I felt responsible for teaching my subject matter. I was told to try to excite kids about the subject, but even that was to be tempered. The important thing was to seem businesslike. In the early days, you sent the message that you were in charge. The important thing then was completion of tasks, usually measured by paper. The documentation was immense and important. This was usually measured by the number of grades in the gradebook. I remember assigning spelling books and having to teach such nit picky rules for grammar and spelling that I ended up checking the answer key occasionally. You know that you have become too detail oriented when you expect the kids to learn something that you as the teacher do not have a working knowledge of. This is how skill oriented we were.
>
> But society has changed. There has been a lot of questioning of the system. When I started, it was in the preriot days of Vietnam. Once Vietnam happened, and all of the challenging of authority and charges that the system didn't care about individuals, and all of the sensitivity to civil rights issues, we started to question ourselves as teachers. What are we doing? What was it all about? The role of the institution took on a more humanitarian mission.
>
> Those teachers who were trained in the old militaristic days saw new techniques as going soft. One teacher I know used to have a "board of education," which was a paddle for punishing kids. It was an actual physical symbol of that old era. My fellow teachers, more than my administrators, sent me the message that this authoritarian approach was what was expected of me. I also took over for a teacher (who was my cooperating teacher) who was very strict. I was taught not to smile a lot. To remain distant.
>
> Now, I come to school, I smile at kids, I remember every name, I say something nice, and I have won my first battle. Your role is to find the catalyst that will

draw them into learning. When you have established a rapport with kids and they read you and respond to you, that's what keeps you going. That relationship with kids is what keeps the whole thing healthy. Kids may be floundering in their private lives, but we seem to have developed better ways to help as a school. (1/6/93)

When Laura was a student and in the beginning of her teaching career, home and school were to be kept separate. Now, in many ways, she was expected to know her students, their families, and their home lives much more intimately than she ever expected when she decided to become a teacher.

Laura saw herself as supporting the long-term life of the school. Laura found value in her teacher education experiences when they helped her meet the expectations of her school community. Since Laura viewed her career as inextricably tied to the history of the school and the aims of the school community, the following explores how Laura's various staff relationships shaped her teaching and the stories she told to guide her teaching.

The Writing Workshop in the Multicultural School

The day before the first day of school, I entered the school cafeteria, grabbed a donut and a styrofoam cupful of weak coffee and took a seat at one of the long tables with the benches attached where the staff were gathering.

The principal entered the cafeteria with an armful of staff and student handbooks and policy materials. As he passed these out, a bright smile on his face, he stopped to ask how one teacher's mother was doing in the nursing home, and how another teacher's son was liking college. After the sheets were distributed, he stood, still smiling, and waited for the chatting to subside. Eventually it did, and he began:

"One of our goals is to work toward becoming a multicultural school. We know that students don't want to be treated differently, and yet they are different."

This draws some snickers from the crowd.

"What I really mean to say is that students want us to be fair with them, to have high expectations for all of them, while still recognizing them as individuals."

He referred to a form he passed out to the staff titled "Market Street School Improvement Plan: Goals and Objectives 1992–1993:"

"Goal #1: School environment: To enhance the school environment which is physically and emotionally safe, nurturing and inclusive of all students.

1. Implement a safety action plan.
2. Develop an all-school theme to build school unity.
3. Assess curriculum and identify teacher strategies that will promote responsible student behavior.

Goal #2: Provide personal support and monitoring for all students.

1. Develop opportunities for students demonstrating talents and gifts.
2. Provide support for teachers to diversify curriculum.
3. Identify strategies for high academic achievement with students and teachers with an emphasis on minority achievement.
4. Provide support to low-achieving students that will address affective and cognitive needs.

Goal #3: Develop responsive curriculum and effective instructional strategies that promote appreciation and respect for people of diverse cultural backgrounds.

1. Computers will be used by teachers and students to develop and implement instructional activities.
2. Computers will be used to support improving achievement for low-achieving students.
3. Integrative curriculum will be used by teams of teachers in the different grade levels.
4. Students will participate in the reading and writing workshop."

I was surprised by the inclusion of the workshop in the school plan. I hadn't realized the extent to which workshop methods were considered "multicultural" by the school administration and staff.

The principal continued, "We need to be concerned about our low CAT test scores in math and language arts. We are over 30 points below those of the other schools in the district. We need to document what we are doing in our programs to combat this. One way we are doing this is through initiatives like the writing/reading workshop."

District documents on minority achievement and multicultural instruction made such claims as the following (Mason City Metropolitan School District [MMSD], 1990, p. 17):

A major reason for student disengagement is the lack of opportunity to express oneself orally and in writing. Self expression offers a special opportunity to recognize the unique experiences and perspectives of all students, but for minority students whose experiences have been so consistently excluded, such opportunities can offer especially powerful educational benefits. Students have few opportunities in school to integrate or internalize what they are trying to learn with their own experience, because they are usually asked to speak or write in fragments of only a few words.

Laura's commitment to authentic writing experiences and the use of writing as a tool to self-understanding seemed to be consistent with school and district expectations for multicultural curricular reform. When I asked one district-level administrator who was in charge of minority achievement goals to describe what she would consider to be an effective multicultural curricular strategy for writing instruction, she responded, "I would encourage them to write their own stories." Laura believed she was doing just that:

We have that open curriculum where they can choose to write the kind of thing they want—poetry or rap or whatever. There are no guidelines. (8/28/92)

The workshop validates all languages and dialects and it also necessitates a tone of respect for all people and all lifestyles. When you talk about how you feel and what happened and you include dialogue and how others reacted to you, it is real. I think multicultural education is real education. I think that it is authentic.

And that leads to another reason why this approach is multicultural—it builds community. That sense of humanity—of living and growing and respecting one another. What makes the workshop more multicultural than other forms of education is that voice of the student coming through and that struggle to be understood by others. Nurturing dialogue, nurturing sharing, the importance of communicating and resolving differences. All of that is multicultural because all of that is the essence of the oneness of us all. (9/27/92)

Laura interpreted the school district's focus on multicultural education as fitting in with the entire schoolwide focus on responsive, child-centered education. To Laura the multicultural education inservices provided by the school district were part of a history of inservice experiences designed to encourage teachers to move away from subject matter–centered curricular philosophies and mechanistic and authoritarian approaches to teaching. In the following, Laura articulates her understanding of multicultural education and minority achievement initiatives at Market Street School:

> Obviously we are involved in not just a districtwide approach but a nationwide approach to minority achievement. The Black and Hispanic groups have a great deal of problems in school. In looking at the socioeconomic situation, a lot of them are transient. Many of them have situations at home that aren't always stable. (9/28/92). Black students require a little more follow-through and attention. And we run into problems like the high rate of teenage pregnancy with black girls. We are trying to help them understand the disadvantages in making choices to become active sexually. But we know that we are working against what they go home to. Often this is really frustrating. (1/27/93)

Whereas district documents pointed to racial demographic shifts within the school population, the staff at Market Street School—from their conversations in faculty meetings to lunch room chatter to casual hallway talk—attended to a different set of demographic realities—the stress that children and their families experienced from living with poverty-level incomes and in low-income neighborhoods. Whereas district reports called on teachers to attend to different cognitive styles in students and to develop curricula that allowed for diverse cultural representations, the faculty and staff struggled with how to gather together the resources that their students' families needed for students to be able to participate in school. Several staff members described what they did on a daily basis as "putting out fires." Many longed for the opportunity to talk about curriculum issues, but felt that their time and energies were consumed by, as Laura called them, "crisis situations" that came up throughout the day.

The staff explained many of their problems with black students—such as the high suspension rate of black male students—as related to the school's highly transient population (the school had 255 student turnovers the semester in which this study took place) and the stresses of low socioeconomic status and family life. Multicultural education, within the staff, came to mean, as the principal put it in an interview, "responding to individual needs by being receptive to different socioeconomic backgrounds, different living situations, different housing patterns, etc" (10/5/92).

Laura believed that child-centered curricula necessitated a close working relationship with students' families. And she believed that many of the problems of her black students had their genesis in black students' relationships with their parents or in their chaotic and unstable home lives. Students like Tina and Bridget were asked to take on what would be considered as "adult" responsibilities. Laura, like many members of the staff, viewed these responsibilities as burdening students and did not see the possible advantages to such ways of "growing up." Families caused children stress; schools did not. The staff, including Laura, was focused on "making up" for black students' home environments. Laura, and her colleagues found themselves attending to "crisis situations" and "putting out fires."

WHAT LAURA'S STORIES SAY ABOUT TEACHING WRITING FROM A MULTICULTURAL PERSPECTIVE

In the stories Laura tells are the conflicting dispositions of her society, culture, and personal biography that act upon her in the present, shaping her views of alternative possibilities in her practice. I provide different contexts—interpretive lenses—through which to understand the stories Laura tells about her students, herself, and the choices that she makes in her practice. This is a complex and partial story of a process of a teacher coming to know her students and developing a theory of literacy instruction with which to guide her teaching. I analyze the limitations and the possibilities of the discourses of writing process theory and multicultural education as Laura came to know them.

The Intersection of Teaching Writing and Motherhood

Laura interpreted the focus on the "whole child" in writing process discourse as being about more than writing development. And, therefore, Laura saw her role as writing teacher as permeating the life of the child as a whole—both in school and outside of it. Not surprisingly, then, Laura relied on her experiences in her role as mother to shape her teaching identity. When reading students' texts, Laura imagined a life context for the child. This was consistent with how she viewed her perspective on her own children as a mother. Laura did not see how her perspectives on child development and on mothering were culturally informed and shaped by her social history.

Laura found in the discourse on workshop approaches a way to react against authoritarian teaching. Writing process theory made sense to her within the context of her career history, one that has been shaped by a historical shift toward acceptance of more progressive practices. When the discourses of writing process theory or workshop approaches are read in terms of a progressive educational history, Walkerdine (1990) points out,

> there is a denial of pain, of oppression (all of which seem to have been left outside the classroom door). There is also a denial of power, as though the helpful teacher doesn't wield any . . . But more than this, the happy classroom is a place where passion is transformed into the safety of reason. Here independence and autonomy are fostered through the presence of the quasi-mother. Children are bewildered because they don't know the rules, use strategies which aren't supposed to exist. Teachers turn out to be more traditional than expected . . . The classroom, then, is a site of struggle. (p. 25)

Walkerdine proposes that working-class and black children create the most conflict in "progressive" classrooms because they are least likely to fit the notion of the ideal child. The dominant culture is taken as "nature" (p.25). And families and children that do not fall within these cultural traditions are viewed as "inadequate" and subjects for "charity" (p.25). Because such pedagogies are based on a view of "normal development," Walkerdine contends that teachers attempt to describe all children and all families according to this vision of the normal.

Writing process instructional theories, even those that encourage teachers to take a social or cultural perspective on literacy development, do not address the issues Laura faced that had to do with differences between her social and cultural identities and accompanying values and those of her students and their families. Sociocultural theories of writing development encourage teachers to be social catalysts (Dyson, 1986, 1991, 1992a, 1992b) or to consider students' cultural identities in the literacy process (Ferdman, 1990) or to "be more sensitive to the diverse perspectives and historically constituted voices and autobiographies that students bring to school" (Wertsch, 1991, p. 21). However, these theorists neglect the processes in which teachers need to engage in uncovering their own biographies. Their personal, social, and cultural histories shape the choices teachers make about what to value in their students' writings. And yet, these aspects of teachers' identities are not addressed in theories of writing instruction, even in those theories that focus on the student-teacher/writer-reader relationship. My work with Laura has convinced me that who teachers are and how they come to believe what they believe must be considered valid points to initiate and sustain teacher inquiry, especially as teachers struggle to cross cultural and social barriers in their work with student writers.

The Promotion of Human Relations as Multicultural Education

Historically, multicultural education in the United States originated in the racial debates and protests of the 1960s (Sleeter, 1992), a view that Laura supports in her story of her career history. Multicultural education was a movement against low teacher expectations of the abilities of students of color to achieve in school, and was a movement against "all-white" presentations of subject matter. Laura believed that she had high expectations for all of her students as writers, and she certainly had no fear of presenting an "all-white" writing curriculum when she allowed them to write their own stories. Teacher race is seen as an issue in studies of multicultural teaching mainly when teachers display overt prejudice toward children of color, fail to understand them, or expect less of them (Irvine, 1988). These studies do not consider how teachers construct their own conceptions of racial issues and experiences of oppressed racial groups based on their own positions within the structure of race, gender and class relations (Sleeter, 1992). Not surprisingly, then, Laura found little in the discourse on multicultural education to provoke her to reflect on cultural differences between her and her students and their families as she thought about her instruction.

Even in school settings, such as Laura's, where "multicultural education" has been a mainstay of teacher development, how teachers' beliefs and values are shaped by their social and cultural experiences is not addressed. By focusing on understanding children's cultures and how they influence students' learning, teachers have not had to face how *their* own culture shapes their learning about students and their instructional responses. Although Laura had been informed about cultural learning styles and the value of certain instructional approaches for certain ethnic groups, she had not been challenged to inquire into her own biography and uncover the assumptions that informed her stories of her students' lives. Sleeter (1992), in her study of a multicultural inservice program, found that most reform movements that claim to be about teacher empowerment—such as multicultural education and the writing process movement—do not "address the identities or social positions of teachers as White upwardly mobile women, whose life experiences usually limit their ability to conceptualize how social institutions function for other people and the strengths and experiences of cultural groups of which they are not members" (p. 216). Her inservice multicultural education program provided Laura with few resources— including theoretical frameworks and inquiry processes—for understanding who her students are and who she is from a cultural perspective.

For the most part, Laura's exposure to multicultural education and writing process theories in her teacher education programs, both at her school and at the local state university, supported rather than disrupted the stories Laura told about her teaching and about particular students and their families. They meshed with the other stories that were told by her colleagues and were promoted by administrative policy statements. Laura's stories were not part of a dialogue with other voices that might challenge and thereby enrich her narratives of herself, her students, and her practices. Using Bakhtin's words, Laura's changes in her practice were limited by a lack of tension between the "authoritative discourses" of her biographical and social history and the more open, challenging "internally persuasive" discourses to which she *might* have been exposed in her teacher education experiences.

To say that Laura's stories were not challenged does not mean that they were conflict-free or unproblematic for Laura. Laura's interpretation of writing process discourses and multicultural education had real-life tensions for her and had real consequences for students' literacy learning in her classroom. She was not supported in a process of considering how both sets of experiences could be part of a process of critique of the variety of discourses influencing her practice—including those of motherhood, progressive education, American family life, and writing process theories. Laura did not see becoming a workshop teacher in this light. Her teacher education program and her relationships within her school context did not support such a process.

I have discovered, through listening to Laura's stories and reflecting on my own experiences (through the mirror of the stories, so to speak), that any theory or approach can become authoritative when the discourses of one's cultural and social experiences are not examined in relationship to the theory. This study highlighted for me as a teacher educator the necessity of taking into proper account teachers' personal perspectives formed from their teaching histories, cultural identities, biographies, and social contexts both within school and outside of school in discussions of teacher interpretation of any theoretical perspective—including those that claim to be "empowering" to teachers, "liberatory" in intent, or "culturally responsive" in structure and content.

ON SHARING STORIES AS TEACHER KNOWLEDGE RESEARCH

> *Social theories are, or should be, first explanations of how the beliefs and values people have, and the choices they have made, sustain and constitute a certain set of social relations between people, whether or not they are consciously aware that their beliefs, values and choices have this effect, and whether or not they intend this effect; and second, proposals of possible worlds (new*

> *realities) that will make for a more humane and just set of*
> *social relationships between people, and proposals for*
> *ways of realizing them. (Gee, 1990, p. 9)*

In the previous section, I discussed my interpretation of how writing process theory was interpreted by Laura within her biography and other discourses of curriculum, teaching, and learning that were supported in the various social relationships that shaped her teaching identity. In doing so, I attempted to fulfill the first purpose of social theory according to Gee. In this final section, I hope to fulfill the second, to suggest a "possible world," a new reality for teacher-researcher relationships and for teachers within teacher education efforts more generally.

I suggest that collaborative storytelling might provide one possible way for teachers to encounter the questions of who they are and what they believe. Stories about teaching practice join the personal and the professional, the biographical and the theoretical, the historical and the present. And when stories are shared with others, and others share their stories, there is a necessary sharing of perspectives on experiences—perspectives that are embedded in our own social and cultural identities. In hearing the stories of others, one's own story is challenged, enriched, brought into like company, or held in contrast. Stories are a way of exploring and extending one's understanding, a way of making more available for critique the discourses that shape our teaching lives.

Collaborative storytelling could extend the current practices of "action research" or "case study" research by teachers on their own practices as a form of inservice teacher education. Teaching stories could be viewed as classroom accounts or personal biographic sketches or critical responses to questions about one's own history as a writer, reader, student, parent, or teacher. Stories could be shared with others in the school community with the intent of being part of a continuing analytic dialogue so that others could become collaborators in the inquiry process. The collaborators, or audiences to stories, would offer ways of making explicit what seems to be implicit about the storytellers' rendition of their experiences. Then the storyteller could respond with a form of critical commentary based on the responses of others. Collaborative storytelling seems to be a possible way to build relationships within school settings that would offer the opportunity for a critique of school and theoretical discourses.

In collaborative storytelling, it is important that all storytellers have a shared interest. We, as teachers, parents, and teacher educators, need places to share our stories with others who share our commitment to students' lives—such as the stories that might have been shared between Laura, Tina's mother, the home-school coordinator, and myself. In doing so, we could all confront our beliefs, values, and identities. This story-sharing process might help us do as Tina's mother recommends: "To work in the helping professions, you need to trace your own values, know where they come from, and be ready to change the values that are no longer reasonable."

TACIT MESSAGES
Teachers' Cultural Models of the Classroom

Mary Lynn Hamilton

*Until we can understand the assumptions in which we
are drenched, we cannot know ourselves.*
—Adrienne Rich, 1979

The study of teacher thinking has often neglected the powerful
influence of culture on teachers' actions and classroom choices
(Hamilton, 1993; Olson, 1988). Rather than examining underlying cultural connections, the research literature focuses on studies
of individual experience (Clandinin & Connelly, 1987; Clark &
Peterson, 1986; Elbaz, 1981; Munby, 1983; Nespor, 1987; Russell, 1987; Tobin, 1990). Few studies highlight the shared beliefs
among teachers (Hamilton, 1993) or the tacit influences on
teachers' thinking and actions. In one significant exception, Olson
(1988) suggests that teachers' actions reflect their culture and that
understanding cultural influences on beliefs is crucial to understanding teachers' subsequent actions. If we are to understand
teachers' thinking about their classrooms, we must consider their
cultural perspectives. And, if we expect teachers to work in diverse
and multicultural settings, understanding teacher thinking and
the ways that their thinking influences their involvement in and
commitment to multicultural classroom contexts becomes vital.

The contemplative world of teachers is difficult to explore because it exists, for the most part, within their heads (Feiman-

Nemser & Floden, 1986), and cannot easily be exposed. Evidence of culture and cultural knowledge can also be difficult to reveal. One way to examine cultural knowledge involves the current work in cognitive anthropology that explores cultural models. This work suggests that members of society share cultural models, taken-for-granted representations of the world within which beliefs are embedded (Holland & Quinn, 1987). In education, these models could be channeled implicitly into the classroom by teachers to affect how students structure their understandings of the world.

This chapter focuses on implicit and explicit messages[1] sent by teachers within one urban elementary school setting and their effects on their classrooms. How teachers convey their messages through nonverbal, or more appropriately, unspoken materials in the classroom represents a particular interest. What do the teachers want to convey to their students? What do they convey to their students? Using these questions as a guide, this chapter describes the messages conveyed by teachers in their classrooms and discusses the cultural implications of those messages—for the students and about the teachers. I first offer definitions and a framework for understanding those messages. Then I present a study of classrooms within an urban school setting to explore the influence of culture and the power of cultural models in the classroom. At the conclusion, I address the power of messages in the classroom.

CULTURE

Culture, as addressed in this chapter, includes two definitional perspectives. The first perspective offers a broad view that examines culture at a societal level. At this level, shared perceptions of class, race, and ethnicity blend with personal experiences to represent the world. The second perspective defines school culture as the experiences that shape teachers' understanding of their actions (Feiman-Nemser & Floden, 1986; Lortie, 1975; Metz, 1983, 1986; Rutter, Maughan, Mortimore, & Oston, 1979; Sarason, 1982) and their students (Tyler, 1987) within a particular school setting. Shared understandings about students among faculty members occur at this level (Page, 1988).

Geertz (1973) defines culture as "historically transmitted patterns embodied in symbols, a system of inherited conceptions expressed in symbolic forms by means of which [people] communicate, perpetuate, and develop their knowledge about and attitudes toward life" (p. 89). Others suggest that culture filters the world through which symbols and ideas flow to provide certain rules (D'Andrade, 1985) and learned meanings (D'Andrade, 1990). Moreover, Eisenhart (1990) views culture as the "collective interpretations of social and material experiences that are more or less shared by members of a group" (p. 22). Evidently, culture provides a screen through which we view our lives and interpret our surrounding world. Advice, correction, and verbal and non-verbal interactions with others (Quinn & Holland, 1987) implicitly furnish the knowledge that supports that screen, best conceived of as a complex of ideas used according to peoples' needs and motives (Price, 1987).

Sociolinguists suggest that talk represents an important way in which people negotiate cultural meaning and accomplish social ends. Children learn culture through the ways they "talk meaning" (Heath, 1986, p. 97) from their environment and information about appropriate behavior given by primary caregivers (Ochs & Schieffelin, 1984). For them, as for all of us, language contains cultural information in the content of discourse as well as the organization of discourse (Schieffelin & Ochs, 1986). All human communities have shared symbolic meanings regarding their social life, regardless of individual behavioral and/or belief variations, because the sharedness is crucial for understanding the messages of social communication (LeVine, 1984, p. 69).

For the most part, school culture represents the culture-at-large, with extra layers of meaning infused into the particular setting through interactions that occur there. Understanding this interplay of school culture and the culture-at-large is critical to understanding what occurs between teachers and students in the classroom. Furthermore, numerous studies (e.g., Blau, 1981; Heath, 1983; Miller, 1986; Williams, 1987) indicate that interactions in schools influence student performance at school and at home.

Cultural Models

Ogbu (1978, 1990, 1991) pushes the notion of culture one step farther, suggesting that members of society must be understood within various frames of reference—including race, culture, class, and gender—that set the tone and tenor of situational understanding. For example, Ogbu suggests that, in addition to the dominant culture, there are two types of minorities in the United States—voluntary and involuntary. Voluntary minorities are ethnic people who have come to the United States in search of a better way of life (e.g., Hispanics from Central America, Koreans, West Indians, and Sikhs). Involuntary minorities (Native Americans, African-Americans, Chicanos from California), on the other hand, became part of the United States through coercion and domination. In each case, their circumstances affect how people respond to life situations.

These different responses to life situations, called cultural models, represent the expected, yet unspoken, mostly unconscious (Kay, 1987), and taken-for-granted aspects of the world. These cultural models contain "shared implicit knowledge" and involve the process of identifying the complex elements of beliefs and knowledge (Holland & Skinner, 1987, p. 79). Furthermore, these shared theories about the world play an immense role in the understanding of recurrent circumstances, events, and situations in various domains of life. Members of a population use them to organize their knowledge about such recurrent events and situations. They develop their cultural models from collective historical experiences that subsequent events or experiences in their universe sustain or modify; they also serve as guides to their expectations and actions in that universe or environment (Ogbu, 1990, p. 523). Cultural models also convey tacit and routine messages (Shweder, 1982) that provide a moral socialization.

For some anthropologists (for example, D'Andrade, 1985, 1990; Holland & Quinn 1987), cultural models are structures around which ideas, beliefs, and/or actions are organized. Importantly, they do not assume that models always translate into behavior, but models do imply a certain level of understanding (Holland & Quinn, 1987). These anthropologists focus on their cognitive organization to examine cultural knowledge (or how group members represent their understanding of their universe inside their heads) and how that organization affects behaviors (D'Andrade, 1984, 1990; Holland & Quinn, 1987). Others, like Ogbu, focus on the construction of a cultural model as it is learned by group members in their language as well as their actions rather than strictly from within an individual's head.

For different groups within their societies, many have their own cultural models—their own understanding of how the system works and their places in that working order—that simply guide actions and interpretations. The white, middle-class model in the

United States coexists with the models of African-Americans, Hispanics, and others (Ogbu, 1990, 1991). There are, however, some distinctions. Voluntary minority groups tend to share their models, like the cultural model of getting ahead, with white middle-class groups.

In contrast, the involuntary minorities' cultural models are often distinct as a result of different perceptions of the system within which they are expected to participate. For example, involuntary minorities use collective effort as a way to overcome barriers to advancement rather than the individual effort often associated with white, middle-class groups and voluntary minority groups. Many involuntary minority group members find that collective relations offer the best possibility for finding success. Furthermore, views of future possibilities, decisions about appropriate behavior, and the development of relationships distinguish between voluntary and involuntary minority groups (Ogbu, 1991).

Studies suggest that successful ethnic minority students have linked their school-based knowledge and strategies of communication with secure, cultural identities (Cummins, 1986) and that students' successes can be undermined by home and school knowledge incongruencies (Heath, 1983; Shor & Freire, 1987). Successful students need links between the public knowledge of school and the cultural knowledge of home and peers (Sleeter & Grant, 1991). In summary, Ogbu (1978, 1990, 1991) and others (McLaren, 1986, for example) find dramatic differences among ethnic minorities and between whites and all ethnic minorities in their behaviors at school, their ways of seeking success, and their methods of communication. In response, this chapter examines the messages conveyed by teachers in the classroom and discusses the possible cultural implications of those messages as they affect students and influence teachers.

FINDING CULTURE

The data examined for this chapter have been collected since 1990 as a part of an ongoing qualitative study of the reculturing process (Placier, 1993) within Bradley Renaissance School, a K–5 urban elementary school in a large, urban, midwestern city. I employed certain methodological strategies that I thought would provide the greatest success in revealing aspects of culture, a concept that can be potentially difficult to document. They included, but were not limited to, many hours of field note–documented

observations in classrooms and throughout the school, and interviews, formal and informal, conducted with faculty and staff. In
this particular portion of the study, I also collected and recorded
information about the physical and the social environment in
every classroom and hallway in the school. Importantly, this was
not an attempt to reduce classroom data to a short, concise list of
behaviors and/or words; rather, it was a desire to capture the
richness of the classroom text.

To collect this specific classroom message data, I drew up maps
of every classroom, hallway, nook, and cranny in the Bradley
Renaissance School building. As I entered each area, I reminded
myself that I must view the classroom as a text, and I addressed
the question "what do the students see when they enter this room
or area?" Consequently, seated in the middle of the room (I completed the mapping during those times when the rooms were
empty or when my presence was unobtrusive), I charted desk
locations, ceiling decorations, window positions, all verbal classroom statements, posters, student work, and so on. In other
words, I recorded anything the students might see when they
entered or occupied the classroom.

Because culture is both powerful and elusive, with historical
patterns and symbols transmitted through language and action, I
focused on words and images in the study of messages in the
classroom. Recognizing that shared language, metaphors, and
key words indicate a shared culture (Price, 1987), I attempted to
uncover some specific forms of symbolic action in which the
shared meanings reside that provide meaning to members of this
particular group (LeVine, 1984) of students and teachers.

Once I collected the data, I had to figure out how to best examine messages conveyed in the classroom. After many readings of
the gathered information, I selected environmental, symbolic, and
self-related elements on which to focus. As I adapted the work of
Gardner (1984) on the acquisition of culture, these elements
seemed crucial to understanding the cultural text of the classroom
and the school. The *environmental elements* represented the physical and social aspects of the world observed. The physical aspect
included artifacts like tools, general art, and structures, and the
social aspect included room arrangements and implicit messages
beyond simple structure. As I observed the school and the classrooms, I included desks (teacher and students), computers, soft
chairs, rugs, other furniture, pictures, and administrivia as a part
of the physical environment. The social environment included the

layout of the room, as well as the locations and use of materials within the rooms.

The *symbolic elements* represented the devices used to transmit cultural knowledge to an individual. These were material (picture and text) or nonmaterial (spoken words and unspoken concepts) elements that captured knowledge and transmitted it from one person to another. During the analysis of my observations, three categories of symbols emerged: instructional, behavioral, and efficacious. The instructional symbols represented some material or nonmaterial elements that transmitted knowledge to students, specifically focusing on subject matter. Topics included: traditional elementary subject matter (social studies, language arts, math), plus colors, alphabet, and seasonal and calendar information.

The behavioral symbols represented material or nonmaterial elements that transmitted behavioral knowledge to students. These symbols included manner phrases, classroom rules, the can't sign, and student rights.

The efficacious symbols represented those elements that transmitted knowledge about efficacy to students. (More details are provided later in the text.) As an important part of the Bradley Renaissance School culture, these symbols included efficacy power statements and classroom shields.

The *self-related elements* encompassed ways in which persons understood themselves in relation to the group within which they were involved through language and/or interaction with others. Three categories emerged from the self-related information: *artifacts* that represented the evidence of self[2] within the room, such as student work or art, student information, student schedules, and birthday information; *symbols* that represented the symbols of self, including student-of-the-week information and group names; and *self* that represented actual evidence of self, such as photos of the students.

In addition, I recorded any multicultural information found in the classrooms in this section, selecting it because I believed that this material offered students an opportunity to see people like themselves. Information received a multicultural label if it represented anything other than the standard white visage, like books on various ethnicities, posters, and information of famous ethnic minority people.

How did I identify culture? Of course, certain actions and communication might occur as a result of gender, class, geographic location, and age, but there are certain cultural parameters established in previous research (Heath, 1983; Ogbu, 1978, 1990; Philips, 1983), and that literature informed my work. Consequently, in this study I considered student-teacher interactions and began to delineate differences and similarities drawing upon already established research.

As a reminder, this chapter focuses on messages conveyed in the classroom by environmental, symbolic, and self-related elements. I decided to exclude classroom interaction and classroom practice because they reached beyond the intended scope of this work. Of course, those elements are important and essential for the full picture of the classroom, but this chapter focuses specifically on the aforementioned elements. Future writing will include a more complete view of classroom experience and will also address student input about the classroom (Hamilton & Fleck, 1994).

Next, I describe the setting and outline the influence of culture on teachers' messages in the classroom.

BRADLEY RENAISSANCE SCHOOL

Built in 1913, Bradley Renaissance School, a red brick building on a tree-lined street not far from a major highway, has watched its urban neighborhood change and grow. Currently the neighborhood includes an assortment of ethnicities and economic statuses, although historically most of the families have been Hispanic families hired by the Santa Fe Railroad. The neighborhood has been a victim of an economic downturn and shifting populations. The school has always been a communication hub for the neighborhood, and the principal attempts to maintain that connection through contact with the PTA officers and other neighborhood members.

In 1990, Bradley School received major funding from a private source that labeled the school an example of current school reform and exciting innovation. The funding offered a renewal of energies and ideas. To signify its rebirth, the school faculty decided to change its name from Bradley to Bradley Renaissance School. One element of the school's plan included an integrated curricular approach based on three beliefs: (1) high expectations for all students; (2) enhancement of all students' self esteem; and (3) an emphasis on a social and multicultural curriculum (Proposal, 1990). The school offered this final element partly because it was the most multiethnic of the elementary schools in the district, containing 6 percent Laotian, 24 percent Hispanic, 29 percent black, and 41 percent white children, all from the surrounding neighborhood. And partly, they offered this perspective because the teachers expressed a commitment to it.

Bradley Renaissance Faculty and Staff

Once the restructuring project received funds, the Bradley Renaissance School staff hired many new (to this school) teachers and voluntarily transferred anyone who requested it. The teachers who agreed to work at Bradley Renaissance School supported similar beliefs about students, positive change, and teamwork. Moreover, the staff were selected for positions at Bradley Renaissance if they were outspoken leaders and committed to students and change. They sought faculty who were articulate about their experiences and their points of views because district personnel are conscientiously watching for successes and failures.

The 32 faculty and staff working at Bradley Renaissance School are 92 percent female (29), 8 percent male (3 men) with an ethnic mix of 13 percent African-American (4), 5 percent Hispanic (2), and 82 percent white (26) and a mean age of 38. They have an average of eleven years of experience and are in their first few years of teaching at Bradley Renaissance School. Prior to their tenure at Bradley Renaissance School, most teachers worked in other urban elementary schools.

These teachers are an exceptionally active group of educators with considerable teaching experience and a desire to attempt innovative techniques and strategies with students and for themselves. They supplement their teacher knowledge with numerous workshops and inservices taken to improve their practice and their classrooms as well as advanced courses at various neighborhood institutions of higher learning.

Bradley Renaissance School Culture

As a consequence of their innovative project, the Bradley Renaissance staff has had the opportunity to build and rebuild a school culture together. In a deliberate, concentrated, and in-depth effort to fuse old and new ideas, the staff has had to struggle with direction. For example, many teachers wanted to follow the dictates of the funding proposal, written by district personnel, but found that they needed to go beyond that outline. The teamwork (each grade level has three teachers that work together) and the collaborative components of the project encouraged the creation of a strong culture, but sometimes individual definitions of teaming and collaboration varied. Yet their work together every day after school contributed to the development of a shared language and collegial bond. Reculturing a school (Placier, 1993) that already had a strong existing culture took time and energy.

From the onset of the project, the Bradley Renaissance teachers shared some language about schooling and students. Evidently their commitment to students developed early in their careers. When faculty members discussed the purpose of the school, they responded with similar words and the identical meaning—all children can learn. For example, responses like "All kids can learn if they have confidence in themselves and if they put forth effort," or "Every child will succeed," or "All children can learn, given time and support; our staff has the power to help students become active participants in their learning" were standard fare. Most teachers demonstrated a high level of commitment to that purpose.

The faculty and staff's exposure to a particular staff development program, entitled the Efficacy Seminar, enhanced their shared vocabulary to some degree. Attended by the entire faculty and staff, this five-day seminar reinforced and explored the beliefs that the teachers brought to the school. Designed to provide participants with an operational model for managing student development, the Efficacy Seminar's essential element equated success with a combination of effort and ability. In reaction to what the seminar leaders identified as the "massive failure" by schools "to develop the potentials of our children," the Efficacy Seminar hoped to analyze and dismantle "the psychological barriers to the development of our children, and to our own development as educators" (from the Efficacy Seminar Handbook). Language like "think you can, work hard, get smarter" was integrated into teachers' vocabularies. Upon completion of the program, the teachers shared their language with their students. In fact, many staff members practiced sharing the language when talking among both students and themselves. For further reinforcement, they designed representative buttons and t-shirts for the students and themselves.

Selected partially because it fit with Bradley Renaissance School's desired multicultural approach to the curriculum, the

Efficacy Seminar attempted to guide the school culture toward an efficacy model of development. This model equates confidence and effective effort with development rather than what the leaders called the American model of development (not called a cultural model), which equates ability with development and promotes a helplessness response in too many ethnic minority students. Moreover, the efficacy model hopes to develop strong positive attitudes toward intellectual competition and encourages students to attribute intellectual successes to ability and attribute their failures to lack of effort. Consequently, the Efficacy Seminar promotes two American cultural models: ABLE PEOPLE SUCCEED and WORK HARD TO ACHIEVE REWARDS. Both represent, to a certain extent, elements of the American Dream—if you apply considerable and worthwhile effort to a particular task, you reap rewards (Sleeter, 1992). In the classroom, for example, you might expect to get an A if you work hard enough.

Thus far, I have discussed culture as the screen through which we interpret the world and cultural models as the implicit representations of that world within which our beliefs are embedded. Additionally, I have begun to detail a study that includes a look at a school's culture that nestles in among the general culture and cultural models. In a classroom and/or in a school, elements of both school culture and the culture-at-large are found. And, of course, the culture-at-large becomes more complex as you look at the cultural models generated from among different groups.

In short, the Bradley Renaissance School culture deliberately revolves around the encouragement of hard-working, confident students who are taught by strong, confident teachers in a school dedicated to addressing the needs of students with a multicultural approach. Or is it?[3]

In the next section of this chapter I discuss the messages conveyed in the classroom using the framework previously described in the methodology because it best delineates the cultural components in the classroom. Once this is completed, I discuss the cultural models that emerge from those messages.

WHAT THE TEACHERS WANTED TO CONVEY

Individually, and as a group, the teachers at Bradley Renaissance School espoused the belief that all children can learn. For many teachers this belief had been a part of them prior to their tenure at

MARY LYNN HAMILTON

Bradley Renaissance, but the Efficacy Seminar reinforced it. When asked to address the school philosophy and their personal directions, all teachers within the school stated the same idea in different ways. Many teachers simply said, "All children can learn." One teacher listed "necessary experiences, confidence, and success" as the essential elements for all children to learn. Yet another teacher suggested that, "assuming all kids can learn (whatever their pace), we're going to give them the best shot by more school time, less hassled teachers (teaming), and a really positive 'can do' attitude." Most teachers, in fact, seemed to echo what one teacher said that the "idea of failure should become nonexistent."

Although not a group-think response, the teachers' beliefs aligned around students and their goals for them. The teachers wanted the students to be the best that they could be. They also wanted the students to feel good about themselves and recognize their value within the school and within society. The language used in the classroom, in slogans, chants, and posters, encouraged this idea. Slogans and chants, called power statements at the school, like "think you can, work hard, get smarter" and "failure is feedback," encouraged children's self-esteem, and "all children can learn" promoted their value in society. The teachers expected efficacious language use in the classroom.

Academically, the teachers wanted success for all of their students. They spent hours designing outcomes and creating or finding activities to match those outcomes. They also expressed a desire to generate a relevant school program for the students, incorporating the students' world into the classroom. They even decided to exchange the traditional grading format for a mastery system that, in their opinions, encouraged success. They wanted this, however, while concurrently wanting their students to be successful in traditional ways, such as achieving high standardized test scores, behaving appropriately in class, and learning textbook subject matter.

They also attempted to encourage a cooperative spirit among students, whereby working together in harmony was the norm. They demonstrated this in two ways. First, the teachers worked in grade-level teams that collaboratively planned and taught classes. These teams of teachers moved along with their students for three years (K–2, 3–5) to better develop relationships with students. As a result, they hoped to model cooperation for the students through their own teaching relationships. Second, the students were arranged in desk or table groups to encourage cooperation. No classes had desk rows.

So, Bradley Renaissance teachers wanted to convey that all children can learn. Further, they wanted to convey ways to build student self-esteem, through the use of power statements, efficacious classroom language, success in the classroom, and a cooperative spirit. They wanted to encourage student success while not drawing attention to that success. But what did they convey?

WHAT THE TEACHERS CONVEYED

Most of the classrooms at Bradley Renaissance School are high-ceilinged, spacious, rectangular structures with at least one wall of windows. Each classroom also has an air-conditioner in one of the windows. The light-colored classroom walls are conducive to brightening the already light-filled rooms.

In contrast, some of the halls are darker in tone, with contemporary pastel colors used to enhance the decor. School art decorates the hallway bulletin boards. Also, two large efficacy statements stating THINK YOU CAN, WORK HARD, GET SMARTER are located in two separate areas, above the principal's office and above the all-purpose room.

Table 7.1 delineates the different elements—environmental, symbolic, self-related—found in each classroom. Table 7.2 delineates the elements found in the hallways and areas not designated as a classroom. For every number represented in a specific category there was a different and individual item identified. For example, under the self-artifact category, every mark represents a different area of student work found within the classroom. Certain items were common to every room, and these items were not included in the tally. These items included clocks, fans, flags, heaters, bulletin boards, and three computers.

Additionally, outside of seasonal changes and student work changes, the rooms mostly remained the same throughout the year. Although all classrooms were visited three or four times during the year, few noticeable changes were documented.

Environment

The physical environment of Bradley Renaissance School resembled the environment found in many schools. The rooms were

Table 7.1.

Elements in Bradley Renaissance Classrooms

Teachers	Environment		Symbol Systems			Self-Related		
	Physical	Social	Instructional	Behavioral	Efficacy	Artifact	Symbol	Self
LCr	5	Desks in groups	12		3	3		
RS	7	Tables for groups	7		1			
AL	8	Soft chair, rug, desks in groups	31		4	2 MC-3	1	1
KW	13	Rocking chair, desks in groups	18			1	3 MC-1	1
1 LB	17	Rug area, soft chair	23	2	2	3 MC-2	1	1
PC	4	Desks in a connected square	5	2	2	3 MC-1	1	1
MC	8	Desks in group, rug	15	2	1	2 MC-4		2
YF	12	Desks in groups	9	9	3	2		
MR	12	Tables for groups	33	4	2	4 MC-1	1	

		Self-Related					
RT	13	Rocking chairs, rug, soft chair, tables for groups	34	2	2		1
AH	7	Rug, tables for groups	8		22	5	
NT	6	Desks in groups	9			MC-1	
MN	8	Tables for groups	8	1	16	3	
DD	5	Desks in groups	8	5	7	1	
MS	16	Tables for groups		4	4	3	
LC	8	Desks in groups	8	2	2	2	
ST	1	Desks in groups	8	1	15	2 MC-8	2
LS	10	Desks in groups	15	2	2	2 MC-9	1
NR	10	Desks in groups	6	1	31	1	1
						MC-3	

Note: The abbreviations in the Teachers category represent teacher identities. The numbers represent how many of each item could be found in each room. In addition, the abbreviation in the Self-Related category indicates how many multicultural representations could be found.

Table 7.2.

Elements in Bradley Renaissance School

Teachers	Environment		Symbol Systems			Self-Related		
	Physical	Social	Instructional	Behavioral	Efficacy	Artifact	Symbol	Self
Lower Hallway	2		1					
Principal's office	4		2			1		
Midfloor hallway	4	1		1	3 MC-2	MC-8		
Social services	25	Tables for kids, soft chair	1	3	2	1		
Kindergarten hallway	2					1		
Library	3		Texts					
Front area	10				1			
Teachers' lounge	10				1	2		
Top hallway	6	Bean bag chairs, rug, tent, stuffed animals	2		1	1		

Note: On this chart, the locations outside the classroom were reviewed and categorized. As with table 7.1 the numbers indicate how many items could be found. The MC abbreviation in the last category identifies multicultural representations.

scattered with the traditional school furniture of desks, tables, and cabinets. Office equipment could also be found in some rooms and hallways. The distinctiveness of each room came from the pictures selected and the social environment established through desk arrangement and comfort areas. Desks or tables in every room were arranged in a cooperative fashion. For example, in a four-desk cluster, the desks were arranged so that the students faced each other. The comfort areas, often designated for reading, usually included rugs and soft chairs or rockers. Pillows were also sometimes included.

Most rooms were quite open, with easy passage among the desks so the students could move easily throughout the room. There were also many classroom tools throughout the classrooms—overheads, paper, pencils—as well as art displayed in the classroom, usually related to subject matter.

When considering what the teachers conveyed to the students through the physical and social environment, I had to look carefully because I knew what the teachers wanted to convey. Initially I saw cooperative settings in every room and felt that the use of cooperative settings was good because it potentially reinforced the notion of cooperative and collaborative work. However, when I looked beyond the environmental setting to the walls and the work found there, there was little evidence of cooperation. Instead, I found students' individual work. Three classrooms had class shields that listed information about the class as a group, but that seemed an anomaly even in those classrooms because they were surrounded by individual work.

I also think the teachers wanted to provide a comfortable space for the students. Often in conversations they would suggest the importance of students needing a safe place to be. And, although they provided conflicting messages about cooperation, the teachers did attempt to offer a comfortable haven for the kids.

Symbolic Systems

The information represented by symbol systems included instructional, behavioral, and efficacious information. Every classroom but one had instructional symbols in them, usually in the form of an alphabet chart, a mathematics display, or another instructionally related outline. Some classes had more charts than others. The one classroom without instructional information was used as a meeting area more than an instructional site. Many classes also had at least one set of rules that established the appropriate behavior guidelines for the classroom. Teachers expected students to have a plan, use effective effort, keep their hands and legs to themselves, respect themselves, raise their hands, and use good manners. Any behavior short of these expectations would be dealt with swiftly.

Many Bradley Renaissance classrooms contained efficacious information in the form of posters or power statements, approximately six statements for every classroom in the school. These statements served as silent reminders of the teachers' and the school's expectations for the students. For example, one poster, an I Chart, stated:

I
Can
Do it
but it requires
thought and effort
on my part.

Another chart stated: Think you can, Know you can, Work hard = Get Smarter. Yet another chart included the Good Day Pledge:

I can have a good day today
and noone can change that.
I can feel good about myself today,
and noone can change that.
I have confidence in my abilities today,
and noone can change that.
I can work hard today, and noone can change that.
I will do my best today,
Think good about myself,
work very hard to get smart, and
understand, appreciate, respect, and accept
myself and others.
And noone can change that.

I placed this information in the symbolic systems section because, although this information was in the room, it might never be explicitly addressed in a lesson. Often it just represented what was considered appropriate and acceptable by the teacher, serving as silent guides for attitudes and beliefs expected in the classroom.

And what was appropriate and acceptable in the classroom? First, many teachers apparently valued instructional information. Particularly in the primary grades, considerable information decorated the classrooms. Often the rooms seemed crowded with information. Certainly the abundance of information conveyed that students have a lot to learn.

The behavior information indicated that the students needed to learn appropriate behavior on their own. Hands, feet, and voices must be kept to themselves, and moving around occurred only when permitted. Only one classroom had any cooperative rules listed. Once again the language revealed the individual nature of the classroom.

The abundance of efficacy statements made clear the teachers' desire to adopt the school culture and promote it to the students. Questions and statements like "Do I have a plan?" "Am I using effective effort?" "Be responsible for yourself," "Always try to do your best work" and "Think you can" attempted to promote self-esteem. Sometimes this information was presented in at least two-foot-high letters. Often the students were bombarded with it. One classroom, for example, had thirty-one separate statements. The students also received contact with these statements in the cafeteria and hallways, as well as in assemblies and other meetings.

These statements were everywhere. What I did not record was the frequency with which these slogans appeared on desks and students' work implements. Many desks also carried efficacy statements (not to mention the shirts, buttons, pencils, and erasers that were found throughout the school).

What did this convey to the students? It certainly sloganized the American Dream. It also seemed to capture the purpose of the Efficacy Seminar and attempted to build student self-esteem. It also seemed to promote an individual perspective because students were to undertake these perspectives on their own, not together. Collective effort among students appeared not to be rewarded.

Self-Related Representations

This category embodied the representation of self in the classroom. At Bradley Renaissance School there were some representations of self in most classrooms. One representation came in the form of student work hung around the room. Many classrooms had at least a few student papers hung in the room. In addition, approximately one-third of the classrooms had symbolic representations of self in student-of-the-week or class names, and one-third of the classrooms (but not the same one-third) had actual representations of self with student photos. Sometimes these pictures were featured in the classrooms and sometimes they were hard to find.

Approximately 50 percent of the classrooms contained multicultural artifacts. In several classrooms, that artifact might simply be a picture of Martin Luther King. In other classrooms, the multicultural representation might be a picture of a undefined totem pole or an antiquated picture labeled "Indian brave." Often these artifacts seemed like a quick addition rather than thoughtful inclusion. One classroom stood out among these classrooms. This classroom had an African-American theme. In this classroom, there were maps, posters, books, and games that addressed the African-American culture. This classroom stood out because it contained a powerful message of self and pride that was missing in many of the other classrooms. Whereas other classrooms seemed to have multicultural representations for decorations, this one classroom seemed to have the information visible for the students, their pride, and their self-awareness.

In a school that promoted a multicultural approach and a commitment to self-esteem, the cultural self seemed to be missing from the classrooms. To begin, many of the teachers were white, and many of the students were not. When looking for a role model who might represent them, there were few represented in the faculty or symbolically within the room or the building.

From the cultural self perspective, the teachers conveyed traditional messages of the dominant culture to the students. There were pictures of white people in the classroom, but few alternatives. Within seven classrooms there were seventeen sets of pictures of anthropomorphized animals. That is, there were pictures of animals dressed in clothing to represent certain messages in the classroom. Some were drawn along with the alphabet, but many seemed substituted for human representation. In one case, there was a set of animals on a career poster with tinted features that seemed to suggest a multiethnic theme, providing a twist on the multicultural perspective.

MESSAGES IN THE CLASSROOM

Bradley Renaissance School's plan centered on high expectations for all students, enhancement of student self-esteem, and an emphasis on a multicultural curriculum. The Bradley Renaissance teachers fervently stated their beliefs about all children learning in relevant settings. However, what I found in the classrooms was quite different. What the school and the teachers wanted to convey in the classroom and what they did convey in the classroom differed. Why? What caused the discrepancies between the stated beliefs and the actions of the faculty?

From the school plan standpoint, I think the teachers tried to convey the high expectations and self-esteem focus in the classrooms but without the multicultural perspective; thus the high expectations and the focus on self-esteem seem misguided. The use of instructional posters and power statements stressed the teachers' desires to have the students succeed and feel good about themselves as they worked. The self-esteem focus particularly came through in the power statements. Certainly in the rooms with many instructional and behavioral messages, the teachers sent messages about the amount of work and the way it was to be done. In those statements, students read how they should feel about themselves and what they should know, but who were they? Very few classrooms explored the students and the cultural and social world in which they lived. One classroom where self was included, Anne's class, had pictures of the community—people and places—labeled and hung in a prominent area of the room. But classrooms where the students and their world were excluded sent a conflicting message of generating self-worth within a world where one's cultural self may not exist.

As I traveled throughout the school and looked within all of the classrooms, the multicultural curriculum was not apparent. A few pictures of a multiethnic nature as well as a few pictures of classroom students do not create a multicultural curriculum. The emphasis on the multicultural curriculum seemed to be a phrase added to the proposal, rather than a perspective addressed within the school. If I use Sleeter's work (1992) or Sleeter and Grant's earlier work (1987, 1988) and talk about distinctions among approaches to multicultural education ranging from the human relations approach to the social reconstructionist approach, the Bradley Renaissance multicultural approach cannot be found. In fact, I suggest that *multicultural curriculum* is a misnomer for the approach taken at this school. There is no evidence, except in the one aforementioned classroom, that the teachers infused dominant culture information with that of ethnic minority cultural information.

When the data were collected and analyzed, I shared my findings with different teachers as a member check. Several teachers said they were not surprised, and many said that they never even thought about it. The teacher with the Afrocentric theme, Lisyl, stated that she felt a commitment to her students to offer an alternative. In her case, her two colleagues (Nona and Stacia) also had multicultural messages in the room because it was a part of a unit they were doing in class. The major difference between her room and the other two rooms was the depth of information. Although Nona and Stacie each had a theme—one was Native American and one was Hispanic—they did not have the books, posters, and games that reinforced the themes. Instead, the Hispanic room had language information displayed, but little else. The Native American room had displays of Native American housing, and that was all.

Other teachers expressed concern about the absence of multicultural information but were not really certain about its place in school, or actually what it was. And finally, a few teachers felt it was the parents' jobs to provide that information for their children.

Along with the multicultural approach, the self was absent from the classroom. The teachers stated that they wanted to create relevant classrooms, but that did not become actualized in the classroom text. Instead, the students saw traditional pictures of the dominant culture—families, contributors to history. The variations on the themes were minimal. If students are to have good self-esteem, they need to see their cultural selves somewhere in the classroom—either in fact (through work or pictures) or in representation (in pictures of others).

Tinkerbell Tenet of Teaching

The Tinkerbell Tenet of Teaching (Hamilton, 1993), whereby teachers believe that something will occur solely on the strength of that belief, like the saving of Tinkerbell in the 1950s version of Peter Pan, appears to be in operation in these classrooms. It seems that the teachers, through the sheer act of believing the students can do it (or acting like they do), are attempting to direct the students in a positive direction. The power statements, particularly by their numbers throughout the school, attempt to convey some message to the students. Everywhere the students are, the slogans are there too. Do the students get it? Do the students believe that they will get smarter by believing in themselves and working hard? I am not sure, but I do know that the teachers would like to believe that.

School Culture Perspective

The Bradley Renaissance teachers clearly attempted to convey the school culture to the students explicitly and in an unspoken manner. Explicitly the students wrote power statements and heard the chants. In an unspoken manner, the power statements fairly littered the classrooms—on desks, on walls, on shirts, and on windows. If students learn information simply from a bombardment of ideas, then the Bradley Renaissance students must have learned these messages well. But did they?

Cultural Perspective

That question raises an important issue about learning culture, and self. If students never see themselves in the class—either in fact or in representation—how valuable can they feel? I think it provides conflicting messages and leaves students wondering what might be true.

In a school where white students are a minority, there should be, at least, a more multiethnic presentation of ideas. Yet at Bradley Renaissance, dominant cultural traditions and approaches to instruction are upheld. Most of the classes are run individually, and the students are taught individually. Collective effort is not a sought-after approach. Differences among students are overlooked rather than celebrated and similarities are also ignored.

The cultural models pursued and promoted within the school—*able people succeed* and *work hard to achieve rewards*—are models most often associated with the American Dream and the "promise of prosperity" John Adams talked about in the 1700s. It is not necessarily that only one group had this model, but that the approach to and attitude about the models differed. The teachers may promote these ideas as individual pursuits of things to attain while the students may see them as adversarial goals. More importantly, if the models are not grounded in their experiences, the students may not even know how to make sense of them. Recognition of these differences is crucial to empowering students. In fact, for some involuntary minority students, belief in the cultural models promoted at the school might create a terrible bind. For example, the bind would occur when, given their relationship with the system, they began to believe that *able people succeed.* As involuntary minority members they may work hard, perhaps like their parents, but not succeed, or to the same degree of success as the members of the dominant culture. And that would undermine the use of the these models (Ogbu, 1991).

SUMMARY

This chapter examined the implicit and explicit messages sent in the classroom of Bradley Renaissance teachers and their possible effects on students. In particular, the unspoken information presented in the classrooms seemed to present the teachers' wishes that the students would be successful, but the messages did not seem to go beyond that. Interestingly, the study of classrooms at Bradley Renaissance revealed discrepancies between what the teachers wanted to convey to the students and what they did convey. They wanted to convey a multicultural atmosphere in which all children can learn and be successful. However, their classrooms and curricula were not multicultural and tended not to represent the children's lives within their four walls. Furthermore, the teachers wanted to encourage cooperative work. In every room, desks were arranged in groups, not aligned in rows. And the encouragement of cooperative effort is important to ethnic minority students. Unfortunately, though, the real individual nature of the classroom is revealed when the room is studied. That lack of representation and encouragement, along with the power of the cultural models teachers bring with them, may interfere with student success.

IMPLICATIONS

Culture in the classroom can be found within the physical environment and the thinking embedded in the design of that environment as well as in pathways through which information is shared and constructed there (Bowers & Flinders, 1990). Teachers can be seen as intermediaries who provide the elements of information, or lack of it, given to each student. In the classroom, students interact with teachers' cultural representations, including classroom materials, interpretations that mirror their own backgrounds, and responses that reflect their biases. Students also learn how to think about something in ways that are learned, implicitly or explicitly, through their teachers. Importantly, teachers may not be aware of the cultural information that they transmit, or that it is being internalized by the students.

We know that successful ethnic minority students have confident cultural identities linked with appropriate school-based knowledge and ways to communicate (Cummins, 1986). We also know that students are disempowered when they lack compatibility between home and school knowledge (Shor & Freire, 1987) because they need connections between public and cultural knowledge (Sleeter & Grant, 1991). This chapter underscores this information and calls again for the need to address teachers' thinking and the ways that their thinking and cultural influences affect their involvement in the classroom.

TEACHERS' CHOICES FOR INFUSING MULTICULTURAL CONTENT
Assimilating Multicultural Practices into Schemata for Instruction in the Content Area

Carmen Montecinos
Deborah L. Tidwell

Over the last thirty years educational reform efforts have focused on reconceptualizing the school curriculum so that it represents the social and cultural diversity of United States society. Various educational associations and accreditation agencies have proposed or mandated guidelines for infusing multicultural content across the curriculum (Martin, 1991). In this chapter we explore the relationship between two areas of teachers' cognition that may influence teachers' responses to infusion mandates: beliefs about multicultural education and beliefs about instruction in the content area. We focus on the case studies of two teachers who expressed a commitment to infusing multicultural content into their language arts instruction and who evidenced sharp differences in their approaches to infusion.

This chapter is organized into five sections. First, we briefly describe the data collection procedure we followed. Second, we delineate the conceptual frameworks informing our interpretations of teachers' approaches to multicultural education and language arts instruction. Third, with those conceptual frameworks in mind we present a description and analysis of how these two teachers, Arnold Larson and Fred Arroyo, approached multicultural education (teachers' names are pseudonyms). Fourth, we draw from information-processing theories of learning to explain why these teachers who shared a commitment to cultural pluralism and multicultural education exhibited divergent approaches to the infusion of multicultural content. And fifth, we explore the implications of this analysis for staff development in multicultural education.

DATA COLLECTION

The data reported in this chapter are drawn from a study we conducted to examine to what extent, and under what circumstances, Iowa's multicultural education mandate had impacted the classroom practices of five secondary language arts teachers (Tidwell & Montecinos, 1993). The five teachers who volunteered to participate in that study had developed lesson plans and objectives to infuse multicultural education across the language arts curriculum. All were tenured faculty at Middleton High School (pseudonym). Arnold Larson and Fred Arroyo were the two teachers who exhibited the most divergent approaches to infusion. The school is located in a city of 23,000 in the state of Iowa. At the time the study was conducted, the school district employed 318 certified teaching staff, 5 of whom were ethnic minorities. Of the 1,652 high school students, 12.7 percent were ethnic minority students, of whom 10 percent were Latino, primarily of Mexican-American descent.

Richardson, Anders, Tidwell, & Lloyd (1991) define beliefs as consisting of "a set of assertions held by informants and realized in the natural language as declarative sentences" (p. 562). Four data sources were used to ascertain and triangulate our interpretations of teachers' cognitions for multicultural education and language arts instruction: a belief interview, a practical-argument interview, a copy of a lesson plan, and a videotaped lesson. Prior to participating in the first interview, each teacher was asked to videotape an instructional period in which he was "doing multicultural education." The first interview focused on questions designed to elicit information regarding teachers' biographies, their declared orientations toward multiculturalism, and the corresponding educational implications they derived from their orientations. At that time, teachers were asked to share with us a copy of a lesson plan in which they were doing multicultural education. To elicit teachers' beliefs in action, a week after the belief interview was conducted the teacher and the researchers met to discuss the teacher's instructional practices within the context of the lesson. During this interview we utilized a heuristic elicitation procedure (i.e., practical arguments) described by Richardson et al. (1991), Richardson and Anders (1990), and Fenstermacher (1986). This technique includes both open-ended questions (constructing teachers' propositions about their own realities) and close-ended questions (establishing interviewer's understanding). As the teacher and the researchers jointly watched the videotaped lesson, teachers were asked questions to elicit their reasoning and rationales for specific instructional choices and interactions within the taped lesson. This involved asking questions such as "Why are you writing students' responses on the blackboard?" "Why are you asking them to read that passage?" and so on.

CONCEPTUAL BACKGROUND

Multicultural Education

Analyzing and interpreting teachers' cognitions about multicultural education is complicated by the fact that "multicultural education" is a concept that means different things to different people. Among its advocates there is a struggle which reflects a widely diverse, and at times contradictory, set of goals, targeted populations, and corresponding educational practices (Banks, 1989; Sleeter & Grant, 1993). In this instance, however, the legal and theoretical framework that underpins Iowa's multicultural, nonsexist mandate provided these teachers with a theoretical context to guide their practices.

The legal framework. Recognizing equity as a cornerstone of quality education, Chapter 256.11 of the Iowa Code and Chapter 281.12(8) of the Iowa School Standards, adopted in 1978, required that a multicultural, nonsexist approach (MCNS mandate) be used in the schools by 1985 (Iowa Department of Education, 1989, 1991). Ideologically the mandate is based on the concept of cultural pluralism and the belief that equity is a basic ideal of the American creed. A rationale for this mandate is the belief that schooling plays an important role in developing healthy intergroup relations. The mandate uses the "tossed salad" metaphor (each ingredient is distinguishable and contributes to the flavor of the whole) to describe the United States's multicultural society that needs to be nurtured by the school curricula. The mandate emphasizes the need to address multiple forms of social diversity as well as the need for systematic input by women and men, minority groups, and the handicapped in developing and implementing programs for the infusion of multicultural, nonsexist concepts across the curriculum.

As articulated in several documents prepared by the Iowa Department of Education, some of the educational goals and rationale envisioned by this mandate include the following:

- · It is important that students see themselves reflected in the school environment in a realistic and positive manner to foster in students the development of a strong, healthy self-concept.
- · It is important that majority students experience a curriculum that reflects the contributions and perspectives of the disabled, various races, gender, and cultural groups to avoid the development of a false sense of group superiority which eventually leads to prejudiced and discriminatory behaviors.
- · Schools must promote equity by openly dealing with the legal and societal constraints that operated to keep some groups either in lower echelons or entirely out of the mainstream.

Approaches to multicultural education. We utilized Banks' (1989) four-level taxonomy to describe the approaches these teachers used to integrate the goals and principles articulated in the MCNS mandate. Banks (1989) postulated that the most frequent approach to integration is to add curricular content that highlights the contributions, costumes, artifacts, and heroes of an ethnic group (i.e., the contributions approach). This approach keeps the structure of the traditional curriculum intact as ethnic content is added as discrete elements, and many times it is limited to celebrating special days. For instance, a language arts teacher taking this approach might ask students to read a book about an ethnic hero in conjunction with the celebration of an ethnic holiday. Mainstream criteria are typically used by the teacher to select the hero, and that hero's life is typically depicted from a mainstream perspective. Banks (1989) defined mainstream perspective as a "focus on White-Anglo Saxon Protestants. This dominant cultural group in U.S. society is often call mainstream Americans" (p. 189).

The second approach, the additive approach, involves adding content, themes, and perspectives to the curriculum without changing its structure, goals, and characteristics. The representation and analysis of ethnic content and materials typically reflect mainstream perspectives as opposed to the perspectives of members of that ethnic group. A literature teacher who followed this approach would add to the list of required readings books written by, and about, the disabled, women, and people from diverse ethnic backgrounds. Each book would be read as an isolated unit without a clear attempt to attain a comprehensive view of how the stories read intertwined to form the collective history of the United States. This teacher would not devote instructional time to help students develop the concepts, content background, and attitudes to respond to the issues raised by these books in ways that resonate the perspectives of the status group depicted.

The transformation approach, in contrast to the previous additive approach, involves the actual restructuring of the curricula. This restructuring purports to infuse an examination of issues, themes, and concepts from multiple perspectives, including mainstream perspectives. A literature teacher using this approach would select a group of novels that addressed a common theme (e.g., physical disabilities). These novels would be analyzed as a collective to see how the lives of people who have and those who do not have a disability are interconnected. Additionally, when including ethnic content, the criterion for selecting a book would not rest solely on the ethnicity of the author. The stories would illuminate ways in which various cultural groups have shaped the macroculture of the United States.

The fourth approach, social action, enlarges the transformational approach by adding components that require students to address social problems. A language arts teacher using this approach would select literature that directly addresses issues of sexism, handicapism, classism, and racism. Students would be encouraged to critically analyze the literature piece to uncover the social conditions that engender those types of social relations. Subsequent class discussion would center around ways of addressing social problems in their local communities and school. For example, teachers could select novels that depict strong female characters in nontraditional roles. Students would later identify gender biases in current schooling practices and propose ways of eliminating gender-based barriers in their school.

Theoretical Orientations in Reading and Language Arts Instruction

The manner in which a teacher approaches instruction in a language arts classroom is a reflection of that teacher's understanding of how learning takes place and more specifically how the reading and writing processes occur. At the secondary level much of language arts instruction focuses on reading tasks to facilitate literacy activities and interactions. Pivotal to this focus is a teacher's beliefs about how reading works (reading process) and the role of the reader/learner and the teacher. Although there have been many theoretical propositions for the interaction of cognition and text, three general models of reading can be seen as representative of the research: a bottom-up (text-based) model, a top-down (reader-based) model, and an interactive reader-text model.

In the bottom-up model of reading, meaning is based in the text, and the job of the reader is to correctly decipher the meaning found in that text (LaBerge & Samuels, 1985). Both structuralists and deconstructionists can be placed in this camp, where the codes or text are the focus of literary analysis (Chatman, 1978; Rosenblatt, 1991). Meaning is derived from the author, the language, and/or the culture. Good comprehension occurs when the deciphered message equally matches the text's intended message. Such a view of reading is often connected to a more skills-based, incremental approach to instruction, highlighting a more synthetic approach for learners (pieces are presented and learners must synthesize for context). In this model instruction involves a more teacher-directed approach, guiding students to appropriate and accurate answers to instructional questions.

A top-down model of reading bases meaning in the mind of the reader. In this model the reader's experiences and knowledge (schemata) form the basis for making meaning of the text (Bleich, 1975; Goodman, 1985). It is highly improbable that a reader's deciphered message from text would ever match the author's exactly. In fact, each reader brings to the reading experience a unique view of the world with a reader-specific purpose for reading which creates a meaning from the text that is similar to, perhaps parallel with, the author's message. Good comprehension occurs when the deciphered message is determined to be meaningful to the reader. Teachers in this model provide a facilitative approach to reading, guiding students to make sense of the text and providing opportunities for them to create meaning from the text.

A more pragmatic view of reading is found in an interactive model whereby the reader's experiences and knowledge interact with the author's meaning (Iser, 1978; Rumelhart, 1985). Such a dynamic creates a negotiated understanding from the text that parallels the author's original message. Prior knowledge and experiences of the reader are highlighted by the teacher as an integral part of making meaning from the text. Good comprehension relies on the interaction of both the reader and the text, where meaning is derived from a reader's negotiated understanding of the author's intended message. Teachers in this model play a facilitative role, helping learners use their own experiences and knowledge in interpreting the author's message.

With these conceptual frameworks for understanding teachers' approaches toward multicultural education and language arts instruction in mind, we describe how Arnold Larson and Fred Arroyo practiced multicultural education. To further contextualize these teachers' approaches we first provide a biographical sketch that highlights some of their personal experiences related to issues of multiculturalism. We characterized Arnold's practice as a bottom-up orientation toward reading and the use of an additive approach to the integration of multicultural content. We characterized Fred's practice as an interactive orientation toward reading and the use of a social action approach to the integration of multicultural content.

"Is just one more thing on the list of agendas": Arnold Larson

Biographical Sketch

Arnold, a forty-nine-year-old white male born and raised in New Jersey, had been teaching at this high school for eighteen years. Arnold's first meaningful cross-cultural experience occurred during his junior year in high school when his family lived in England for a year while his father was on a Fullbright scholarship. Later in college he socialized with Jewish classmates and learned about their traditions and beliefs. At that time he considered the idea of converting to Judaism. In college he also participated in an exchange program between his all-white college in Pennsylvania and an all-black college in Virginia. Of that experience he said: "Going down to Hampton Institute was fun, it was interesting. I wouldn't say it was a life changing kind of thing. I wasn't prejudice before I went and I wasn't after I went."

His first teaching job in a town on the U.S.A.–Canadian border gave him an opportunity to witness the French-Anglo tensions across the border in neighboring Ontario. At the time of the interviews, through his church, Arnold was involved in a cross-cultural exchange with an African-American church in Oklahoma. When it came to addressing some of the ethnic tensions found in his own town, Arnold took the role of a concerned spectator:

> In Middleton the ethnic population has changed. It has always had a significant ethnic population, Mexican-American, Latino and is increasing. The white community in town doesn't know what to do, doesn't know how to handle that. . . . I don't think we do a good job of making as many opportunities available to Latino children.

When asked about his formal training in multicultural education, he reported attending a few inservices but not having been involved in any serious work in this area. He vividly recalled his anger when he was first exposed to substantive African-American literature. One of the courses he took for his master's in English composition was a two-semester course in Afro-American literature: "I remember being just furious at one time that the works that we were reading I had never read before. They had never been shown to me before." When asked why he had not been exposed to that literature earlier, he said: "I just think it is just Mr. Benign Neglect. Nothing malicious, no reason to include literature that some people had found inferior, or not worthy of inclusion. It is always hard getting into the canon."

Beliefs about Multiculturalism

A descendent of Finnish and Swedish immigrants, Arnold greatly regretted that his parents' heritage had been prey to the melting pot ideology:

> When my parents were growing up the metaphor was the melting pot. Now we are getting into the metaphor

> of diversity, the salad bowl. I think it is a better meta-
> phor. The sameness is pretty boring; that Latino culture
> has a lot to offer. If we make it a melting pot then whose
> dignity or worth do we strip away in order to become
> like some else? If we take the melting pot of the domi-
> nant white society, then take every other culture that
> comes in to it and say you have to come to the white
> dominant society, then everyone who comes loses.
> And I am not sure the white society gains.

His embracement of cultural pluralism was also evident in his description of the benefits of an education that was multicultural. He felt that multicultural competency was an essential skill for living and working in a diverse society. He argued that students who had not developed these competencies would be "less able to relate to people. I think in a community in which you have any kind of background, with people of different backgrounds, in any line of work it is more helpful if you have some awareness of, if not their culture, other cultures so you are aware of cultural difference."

Arnold thought that his job as an educator was to create oppor-tunities for young people. Multicultural education helped him do his job as an educator: "[It] can affirm a person, that you have value and worth of yourself. That might be very hard to see in a society in which you are a minority or in which you face prejudice every day, some overt, sometimes hidden." Consequently, the goal of multicultural education was to create a more humanistic educational system: "I think multicultural is in the same track that, mmmm, trying to open up schools to distinct racial minor-ities was in 50s, 60s, 70s. It is a more humanistic way, a more open way of seeing people as human being. A more liberal, I suppose."

Integrating Multicultural Content

Arnold understood that there was a tension between the way he practiced multicultural education and the way he thought it should be practiced. As described below, he followed Banks' addi-tive approach while recognizing its shortcomings and the need for a different praxis. This tension appeared to emerge from the chal-lenges he thought teachers encountered when trying to integrate multicultural content. The difficulties Arnold articulated stemmed from three interrelated sources: structural constraints, his ap-

proach to language arts instruction, and the need to fulfill competing educational objectives.

Structural constraints. First, Arnold noted some structural constraints placed on teachers by Iowa's Department of Education.
The state had multiple agendas competing for the same resources
and time:

> Don't have an awful amount of time . . . . I am not
> begging the questions. It is just, you know, we have this
> mandate, we also have 200, 28011 that we are trying to
> respond to, I think that is a mandate for districtwide
> assessment reporting. We have the AIDS awareness,
> you know the list goes on, we are now going into "tech
> prep," we have an inservice next week. So there isn't
> time to spend on any one issue, in any substantive
> way, it is all a band-aid.

This lack of time was seen as critical because he recognized
that taking the mandate seriously required a substantive change
in the curriculum. To accomplish this, he said, the faculty needed
to address some problematic questions:

> I think that if you really wanted to do a multicultural
> approach you need to do a rewriting from the ground
> up. We need to have some time to get together, to talk
> about what we think is important. Why, why do we
> want to do this beyond it being a trend? You know, are
> there reasons to be taking multicultural approaches in
> our particular community? Would we want to look at
> our cultures that are part of our community and what
> they are?

Approaches to literature instruction. Arnold's understanding of literature instruction presented a second challenge for the integration of multicultural content. The conduit between his beliefs
about multiculturalism and his practice was his understanding of
the teaching of literature. Arnold's approach to literature instruction was based on the belief that there is meaning in the text to be
retrieved by the reader, and instruction, therefore, must be geared
toward helping students retrieve this meaning. His bottom-up approach was clearly illustrated in the way he explained the multicultural lesson plan he prepared for us to see.

The lesson he videotaped was the first of a series of class periods in his twelfth-grade English class devoted to the poem "Middle Passage" by the African-American poet Robert Hayden (1968). All students in the class were white, and two of them were foreign exchange students from Europe. Arnold indicated that he selected this poem as an example of multicultural infusion because it was a poem written by an African-American and it provided a different point of view about "American black history."

Arnold started instruction by asking students to skim over the poem. Later he directed a question-answer activity with his class in which students were asked to express what they knew about slave trading and its historical context. To validate the students' contributions, he said, he wrote on the chalkboard all the ideas expressed by them. He stated that his efforts were geared toward helping students become aware of the times because "how can you understand or get into something when you have no idea of the background . . . what some of the history of it is?" Additionally, by prompting students to make explicit their views, he wanted to see "if there are any prejudices that are going to come up when they think about slavery." He was also interested in having students reflect on how their own ethnicity colored their views and interest in this poem about slavery.

His emphasis on understanding the historical context created a tension between his beliefs and his practice. Numerous times students would make comments dealing with contemporary issues of racism and prejudice. When that happened, Arnold would respond by shifting the conversation back to the past: "Dealing with racism and prejudice today got us away from the poem. That's the whole issue. Does it get you away from the poem? To some extent it does."

It was important to Arnold that his students clearly understood the correct message provided in the text. His role as the teacher was to monitor and confirm students' understandings of the passage and to provide instructional direction for those who had missed this correct message. He also wanted to point out to students how little they knew about the facts surrounding slavery, how narrow their focus was. This in turn would help them see the new facts that the poem was going to bring out. For example, he wanted them to see that slavery was not a southern problem. All this work was necessary so students could hear the poem's message: "What is this poem telling us? Because this poem is going to tell us a lot of things we do not want to hear but I want it to come from the poem." When we asked Arnold what the poem was going to tell students, he said: "The poem is really going to use slavery in passages of metaphors for race and relations in these countries. . . . The poem is going to tie up that these people are basic immortal humans, a wish that is not black, not green, not yellow. It's a wish for freedom."

Consistent with his belief in the need to accurately represent the text's meaning, both in students' responses and in teacher's instruction, Arnold's selection of literature was limited to pieces that were situated in a historical time and/or reflected a culture that he was knowledgeable of:

> It is very difficult to bring in world literature. You know we have books that have some Japanese, some Chinese. We are just playing "drips and drabs." That is ridiculous. How can we understand a Japanese poem which is already a translation from Japanese to English and have no cultural base to even begin to understand what is going on in that poem? Can we retrieve it? That is impossible.

At another point he added: "See, it is very hard if I wanted to include, I do very limited Native American literature. It's very hard as a white to have much of an understanding of Native Americans. Native American religion, Native American culture. So it is very difficult."

The following tension emerged between his beliefs and his practice. On the one hand Arnold thought it was important that students made explicit their views about the concept addressed in the poem, slavery, since their views were going to color their understandings. On the other hand, he also wanted students to listen to what the poem was saying to them (the truth in the text), not what they thought the poem was saying to them (students' own construction of meaning). A tension emerged when he asked students to hear the "author's voices" without having had the opportunity to develop the "content background nor the attitudinal sophistication to respond to them [those voices] appropriately" (Banks, 1989, p. 196). This unresolved tension is one of the primary reasons why we categorized Arnold's practices as additive and not transformative. In principle he was interested in enabling students to see issues from the perspective of the ethnic group depicted, which is a characteristic of the transformative approach.

In practice, however, he failed to provide students with the appropriate tools. As described below, the relationship he saw between multicultural education and language arts goals as well as his beliefs about the possibilities of seeing things through someone else's eyes can account for the lack of content development.

Competing educational objectives. The third source of constraint that Arnold faced was in the struggle to address many different and often competing educational objectives. When he tried to integrate multicultural content into his courses, he saw a crisis in American education that went far beyond multiculturalism. As Arnold noted, his concern and commitment toward multicultural education were secondary:

> The biggest problem I have is trying to get kids ready for college . . . students from the dominant society have no sense of cultural heritage or background which is a significant loss. Lots of stuff coming out in the last couple of years on loss of cultural cohesiveness which is due to a loss of understanding our roots and our backgrounds, even western civilization. We are suffering from a tremendous lack that way, it is very, very hard to see any time to bring in more. You know, very, very hard.

Arnold made a clear distinction between multicultural education and literature instruction. He explained that he asked students to read a passage several times so they could learn to identify the structure of the text and the seven to ten personas of the poem. Doing this was like putting a puzzle together, looking for clues in the text: "That is what they are going to have to do next year [in college]. You can't go in and say you don't know. This is now into the teaching of the course rather than the multicultural . . . we are not emphasizing the multicultural nature."

The Mandate's Impact on his Teaching

According to Arnold, the mandate to infuse multicultural education had influenced his practice. The mandate had made him rethink his selection of literature and include new readings: "I am probably working harder at bringing nonsexist stuff. So much literature . . . is not all written by male but very frequently has . . . it reflects the culture of its time, western culture reflects male values for a long time. I try to make sure that I am bringing in plays or bringing in poems, in works that show strong women characters." When he was asked if this emphasis was related to the mandate, he responded: "See, that is also where you can bitch and moan at the state all you want to but if you do not get some stimulus from some place, things aren't going to happen either."

From Arnold's perspective, how teachers interpreted and integrated the mandate into practice could be traced to teachers' individual commitments and beliefs: "A liberal point of view rather than a conservative one if you want to put it in political terms. A real sense that inclusion, by its nature, is stronger than exclusion."

Overview of Arnold's Approach

Arnold's approach to reading instruction reflected primarily a bottom-up orientation toward the construction of meaning. At some level he thought that the information presented in the poem would speak for itself, or, as he put it, "the poem is going to tell us things." As Banks (1989) notes teachers who use an additive approach, such as Arnold, do not provide the explicit instruction that would allow students to understand issues and concepts from the perspectives of the group being depicted in the text. This leaves students to interpret the poem from mainstream and Eurocentric perspectives; thus many times what students "read" ends up reinforcing stereotypes and prejudices they have brought to the text. Arnold seemed to recognize this when he was attempting to gauge through his questioning of students if any prejudice was going to come up. He did not, however, spend much instructional time giving to students information that would help them reconstruct their understandings of slavery; he hoped the poem would do that.

"I want them to see how a problem can be solved": Fred Arroyo

Biographical Sketch

Fred Arroyo, a forty-four-year-old male Puerto-Rican from New York, had been teaching at this school for six years. He grew up in the tip of Spanish Harlem at a time when Spanish-speaking children were punished for bringing their language into the school grounds. As a result of this, he went from being a bilingual child to being an English-only adult. Needless to add, he felt a great sense of loss over this.

His professional life was cast early by his stepfather and school counselor. Fred wanted to be an actor, but his stepfather did not allow him to attend New York City's Performing Arts High School because "he thought if I went I would become a homosexual." His school counselor reinforced his parents when he suggested that Fred become an "x-ray technician because that was a good job for a Puerto-Rican." As it will become evident later, this desire to become an actor permeated his pedagogy for language arts instruction.

In the sixties Fred was actively involved in the civil rights movement. Through a political organization he had participated in the "rewriting of history [books] . . . to make it more meaningful." After working as a lab technician for a few years, in 1968 he joined VISTA (Volunteers In Service to America) and worked on Indian reservations in South Dakota. Although he had a one-year assignment, he stayed for three years helping both with economic development projects and cultural work. He helped the people rewrite the history books used in the reservation schools. From there he went to work at another Indian reservation in Minnesota: "I wouldn't trade those years for anything—that was an experience. I use that experience in my classroom too when we do a unit on *When the Legends Die* (Borland, 1963) and I do an Indian unit with the class."

When asked about his formal training in multicultural education, he reported attending a couple of inservices offered by the district. By and large, he thought that "any multicultural training, formal training I've gotten is the reading, my past experience, what I feel, what's going on."

Beliefs about Multiculturalism

When Fred was asked about his philosophy regarding multiculturalism, he indicated that in principle he agreed with the melting pot theory although "in the practice I don't always see it." He had not heard the tossed salad metaphor. After we discussed it, he became quite convinced that it was a better metaphor for the society he envisioned: "I like the mixing, so I'd probably go with the salad bowl. I think the melting pot idea is just an idea, it's ideal but when it comes down to it . . . growing up in that atmosphere seeing that it was almost one-sided and almost forced assimilation. And then working with the Indians I definitely saw that, the forced assimilation."

Fred believed multicultural education was needed because the world had become a global village. He stated, "We are not America, the isolated country." Not receiving a multicultural education, he argued, would limit a person, would disable the person in the global sphere. In the United States, he noted, people always expect others to adapt to them: "They visit a foreign country and then expect people in that foreign country to speak in English. Yet we get people from other countries here and they know English."

He understood that one goal of multicultural education was to create "awareness, pride, insight . . . to realize that we are all in this planet but we all don't have to be the same." The purpose of creating greater insight was to "give people an opportunity . . . stop the fighting, the jealousy."

Multicultural education should help students become sensitized to the plight of the disenfranchised and those who were victims of prejudice. He firmly believed that teachers should go beyond creating awareness of a problem and engage students in problem solving. He wanted them to "see how a problem could be solved . . . because they are part of the world! There are problems, these are young kids, this is the next generation. Let's hope that they do not screw up the way we screwed up."

Fred thought that multicultural education should address multiple forms of social diversity that were linked by the common thread of being "not in the norm." For example, he argued that issues of ethnicity, handicapism, and homophobia were all linked by "the ignorance, the disenfranchised, the stereotyping." He thought that the term *multicultural* should target the "humanity of people."

Integrating Multicultural Content

In contrast to Arnold, for whom the road from theory to practice was fraught with barriers, Fred's road was a wide-open passage. There was a congruency between his theoretical beliefs about multicultural education and his classroom practices. What largely made this congruency possible was his orientation toward reading and language arts instruction. By following an experiential approach, Fred believed any piece of literature could be used as a vehicle to foster sensitivity, awareness, and problem solving. He also thought that the goals of multicultural education were an integral part of the goals of schooling in general and multicultural education in particular. As described below, his interactive approach to reading instruction and his conceptualization of educational goals translated into practices that reflected Banks' (1989) social action approach.

Teaching as an experience. The lesson Fred videotaped was a class period devoted to the play *The Miracle Worker,* the story of Helen Keller (Gibson, 1960). As he discussed his approach to this lesson, he stated: "You can teach it as drama, just plain drama . . . [or] you can teach it as an experience. And I want the students to experience what it is to be handicapped." When asked to elaborate on what he meant about teaching as an experience, he said:

> So they can feel empathic, so they can feel involved with the character. Again, they can become aware of a minority situation. In this case it is handicapped. But like every other thing, people do not ask to be a minority. People are labeled a minority, and they are put in that situation of becoming that label. So I wanted students to become aware that this is a minority group that is even in Middleton, and we ignore it.

Students in his ninth-grade English class had read *The Miracle Worker* before the class period Fred videotaped. He stated that he selected this play for multicultural education because handicap is a form of minority status and "handicapped is one of the most ignored groups in the country." In society and in the school, handicapped people were invisible. "You know they are there, but you do not see them."

He started his lesson by lecturing to students about the differences between the terms *disability* and *handicap.* He then focused on the scene in which the family suggests putting Helen in an asylum and Ann describes to the family what it is like to be in an asylum. He asked students to comment on what Helen's family wanted to do with her because "this is where we get into prejudicism." The conversation then drifted to students' feelings about Helen and what "we do with handicapped people, we shove them aside." At this point students were assigned to take different roles and read their part aloud, so they could "get more empathy . . .

plays should be read aloud to get the experience . . . I guess that is the dramatist in me. If this class was not as full, I would have them reenact the scene."

After students read the scene, Fred gave a lecture on how prejudicism started. He tracked it from primitive tribes, to euthanasia among the Greeks and the Romans, to the creation of "clowns" in the Middle Ages, and concluded it by "bringing it down to our system now." He used as an example the situation that would be faced by a student in a wheelchair attending that school in case a fire broke out. The purpose behind the kind of questioning Fred illustrated below was to "sensitize so they can go back to the school board and say 'Do something about this!'" "Because the school is not built for handicapped. There's only one elevator, there is no ramp, even the doors are terrible. . . . And I ask the kids that, 'Well what do you do if you have a student [in a wheelchair] up there?'"

As we were watching the tape with Fred, suddenly the television screen went black. Fred reported that at this point in the lesson he had turned the classroom lights off and had asked students to look at the ceiling, to help them experience "how a blind person sees." Afterwards he told students about a previous time when he had done this activity with a class that had a deaf student. He failed to warn the student that he was going to turn the lights off and the student got very scared. As he was relating that story to the students, he said, "As a teacher I learn from you guys." His reason for telling this story to the students was to present himself to students as "a human, as someone who made mistakes."

At an earlier meeting he had asked students to learn to use sign language. When one student had asked why they needed to do that since they were not Helen Keller, Fred said to the student: "Helen Keller did not ask to be blind or deaf either and she had to learn and I want you to learn how to do it. That's a little bit insensitive. People do not ask to be put in those situations." The class period ended with students practicing sign language with each other.

Selecting literature. Fred's experiential approach enabled him to use any literature piece to address multicultural content. He thought that "culture could be defined as what people practice, what's traditional, or what's folklore." From this standpoint, Fred found multicultural education lessons in many of the texts he used: "You can pick out things that are multicultural in almost any piece of literature that you go through. And you couldn't be any more multicultural than Shakespeare, even to the point of prejudices." He stated that when teaching *The Merchant of Venice* he could bring up the issue of anti-Semitism, and with *Othello* he could address the issue of mixed marriages.

Seizing the moment. Probably the most striking quality of Fred's practice was his ability to seize the moment and engage in multicultural education as the "need arises." His experiential approach gave students the authority to trigger specific contexts for instructional content. For instance, he described an incident in which an Anglo student in his speech class had complained about a Spanish-speaking Latino student who was getting extra help from a teacher's aide. After he listened to the complaint, he asked the Latino student to give a speech in Spanish to the class and asked the Anglo student to describe what she had learned from the speech. Next he asked the Latino student to give the speech again, but this time a bilingual student sat next to the Anglo student and offered simultaneous translation. This provided an experiential-based instructional moment for a student to better understand the context of learning for non-English-speaking students.

Fred's ability to seize the moment went beyond classroom incidents, as he brought into the classroom events that happened in the local community. Especially in his speech class he felt it was important that students thought about current issues. "I feel they should be aware . . . because they are the ones who are going to make the decisions." For instance, a few months before we interviewed him a fight had broken out between some African-American and some Mexican-American youth at the YMCA in town. The YMCA authorities at hand decided to ask all of the African-American and Mexican-American patrons to leave the premises, even those who were in a different part of the building and were not involved in the incident. The white patrons were not asked to leave. Fred said: "I wasn't there but, boy, if I was there I would have protested like crazy. And we talked about that in class." The class discussion was geared toward understanding what happened and to help students uncover ways in which the situation reflected prejudices. Additionally, he asked students to think, "Ok, next time this happens what can we do about it? . . . Let's work on solving that problem."

The Mandate's Impact on Fred's Teaching

Fred had come to Iowa after working as a teacher in Minnesota where multicultural education policy had already been implemented. He thought that the mandate had provided him with opportunities to expand his teaching and his knowledge: "It's made me more sensitive . . . not that I didn't have it before. . . . It also gives me a lot of latitude. Multicultural helps me as a teacher to expand my knowledge. Not only that, but to expand my students' knowledge. Whatever I have available or at hand I can use." To meet his goal of expanding his students' knowledge, he would use "whatever comes up . . . and I'll go for it. If it's my background . . . if it's something I have read someplace . . . some person I've met where I've learned something from that person . . . what I've learned from my class, from students, from their backgrounds."

Overview of Fred's Approach

We interpreted the practices Fred showed to us in his videotape, as well as the other activities he related to us, as evidence of an interactive approach to reading instruction. As suggested by Rumelhart (1985), teachers using an interactive approach provide instructional activities that will highlight prior knowledge and experiences that can help make the text meaningful to the reader. Because of the negative attitudes that society at large has toward people with disabilities, Fred thought that most of the students would read the text and construct meaning through prejudicial schemata. His classroom instruction, therefore, was geared toward restructuring the initial understandings students had about people with disabilities. He used cognitive approaches such as discussing the history of prejudice as well as experiential activities such as turning the lights off.

Teaching a unit from a social action approach involves the following components: Pose a question, collect data, value inquiry, and social action (Banks, 1989). These components were present in Fred's lesson: (a) he asked students to think about the way in which handicapped people were treated in society at large as well as in the school, (b) he provided to students information regarding the conceptual distinction between handicap and disability and the historical treatment of people with handicaps,

(c) he asked students to do role-playing to examine their own feelings about Helen's condition, and (d) he challenged students to take action. Fred, however, did not go as far as suggested by Banks (1989) since part of the course requirements did not involve actually going to the school board with a request to make the school more accessible to people with disabilities. His explicit focus of decision-making and action focused more on changing individual student's behaviors and not necessarily in changing wider social practices that created barriers for people with disabilities.

TEACHERS' COGNITIONS FOR MULTICULTURAL EDUCATION: AN INFORMATION-PROCESSING ANALYSIS

For many inservice teachers, responding to educational policies mandating the curricular infusion of multicultural content involves learning new practices. The information-processing theory of learning postulates that the acquisition of new knowledge is always mediated by prior knowledge that has been stored in memory in the form of a schema (Anderson, 1984; Bartlett, 1932). This schema aids the learning process by performing several functions. For instance, the schema facilitates the assimilation of new information by providing a framework to construct a meaning that is plausible and consistent with what the learner already knows. In the process of assimilating new information the learner typically alters the new information to make it consistent with the expectations built into the existing schema. Similarly, through the process of inferential reasoning, schemata enable the learner to construct the details necessary to fill knowledge gaps implicit in the new information. Over time, the acquisition of new information helps people reconstruct existing schemata.

The effects of schemata in processing new information suggest a framework for examining teachers' cognitions for multicultural education. More specifically, it suggests that teachers who are asked to incorporate multicultural teaching practices into their instructional repertoire will *adapt* these practices to make them fit with their existing pedagogical understandings. This process of adaptation, as suggested by Piagetian theory, involves the processes of assimilation and accommodation (Good & Brophy, 1990). Below, we use these processes to explain the differences we found between Fred's and Arnold's approaches for infusing multicultural education in the English language arts.

Both of these teachers shared a commitment to multicultural education and reported having received little professional training on multicultural education. They also shared the understanding that infusing multicultural education in the English language arts should make audible the voices of those who have been left out by the prevailing canon. Fred's existing schemata for teaching and learning in the language arts translated into making these voices audible through Banks' (1989) social action approach. For Arnold, on the other hand, the pedagogical implications of changing the canon through a social action approach involved adaptational demands that could not be met within his existing instructional repertoire. His instructional schema could more easily assimilate Banks' (1989) additive approach to infusing multicultural content. What is noteworthy is that, although these teachers had never heard or read Banks' typology, their approaches closely resembled Banks' characterizations. It is also important to note that neither one fully embodied the approach as described by Banks (1989) because their practices were permeable to elements of the other approaches. Below we describe the relationships we saw between teachers' understandings about language arts instruction and their approaches to multicultural education.

Fred, who saw language arts as an ongoing, lifelong pursuit of experiences through the arts, approached multicultural education as an inclusive program in which all students informed one another about their differences and their similarities. Fred's goals for language arts were realized through multicultural education, and his goals for multicultural education were realized through language arts. He understood the goals to be an ongoing representation of the purpose of schooling and teaching: to bring students' understandings and past experiences to address problems and to create new and better understanding of their own realities and the world around them.

Fred's experiential approach to teaching made it easy for him to focus on helping majority students experience a curriculum that reflected the perspectives of the disabled, various races, gender, and cultural groups. His definition of "majority" in this case involved the "able" majority. In his teaching, he was very intentional about disrupting the development of a false sense of group superiority, which leads to prejudiced and discriminatory behaviors. Fred saw his role as more of a facilitator of learning, providing contexts and situations for students to think about and relate to in their own language and through their own experiences.

From this approach, Fred was less able to provide concrete absolute information to students, but was more able to allow students to struggle through and solve their own understandings of such issues as equity, prejudice, and the creation and shaping of ideas and beliefs. For Fred, engaging in a social action approach to multicultural education, therefore, did not require dramatically changing what he was doing before the MCNS mandate came along.

In contrast to Fred, Arnold could make a clear distinction between his goals for multicultural education and his goals for language arts instruction. His language arts goals included learning about the structure of texts, identifying the voices in poems, and so on, with an underlying focus of giving students the skills to succeed in college. Multicultural goals involved expanding one's knowledge of the perspectives and experiences of various ethnic groups. Arnold would incorporate multicultural material and discussion in his language arts instruction as long as it did not interfere with his language arts instructional goals. He saw multicultural education as something to add if applicable to his main task of preparing students for college.

Arnold understood that multicultural education required him to include literature written by female and ethnic minority authors. The process of including new voices, in turn, required him to enlarge and expand his own knowledge base for teaching. Arnold saw his role as a teacher as one who dispenses information and provides correct views and understandings of literature (in the case of language arts) and correct views and understandings of others (in the case of multicultural education). To accomplish this he and his students needed to become knowledgeable about the experiences, histories, and contributions of the various ethnic groups to be represented in the curriculum. The beliefs in which he embedded his practice, however, greatly limited what literature he could actually teach in his classes.

Arnold believed that, in order to correctly interpret Hayden's poem, students needed to have awareness of the cultural and historical background of slavery. In contrast to Fred, Arnold asked students to describe what they knew, without giving them additional information to reconstruct their own schemata. This can be traced to his understandings about schooling and language arts instruction. First, Arnold's belief that one can never really understand "cultural others" or see things from their perspective probably made the task less important in his mind. Second, he believed that multiculturalism was secondary to his job of getting kids ready for college; therefore, spending too much time developing the background would detract from this task. He had students read the poem as a way of exposing them to good literature written by an African-American. His intention was not to help students understand the nature of contemporary U.S. society. And third, Arnold believed that his role as the teacher was to monitor and confirm students' understandings of the passage and provide instructional direction for those who had missed the "correct" message. Taken together, these beliefs, in a sense, forced Arnold to stay within the boundaries of the additive approach.

The way in which each teacher presented his lesson and discussed his teaching was consistent across language arts and multicultural education, forming two broad categories related to the context and design of instruction. Arnold taught the lessons incrementally, teaching specific skills or pieces that students then brought together in studying the whole unit. The context of the lesson to the *whole* was provided in summary, framed within the closure of a unit. Fred taught the lesson more holistically, providing a context a priori, relating the lesson to the *whole* as an ongoing process, and continuing to update and validate contexts as they developed.

Those teachers, like Arnold, who see the world of instruction as the combination of incremental pieces see multicultural education as the accumulation of parts to form a limited sum (meaning that only so many pieces can be brought together to create a whole). Multicultural education is seen as an addition to the already burdensome amount of teaching being asked of them. For these teachers, time and materials become the greatest factors in determining how effective they can be in classroom instruction. Those teachers, like Fred, who see instruction as a collective whole view multicultural education as part of good language arts instruction and vice versa. For these teachers, the greatest factor in determining effective instruction is their ability to get students problem-solving and thinking about the world around them, using each lesson as the vehicle for learning and the students' lives as the context.

IMPLICATIONS FOR STAFF DEVELOPMENT FOR MULTICULTURAL EDUCATION

The evidence collected from these case studies suggests that there is a relationship between teachers' beliefs about instruction in the content area and their choices for multicultural education. From our analysis of these two case studies we have concluded that these two teachers' approaches to multicultural education differed, to a large extent, because they were embedded in different orientations toward instruction in the content area. As noted by Yin (1989), the findings from case studies are not generalizable to populations, but they are to theoretical propositions. The interpretation we have proposed for the differences observed between these teachers is in agreement with schema theory and information-processing models of learning. Simlilarly, the interpretation offered is consistent with previous studies that have implied that teachers adapt educational practices suggested by new policies in order to make them correspond with their prior beliefs (Darling-Hammond, 1990). This interpretation is also in agreement with previous research on effective inservice training. For instance, in the context of math education, Good and Grouws (1979) found that teachers who showed the highest implementation of the new practices following training were those who found the new practices congruent with their values and teaching styles. Stallings, Needles, and Strayrook (1979) conducted an inservice with secondary remedial reading teachers. These researchers concluded that teachers changed their prior practices and incorporated the new practices when they were able to adapt these to their own settings. Further research needs to be conducted to see if the relationship of instructional practice and belief proposed here occurs among other teachers, both in the context of language arts instruction and in other content areas.

The findings of this study and the previous studies cited raise questions about the development of effective strategies for multicultural teacher education. Information-processing theories of learning suggest that all instruction must build upon a learner's prior knowledge, which is organized into a semantic web or schemata. Current strategies for multicultural teacher education follow this advice (Zeichner, 1993). As reflected in the research literature, instructional emphasis has been placed on strategies that elaborate upon teachers' schemata about diversity, their views of culturally different learners such as their learning styles, and so on. What this study suggests is that if, indeed, teachers' practices for multicultural education are embedded in their broader beliefs about learning and instruction in a content area, then staff development must also involve strategies that elaborate upon these schemata. These schemata present important individual differences to be considered when inservicing teachers to engage in the types of curricular transformations advocated by Banks (1989) and many other proponents of multicultural approaches to schooling (e.g., Gay, 1989; Sleeter & Grant, 1993).

For some teachers, like Fred, adopting practices recommended by transformative approaches to multicultural education involves primarily a process of assimilation and to a lesser extent accommodation. For others, like Arnold, however, adopting these practices involves primarily a process of accommodation and to a lesser extent assimilation. In other words, when working with teachers like Arnold, strategies for multicultural teacher education need to be geared toward developing new understandings of learning and teaching in the content area. Staff development practices for promoting conceptual changes among teachers can be derived from the research literature on factors affecting meaningful learning (Good & Brophy, 1990). A suggested staff development program for language arts teachers would involve a course infusing multicultural education and language arts methods. Course content and pedagogy that explicitly aimed at restructuring teachers' understandings about instruction in the language arts to accommodate a transformative approach to multicultural education should involve the following components:

1. Teachers are presented with various conceptual frameworks for literature instruction.
2. Teachers are presented with various conceptual frameworks for multicultural education.
3. To process the information conveyed by these frameworks, teachers can be asked to do the following:
   - Locate their current and ideal practice on these conceptualizations
   - Examine the assumptions and implications implicit in each conceptualization
   - Examine the cause-effect relationships among the ideas within a conceptualization
   - Examine implications for multicultural education within each conceptualization of reading instruction
   - Examine implications for reading instruction within each conceptualization of multicultural education

- Become aware of possible conflicts and contradictions between their beliefs about content area instruction and their beliefs about multicultural education
4. Finally, teachers need to integrate concepts into a schema for infusing a transformation and social action approach to their language arts instruction.

Additional content should involve what has become part of the standard curriculum for multicultural teacher education. As documented by Zeichner (1993), course content is most effective when it (a) addresses the dynamics of prejudice and racism both at the individual and institutional level; (b) provides ethnically based characterizations of students' learning styles and corresponding teaching styles; (c) provides descriptions of the histories, cultural patterns, and perspectives of various status groups; (d) helps teachers deconstruct and reconstruct their views about the school achievement of culturally diverse learners; (e) provides activities that promote intergroup contacts; and (f) provides exposure to multicultural resources. Effective inservice for multicultural education, of course, is not only a matter of adequate content; attention must be paid to pedagogy. As noted by Mohlman, Coladarci, and Gage (1982), staff development will be more effective in promoting the adoption of new practices when it involves a highly interactive, supportive atmosphere in which philosophical objections and difficulties can be worked out during the training sessions.

THINKING ABOUT HOW TO CHANGE THINKING

TEACHING CONCERNS REVISITED
The Multicultural Dimension

Patricia L. Marshall

The literature related to teacher classroom behaviors is replete with discussions of how teacher actions toward students are directly influenced by the cultural background of the students. In particular, various writers have described how cultural elements such as race (Kozol, 1992), class (Friedman, 1976, cited in Dusek & Joseph, 1985; Rist, 1970; Weinstein & Middlestadt, 1979, cited in Dusek & Joseph, 1985), and gender (Brophy & Good, 1974, cited in Irvine, 1990; Brophy & Evertson, 1981, cited in Irvine, 1990; Irvine, 1986, cited in Irvine, 1990) influence how teachers interact with students. Although much is known about teacher-student classroom interactions, less research has been generated that specifically describes the nature of the thinking that undergirds why teachers interact with particular students as they do (see the introduction to this volume).

The nature of teacher thinking about what occurs in classrooms has potential to reveal much about teacher perceptions about schooling. The concept of teacher thinking has been described by Clark and Peterson (1985) as a combination of teacher planning, interactive thoughts, and theories and beliefs. For this discussion, *teacher thinking* refers to those professional concerns teachers express about aspects of the teaching role.

There is a considerable body of literature that reveals that concerns teachers hold about their work may influence how they approach aspects of their work. Included in this literature are explorations of the concerns of second-career beginning teachers (Boccia, 1989), teacher concerns about changes and the introduction of technology in schools (Cicchelli & Baecher, 1987), stages of teacher concerns (Fuller, 1969; Fuller & Bown, 1975), concerns of preservice science teachers (Gunstone, Slattery, Baird, & Northfield, 1993), concerns about innovations in schools (Hall & Loucks, 1978), concern stages of physical education teachers (McBride, 1985), and early field experiences and preservice teachers' concerns (Tanner, 1982). Conspicuously absent from this literature is attention to the reality of cultural diversity in schools and the impact student diversity may have on teacher thinking, or concerns as it were, about their work in schools.

This chapter is an examination of the concept of teacher concerns as it relates to the peculiarities inherent in working with culturally diverse student populations. The concept *multicultural teaching concerns* will be explored and used as a conceptual framework from which to interpret teacher thinking about multicultural education and teachers' work in culturally diverse school settings.

A RECENT HISTORICAL PERSPECTIVE OF TEACHING CONCERNS

The work of Frances Fuller spawned a plethora of literature and research related to the professional teaching concerns of classroom practitioners. Her study, *Concerns of Teachers: A Developmental Conceptualization* (Fuller, 1969), focuses attention on the idea that teacher concerns about work in classrooms form consistent patterns that increase in complexity as teachers develop from novices to mature professionals. The developmental foundation of Fuller's work was based on psychological stage theory.

Fundamental to stage theory is the belief that progression from the relatively simple to the more complex modes of human functioning (e.g., cognitive skills, moral reasoning, ego development) occurs in a predictable sequence. Stages cannot be skipped and complete resolution of conflicts in early stages must be resolved before progression to more complex stages can be successful (Sprinthall & Thies-Sprinthall, 1983a). Feiman and Floden (1981) indicate that Fuller's earliest work on the teacher concerns conceptualization "connect[ed] stages of concern with Maslow's hierarchy of needs" (p. 7).

Fuller (1969) identifies three levels of teacher concern: preteaching phase, early teaching phase, and late teaching phase. Subsequent research on teacher concern levels (for examples see

Fuller & Bown, 1975; Fuller & Case, 1972; Fuller & Parsons, 1972; Fuller, Parsons, & Watkins, 1974; Parsons & Fuller, 1974) resulted in development of the *Teacher Concerns Statement.* The three concern levels were revised and eventually described as *survival (self), teaching (task),* and *pupil (impact).* Fuller and Bown (1975) differentiate among these three levels in the following manner:

> Survival concerns . . . are concerns about one's adequacy and survival as a teacher, about class control, about being liked by pupils, about supervisors' opinions, about being observed, evaluated, praised, and failed.

> Teaching concerns . . . are about having to work with too many students or having too many noninstructional duties. . . . These frustrations seem to be evoked by the teaching situation.

> Pupil concerns . . . are . . . about recognizing the social and emotional needs of pupils, about the inappropriateness of some curriculum material for certain students, about being fair to pupils, about tailoring content to individual students, and so on. (pp. 37–38)

Data from Fuller's 1969 work as well as subsequent teacher concern research never corroborated a definitive claim of stage progression among the levels of concern. Fuller and Bown (1975) note that "whether these really are 'stages' or only clusters, whether they are distinct or overlapping, and whether teachers teach differently or are differentially effective in different stages, has not been established" (p. 37). Despite questions surrounding the idea of a psychological stage progression among concern levels, the developmental foundation suggested that concern differences were apparent between beginning teachers and experienced teachers. Fuller and Bown (1975) indicate that these differences were reflected in the manner in which teachers direct their professional energies. Feiman and Floden (1980) note that although novice teachers express task and impact-level concerns, their *energies* are largely directed toward resolving survival (self) concerns. Conversely, because of their familiarity with the teaching role, experienced teachers have fewer survival concerns; their professional energies tend to be directed toward attending to teaching tasks and meeting the needs of students.

Other researchers have explored the implications of Fuller's (1969) teacher concern developmental conceptualization. For example, Katz (1972) revisits the developmental stage theme in her description of the professional maturation stages of preschool teachers. Closely paralleling Fuller's (1969) earlier efforts, Katz identifies *survival, consolidation, renewal,* and *maturity* as specific stages through which preschool teachers must progress as they develop from novice to master teacher. Katz (1972) cites concerns expressed during particular stages of preschool teacher development. Those concerns identified during the survival stage correspond to concerns about self, and concerns during the consolidation and early renewal stages reflect a combination of teaching task and student concerns. Late renewal stage and maturity stage preschool teachers express concerns about the impact of their teaching.

Kazelskis and Reeves (1987) and Reeves and Kazelskis (1985) explore the nature of teacher concerns utilizing the Teacher Concerns Questionnaire (TCQ) developed by George (1978; cited in Kazelskis & Reeves, 1987) and based on Fuller's 1969 study as well as subsequent teacher concerns research completed at the now defunct Research and Development Center for Teacher Education at the University of Texas, Austin. Referring to the TCQ as "the Fuller-George concern hierarchy model," Kazelskis and Reeves (1987) indicate that teachers at all experiential levels express concerns across the various dimensions. Their research supports the suggestion that the levels of teacher concern may not be as lockstep and predictably ordered as suggested in the original conceptualization. Further, Kazelskis and Reeves (1987) deemphasize the significance of the Fuller-George hierarchy of self, task, and impact concern levels. In their study of the hierarchy of concerns between preservice and inservice teachers, Kazelskis and Reeves (1987) note,

> The preservice teachers did express greater concern for self-evaluation than for task, and there was a higher level of concern for task expressed by the inservice teachers. However, the levels of self and task concerns expressed by the inservice teachers did not differ; and, the levels for impact concerns were higher than either

for self or task concerns with respect to both the preservice and inservice groups.

Kazelskis and Reeves (1987) indicate that the Fuller-George
model lacks empirical data to support the notion of a hierarchy
among teacher concerns. They call for more research into teacher
concerns.

Despite subsequent research that has called into question the
hierarchy of teacher concerns, extant research on this topic has
made an important contribution to teacher education. In this regard, the overall significance of the original developmental conceptualization of teacher concerns (Fuller, 1969) was that it challenged teacher educators to reexamine both the theoretical and
the practical aspects of teacher education. Fuller (1969) observed
that much of what occurred in teaching methods courses may not
have been relevant to the real-life dilemmas facing classroom
practitioners at that time. This observance was provoking in its
day; however, explorations into the relevance of the methods
course continues to be the bane of teacher educators.

Culture and Teacher Concerns

Fuller's 1969 study has attained germinal status within the
teacher concerns research. However, Fuller herself identifies one
study whose publication predated her work by over thirty-five
years. This sole citation broaches the impact of cultural factors
(i.e., student social background) on teacher concerns. Fuller
(1969) notes, "New teachers in England complained in 'extensive
correspondence' about . . social background of schools in which
they taught, . . . and about depressing effect of neighborhood
areas and aggressive attitudes of parents toward teachers" (Phillips, 1932, as cited in Fuller, 1969, p. 209) Curiously, although
noted in her 1969 study, the possible impact of cultural factors
(e.g., race/ ethnicity, social class of students taught) on teacher
concerns was never incorporated into the Fuller's developmental
conceptualization (Fuller, 1969; Fuller & Bown, 1975). However,
it seems that to some degree Fuller may have wondered about the
impact of cultural factors on teacher concerns.

Exploring the implications of her developmental conceptualization, Fuller (1969) asks, "Is concern phase a function of the
person, of the situation or of both?" (p. 222). Then, reflecting upon
this feasible connection, she poses the crucial question, "If con-

cerns are related to characteristics of the person and/or the situation, what are these characteristics?" (p. 222).

TEACHER CONCERNS AND CONTEMPORARY DIVERSE STUDENT POPULATIONS

The climate of an ever-increasing student diversity presents challenges for students and teachers alike. Among the greatest challenge is the *absence of synchronization* (Irvine, 1990) between the culture of schools and the culture many students of color bring to schools.

That student needs differ based on the differences students bring to schools is obvious. Equally apparent is the fact that some students enter schools with the prerequisite skills, abilities, and attitudes that predispose them for a basic level of school success. However, less apparent is that many students find their experiences and interactions in schools highly stressful. Specifically, children and youth from poor and minority backgrounds (to a degree that is disproportionate to their populations in schools) have experiences in schools that are believed to impede their success in schools (Irvine, 1990; Kozol, 1992).

Although success is not assured any student, many students from minority cultures discover that success in school is inextricably tied to the extent to which they can emulate the behaviors, attitudes, and speech patterns of the majority culture (Irvine, 1990). To this end, many minority culture students must become proficient in demonstrating personal attributes that are different from (and in some cases incongruous with) those they have acquired through membership in their own cultural group.

Arguably, the absence of cultural synchronization for students also presents professional challenges (or concerns) for teachers. In school settings where pluralism is highly apparent, some teachers may sense an atmosphere of persuasion or coercion aimed at heightening their cultural sensitivity and awareness. To the extent that teachers themselves use cultural awareness as a measure of their effectiveness (or lack thereof) with culturally different students, they may experience anxiety about their work in contemporary schools.

Locke (1988) proposed that teachers must develop certain levels of cross-cultural awareness to be effective in teaching students of color. Among the levels noted in his *cross-cultural awareness continuum* are self-awareness; awareness of racism, sexism, and poverty; awareness of individual differences; and awareness of other cultures. He noted, "As a teacher encounters a culturally-different student where some cultural awareness is lacking, the teacher must return to an earlier awareness level, explore the awareness at that level, and then proceed along the continuum to teaching effectiveness" (p. 131).

The suggestion that teachers may have unique concerns about working with students of color seems plausible. This is because some factors endemic to working with students of color may arouse professional concern. Many students of color demonstrate culturally influenced *ways of being* (i.e., personal interaction patterns, language forms, and learning styles) that differ considerably from those to which many teachers are accustomed (see Anderson, 1988; Kochman, 1981; Vasquez, 1990). Teachers unfamiliar with these distinct ways of being are likely to develop concerns about their interactions with students of color. As such, these concerns could be said to be peculiar and specific to teachers' work with students from these backgrounds.

Teachers may prioritize their professional concerns and, perhaps by default, prioritize their interactions with students. The dissimilarities between the culture of school and the home culture of certain students may result in these same students presenting different professional challenges for teachers. Because of this perceived challenge, such students are likely to be treated differently by teachers.

Irvine (1990) noted that teachers differ in their interactions with students on the basis of various factors, including time of school year and grade level of students. However, research related to teacher expectations for students indicates that teachers alter their expectations for students (and subsequent interactions with those same students) based on personal characteristics of the students (Irvine, 1986, cited in Irvine, 1990). Immutable characteristics of students (i.e., race, gender) and perceptions of student physical attractiveness have been determined to impact teachers' interactions with students (Cornbleth & Korth, 1980, cited in Irvine, 1990; Washington, 1980, cited in Irvine, 1990). Hence there is significant research to support the notion that teachers behave differently with students based on given student characteristics. Conspicuously absent from the literature is an exploration of the nature of the specific concerns teachers have about working with students from diverse cultural backgrounds.

PATRICIA L. MARSHALL

MULTICULTURAL TEACHING CONCERNS

The nature of teacher concerns as related to culturally diverse student populations was examined by Marshall (1993) in a survey of preservice education majors and experienced teachers. An equal number of preservice education majors and experienced teachers (N=206) were selected to respond to a four-item questionnaire about concerns specific to working with diverse students. The questionnaire items were worded to elicit responses that would reflect a general measure of cross-cultural awareness as described by Locke (1988) and concern stages as described by Fuller and Bown (1975) and Katz (1972). Two forms of the questionnaire were developed to correspond to the different teaching experience levels of the subject groups. Subjects responded to the four items by identifying questions or concerns they have about working with diverse student populations. Over 300 responses were submitted. These responses were analyzed, and duplicate or ambiguous items were eliminated. A series of analyses by a group of judges resulted in the original 300 responses being reduced to 64 different items. Four common themes or categories of concern emerged among these items. These were *familial/group knowledge, strategies and techniques, interpersonal competence,* and *school bureaucracy.* A description of each category is presented in Table 9.1.

Subsequent to the analyses of the four-item questionnaire, the 64-item Multicultural Teaching Concern Survey (MTCS) was developed. The MTCS is designed to assess the intensity of concerns about working with diverse student populations across the four concern categories. Subjects complete the MTCS anonymously. Different forms of the survey are color-coded to correspond with the different professional experience levels of the two subject groups. Items for each concern category are rated on a five-point Likert-type scale ranging from *an extremely important concern for me at this time* (5 points) to *an extremely unimportant concern for me at this time* (1 point). The item ratings within each category are summed to yield four subscores. Mean scores for each category are obtained by dividing the category score by the total number of items within the particular category. A higher category mean score represents a more intense level of concern for the particular category. Table 9.2 presents Form A (for preservice education majors) of the MTCS.

Two hundred sixty-three MTCS surveys were distributed, 151 (57 percent) were returned, and 146 were useable for the analysis.

Table 9.1.

Multicultural Teaching Concerns Categories

Category A "Familial/Group Knowledge" Concerns about the completeness of teachers' knowledge about diverse students' familial/group culture and background
Category B "Strategies & Techniques" Concerns about utilizing "proper techniques" and including the most appropriate "diverse" content in curriculum
Category C "Interpersonal Competence" Concerns about the impact of personal attitudes, actions, and/or beliefs on interactions with diverse student populations
Category D "School Bureaucracy" Concerns about whether the structure of schools (e.g., grouping patterns) and the actions of other school personnel impact efforts to implement multicultural education in schools

Table 9.2

Multicultural Teaching Concerns Survey: Form A

Directions: Below are questions some preprofessionals have posed about working with culturally diverse students (e.g., African-American, Hispanic, Native American). These questions may or may not be of concern to you at this point in your professional preparation. Read each question and then *circle the number* that represents the degree of concern the question holds for you. Use the following scale:

5—an extremely important question for me at this time
4—an important question for me at this time
3—a somewhat important question for me at this time
2—an *unimportant* question for me at this time
1—an extremely *unimportant* question for me at this time

* * * * * * * * * * * * * * * *

1. Will I be biased in favor of divese students?	5 4 3 2 1
2. In what specific ways does family culture affect diverse students' performance in school?	5 4 3 2 1
3. How should I vary my teaching methods when dealing with culturally diverse students?	5 4 3 2 1
4. What happens when teachers fail to see their own prejudiced behavior?	5 4 3 2 1
5. Are diverse students' home environments adequate models for academic study?	5 4 3 2 1

Table 9.2 Continued

Multicultural Teaching Concerns Survey: Form A

6. What skills do I need in order to lessen the white students' prejudices from surfacing in my classroom?	5 4 3 2 1
7. What type of values and behavior patterns are characteristic of diverse students' families?	5 4 3 2 1
8. How can I help all students relate to those who have different backgrounds in my classroom?	5 4 3 2 1
9. Is it realistic to expect that one teacher will be able to meet the needs of various diverse groups assigned to the same class?	5 4 3 2 1
10. Will I inadvertently offend my diverse students?	5 4 3 2 1
11. Will diverse students try to label me "prejudice" without provocation?	5 4 3 2 1
12. Will I stereotype students on the basis of their race?	5 4 3 2 1
13. What kinds of things can I do to meet both the academic and the emotional needs of diverse students in my class?	5 4 3 2 1
14. Will culturally diverse students be comfortable with me as their teacher?	5 4 3 2 1
15. How do I attend to the needs of diverse students and simultaneously meet the needs of all the rest of the students in my class?	5 4 3 2 1
16. Will my own beliefs interfere with the actual content I will be teaching?	5 4 3 2 1
17. Will diverse parents be prejudiced against me?	5 4 3 2 1
18. What names will diverse students prefer I use when referring to their particular racial/ethnic group?	5 4 3 2 1
19. Will my point of view about diversity be vastly different from that of my diverse student population?	5 4 3 2 1
20. Should all teachers learn the skills and information needed to implement multicultural education?	5 4 3 2 1
21. What are diverse students' concerns about discrimination in the society?	5 4 3 2 1
22. What are some techniques for motivating diverse students?	5 4 3 2 1
23. Will my diverse students be prejudiced against me?	5 4 3 2 1
24. What can teachers do to insure that students in need of financial or nutritional assistance receive it in a dignified manner?	5 4 3 2 1
25. Will I relate to diverse students well considering my background is so different from theirs?	5 4 3 2 1
26. What specific techniques and materials motivate diverse students?	5 4 3 2 1
27. Will I show favoritism to white students or students from my background?	5 4 3 2 1
28. Do diverse students receive adequate support in their homes?	5 4 3 2 1
29. How does discrimination impact diverse students' ability to grasp concepts?	5 4 3 2 1
30. What are the special needs of diverse students?	5 4 3 2 1
31. Do diverse students need a different type/approach to teaching that more closely resembles their own culture in order for them to learn?	5 4 3 2 1
32. Should schools be expected to cure the problems of the larger society?	5 4 3 2 1

Table 9.2 Continued

Multicultural Teaching Concerns Survey: Form A

33. What can I do to help students understand that being different does not mean being inferior?	5 4 3 2 1
34. How can I manage tensions between different racial/ethnic groups in my class?	5 4 3 2 1
35. Will I go overboard trying to be sensitive to diverse students?	5 4 3 2 1
36. Do diverse students perceive themselves as victims of discrimination and prejudice?	5 4 3 2 1
37. Will diverse students accuse me of discrimination?	5 4 3 2 1
38. What are the methods and techniques that appeal to all students regardless of their cultural background?	5 4 3 2 1
39. What should I do if the techniques I use with diverse students do not work?	5 4 3 2 1
40. How do I incorporate multicultural education when the teaching/learning resources present white-American perspectives?	5 4 3 2 1
41. How do I effectively teach a class of students whose ability and experiential levels are widely diverse?	5 4 3 2 1
42. How do I deal with the attitudes of intolerance toward diverse students as expressed by my colleagues?	5 4 3 2 1
43. Is formal course work available to help teachers learn about diverse cultures?	5 4 3 2 1
44. Will culturally diverse students perceive me as biased simply because my background is different from theirs?	5 4 3 2 1
45. How does discrimination impact diverse students?	5 4 3 2 1
46. Is it possible to teach the history of all the different races and cultures?	5 4 3 2 1
47. What are some of the ways to integrate multicultural education into the classroom?	5 4 3 2 1
48. Will my personal feelings about diversity influence how I interact with the students in my classroom?	5 4 3 2 1
49. How does the home environment of diverse students impact their receptivity to school?	5 4 3 2 1
50. Will I be able to be myself when working with diverse students without appearing uncaring and aloof?	5 4 3 2 1
51. How do I make lessons and content relevant to diverse students?	5 4 3 2 1
52. What criteria do I use in selecting materials related to diverse cultures?	5 4 3 2 1
53. What are the most effective methods for teaching diverse students?	5 4 3 2 1
54. What impact does race have on diverse students?	5 4 3 2 1
55. Do parents of diverse students possess high expectations for their children?	5 4 3 2 1
56. Can I just act normally and still be "sensitive" to diverse students?	5 4 3 2 1
57. Should teachers be held responsible for the lack of enthusiasm in students who have already been negatively labeled in earlier grades?	5 4 3 2 1
58. What problems exist in diverse students' homes that impact how they respond to learning?	5 4 3 2 1
59. Do diverse students have appropriate adult role models at home?	5 4 3 2 1

Table 9.2 Continued

Multicultural Teaching Concerns Survey: Form A

60. In attending to multicultural issues, will I be engaging in reverse discrimination?	5 4 3 2 1
61. What happens when the policies of the school district contribute to inequitable school experiences for diverse students?	5 4 3 2 1
62. Will the parents of diverse students accept me?	5 4 3 2 1
63. What is the structure of nonstandard dialects spoken in homes of diverse students?	5 4 3 2 1
64. What strategies should I use when working with diverse students?	5 4 3 2 1

Ninety (62 percent) of the useable surveys were from preservice education majors, and 56 (38 percent) were from experienced teachers. Ages ranged from 19 to 67 years; the median age was 22 years. One hundred-nineteen (81.5 percent) females and 27 (18.5 percent) males responded to the survey. Racial and ethnic designations were noted as 126 (86.3 percent) white/Euro-American; 13 (9 percent) black/African-American; 4 (2.7 percent) Hispanic-American; 1 (0.7 percent) Asian-American; and 2 (1.3 percent) other, nonspecified. Forty-four (78.6 percent) of the experienced teachers had taught for ten or more years. All subjects (100 percent) indicated that they expected to teach (or currently teach) culturally diverse student populations. Eighty-six (96 percent) of the preservice education majors and 55 (98 percent) of the experienced teachers indicated that African-American students would be or are the primary group of nonwhite (culturally diverse) students they expect to teach or currently teach.

MTCS: Preliminary Findings

An exploratory factor analysis solution using the maximum likelihood procedure with orthogonal varimax rotation was used to examine the factor structure (Marshall, in press). Factor loadings for the 64-item MTCS are presented in Table 9.3. Those items that received a significant loading on two or more factors were not considered in the interpretation of the factors. Instead, only those 31 items loading high ($\geq$ .30) on a single factor were used in the interpretation.

The factor structure revealed that the descriptions developed during the four-item questionnaire analysis were appropriate to

Table 9.3.

Factor Loadings for 64-Item MTCS

MTCS ITEM	FACTOR 1	FACTOR 2	FACTOR 3	FACTOR 4
1	.40	.11	.35	−.05
2	.02	.26	.16	.44
3	.20	.56	.16	.15
4	.24	.06	.29	.26
5	.12	.15	.03	.55
6	.11	.39	.35	−.02
7	.16	.32	.09	.49
8	.05	.43	.23	.21
9	.38	.22	.23	.26
10	.58	.32	.07	.13
11	.78	.08	−.13	.08
12	.63	.10	.09	.03
13	.18	.61	.07	.23
14	.58	.36	.12	.08
15	.33	.49	.08	.14
16	.50	.15	.13	.02
17	.70	.20	.00	.08
18	.44	.32	.05	.23
19	.49	.27	.20	.28
20	.10	.31	.34	.21
21	.09	.44	.50	.25
22	.05	.65	.09	.32
23	.73	.21	.11	.07
24	.15	.43	.26	.18
25	.53	.31	.27	.13
26	.13	.64	.15	.15
27	.71	.06	.25	.14
28	.14	.31	.17	.66
29	.20	.36	.39	.46
30	.10	.54	.19	.34
31	.24	.51	.31	.25
32	.27	.00	.42	.12
33	.14	.37	.60	.07
34	.35	.34	.51	.02
35	.61	.11	.43	.13
36	.50	.19	.59	.17
37	.77	.13	.26	−.01
38	−.02	.46	.21	.20
39	.27	.49	.19	.45
40	.31	.42	.35	.17
41	.21	.59	.28	.14
42	.21	.27	.60	.14
43	.11	.46	.49	.17
44	.70	.17	.29	.07
45	.28	.30	.67	.22
46	.12	.29	.42	.12
47	.11	.51	.35	.16
48	.49	.09	.45	.21
49	.11	.25	.21	.74
50	.65	.04	.22	.24

Table 9.3. Continued

Factor Loadings for 64-Item MTCS

MTCS ITEM	FACTOR 1	FACTOR 2	FACTOR 3	FACTOR 4
51	.24	.63	.10	.25
52	.17	.69	.15	.24
53	.19	.79	.10	.13
54	.29	.20	.63	.31
55	.16	.25	.16	.58
56	.57	.01	.32	.27
57	.25	.10	.31	.25
58	.09	.43	.18	.64
59	.17	.23	.09	.78
60	.63	−.02	.24	.15
61	.20	.32	.53	.17
62	.59	.14	.19	.36
63	.15	.20	.33	.35
64	.21	.73	.20	.23

explain the four multicultural teaching concern categories. Names for the categories were retained, with the exception of Category C. For this category the term *interpersonal* was replaced with *cross-cultural*. The latter term was chosen because it is more descriptive of the general emphases of items loading high for this category.

Factor 1 corresponds to Category C (*cross-cultural competence*); Factor 2 to Category B (*strategies and techniques*); Factor 3 to Category D (*school bureaucracy*) ; and Factor 4 to Category A (*familial/group knowledge*). Eleven items each were retained for Factors 1 and 2, and four and five items respectively were retained for Factors 3 and 4. All but two of the retained items received factor loadings above 0.40. Actual loadings range from 0.31 to 0.79.

Items in factor 1, *cross-cultural competence,* imply two over-arching questions: "What do culturally diverse students think of me?" and "What do I think of culturally diverse students?" Items loading high on this first factor collectively reflect those anxieties teachers experience about their ability to interact honestly and equitably with diverse students. Teachers express concern about their ability to judge students fairly without regard to cultural background, and to be judged fairly by students without regard to cultural background.

Factor 2, *strategies and techniques,* describes concerns about selecting and incorporating the most appropriate teaching resources, materials, and tactics that will positively impact learning outcomes for diverse students. Several of the items in this second MTCS category reveal concern about culturally relevant lessons and content.

Factor 3 is identified as the *school bureaucracy* dimension of multicultural teaching concerns. These items reflect problems, issues, and phenomena related to the universe of schooling that are beyond what teachers alone can be expected to address in classroom settings. Additionally, items in this third factor demonstrate concerns teachers have about the extent to which the structure of school impedes their ability to effectively meet the needs of diverse students.

Finally, items loading high for Factor 4, *familial/group knowledge* are directly related to the impact of diverse students' family or ethnic/racial group culture on the schooling experience. The items reflect the extent to which teachers perceive gaps in their own knowledge about the family or cultural group background of their diverse students.

To some extent, the results of this study parallel the findings of extant research on teacher concerns. In this regard, the data indicate that three of the MTCS categories roughly coincide with the basic three-level concern conceptualization discussed by Fuller and Bown (1975). An exploratory factor analysis revealed that *cross-cultural competence* items are comparable to self concerns and *strategies and techniques* items correspond to a combination of task and impact concerns (Marshall, in press). Although these similarities are indicated, findings suggest that teacher concerns about working with diverse student populations do differ from other reports of teacher concerns in two substantive manners.

First, this study revealed subdimensions within the *cross-cultural competence* (self concerns), and a combination of emphases in *strategies and techniques* (impact/task concerns) dimensions. As a result of this latter finding, the order of prominence among MTCS categories suggests a *self/impact/task* sequence with the impact and task levels not being clearly delineated. This contrasts sharply with the self/task/impact sequence that has been supported in previous research.

Second, two new concern dimensions were revealed: *school bureaucracy* and *familial/group knowledge*. Introduction of these new dimensions may suggest a need to consider five (as opposed to three) dimensions of concern for teachers working with diverse student populations. These new concern dimensions as well as the subdimensions within the other MTCS categories most likely

PATRICIA L. MARSHALL

emerged because of the specific focus of this study on cultural diversity.

Results of this study suggest that teachers' concerns vis-à-vis their work with culturally different students are substantively different from the general concerns teachers have about working in schools and, ostensibly, with majority culture students. This difference is apparent despite the fact that the *cross-cultural competence* and *strategies and techniques* categories roughly correspond to the standard three-level concern conceptualization as presented by Fuller and Bown (1975).

MULTICULTURAL TEACHING CONCERNS: IMPLICATIONS FOR TEACHER EDUCATION

This study of the nature of teacher concerns about working with culturally diverse students has identified a new dimension of teacher concerns that warrants further exploration. The concept *multicultural teaching concerns* continues to evolve, identifying specific aspects about working with diverse student populations that, to some extent, reflect teacher thinking about multicultural education. To this extent, future research related to multicultural teaching concerns may be able to influence the design of multicultural study in teacher education.

Teaching Concerns as Part of a Conceptual Base for Multicultural Education

Multicultural educators aspire to facilitate students' ability to engage in substantive critical analysis of various aspects of schools, and to affect change that will result in equitable schooling experiences for all learners. Yet certain challenges, which may reflect particular student thinking about multicultural education, can serve to undermine this goal. Among these challenges are the limited knowledge about diversity in U.S. society that many students bring to the study of multicultural education (Ladson-Billings, 1991); misconceptions about multicultural education (Marshall, 1994a); dysconscious racism and other uncritical habits of mind (i.e., perceptions, attitudes, assumptions, and beliefs) (King, 1991); and limited intellectual capacity to engage in substantive analysis of multicultural issues (Bennett, Niggle, & Stage, 1989).

Although student thinking about multicultural education may contribute to the challenges faced by multicultural educators, the multivariate structure of multicultural education as a field of study (Banks, 1993) and the overall philosophy of multicultural education (Gay, 1994) may inadvertently present overwhelming challenges for some students. As such, courses in multicultural education may need to be structured in such a manner that they meet students "where they are" and then facilitate student growth to "where they need to be."

Bennett, Niggle, and Stage (1989) considered this phenomenon of meeting students "where they are" in a study of student knowledge of multicultural education at the beginning and end of an undergraduate course in multicultural education. Applying a cognitive developmental framework to the design of the course, Bennett, et al. (1989) proposed that *matching* instructional strategies and content with the intellectual abilities of students would facilitate students' learning multicultural content. The researchers reported that those students whose cognitive development demonstrated the least dualistic orientations (i.e., the tendency to view the world in absolute "black-and-white" terms) also had the greatest knowledge of multicultural education at the beginning and conclusion of the course. Similarly, lower social distance scores (i.e., more positive attitudes toward persons differing from self) were positively correlated with gains in multicultural knowledge (Bennett et al., 1989).

Although Bennett et al. (1989) suggest a cognitive developmental framework for the structure of multicultural education courses, they do not explore the notion of facilitating the development of student thinking to more complex cognitive levels. Thies-Sprinthall and Sprinthall (1987) suggest that the ability to function at more complex stages across varying cognitive dimensions (e.g., conceptual functioning, moral reasoning, ego development) is evidenced in the ability to perform the most complex tasks involved in helping professions such as counseling and teaching. They note that "at a higher stage level there is more humaneness, a greater ability to empathize, to symbolize experience, and to act on democratic principles" (p. 69).

Multicultural education is composed of several dimensions, including content integration, knowledge construction, and prejudice reduction (Banks, 1993). Successful implementation of these dimensions may only require augmentation of one's current knowledge base. However, other dimensions (e.g., equity pedagogy, empowering school culture and social structure; see Banks, 1993, p. 5) demand the complex stages of conceptual and moral exploration reflected in complex levels of humaneness and commitment to democratic principles. Teachers whose thinking reflects simplicity across these various cognitive dimensions may actually be unable to engage in the more complicated aspects of this multidimensional field of study. As such, they may be unable to think about multicultural education from emancipatory perspectives.

Therefore, multicultural education courses should be designed to not only match student functioning level with course content and teaching strategy, but they should also *promote cognitive growth* among students. To promote growth, deliberate mismatches between student cognitive stage, course content, and teaching strategies must be undertaken.

The concept of *multicultural teaching concerns* may play a significant role in the exploration and ultimately the design of multicultural education courses based on cognitive developmental theory. In this regard, multicultural teaching concerns provide insights into where students are in their thinking as related to working with diverse student populations.

For example, *cross-cultural competence* concerns suggest a preoccupation with one's ability to interact with students who differ from oneself, whereas *strategies and techniques* concerns suggest thinking related to delivering content in a most effective manner to diverse students. Neither of these multicultural teaching concern emphases implies teacher thinking that reflects an inclination to engage in critical analysis of the inequities in schools. Rather, preoccupation with these particular concerns may actually preclude the ability to become immersed in the transformative goals endemic to a substantive study of multicultural education.

Analysis of the items that loaded highest within the *cross-cultural competence* category (see Table 9.3) suggest concern with the extent to which diversity in the school environment could complicate or detract from the teacher's development as a professional. Thus a teacher whose thinking is focused on *cross-cultural competence* would likely attempt to deemphasize cultural pluralism in schools, that is, "not see color." Ladson-Billings (1992) addresses problems endemic to school environments where teachers opt to ignore cultural diversity. Similarly, Irvine (1990) notes that the absence of cultural synchronization many students of color experience in schools may be a direct result of benevolent attempts on the part of teachers to deemphasize cultural difference.

Multicultural education courses that are based on a cognitive developmental perspective should provide teachers whose concerns about working with diverse students are concentrated within the *cross-cultural competence* dimension with experiences that help them better understand *themselves* as racial beings. In this regard, course activities should be designed to help teachers perceive cultural diversity as a reflection of the similarities and differences and the natural order of the human mosaic.

Similarly, teachers whose thinking is focused on *strategies and techniques* might be said to be most developmentally receptive to learning specific how-to's for working with diverse students. With intermittent critical analysis of such concepts as cultural styles and cultural synchronization, such teachers may eventually be coaxed into exploring other dimensions of multicultural education. However, if their immediate need to find useful instructional techniques is not addressed, then they will probably be unable to focus on the more complex dimensions of multicultural study.

Overall, experiences designed to directly match *cross-cultural* and *strategies and techniques* concerns would probably be more beneficial and more developmentally appropriate as initial multicultural course content than attempts to examine transformative goals of multicultural education.

Conversely, the multicultural teaching concerns related to the *school bureaucracy* and *familial/group knowledge* categories suggest an inclination in thinking about multicultural education that would at least be prerequisite to engaging in the more complex dimensions of this field of study. Moreover, these two categories suggest new dimensions to teacher concern research. Specifically, MTCS items that loaded highest on the *school bureaucracy* category reflect a macroperspective awareness about those issues in schools that affect the experiences of culturally diverse students. *Familial/group knowledge* concerns indicate interest in learning more about the family and cultural group experiences of diverse students that directly impact the schooling experiences of students.

Students whose thinking about multicultural education is focused on these categories may be more developmentally inclined to explore the more complex dimensions of multicultural education identified by Banks (1993). Moreover, those students who can focus on the *bureaucracy of schools* may also be prepared to examine how schools disempower them as professionals. They may be the students who are more inclined to appreciate and critically examine the connectedness between various dimensions of oppression and discrimination and their impact on individuals and schools as societal institutions (Sleeter & Grant, 1994).

Finally, in the context of the developmental multicultural education, mismatches can be provided for students by incorporating teaching techniques that carefully guard against cultural aversion (see Irvine, 1990) among teachers, and that provide guided reflection upon new experiences. Marshall (1994b) describes the issues exchange activity in a multicultural education course as a mismatching experience designed to help students engage in the equity pedagogy and reconstruction goals of multicultural education study.

CONCLUSION

Since Fuller's 1969 study, the notion of teacher concerns has consistently provoked interest among teacher educators. This may be because it answers the need to assess the relevance of teacher education. Similarly, multicultural educators search for answers to their relevance query. In exploring the nature of teacher thinking about multicultural education, we aim to better comprehend how we might more effectively reach the ultimate goals of multicultural study.

The present study examined teacher thinking as it relates to teacher concerns about working with diverse student populations. The data revealed that teacher concerns about working with diverse students are multidimensional. Moreover, these varying dimensions may provide insights into how to configure developmentally appropriate courses in multicultural education.

The data from this study also revealed that more research is needed in connection with the concept *multicultural teacher concerns*. This latter revelation was probably most evident in one teacher's response to the initial MTCS four-item questionnaire. She noted,

> Unfortunately, I cannot help you with these specific statements. I don't really have any questions or concerns about working with people who are culturally diverse. I do worry that my lessons cannot reach people who are hungry or pregnant or worried about family members. I also am concerned about a seeming cul-

tural norm to have sex with multiple partners as a form of entertainment, but I don't see that my concern affects my teaching. Is that what you are asking? I do vary my teaching styles, but I do so to benefit everyone not just the "culturally diverse." My interactions with students don't reflect their diversity either. I'm not sure what sorts of responses you are seeking. . . . (anonymous teacher response to 4-item questionnaire)

Clearly, the nature of teacher thinking about multicultural education is very complex. Hopefully, this study will evoke continued interest and exploration in this particular dimension of the issue.

USING A CONSTRUCTIVIST APPROACH TO CHALLENGE PRESERVICE TEACHERS' THINKING ABOUT DIVERSITY IN EDUCATION

Teresita E. Aguilar
Cathy A. Pohan

Course work in multicultural education, cultural diversity, human relations, and related topics has increasingly become a requirement in teacher preparation programs and teacher certification and recertification programs. This movement is driven by multiple factors, including changing demographics within public schools, educational discrepancies (i.e., dropout rates, graduation rates, academic achievement, educational opportunities and access), legislative action, political interests, and the recognition of a predominantly white, middle-class, and female teaching force with limited knowledge or experiences with diversity. Central to this emphasis in multiculturalism and diversity in teacher preparation curricula is the notion that we may need to reconsider or challenge how we have historically prepared teachers. As we recognize our increased cultural diversity and acknowledge the failure to educate or promote education about this diversity, the seriousness of the matter is intensified.

The question of how to prepare effective teachers for a more notably diverse society and classroom becomes critical to teacher preparation programs. It is undoubtedly naive to expect that a single course in multicultural education or diversity could accomplish such a monumental task. Indeed, this notion has been challenged elsewhere. Our focus is on a more broadly defined multi-cultural education curriculum within teacher preparation—whether that includes a series of multicultural courses or more infused, integrated curricula. In this chapter, we review the charge of multicultural education within teacher preparation programs. We provide a summary of attributes of an educator who is competent in addressing diversity as subject *and* object of education. The selected attributes provide a framework for extended discussions of critical professional beliefs about diversity in education and a multicultural knowledge base. We also discuss the need for increased and meaningful cultural experiences to enhance the effectiveness of multicultural education. We strongly advocate the use of a constructivist approach in the design and implementation of a multicultural curriculum, and provide specific examples of educational activities to illustrate this approach. The ultimate purpose of such a curriculum is to develop multicultural or cross-cultural competence among preservice teachers.

PREPARATION FOR DIVERSITY: A CHARGE FOR MULTICULTURAL EDUCATION

There are numerous interpretations and associated approaches to multicultural education (Sleeter & Grant, 1988). The schools of thought range from a distinct multiethnic emphasis (Banks & Banks, 1993; Gay, 1983) to a more radical, antiracist education (Nieto, 1992). This implies that there is not universal agreement on what multicultural education is or ought to be. We suggest that multicultural education in teacher training has a distinct purpose, one that is different from educating society about diversity. The central multicultural issues for preservice teachers are necessarily driven by the need to acquire cultural competence leading to more effective teaching. We begin our discussion with an overview of several proposed attributes of a multicultural educator. The development of these attributes is reviewed in light of the cognitive characteristics identified in the literature.

Attributes of a Multicultural Educator

The literature on multicultural competency suggests that an effective multicultural educator possesses several characteristics that can be categorized into four interdependent psychological dimensions: (a) *attitudes and beliefs* that are consistent with and supportive of multiculturalism and into which knowledge can be incorporated and upon which skills can be built; (b) *declarative knowledge*, or general facts about cultural and social diversity, including knowledge about diverse learners' needs and inequalities in education, and the relationships among those facts; (c) *procedural knowledge*, knowledge of essential or effective skills for use in and beyond the classroom which take into consideration an understanding of declarative knowledge; and (d) *conditional knowledge*, or knowledge of when and why certain procedures are to be applied, and the will to carry them out.

We have recategorized these four dimensions into two: beliefs and knowledge. This tactic establishes a two-dimensional core upon which to base multicultural education. To merely focus on increased knowledge, for example, would be insufficient and would fail to bring about a change in attitudes or behaviors (Byrnes & Kiger, 1989). Further, given the controversial and inconclusive research on attitudes (see Grant & Secada, 1990), we have chosen to limit our discussion to beliefs about diversity, rather than a more broad concern for attitudes and attitude change. The combination of the three knowledge dimensions serves to identify and propose a more comprehensive multicultural knowledge base for teacher preparation. The role and significance of beliefs and multicultural knowledge are briefly summarized.

BELIEFS ABOUT DIVERSITY

Attitudes, beliefs, and expectations can guide and direct teachers' responses toward various students (Grant, 1985; Pajares, 1992). Substantial evidence shows that stereotypes are assigned to students according to race (Guttmann & Bar-Tal, 1982; Hale-Benson, 1982; Nieto, 1992), social class (Baron, Tom, & Cooper, 1985; Cooper, Baron, & Lowe, 1975; Nieto, 1992), and gender differences (Brophy & Everston, 1981; Brophy & Good, 1970; Sadker, Sadker, & Long, 1993) (see also Oakes, 1985; Palardy, 1969; Rist, 1970). These same studies reveal discrepancies in the amount and type of student-teacher interactions, curricula, and academic outcomes for students from diverse backgrounds. Some teachers hold beliefs that white students and students of color from lower socioeconomic backgrounds cannot perform as well as their middle-class counterparts. Since school failure is the result of a complex interaction between teachers, schools, communities, and society, we must challenge low academic expectations that are linked to teachers' negative and stereotypical beliefs about groups of students.

Teachers' beliefs refer to the implicit assumptions held about students, classrooms, and the curriculum (Kagan, 1992). Stereotypes may be based on a set of beliefs that ultimately affect teacher expectations (e.g., low-income students are low achievers). After reviewing twenty-five teacher belief studies, Kagan (1992) concluded that "teacher beliefs usually reflect the actual nature of the instruction the teacher provides to students" (p. 73). Several scholars have found that teachers' beliefs are consistent with their daily practices and interactions with students (Brophy & Evertson, 1981; Gudmundsdottir, 1991; Hollon, Anderson, & Roth, 1991; Janesick, 1982; Morine-Dershimer, 1988; Pajares, 1992). Rennie (1989) concluded that patterns of student participation and the nature of instruction are largely determined by teacher belief. Given the potential relationship between beliefs and actual practice, it seems paramount that we gain a better understanding of preservice teachers' personal and professional beliefs about diversity.

Preservice teachers enter teacher education programs with a particular set of attitudes and beliefs toward their own and others' culture. Some parts of the belief system are valid, but other parts are based on myths, misconceptions, or ignorance. To help prospective teachers understand, respect, and affirm cultural differences, schools of education must begin "where the learner is," targeting both the cognitive and affective levels of each candidate, and build from this beginning point toward a more mature level of multicultural awareness and sensitivity (Ross & Smith, 1992). Teacher candidates must be challenged to analyze the perceptions and beliefs they hold about their own group and other groups if they are to become effective multicultural educators.

Multicultural Knowledge Base

A comprehensive multicultural knowledge base should, at a minimum, consider various types of knowledge needed by competent multicultural educators. Combining declarative, procedural, and conditional knowledge bases for multicultural education provides a comprehensive grounding in the thinking and practice of teaching in a diverse context. Since multicultural education is an emerging field, a comprehensive knowledge base has not been clearly established. The question of what knowledge is (and what multicultural knowledge in particular is) was recently posed by Banks (1993). Essentially, he argues for a constructivist approach to the creation of knowledge and then categorizes knowledge into the following typologies: personal/cultural, popular, mainstream academic, transformative academic, and school knowledge. Ultimately, he fails to specify or more narrowly define a knowledge base needed by (multi)culturally competent educators. In his rejoinder, Chesher (1993) challenges the absence of a clear explanation of what is or ought to be considered essential multicultural knowledge. In a perusal of multicultural textbooks and journal articles, several themes or topics were repeatedly suggested for inclusion within the curriculum. Among the major categories included consistently were knowledge of the following

1. Diverse cultural (i.e., multiethnic) or social (i.e., gender, social class, sexual orientation) groups
2. Educational practices or services pertaining to diversity
3. Historical policies and legislative mandates directly affecting diverse groups
4. Historical, theoretical, and practical implications of multicultural education

One could easily consider these themes within the previous framework of declarative, procedural, and conditional knowledge to identify the content and context upon which preservice teachers ought to develop their multicultural knowledge base.

Building upon the four major identified themes listed above, a multicultural education knowledge test (Aguilar, 1995) was developed to assess the extent of knowledge respondents have for thirty-five specific topic areas relevant to multicultural education (see Table 10.1). The test assesses the respondents' perceptions of depth of knowledge about the selected topics, without having to spell out exactly what they "know" (i.e., factually) or how they came to know (about) each listed item.

The initial test results indicate that a range of knowledge bases exist from minimal to extensive, and the bases vary predictably with level of education, completed course work in multicultural education and diversity, and personal experiences with diversity. This measure illustrates one method of identifying and proposing a thematic knowledge base for multicultural education, suggesting a representative list of key or central multicultural issues or topics. The measure is designed to serve as a diagnostic gauge to identify areas of deficiency in knowledge or awareness.

Given the historical absence of multicultural issues, perspectives, or content within mainstream educational settings, it is not surprising that most preservice students' multicultural knowledge bases are quite limited. Like beliefs, knowledge can be based on incorrect information. Establishing and strengthening one's multicultural knowledge demands hearing and understanding multiple perspectives and realities about topics or issues related to cultural diversity and multiculturalism. This challenge is perhaps more easily met through a constructivist approach than through an objectivist one.

Cultural Experiences as Cultural Contexts

We propose that beliefs supportive of diversity and a sound multicultural knowledge base are enhanced through bi-, multi-, or cross-cultural experiences. Triandis (1971) argues that direct, personal experience can bring about a change in one's attitudes toward someone or something. Cross-cultural experiences might also occur vicariously through visual media, literature, and direct observation. Direct or vicarious experiences serve to enhance the transition from initial to reconstructed realities about diversity.

As dissonance occurs, an individual is forced to reorganize his or her beliefs. Consider an individual who believes that all members of the lower economic class are lazy. When she or he meets someone from this group who does not fit this description, the individual is likely to experience some dissonance. This experience may require him or her to reorganize existing beliefs about members of the lower class. Still further, a *pleasant* experience with a member of the lower economic class will likely affect alternative views of other members of the lower economic class (Triandis, 1971).

Without meaningful, direct, and positive experiences with diverse others, one's knowledge and beliefs about cultural diversity may be limited to images (i.e., media) or the often negative experiences expressed by others or experienced by oneself. Although the images might be useful, the more direct experiences tend to challenge those areas of negative images in a more meaningful way. Enhancing cultural competence through contact with

Table 10.1.

Multicultural Education Knowledge Test (Version C)

INSTRUCTIONS: Circle the number which best assess the extent of your knowledge for each topic.
None = complete unfamiliarity
Minimal = some familiarity
Average = ability to discuss the topic
Extensive = ability to debate/explain/lead discussion on the topic.

MY KNOWLEDGE ABOUT . . . IS	NONE	MINIMAL		AVERAGE		EXTENSIVE	
1. Multicultural teaching practices	1	2	3	4	5	6	7
2. History of African Americans	1	2	3	4	5	6	7
3. Special education services	1	2	3	4	5	6	7
4. Hispanic American groups	1	2	3	4	5	6	7
5. Civil Rights legislation	1	2	3	4	5	6	7
6. Standardized test bias	1	2	3	4	5	6	7
7. Systemic racism in public schools	1	2	3	4	5	6	7
8. Immigration laws	1	2	3	4	5	6	7
9. Asian American cultural groups	1	2	3	4	5	6	7
10. Native American tribes	1	2	3	4	5	6	7
11. Educational tracking	1	2	3	4	5	6	7
12. History of multicultural education	1	2	3	4	5	6	7
13. PL 94-142	1	2	3	4	5	6	7
14. ESL programs	1	2	3	4	5	6	7
15. Religions other than own	1	2	3	4	5	6	7
16. Prominent people of color	1	2	3	4	5	6	7

17. Bilingual education	1	2	3	4	5	6	7
18. Lower income lifestyles	1	2	3	4	5	6	7
19. Social class educational barriers	1	2	3	4	5	6	7
20. Multicultural environments	1	2	3	4	5	6	7
21. Cultural identity development	1	2	3	4	5	6	7
22. Multicultural education resources	1	2	3	4	5	6	7
23. Gay and lesbian lifestyles	1	2	3	4	5	6	7
24. Human relations	1	2	3	4	5	6	7
25. Cross-cultural communication	1	2	3	4	5	6	7
26. Oppression in education	1	2	3	4	5	6	7
27. School funding practices	1	2	3	4	5	6	7
28. Etnic community resources	1	2	3	4	5	6	7
29. Multicultural curricula	1	2	3	4	5	6	7
30. Women in American history	1	2	3	4	5	6	7
31. American Disabilities Act	1	2	3	4	5	6	7
32. Multicultural education scholars	1	2	3	4	5	6	7
33. Ethnic groups in America	1	2	3	4	5	6	7
34. Title IX, Education Amendments	1	2	3	4	5	6	7
35. Second language acquisition	1	2	3	4	5	6	7

Source: Aguilar, T.E. (1995). Do not use without written permission of author.

others is particularly significant when you consider that the typical preservice teacher (i.e., white, middle-class, female) has limited culturally diverse experiences.

A Preliminary Model

The model shown in Figure 10.1 illustrates the relationships among the variables of beliefs, knowledge, and cultural experiences as a foundation for multicultural education in teacher preparation programs. We suggest that interactions occur when one or more areas are altered. For example, a change in knowledge usually affects a change in beliefs. The "initial reality" demonstrates where preservice teachers begin. Following multicultural educational experiences, if they are indeed effective, there should be a transition to a "reconstructed reality" of multicultural and diversity issues.

One clarification of this model is in order: students come to the formal educational situation with an initial reality about various multicultural issues or topics. There are, for example, preconceived notions about diversity, often based upon stereotypical

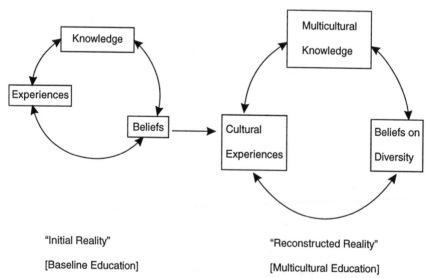

"Initial Reality"

[Baseline Education]

"Reconstructed Reality"

[Multicultural Education]

Figure 10.1 Transition from Initial to Reconstructed Reality about Diversity

data. If this is the place where preservice teachers are, then this is where the teacher preparation program needs to begin. This approach recognizes the current, existing reality of the students.

Constructivists view reality as internally mediated. That is, an individual's prior knowledge, beliefs, and existing frames of reference are weighed heavily in the development of knowledge and in defining reality (Jonassen, 1991). In contrast to an objectivist view of learning as reception of knowledge from an outside source, a constructivist perspective sees learning as knowledge formation (Alkove & McCarty, 1992; Brooks, 1990; Jonassen, 1991). Learning, then, becomes the creation of knowledge, particularly that which is meaningful and is understood within a given context. Learning is NOT the acquisition of "facts and figures" in the *absence* of meaning or context.

The next sections of this chapter articulate and defend the use of a constructivist approach to multicultural education, providing specific examples of educational programs and activities. These examples serve as illustrations rather than as blueprints. The constructivist approach suggests a process, and one which will vary in specific tactics in response to the needs, levels of awareness, and thoughts of the students as individuals and as a group.

A CONSTRUCTIVIST APPROACH

Believing that learners construct knowledge through the processes of *reflection, inquiry,* and *action* (Fosnot, 1989), constructivists focus on the development and utilization of the cognitive processes for acquiring, judging, and organizing new information. The implicit goal of instructional strategies therefore is to engage or enhance student thinking, not to supplant it (Salomon, 1979). Once a teacher conceptualizes what the students presently believe, the teacher's task is to plan instructional activities that prompt disequilibrium and, subsequently, self-regulation.

Constructivists argue that the most effective learning takes place in context (i.e., real-world environments), and that the context becomes a significant feature of the knowledge base associated with that learning (Jonassen, 1991). "Interrelatedness of concepts is emphasized, by providing a variety of perspectives on the content, and by using case-based instruction that provides multiple perspectives or themes inherent in the cases" (Jonassen, 1991, p. 11). Brooks (1990) suggests four dimensions of a constructivist classroom: (a) structuring curriculum around primary concepts instead of a long list of behavioral skills and objectives; (b) un-covering alternative conceptions or misconceptions; (c) attempt-ing to understand the learner's point of view; and (d) providing a context of growth and cooperation, in which conflict can be the source of developmental progress. Indeed, Prawat (1992) warns that the constructivist approach places much greater demand on both "teacher" and "student," as they become colearners with a shift from a traditional telling and listening relationship.

EXAMPLES OF CONSTRUCTIVISM IN MULTICULTURAL EDUCATION

Two examples are selected for illustrating a constructivist ap-proach in teacher preparation used to develop cultural com-petency. The first is built around the issue of "racism" and the second around the use of "cultural immersion." The cultural im-mersion experience was designed to enhance cultural compe-tence through knowledge development, through a challenge to preexisting beliefs, and through direct experience. For both exam-ples, we describe the primary concepts being addressed, consider unique aspects of these primary concepts (including misconcep-tions), recognize multiple perspectives and points of view, and encourage learners to move beyond their initial perspectives or understanding of the primary concepts. These efforts are parallel to Brooks' (1990) suggestions for a constructivist "classroom."

Educational Activity 1: On Understanding Racism[1]

A rationale for the study of racism. The topic of *racism* is often addressed within multicultural education courses and texts, with varying degrees of attention. Nieto (1992) argues that race and racism are essential areas of study in multicultural education, enhance one's understanding and appreciation for cultural diver-sity, and lead to the development of culturally competent educators.

An analogy is offered to illustrate the relationship between un-derstanding racism and engaging in *multiethnic* education.[2]

> A preservice teacher with limited educational or per-sonal experience with racial diversity is asked to read James Baldwin's (1988) essay "A Talk to Teachers." This student has never formally studied racism, and

she thinks that racism is "something of the past" or "something that happens mainly in 'the South.'" She reads his essay, and is incredibly uncomfortable and even offended by his words. "What's he so angry about?" she exclaims in class. He should just "get over it!"

The sentiment here is that Baldwin should not criticize the United States, particularly on the issue of racism. After all, it really isn't as bad as it used to be. Are Baldwin's words read differently by the student who has some sense of the history and politics of racism? Do the words cause a different reaction for the student familiar with multiple perspectives on racism?

We would argue that having an understanding of issues such as racism must precede learning about diverse and specific cultural groups. At the very least, the "isms" around issues of race, class, and/or gender should be integrated into the learning about diverse cultural groups. In other words, learning about racism and oppression should coincide with learning about historically excluded or underrepresented groups in our society. To attempt to teach about selected ethnic groups without regard to social oppression fails to provide a context for the significance of this educational component within teacher preparation (Giroux, 1988).

Given the limited exposure most preservice teachers have concerning the study of racism, it is generally easy to prompt disequilibrium in learning about racism. In using a constructivist approach, the initial task is to assess students' preexisting beliefs and notions about racism. A challenge in addressing racism in a predominantly white institution or within a predominantly white student population is that, more often than not, students express that racism *has not been* a factor in their lives ("There were no people of color in my hometown." "Race was not a 'problem' in my community."). In essence, they would suggest that they have no context for understanding racism. This is often "the place" where many preservice teachers begin on racism.

Racism from a white perspective. Too often, discussions of racism focus on the negative consequences and historical accounts that tend to create the "color line" between "us" and "them." From this perspective, racism appears to be a social problem for people of color. It can lead to feelings of resentment or guilt among white students, followed by self-disclaimers (it is *not* our fault). Indeed, at this point, white students may report feeling alienated or attacked for something with which they feel they have nothing to do. If white students are to make sense of racism, they will need to practice seeing racism from multiple perspectives rather than as a dichotomous social issue.

Thus a critical challenge is to enhance all students' ability to view racism from the perspective of a white person or a person of color, from a societal or institutional level, from an individual level, and so forth. Essentially, the exercise becomes one of changing the lens of a camera to photograph the same object or subject. The photographer, in this case, is asked to change the tone, lens, angle, distance, and depth of the same object or subject to deliver a series of different photographs reflecting multiple truths or realities of the "same object/subject" (i.e., racism). Christine Sleeter (in press) has written about her experiences in teaching about racism and oppression with a predominantly white student body. She describes the struggle of reaching her ultimate goal of helping her white students see racism and other forms of oppression from different perspectives. Among her efforts are the design of vicarious experiences intended to illicit a more personal awareness of the selected issues (via films, readings, past experiences); opportunities for direct contact with persons culturally different from her preservice students; literature that attempts to illustrate social ills from a personal perspective; simulated experiences of unequal power bases; reflective writing; and creating a collective knowledge base. Although she describes some rather encouraging works produced by her students, works portraying a critical analysis and understanding of social inequities in education, she also concludes that unless the intellectual advances merge somehow with the "gut level" of denouncing discrepancies, change in schooling will be minimal, at best. The challenge, then, may well be to complete the circle by connecting a reconstructed reality of racism in schooling *with* historical and contemporary institutional views on racism, *to* the mediating role of the future teacher perpetuating racism in educational settings.

Seeing multiple views of racism. In addressing multiple views of racism, it is helpful to use diverse images and analogies that intentionally take the focus away from racial *differences*. In fact, it has been useful to use other objects to create a comfort zone for a more gradual transition to discussions on race and racism. Some of the "tools" used to accomplish this transitional study of racism include shoe size as category and identifier, and photographs and negatives as ways of viewing the picture of racism. These images are points of departure for looking critically and perhaps even somewhat simplistically at how race is used to perpetuate racism.

1. *Shoe size as category and identifier:* Everyone in the room is divided into groups according to each individual's shoe size (or other physical identifier). Next, each group proposes a rationale for this shared phenomenon. The students discuss other (physical, cognitive, emotional, etc.) traits that they believe they have in common with other members of their group and which, if any, of these additional traits or characteristics are associated with shoe size. This exercise is an excellent lead-in to discussions about dividing people by physical traits (race, weight, hair color, etc.) and about ascribing other characteristics, personalities, or adjectives to people with a given physical trait. This discussion may serve as a basis for understanding the "logic" of stereotypes: a basis for understanding differential life experiences as a function of visible physical traits, or as a way we *give social meaning to physical conditions.*

2. *Viewing racism:* We begin with an image of racism as a picture, and the challenge is to see it from multiple perspectives. Students are asked to imagine that they have each been given a roll of film, a camera, and a task of photographing various forms of racism (e.g, institutionalized, individual, internalized). They take their pictures, have them developed, and now have the envelope with negatives and photographs.

   We often begin the task of seeing racism by viewing the "negatives." Students are asked to imagine holding their negatives up to a light. The essence of the picture of racism is captured. Students are reminded that the negative shows an opposite image (in terms of color) than will be seen in the actual photograph. Thus the negative can only give you *part* of the picture.

Students are asked to shift to the developed photographs. The image is complete only after one goes
beyond the image posed by the "negative." The parallel is thus drawn to racism. If we only discuss the
negative images or consequences of racism, we fail
to acknowledge that there is some positive gain for
some people in the overall picture. One reading
used to illustrate this picture is Peggy McIntosh'
(1989) writing on white privilege. Essentially, she
reminds us of what happens (or does not happen) to
white persons because of their race. She has noticed, for example, that when she accomplishes
something, she is not openly acknowledged or
praised as being a "good reflection of her race," or if
she moves into a new neighborhood, the neighbors
aren't afraid her presence will "devalue" the surrounding property. Thus, to actually view racism, it
is not enough to merely focus on the negative, for
that is an incomplete picture of the concept.

A reconstructed reality of racism. The concept of racism is generally
discussed early in the semester, and is considered a building block
to future critical discussions of diversity and various forms of
oppression. The groundwork is thus established to consider individual and societal analyses of various topics and concepts in
multicultural education.

Rarely does a learner retain his or her initial reality about racism following the classroom experiences provided on this topic.
The following excerpts from student evaluations and other forms
of feedback reflect a preliminary movement toward a reconstructed reality and an appreciation of racism in our society and,
more particularly, in our schooling.

"Until I took this class I didn't understand racism
and my role in it. For this alone I will be forever grateful. Now I feel I can begin to do something to help
alleviate this ism."

"This course opened my eyes to a lot that goes un-
noticed, such as racism and prejudice."

". . . made me think about what it meant to be
'white.' "

"It made me think and consider where I'm coming from. I don't consider myself racist but will have to look closer, since I was uncomfortable at times."

". . . I think now I know racism is a very serious issue. I never thought it was that big of an issue, but it definitely is."

"Helped me realize the depth and pain of racism and prejudice . . . but we can all do something about it."

"My outlook on issues of diversity has changed. I see people in a different light. I used to just look at diversity, knowing that it existed all around me, and ignore it. Now, I've become more aware of all kinds of diversity and am paying attention to the effects it has on people. It is beginning to anger me, whereas before, I was indifferent to it. The one final thing I would like to get out of this class is the knowledge of what I can do to aid in stopping or helping those who are discriminated against. . . . I want to know I can do my part."

Educational Activity 2: Cultural Immersion

A rationale for cultural immersion. Knowledge alone is insufficient to bring about change in one's attitudes or beliefs (Byrnes & Kiger, 1989). However, when new knowledge is introduced in combination with direct, personal contact, a change in one's attitudes or beliefs is more likely to occur (Grant & Secada, 1990; Triandis, 1971). Given that the typical preservice teacher has had limited cross-cultural experiences, cultural immersion can be an extremely powerful tool in teacher preparation programs. Consistent with a constructivist approach, cultural immersion presents students with a real-world (i.e., learning in context) experience in which they can develop multicultural competence.

A cultural immersion experience was designed by the authors to provide a "laboratory" beyond the traditional classroom in which cultural dissonance and personal disequilibrium could be established and developmental progress facilitated. The summer experience of four and one-half weeks entailed giving ten education majors from a midwestern university the opportunity to study and live within a predominantly Mexican American, rural community in the U.S. Southwest.

Creating a culture specific knowledge base. The processes of reflection, inquiry, and action took place on a number of levels and through a variety of activities. Each student kept a journal of the immersion experience, which included responses to guiding questions. Using excerpts from their journals and notes from debriefing sessions, the following notations illustrate some of their initial realities about Mexican culture and the host community, including reflections upon their initial realities. Their direct contact may have forced these initial notions to be challenged.

> "I wondered how I would get along, expecting everyone would speak Spanish, not English. But, man, people didn't speak Spanish."
>
> "I thought there would be more oppression and with it hopelessness, but it wasn't like that."
>
> "Another stereotype I had was that this community would be more Anglicized. I thought they would be more assimilated, but they were more acculturated. They had the attitude: 'This is who we are and we are proud to be who we are.'"
>
> "If someone would have asked me what I knew about Mexicans, I would have said, 'They are farmworkers, they eat burritos, wear sombreros, and use the bottle.' What I saw was quite different. We have lots of similar values in terms of what is important and what is not."
>
> "I couldn't sleep the first night—there were spiders all around me. I felt like a f_____ princess. I literally had to beat myself and remind myself of why I was here."
>
> "I didn't know what to expect. You didn't tell us much. So much of what I built up was based on past experiences. I thought I was pretty laid-back (i.e., having no stereotypes), but I found out that I was clueless in regards to a culture that is thriving in America. I am envious of the Mexican culture—the family and unity."

A set of required and optional readings on Mexican culture and Mexican American schooling was given for their reflection and reactions. In addition, lectures and presentations by community leaders provided information about the local culture. The option to write a short biography on a local resident provided yet another means to acquire additional knowledge about the community, culture, and selected individuals. During the course of the immersion experience, several primary concepts were addressed or challenged by the preservice teachers. The following list includes several concepts that students began to think about in different ways (from their initial perceptions): Mexican culture, family, children, home, cultural art, teacher or teaching, poverty, language and bilingualism, assimilation, acculturation, and community. In some cases, students chose to write about these concepts in their journals. In other instances, they chose to bring them up in debriefing sessions or in less formal discussion sessions. Overall, these experiences provided students with the opportunity to ask questions, reflect upon their initial knowledge (and beliefs), and reorganize or reconstruct their preconceived notions about both rural, southwestern culture, and Mexican (American) culture. Consistent with a constructivist approach, the immersion experience was designed to provide opportunities for students to acquire multiple perspectives of Mexican culture. Two major strategies for the immersion experience were to provide for individual and group cross-cultural experiences.

Individual or personal immersion. Perhaps the most powerful means of achieving individual or personal immersion was through living with a Mexican American host family. Each participant was taken in as a "temporary" family member by one of the local families and participated fully in family life. The students very quickly became a significant part of the "extended family," not just a temporary member. In addition to living with a local family, participants were integrated into community life through a number of different activities.

Community immersion or integration. Beyond the more individualized immersion experiences, there were three areas of shared, community-based immersion within this experience.

1. *Community activities:* The students participated in a variety of community and family events, such as birthday parties, weddings (ceremonies, receptions, dances, etc.), home movies, basketball parties (national playoffs) or day trips (e.g., shopping malls, metropolitan areas, Mexican border towns). The community also arranged for several special events

specifically designed for the university students. Among these were touring a mine where many locals were employed; four-wheeling through the surrounding area and having a full-course picnic; participating in the annual Fourth of July parade; and being serenaded with "las mananitas" and other traditional Mexican folk songs.

2. *Community volunteer:* In the spirit of giving, the university students were encouraged to volunteer their services in the community. Some helped with a reading program at the local library, and others volunteered at the local swimming pool, Little League games, the senior citizen's center, and other local establishments.

3. *"Cultural Enrichment through the Arts" program:* The preservice teachers, along with local and regional Mexican artists, designed and implemented a three-week Mexican art program that was educational and recreational in nature. The "Cultural Enrichment through the Arts" program[3] was probably the most significant way in which we gave to the community as a whole. Since the school district had not had an art program for some time, this was a unique opportunity to nurture creativity and affirm the children's' Mexican American heritage through Mexican art forms.

Experiencing cross-culturalization. In this immersion experience, students were encouraged to find or to create their own place in this predominately Mexican American community. It was a unique experience in rural, southwestern, mining culture as much as it was an experience in ethnic culture. It was not international, yet certainly it was "foreign"—it provided an additional snapshot of American pluralism. Further, the "laboratory" experience provided by the development of a summer arts program added another dimension to these students' study of schooling in nontraditional contexts. Students took on the roles of both a "local" and an "outsider." As a "local," each person became a member of the family—being called daughter or son, and referring to the host family as "my parent(s)." Students began to attempt to view things through the eyes of the locals. As an "outsider" (i.e., being from the Midwest), students analyzed the culture and community from the perspective of a midwesterner (and often from a white, middle-class perspective). Additionally, in this role university students were able to see themselves through the eyes of the local youth. Switching back and forth between these roles provided students with a unique opportunity to reflect upon and reconstruct beliefs and knowledge about both rural, southwestern culture and Mexican American culture. Clearly, it was an exercise in considering multiple perspectives of this particular cultural group. Students were actively involved in the community, volunteering at a number of agencies and recreational activities. The themes of *giving* (i.e., serving others, placing the needs of others above your own) and *respect,* which are often considered characteristic of the Mexican culture, were placed at the forefront of the cultural immersion experience. When planning, we constantly challenged ourselves to think of what would be best for "the community." This was particularly challenging for those students who (a) were still rather egocentric in nature, and (b) would have preferred to have been handed a prepackaged program to implement. Again, students were encouraged to reflect upon their experiences and to construct their own beliefs about Mexican culture, children, teaching, learning, and classroom management. Much of the inquiry and reflection took place in daily debriefing sessions after lunch, but many students also chose to work through their thoughts and feelings in their journals.

Reconstructed reality about Mexican culture. Clearly, several experiences during the few weeks of direct contact in this rural community forced students to challenge, reorganize, or reconstruct their initial beliefs or realities on a number of issues. Beyond being guests in the community, the students were also held in high esteem as future teachers, as leaders in the summer youth program, as willing and enthusiastic learners, and as "adopted" sons and daughters of the host families. Recognizing this high social status perhaps added to the disequilibrium and dissonance, since students are not often treated with such respect and appreciation.

Comments toward the end of the experience illustrate the added depth of the students' thinking about the experience and their personal beliefs.

> "I didn't feel the hopelessness I thought I might. People work hard and struggle, but there is a strength within them. I didn't see much giving up . . . I had to

overcome the sympathy syndrome toward poverty and people living in shacklike homes. What is poverty? How do you define it?"

"I didn't only learn about the Mexican American community, but I learned about the Anglo community as well. . . . Anglos seem to have an outer shell that is hard to get through."

"I was envious of the people in [the community] because they know about their culture. As an African American, I don't. It made me want to know about myself more. Family unity and closeness is very similar to what I have experienced in my own culture."

The selected examples of discovering racism (Activity 1) and becoming culturally immersed (Activity 2) in an unfamiliar cultural setting have been described as using constructivist approaches designed to challenge teachers' thinking about multiculturalism and pluralism. In both examples, learners were able to engage in the processes of reflection, inquiry, and action at their own pace and from their own personal points of departure. Certainly the immersion experience is easily seen as an opportunity to learn *in context*. So, too, is the experience of using imagery as a context for learning about racism with a predominantly white student population in a predominantly white institution and state.

SUMMARY AND CONCLUSIONS

In our own thinking about preparing teachers for becoming culturally competent educators, we have looked critically at how we approach and define multicultural education. As we view it, multicultural education in teacher preparation programs ought to be about preservice teachers having an opportunity and forum for developing their (multi) cultural competence. Integral to the development of multicultural competence is the possession of beliefs that are consistent with and supportive of pluralism in America and the acquisition of a broad, well-grounded multicultural knowledge base.

Given the potential relationship between teachers' beliefs and actual classroom practice, teacher candidates must be challenged to analyze the perceptions and beliefs they hold toward their own and other groups if they are to become competent multicultural educators. Additionally, much learning occurs vicariously (through films and videos, reading, direct observation). For example, beliefs and attitudes are formed on the basis of information about or direct observation of an individual or group. We recognize that a base of multicultural knowledge is essential in the development of multicultural competence, because knowledge has a potential relationship to beliefs and behavior.

We proposed a model (see Figure 10.1) to illustrate the relationships among the variables of beliefs, knowledge, and experiences as a foundation for multicultural education in teacher preparation programs. The teacher preparation program needs to recognize the current, existing reality of the students, particularly with respect to diversity.

We advocate utilizing a constructivist approach to multicultural education that focuses on facilitating the (re)construction of a multicultural knowledge base and the (re)construction of personal beliefs about diversity through the processes of reflection, inquiry, and action. In other words, a teacher's task is to assess what students currently believe (their initial reality) and to plan instructional activities that prompt disequilibrium and subsequently self-regulation (facilitating a reconstructed reality).

To illustrate a constructivist approach to multicultural education, we introduced two examples currently being used to enhance students' understanding and appreciation for cultural diversity (seeing multiple views of racism, and experiencing cultural immersion). We believe that a solid understanding of racism in the United States ought to precede learning about diverse groups and is essential to developing multicultural competence. Further, we described the implementation and results of a cultural immersion experience designed to enhance cultural competence. As individuals' multicultural competence develops, perhaps they will be more likely to increase their own willingness to cross additional, unfamiliar cultural boundaries, and eventually serve as bridges for those who might otherwise avoid such a journey. Indeed, this is an implicit goal of our approach to multicultural education in teacher preparation.

LEARNING TO TEACH IN CROSS-CULTURAL SETTINGS
The Significance of Personal Relations

Linda Valli

Statistics now widely reported in the literature indicate the rapidly changing composition of students in K–12 classrooms. By the year 2000, one out of three students is projected to be an ethnic minority (Banks & Banks, 1989). In contrast, the demographic profile of K–12 teachers has remained stable and homogenous. The majority of teachers are white, married females. According to data collected by American Association for Colleges of Teacher Education, future teachers will mirror this population. They will be white females who went to small town or suburban schools and who intend to teach middle-class students in similar settings (Zimpher & Ashburn, 1992). This cultural mismatch heightens concern that schools will be even less equipped than they are now to provide ethnic minorities with equal and adequate educational experiences.

Although we know that most preservice teachers prefer to teach middle-class students in similar settings, we have little elaborated knowledge of their perceptions of, concerns about, or experiences in culturally diverse schools. Lacking this empirical knowledge, the teacher education curriculum has been left without a solid conceptual basis for incorporating diversity issues. Typically, information about cultural diversity is taught in a separate class or infused in professional education courses. Unfortunately, these approaches can have perverse effects, actually reinforcing the stereotypes they were meant to overcome (McDiarmid, 1992).

This study tracks the experiences of a small cohort of student teachers throughout their semester internship. Its purpose is to explore their initial perceptions and experiences of successfully teaching in cross-cultural settings. An underlying assumption of this study is that teaching in cross-cultural settings raises issues for new teachers that they would not otherwise encounter. Learning about student teaching problems and successes can assist teacher educators in constructing a more meaningful professional preparation curriculum. The theoretical basis for this assumption is constructivism, which posits that for learning to be meaningful, for it to make a difference in one's worldview and social interactions, implicit beliefs must be engaged and reconsidered. This constructivist orientation has informed the growing body of literature on teachers' socialization, the development of professional perspectives, and teaching beliefs (Weinstein, 1989). But with few exceptions (see, for instance, Ross & Smith, 1992), little is reported in the literature regarding beginning teachers' diversity beliefs that are derived from actual experience. Generally studies are based on hypothetical cases (Paine, 1990) or brief intervention strategies (McDiarmid, 1992).

METHODOLOGY

Data were collected throughout the student teaching semester. Two white females were assigned to McDuff, a junior high school whose student body was approximately 95% African-American. Four white students (three females and one male) were assigned to Crandall, a senior high whose racial/ethnic compositions was 40% African-American, 30% European-American, 15% Hispanic-American, and 15% Asian-American. I occasionally draw on the voices and experiences of two other student teachers: one who was part of this cohort group but student teaching in a less diverse school, and one who had been assigned to McDuff the previous semester. Only one student, Matt, had taken a specific course in multicultural education. The others had been briefly introduced to diversity issues through their education courses: foundations, psychology of education, and methods. The emphasis of most of their liberal arts courses was mainstream Western culture.[1]

The findings of the study are based on classroom observations, teaching videotapes, formal interviews, student papers on teaching beliefs, seminar discussions, and casual conversations with a small cohort of student teachers. My interest in this issue started with comments I heard about "city" schools. Many of our students had negative impressions of them and concerns about teaching in them. I began to collect these stories in an informal journal and then generated an open-ended set of questions which I used for taped interviews and for teaching belief papers. Types of questions were "What were your first perceptions of and experiences in this school?" "Have any of these perceptions changed?" "What does it take to be a successful teacher in this school?" A common practice was to tape an interview with students based on information from their papers. I then used standard ethnographic coding procedures to analyze the papers, transcribed interviews, and fieldnotes for themes related to perceptions and changing perceptions of cultural diversity. These themes were confirmed by others who read this chapter: two of the student teachers, one of the university supervisors, and a graduate assistant. The graduate assistant also independently verified themes from student seminar papers and transcribed interviews.

My initial analysis of the data indicates that all the student teachers began their internship semester with apprehensions and misconceptions about their assigned schools. These apprehensions included inability to control and relate to students. Student teachers were also concerned that they would receive some challenges because of their race. Six of the seven students were able to break through their initial fears and cope with confrontations by risking personal relations and revelations with their students. They told students about themselves, asked students about their interests, histories and cultural practices, reacted with humor when called racists, and sought out culturally sensitive curriculum materials. Their pupils came to see these actions as caring about them as individuals and responded with more engaged learning behaviors. The student teacher who had the least successful experience was never able to establish close bonds with her students. Her body language, tone of voice, and referential language all suggest a view of student as "other."

These findings support Erickson's (1987) contention about the importance of teacher-student trust in cross-cultural settings. However, neither the content of that trust nor the way it is constructed is elaborated. This study indicates that building personal relations with students is a significant aspect of the politics of trust and challenges work that deemphasizes the importance of affective aspects of teaching. The study further indicates that not enough emphasis is placed on the significance of personal relations in cross-cultural teaching. In a recent review of the literature, Zeichner (1993) summarizes "aspects of successful teaching for poor students of color" (p. 7). That summary includes high expectations, scaffolding, teacher knowledge, teaching strategies, parent involvement, and assessment. The only reference to the importance of personal bonds came from a private correspondence with Ladson-Billings, whose ethnographic work on culturally relevant teaching suggests the significance of relationships for Afro–North American students (Ladson-Billings & Henry, 1990). An earlier study of Indian and Eskimo students came to the same conclusion (Kleinfeld, 1972). What this small body of research suggests is that prospective teachers will not be able to scaffold, communicate high expectations, or develop culturally-responsive teaching strategies unless they first establish personal relations with their culturally diverse students.

The data analysis begins with the student teachers' apprehensions and misconceptions about their initial teaching experience. In contrast to their "happy, safe, and normal" world, the schools they were entering were "dangerous, disorienting" places. After describing and trying to account for these perceptions, I look at ways in which they began to change. Almost always this change involved student teacher attempts to establish personal trusting relations. Description of this interpersonal work is the heart of the chapter, work that included sharing personal stories, showing interest in students' lives, handling confrontations, and planning multicultural lessons. The chapter ends with some implications for teacher education reform.

APPREHENSIONS AND MISCONCEPTIONS

Like so many student teachers, this group of secondary education interns had few prior experiences in multicultural or predominately black schools. Most of them had attended white, middle-class, suburban public or private schools. Their upbringings had given many of them a "sheltered" or "slanted" view of the world, that of a "happy white community" in which there were few or no people of color:

"I just assumed that everybody was pretty much, like you would say, Irish Americans."

"[I] grew up in a totally nonculturally diverse setting and every single person was white. Every single person was Christian."

"I always associated diversity with problems. . . . I always thought the more diverse a school was, the more problems they're gonna have. . . . I'd always pictured the world as predominantly white, and it wasn't."

These students were concerned that they would not be liked because they were white and that they would have little control over their classes: "I went in with some assumptions . . . that the students were all going to be mean to me, and they weren't gonna like me because I was white . . . and just . . . like that I would probably come up crying because of all the violence in the school, and not being able to handle myself." As one student admitted, "Those preconceptions were because the students were black. I was not sure if they would accept me. I will admit the students' color scared me in the beginning which triggered all of the nervous feeling. . . . I felt that there might be some tension because of our racial differences." Matt felt he had to "defend" himself from students, who would be thinking, "Who is this white person coming into our black school?"

For these students, the "normal" school population was white, Christian, and American—terms that were at times interchangeable in their minds. By definition, then, the schools they were entering were abnormal. Schools composed mainly of African-American students were automatically labeled inner city and dangerous. Students who attended those schools were perceived to be of one type. The preservice teachers initially perceived little social class, ethnic, or academic variation among them. Their thinking occurred in couplets (suburban = white; urban = black; black = poor; urban = inner city; inner city = violent) and in dualisms (black vs. white; urban vs. suburban). One student drew a distinction between "Hispanic-Americans" and "American-born Americans," and when asked "Who is American? Who do you mean by American students?" responded, "Like, Caucasian—white Americans." It is no surprise, then, that when this student teacher came across a group of African-American male students diligently at work in the school library, she eyed them suspiciously: "They must be up to no good!" The equation in her mind was "black male adolescents = poor students and delinquents."

In addition to their sheltered upbringing, several factors reinforced stereotyped and dualistic thinking. There were frequent news reports of drugs, weapons, and violence in area schools; stories of security guards and newly installed electronic security systems; and remarks from families, friends, and roommates such as "I can't believe you're going to teach [there]! You have to get out of that," or "Oh, good luck teaching there! The students are always fighting." Sometimes students mistakenly presumed that Crandall, the suburban school to which they were assigned, was white. For these students, the initial experience of entering a crowded hallway of mostly Black and Hispanic students was one of shock and disorientation. One student said she felt as though she stuck out "like a sore thumb":

> I just got just overwhelmed by. . . . I wasn't . . . I wasn't used to that many minority students, and I guess I just . . . I never pictured myself as prejudiced, I still don't but I was kind of like, "Wow! Like, wait a minute." You know? Walking around with all these kids it's like, you know, heads above me, and I just wasn't prepared for that all. I just wasn't ready.

Initial experiences with students—or stories of other teachers' experiences—also shaped apprehensive perceptions. One student heard rumors among the English department faculty that her lowest-track classes were "inhabited by numerous delinquent students who will not cooperate within the classroom and who are not interested in learning." She was directly told that one of her students "had so angered a teacher of twenty-something years that he lost his temper and struck the student (resulting in the loss of his job)." Students were told about "bad" classes and cautioned not to take on black kids, who might hit you in the face. They were also warned not to get in the middle of a fight since they couldn't be sure students weren't carrying guns or knives. These fears were reinforced by the unpredictable, scowling, or disruptive behavior of individual students. When the school's top wrestler began shoving desks and pushing other students, Christine worried, "So how was I (all 5'2" and 120 pounds of me) going to keep control?"

Gender was a complicating factor for other female students. Alicia felt sexually and racially harassed when a group of Puerto Rican students whistled as she passed them in the hall, and Jessica carried similar memories from a previous field experience in a different school. African-American high school males questioned her presence in their school as she walked through the halls. Like Alicia, Jessica, a youthful-looking blond, had been mistaken for a high school student: "Every time I had walked through the front doors, students would have some kind of nasty or rude comment to make about my color or sex. That had shaken me up a bit and I did not want to go through that again. Those students had intimidated me." She feared that these types of encounters would be repeated at the junior high to which she was assigned and would prevent her from being a teacher:

> I kept imagining . . . what my days . . . were going to be like. . . . At first I visioned the worst. I kept thinking of my experience at St. Joseph. I saw the students just not paying any attention to me, talking while I was talking and just not giving me any ounce of respect. I proceeded to go out and purchase two books on discipline in the Middle School years.

Worrying that there would be a lot of chaos in her assigned placement and that students could physically hurt her, Jessica armed herself with discipline techniques.

ESTABLISHING TRUSTING PERSONAL RELATIONS

Overcoming these fears, apprehensions, suspicions, and stereotypes was essential if these young interns were to have a successful student teaching experience. How did this occur? Certainly the support of administrators and other teachers facilitated the induction process. Not all teachers told horror stories. Many positively mentored the interns, introduced them to students, and initiated them into the school's culture. Fears were also allayed when students saw that buildings were secure, criminals did not roam the halls, and that their pupils were calmer than they anticipated. Not even potentially threatening situations alarmed the interns once they trusted the school administration's ability to handle them. This is a story that Jessica told:

> One day, the kids were telling me that the . . . prior weekend there had been a fight between one of the students at McDuff and another student at another school, and the other student at the other school hap-

pened to be part of a gang. So on Monday morning, or Monday afternoon, the gang was coming back to find this student and beat him, or whatever. And I remember [the principal] calling every class down and escorting them out the back door, and I had to be escorted out the front door to my car because they were afraid that something might happen. . . . But after having been there, you know, eight or nine weeks or so, it wasn't . . . it didn't bother me.

This, however, was not the main type of story I heard from students. In reading their seminar papers, remembering seminar discussions, and listening to the tape recordings of our interview sessions, I was continually struck by the language of personal relationships. In one way or another, they talked about creating an environment of mutual trust and respect. Their own discourse often focused on what they did to break down barriers which, they came to realize, were often of their own making. The process of establishing trusting relations involved removing these obstacles. This was done in various ways, chief among them being risking personal revelations, expressing interest in students as persons, handling direct confrontations, and enacting a culturally responsive curriculum. So although the support of teachers and administrators laid the foundation for a successful semester, it was not the primary factor. The student teachers themselves had to work hard at constructing relationships with their students. They had to be able to deal with confrontations, banter with students, and discuss personal—including racial—matters. Their willingness to engage with students in these ways established the connections necessary for them to overcome barriers to teaching in these settings.

Risking Personal Revelations

Pupil relations often present a quandary for student teachers, especially at the high school level. Sometimes only four years older than their pupils, they find themselves wanting to casually relate to their pupils, but pull back for fear of not seeming professional. How to be teacher and friend (or whether to be friend) is a constant tension. On the one hand, they want respect and believe they must distance themselves and establish rules to earn it. On the other hand, they want to be liked. They want students to affirm their person as well as their professional role.

This tension was increased for these white student teachers in their culturally diverse and predominantly black schools. Initial fears of being neither liked nor respected were intense, making it more difficult, but more important, to quickly and skillfully find ways of establishing connections that balanced the personal and professional. Seminar discussions indicated that the interns were consciously working out this dilemma. Sometimes they were too friendly; sometimes too distant. The greater danger, however, appeared to be distance: the failure to let their pupils know they cared about and trusted them enough to let them into their own personal lives.

Classes, cooperating teachers, and individual pupils often gave the interns opportunities to connect through personal stories. The interns talked about their families, the kind of schools they went to, where they lived, their university experiences, job interviews, hobbies, and so forth. On her first student teaching day, for instance, Alicia, whose "anxiety grew" as she made her way to her classroom, was immediately put at ease by her classes and cooperating teacher. Mr. Johnson told her about the school and students, walked her around the school, introduced her to other faculty members, and had her spend the first day in front of the room talking to his classes.

> Mr. Johnson introduced me, and then we just kind of, you know, talked. . . . They asked me questions about where I went to school, where I was from, and, you know, I did the same with them. . . . It was nice.

> I realized that my fears were senseless. All of the students were polite and friendly. I wasn't being looked down upon in the hallways but smiled at. Once I was at Crandall for a couple of weeks, those same faces that used to intimidate me were now the familiar faces of many of my and the other student teachers' students.

About three or four weeks into the semester, Jessica decided to spend some classtime telling her junior high students about herself: "I just knew they were dying to ask me questions." She had regularly engaged in casual conversation with them about sports or news events as they entered the room, but felt that even more personal connection was necessary. Feeling that she was spending too much time quieting or reprimanding her students, Jessica told Mr. Varnum, "I just feel like I'm bitching all the time at these students, and it just seems too tedious for me." Letting students ask her personal, but not unbounded, questions seemed to create a more friendly, less tedious environment in which Jessica felt "much happier." Her "loosening up a bit" was appreciated by students, who candidly told her on the last day of class: "When you first came in here we didn't like you because we thought you were so strict and so mean, but then you were really cool." Having been intimidated by race differences, Jessica had armed herself with classroom management books and a list of rules. Because of this fear, she also misinterpreted her cooperating teacher's suggestion to structure lessons carefully as advice to maintain a highly structured (teacher-controlled) classroom which put her at an uncomfortable distance from her students. By allowing the person of Jessica to come through the role of Ms. Stevens, Jessica began to establish some much-needed connections. The student teachers took the risk, in other words, of presenting themselves as real people who were open and, thus, vulnerable.

Sometimes "connecting" occasions took a light "racial" turn, as when Claire's students teased her about her "white" taste in music and lack of rhythm or when Helen's asked if it "felt different to be white." Her junior high girls were so fascinated with her straight, blond hair that they often touched it and asked if she used a perm to straighten it or baby oil to get it so soft. During his pre-student teaching experience at McDuff, Matt's junior high students pointedly asked how he felt about being in a black school. He responded and just as directly asked how they felt about having a white teacher. Matt spent many class periods after that engaged in discussions about race, which was an important aspect of self-disclosure. The junior high students in particular, some of whom had never had a white teacher, seemed to need to explore that aspect of their relation with the student teachers. Talking about race, especially with a white person, was a rare experience.

There were also occasions when self-revelations were evoked in a private, almost counseling-like context. One such occasion occurred when Christine's student Shanita returned to school after being institutionalized and labeled schizophrenic. Following a violent school incident, Shanita told Christine that she was ashamed and worried about future episodes. Empathizing with her fear, Christine decided to share her own story of demolishing her bedroom one day when, as a young girl, she had stored up too much anger. Christine assured Shanita that she wasn't a freak, but that she did need "to develop skills in coping with anger and stress." This advice echoed that which was given by Shanita's doctors. As the semester went on, Shanita became better at resolving ("though not ignoring") problems with other students. She also "chose speech topics that revealed the problems against which she was struggling." Her classmates listened closely to her and many "became very protective and sensitive to her problems." By connecting with Shanita through an empathic disclosure, Christine seemed to open up a space for Shanita to deal with her anger and turmoil.

The interns' willingness to share their lives seemed to make a big difference in their comfort level with students and in their students' feelings about them. Claire, whose reputation spread among her peers for her ability to connect with her students, concluded about her intern experience: "I could not believe how interested they were in my own life. . . . I let them know about my painting and I would talk about that and how I was doing it, and they would ask me how it was coming, and things like that. . . . I really developed a special relationship with many of my students. I think when you share your own thoughts and ideas and personal stories, the class becomes more accepting and doesn't look at coming to class as a chore."

Evoking Student Voice

As many of these incidents indicate, the telling of stories was often a reciprocal event. While student teachers had to be trusting enough to let students into their lives, they simultaneously expressed interest in their pupils' lives. As indicated earlier, learning about their students helped decrease their apprehension. As Alice admitted, "I had to get to know them before I could feel that comfortable around them and realize that, you know, it [my fear] was stupid." Listening to student stories (consciously evoking their voices) also provided a way for student teachers to express personal concern and caring, to engage students in classroom activities, and to learn from their students. Referring to her students, Jessica, for instance, reported: "They told me that they really thought I took a genuine interest in them as people and not just as students." Throughout the semester, the student teachers constantly referred to how much they were learning because of cultural differences. Their obvious enjoyment of their learning role reversed the typical teacher-student relation and occasioned deeper trust and respect.

The studio setting of the art room provided Claire with multiple opportunities to express personal interest. She never spent class time at her desk. Except for the time she introduced and explained new projects, Claire walked the room, monitoring and assisting with projects. During that time, she tried to do more than comment on design and composition. In fact, that was often merely the occasion to engage in more personal discourse. "I never sit at . . . I never used the desk, only to take attendance, and then I'm always walking. . . . I always make sure I hit every table, and I talk to everybody. And, of course, you know, watch what they're doing on their project."

So while never losing focus on the task at hand and constantly being wary of "not being too much on their level," Claire would talk with students about work and home lives, music concerts and preferences, and so forth. Since her students often chose to seat themselves according to their native language, Claire could recruit the more fluent English speakers in translating her conversations with those who had not yet developed much proficiency in the English language. In this way she was able to express interest and concern; she could attend to her students as both students and persons. Developing friendships and getting to know students on a personal level was Claire's most important student teaching accomplishment: "I got to know them as individuals, each student as an individual, and I think that's important. . . . I knew a little bit about each one. Like what sports they played, and what they're interested in beside just coming to art class, and things like that. Not really so much what race they were or language they spoke. You kind of forget about that after awhile."

Other student teachers, whose classes were more formally structured around direct instruction, group discussion, and individual presentations, had to find other ways of expressing personal interest in their students' lives. They were able to do this through group discussions, individual projects, and before- or after-class conversations. Alicia, for instance, tried to bring students' personal experiences into her discussion of literature. "I showed an interest in their interests, and they appreciated the personal touch I tried to give to my lessons." Matt gave students a lot of choice on social studies projects. He often distributed lists of possibilities. Christine, who taught drama and public speaking, encouraged students to draw on meaningful life experiences for their speeches: "I always encouraged them to share something of importance to themselves within the class, and in this way, we got to know the students through introduction, demonstration, information, and personal narrative speeches."

Learning about students' interests was also a way of decreasing school alienation and engaging students in class assignments. Christine's writing focused extensively on this matter. By speaking privately and personally to students, Christine was able to encourage class engagement from withdrawn students. Latika, a Nigerian student, had developed the habit of resting her head on her desk. After Christine privately encouraged her to contribute and promised help in improving her English, she began smiling and interacting with peers and participated frequently. She became personable and confident about classroom assignments. Christine also convinced Terrance, who missed the first few weeks of schools due to chicken pox, that failure wasn't inevitable. To do this, she had to discover his area of interest (basketball), become knowledgeable, and initiate basketball conversations before he was willing to come to school early for tutoring and missed assignments.

Privately initiated conversations also helped Christine engage students who had been regularly rude and disruptive. As with Terrance, Christine connected with Hakim over sports. This time she was fortunate to have some knowledge of the sport he participated in: wrestling. After talking to him about "the different holds, the strict training regimen, and about the ridiculous starvation diets of a wrestler," Christine was consistently greeted with "high-fives" at the start of each class. Hakim created few disruptions in class after that and also "convinced several of his peers to cooperate with me."

Christine had similar success with Anissa, a student she described as "extremely intelligent" but who constantly disturbed her cooperating teacher with "rude comments." Christine decided to speak to Anissa each day during her pre–student teaching observation period. She commented on what a "great outfit" Anissa was wearing, explained why she was there, and so forth. Anissa began to gradually confide in Christine, telling her about "her friends, her interests, and her horrible living situation." When Christine assumed responsibility for teaching this class, Anissa moved to the front and became involved in classroom activities. The two became good friends. When Christine commented about her transformation, Anissa responded that she hadn't known she had any intelligence before this. She promised not to waste it. In her final seminar paper, Christine commented: "It is difficult to believe that my relationship with Anissa began with a simple comment about an outfit." She described personal relations as the "one real disciplinary tool which worked effectively for me. . . . I found that with the relationships that we had formed . . . they did not want to interrupt or disappoint me. Many of these students even stopped their peers from misbehaving so that I did not have to waste so much time or energy on disciplinary measures." In a casual conversation with me just before her graduation, Christine said she could not believe how quickly paying a little attention to some students could make a difference in their reaction to her.

By deliberately evoking student voice, the interns placed their students in the role of teacher. Everyone in the classroom became learners together.

> "Perhaps that's yet another reason why I want to teach at a school like Crandall. Every day is different, and every day I learned something new about my students."

> "I just got all excited in this environment that I had never been in and learned all these new things. . . . every day I learned. . . . And they liked the fact that they could tell me . . . teach me new words, or show me new music."

Helen's students delighted her with superstitions and myths from their cultures, and Evelyn's informed her about Africa: its size, diversity, traditions, and rituals. "One of the boys was talking about when they reach a certain age, they'll have kind of a group blessing, and they're saying, 'Now you have all the responsibilities of an adult, and you have the privileges of an adult.'"

Matt found Crandall High to be an ideal situation for creating a multicultural curriculum. His culturally diverse students served as resources for himself and each other: "Like if I was teaching on Jainism I had a Jain student come in that could talk to them." He bemoaned his own limiting monocultural education "because so many misconceptions form out of not knowing, not experiencing. Where I grew up, it was a terrible, terrible racism."

Art projects were an excellent opportunity for Claire to encourage cultural expression and learn from her students. Fortunate to have a cooperating teacher who had just finished writing a book about teaching multicultural art, Claire was amazed at the variety of work her students produced: "You know, you teach this one lesson and then students interpret it all different ways, and it's just great, and it inspires me in my work." She talked about different uses of color and symbols and different orientations to perspective and design. Like Matt, she also encouraged her students to be resources. A Somali student acted as informal judge of the African masks her fundamental's class produced: "He could point out which part of Africa each of the masks came from just by observing the shape and design of the masks! What an excellent resource to see if our masks were authentic!"

The interns' definitions of a good teacher often included learning from their students: "Let them teach you something. That seemed to work a lot. Me asking them questions rather than them always asking me questions and letting them know that I do want to learn more about them, and that I don't know everything about different [cultures]." Other student teachers similarly observed that students like teachers who get them involved, who show an interest in their lives, and who are having a good time. They tend not to like those who are all work, can't relate to their personal lives, and "remain distant."

Coping with Confrontations

Sharing stories about themselves and eliciting stories about their students were not, however, enough to cover the cultural space between the student teachers and all their pupils. The issue of cultural difference continued to crop up—sometimes humorously, at other times more seriously. In both types of situations, the student teachers had to be willing and able to handle racial texts and confrontations.

Claire seemed to maintain the most lighthearted interchange with her students. The informal climate of the art studio enhanced her inclination to engage, relate, and interact. In most classes, Claire played background music as a way of prompting more "right brain" activity. She wanted to release the intuitive rather than the rational. Students took turns selecting the music, much of which was unfamiliar to Claire. This often resulted in student laughter and comments such as white people "can't dance" or "can't sing it right." Rather than be offended, Claire laughed along with her students and commented in her interview about the importance of humor. When students used terms outside her frame of reference like *lunchbox, BAMA,* and *carrying,* she treated them as learning opportunities, expressing interest in the new adolescent lexicon.

Becoming adept at "carrying" was a way Matt connected with his students. At first thinking it was mere rudeness, Matt eventually found out that "carrying" is more a demonstration of verbal skill: having the ability to "carry" the conversation to higher levels of "friendly insult." During his first weeks at Crandall when a student said something sarcastic like "Oh, nice pants, Mr. G." he would just ignore it. He wasn't pleased with his response, thinking it somehow "didn't look good," but was at a loss about an appropriate respond. Fortunately a "carrying" event occurred in front of another teacher, who let Matt in on its mysteries. Although Matt was initially uncomfortable with this type of verbal interaction ("I can't believe I told that kid that!"), he eventually became so proficient that a student remarked, "You didn't have to carry me *that* much!" Matt learned that friendly banter did not necessarily diminish teaching authority. He remained wary, however, of teachers who seemed to cross the line.[2]

Not all the interns mentioned "carrying," but in one way or another, they were all expected to be adroit and comfortable with racial and cultural expressions. Jessica, a fair-skinned blond, evoked a round of appreciative laughter as she waited outside the school building one day after school. A friend, who came to pick her up after school, drove past her as she stood in the midst of her African-American students. "I can't believe it," she joked. "It's not like I don't stand out in this crowd!" Claire got a similar humorous response in a painting class following her use of the Spanish "negro." As she wrote in a seminar paper about this unintended incident:

> I was trying to communicate with a Hispanic student and tell him to use some black. The Spanish word for black is negro so I repeatedly used the word, and every time I did, my student Leroy kept saying "what". Finally I said to Leroy, "I haven't been asking you anything, why do you keep saying what?" His reply was, "Don't you keep saying negro?!!" At that point we all lost it.

Student teachers seemed to do better when they acknowledged rather than ignored racial differences. Pretending that differences did not exist put more distance between the interns and their students. Dealing with their own whiteness—and students' color—was a way of connecting. It helped address student concerns about teacher prejudice and discrimination.

These concerns about prejudice often came when students felt that they might be or had been treated unfairly. Student "tests" or accusations of prejudice were more prevalent at the predominantly black junior high than it was at the multicultural high school. Incidents occurred at both places, however. At the end of her student teaching, Jessica wrote:

> The students told me that they found it sometimes difficult to have a white teacher. . . . They said that because they were black and I—white, I would grade them harder and smother them with work. . . . I asked them why they thought that way. They responded honestly. They thought that I might have had something against black people because they picked up on my hesitation when I was doing my observations.

Other interns reported similar incidents of hearing themselves or other white teachers called prejudiced or racist. This occurred both in "stage whispers" behind their backs and in face-to-face confrontations. They received remarks such as "If a white teacher hadn't suspended me. . . . I heard you were a racist. . . . I got this bad grade because I'm black and she's white. . . . They don't respect you because of your complexion. . . . He's trying to make me white. . . . You're just yelling at me because I'm black. . . . All the book [*Sing Down the Moon*] made me do is hate white people more. . . . Black History month is just something to shut us up with. . . . You whites think you are better than us because you enslaved us for hundreds of years. . . . Blacks are superior because any time there's a baby born between a white and a black person, the baby turns out black, so that means black genes must be better."

Interns did well to seize opportunities when they could. Sometimes simple rejoinders were helpful. Student teachers reported such remarks as "Look, do you think I would be teaching in this school if I were racist?" or "Other students got good grades and *they're* black!" It seems that some students needed to actually hear their teachers deny being racist. It was an issue that for some had to be dealt with in a direct confrontational manner. This usually happened with younger students who had almost no prior contact with whites. It seems as though the teachers had to assure their students that they could relate to them as a person and not an inferior classification.

Generally, however, concerns about racism required more prolonged interactions. A number of the student teachers commented on the need to prove that they weren't racist and to establish trust before they could engage in sensitive discussions with students about race relations. In an early discussion McDuff students had about *Eyes on the Prize*, Matt experienced what he called "hostility towards . . . all whites in general." He spent a lot of time talking with students about the civil rights movement but also had to field comments about the Mike Tyson trial, the superiority of black genes, and his own beliefs about racism. Believing that many of the students had never had the opportunity to discuss such matters with a white person before, he encouraged open conversations and personal questioning: "I tried to ask them why they felt this way and talked to them about my culture and where I came from, and how I feel, and try to get them to talk about how they felt." These conversations seemed to persuade students that Matt was trustworthy and that not all whites were racists who belonged to the Ku Klux Klan.

Some students, however, stood firm in their accusations of racism. Christine in particular seemed to be confronted by vocal and volatile students. But rather than distance herself, punish students, or ignore comments, she entered the fray, refusing to be defeated, dismissed, or disempowered. Her most difficult challenge was Alonzo, an unusually talented student who, refusing to do any work, constantly referred to her as "master" and referred to drama as "white man's stuff."

On the first day of class, Alonzo insisted on being called "Big Pimp" and refused to respond to his real name. He wanted to be paid to do assignments, asked Christine how she could still use the ball and chain on him, and ignored work with the remark "I am no longer your slave. . . . Three hundred years ago, my father didn't get to write, and now you take away my freedom by making me write." Arguing to the contrary that she was trying to "aid in his liberation," Christine later wrote that "the hardships of those who had been so unjustly enslaved seemed somehow diminished by this student trying to get out of his assignments." The semester continued as a struggle. Christine persisted in presenting education and drama as important to blacks; Alonzo persisted in his counterarguments and resistance. Although she felt her success to be limited, by the end of the semester Alonzo finally did a presentation which, Christine writes, "brought the house down."

Enacting a Responsive Curriculum

Many educators have promoted the importance of a culturally responsive pedagogy. Most have been in the context of raising student self-esteem, promoting cultural identity for marginalized groups, or correcting a Western-dominated view of the world (Banks & Banks, 1989). From my interviews with these student teachers, I began to consider another reason, one that is less cognitive and more relational. By developing a curriculum that was multicultural and attending to various learning styles and needs, the student teachers were communicating to their pupils in yet another way that they cared about them. They cared about them as students, so they wanted to help them be academically successful. And they cared about them as people, so they attended to meaningful cultural constructions.

Also missing from much of the literature on multicultural education is the importance of the curriculum to the teacher as well as the students. These young teachers were learning, relearning, and unlearning in ways that were as significant for themselves as they were for their students. Claire enjoyed creating a multicultural art curriculum so she could select areas she did not know much about and learn with her students. Matt talked about relearning history as he taught: "When I took a world history course, all I learned was Western history." Jessica expanded this theme: "I just went to such a good high school and I thought I got such a great education, but I just got one version of history, and there were so many . . . I did not even celebrate Black History Month, I didn't learn about any famous black people, and I think that that's . . . that is being deprived." She felt challenged to become a "more well-rounded teacher and person" by teaching with an Afrocentric focus.

Claire did extensive research at the Museum of African Art, from which she brought back to her students African art books and audiotapes of African music. Jessica taught units on race relations and civil rights, incorporated the roles of blacks and women in the American Revolution, and reexamined slavery from the slave's perspective "as opposed to the European-white male story." As project choices, Matt included the Hispanic or Mexican influence on the cowboy and the role of women on the Western

Plains. He set up simulated debates between W.E.B. DuBois and Booker T. Washington and, in the unit covering the Spanish-American War, engaged students in considering why Mexicans might call these events the American invasion. He also covered racial segregation in the military, the role of the 93rd Division in World War II, and the treatment of black soldiers when they returned home as heroes. Helen discovered there were only four minority writers in her literature anthology and so supplemented poetry in the text with rap and poetry written by minorities.

Several courses to which student teachers were assigned lent themselves to individual or group projects. The student teachers often encouraged their pupils to be culturally expressive in these curricular spaces. Matt and Alicia both engaged their students in heritage projects. For Alicia, "the results were amazing. We heard stories from all over the world: Africa, Haiti, Japan, Vietnam, Spain, Ireland, Italy, Russia, Czechoslovakia, Romania, the list went on and on." Claire had her art students paint symbolic self-portraits after they studied Frida Kahlo, a Mexican artist. Like Alicia, she marveled at how much she learned by questioning her culturally diverse class about their symbols. "Many symbols were cultural icons that I never knew about."

More than any other student teacher, Matt had given the nature of the curriculum considerable thought. Although the English and art student teachers at Crandall High School were impressed with the multicultural nature of the curriculum and those at McDuff called their curriculum Afrocentric, Matt had the impression "that some teachers included other cultures in their curriculum just because they were told they had to by the higher administration." Instead of consistently grappling with the question "What are we trying to teach?" Matt found teachers covering multicultural content "quickly" and briefly "so they could add enough questions about women and minorities on the final examination to appease school district authorities."

Balking at this approach to curriculum construction, Matt talked about how multicultural education has to be authentic, how you can't spend hours discussing "this obsolete [white] person that I never even heard about" and then spend only two or three minutes on Booker T. Washington. Based partially on these experiences, Matt developed a framework for successful teaching in culturally diverse schools that included respecting students' backgrounds, discussing different cultures in the curriculum, giving students opportunities to explore their culture and other cultures, and honestly dealing with current cultural issues. "Students can tell when you include information about culture as a token fact or activity."

With one of his students who exhibited deep-seated school alienation (boredom, disenchantment, inattentiveness, and sarcasm), Matt made special arrangements. Concerned at first that the student was only interested in his own culture, Matt eventually decided that "Antoin probably has learned a lot about the mainstream culture through his experience in a white dominated society." Matt decided to let Antoin "investigate more about his culture and let his contribution to the class be through this route." Matt let Antoin develop his own project and decide who would be involved, what it would include, and how it would be evaluated. As a result of this individual and cultural accommodation, Matt claims that Antoin became more attentive, participated more, and did better on tests and quizzes: "I think what needed to happen was that he had to realize and I had to show that I respected him and his heritage. Once I gained his respect, the lines of communication were open and he was willing to learn not only about his culture, but also about my culture and the culture of his classmates."

Helen had similar concerns about students wanting to learn *only* about their culture. She worried about this because she saw disinterest in anything that wasn't "about them" and a tendency for students to negatively stereotype other groups. She believed that learning about other cultures would help her students interact better in the outside world. But like Matt, Helen eventually decided that "if [students] gain an appreciation of their own culture first, then they will be able to appreciate others more easily." Perhaps what these students are really learning is that the teacher respects them enough to care about including their culture in the curriculum.

But implementing a multicultural curriculum did not always result in more engaged learning or improved classroom relations. The student teachers had to be prepared for the limitations and unanticipated consequences of their actions. During a unit on personal narrative speeches in a culturally diverse class, Christine reported an incident which "absolutely horrified me. It made me aware of the fact that racial barriers are still very real, despite the illusion of peace and harmony which generally exists within my classroom." A Guatemalan student, Ramona, told about coming to America. Overcoming her reticence and second-language problems, Ramona narrated the story of a family who entered the U.S. illegally to save a dying sister, "traveling in subhuman conditions so they would not be discovered by the police." These controversial words struck a nerve in some of Ramona's classmates, who interrupted with shouts of "spic." Feeling she could neither ignore the comments nor handle the disruption merely by assigning detentions, Christine recalled two other speeches that day which focused on racial tensions. One African-American student had spoken about being harassed by police, another about being called "nigger" in a restaurant.

Christine reminded the class about the speeches and asked who had experienced racial discrimination. After several students told their stories and how such treatment made them feel, Christine pointed out the similarities of humiliation and degradation, despite differences in background and culture, and the need to create "at least one environment in which each individual could feel safe from racial discrimination." When students responded that nothing could be done to stop racial hatred and racism in the United States, Christine mentioned the cross-cultural friendship patterns in the classroom, their willingness to defend each other and "to fight against the ignorance which lies at the root of racism by simply getting to know one another." Asking again what they could do to eliminate racism, several students responded: getting to know people from various cultures, refusing to use racial slurs and insults, and bringing their culturally different friends into their neighborhoods and homes. Although Christine's attempts to provide a culturally responsive curriculum had the unintended effect of eliciting cultural insensitivity, she was able to use the occasion for deeper lessons on race and racism. This type of spontaneous pedagogy is difficult, however, for even the most experienced teacher.

Although few student teachers encountered a situation as volatile as Christine's, they all found themselves having to be flexible and adaptable in responding to student needs. Conscious of both individual and cultural differences, Matt deliberately varied his teaching style. "On one day I might lecture using advanced organizers, the next day I might use a cooperative learning strategy." Frustrated that other teachers let a Spanish-speaking student do other work in class or "sit and do nothing," Jessica was determined to help Carla learn history. She moved her next to a bilingual student who could be an interpreter, met with her two days a week after school, and let her take tests orally: "This system has worked wonderfully so far. She is more involved in the class and puts the effort in that I expect her to." Jessica also kept "un-engaged" students after class. If they needed extra help, she met with them before or after school. If the problem was personal, she "laid off," but reminded them of their responsibility. Determined not to let any students submit incomplete assignments or get poor grades, Jessica tried not to move ahead until students felt comfortable with the material they were having trouble with.

Claire approximated that she had fifteen ESOL (English for Speakers of Other Languages) students in any given class. Not anticipating this language barrier, Claire kept searching for new ways to explain lessons. She used a lot of visuals, and constantly walked around the room so she could pick up on what students did not understand. Like Jessica, she employed bilingual students to interpret and picked up a few Spanish words herself. She also regularly prepared a handout with step-by-step instructions for each art project.

In addition to being demanding and accommodating in their teaching relations, the teacher found that fairness seemed to be an important part of the pedagogical relationship. Rather than using normative grading, Claire carefully constructed an elaborate, individualized grading system. Each art project received four grades. One was always effort, and the other three depended on project objectives: techniques, color schemes, composition, and so forth. Claire believed it was important that students see a grade for effort, that "they know that you know that they tried."

Student evaluations at the end of the semester confirmed Jessica's impression that the reason students respected and listened to her was that she was fair. Though not "lenient," she gave students second chances and opportunities to make up work. Foremost in her mind and in her relations with students was their academic success. Her notion of fairness was closely linked to her belief that she was there to help all students succeed. Believing that she should give everyone "equal treatment and time" (supplemented by out-of-class assistance), Jessica took issue with other teachers on a required History Day project. Her objection was "the special treatment that certain students have received over other students. . . . I am not crying foul play nor implying "favoritism." Yet the extra attention some students have received for the duration of the project preparation is an issue that is of great concern to me."

Since the projects were part of a local and national competition, teachers felt pressure to win. This reflected well on the school and the teacher. To accomplish this goal, Jessica perceived that teachers worked with individual students and groups with "potential" and "completely neglected" other students. This pattern violated Jessica's sense of equity and her belief that learning best occurs when it involves discovering things for yourself, not getting "all of the tips from the teacher." She was especially troubled because these projects counted for as much as 50 percent of student grades for the third marking period. So, departing from accepted practice, Jessica tried to give all the students equal time and treatment." She walked around and answered questions, but "never did I spend half a class period trying to help a group fix up their board."

DISCUSSION

The misconceptions and apprehensions of preservice teachers must be pedagogically engaged. Otherwise, as constructivist theory indicates, there is little hope for the kind of cognitive transformation that occurred in the student teachers reported in this study. Their negative stereotypes and fears, their dualistic thinking about race, and their sheltered worldviews were immediately challenged by their internship placements and nonthreatening seminar discussions. The students learned that they *could* teach in cross-cultural settings, that, in fact, they liked teaching in these settings, that personal relations were a prerequisite to teaching success, and that diversity and interracial discourse were not problems to avoid, but resources to treasure.

This is not meant to suggest, however, that these student teachers did everything right or that their actions solved all the educational and social problems that accompany cultural diversity. Matt realized early in the semester, for instance, that the purpose of learning was not self-evident to students. So he discussed with his classes why they study history and "what kind of history" should be studied. Reasons students gave for studying other cultures included ending racism, understanding different cultures, breaking down barriers, and being more educated. But not all students bought into this ideology. A small group of African-American males shunned other black students who were academically successful and failed their classes in disproportionate numbers. They muttered comments about classmates such as "Well, what is he doing? What is he tryin' to show?" and about teachers, "He's tryin' to make me white." Matt was frustrated by the absence of minorities among the faculty and attributed student alienation to the perception that education was white imposition: "I think one of the reasons [for failure] is 'cause they don't see it as. . . . They see it as something that the white race is forcing upon them. But if they see that you can succeed, you can keep your culture, and you can . . . and it is part of the African-American culture to become educated, and to . . . you can succeed, that it's possible." Although the student teachers were not successful in relating to all their students and seldom moved beyond a white, middle-class construction of schools as meritocracies, the situations in which they experienced most success involved establishing trusting relations. As Ladson-Billings and Henry (1990) discovered in their study of effective teachers, "Culturally relevant liberatory pedagogy is as much about relationships as it is about pedagogy per se. . . . without the relationship, there is no real teaching and learning" (p. 85).

Informed by constructivist theory, this chapter suggests that teacher educators, cooperating teachers, and supervisors need to work with student teachers to help them voice and overcome apprehensions about student teaching in cross-cultural settings. When prospective teachers are helped to understand the importance of personal relations and to develop interpersonal skills, more teachers are likely to want to teach in culturally diverse schools and will be able to teach in them successfully.

Teacher education programs should assist students in directly confronting their own racial ignorance, fears, and stereotypes. They should help prospective teachers situate their own feelings and their students' questions in the larger context of U.S. racial history. This can be done through autobiographies, case studies, role-playing, early field experiences, seminar discussions, and more rigorous attention to diversity issues throughout the liberal arts curriculum. To help overcome stereotypes and perceptions of "the other," prospective teachers can read short stories and autobiographical sketches representing a variety of cultures. They can also shadow and interview students in their field placements and write educational position papers from culturally diverse perspectives.

Field experiences should be carefully monitored to prevent unintended learning. Field sites and past student experiences should be described to help interns deconstruct their prior conceptions. Giving preservice teachers real roles to play in the classroom will prevent them from feeling like "outsiders" and establishing distance from their students—distance that will later be difficult to overcome. Field sites should also be carefully selected. They should have a strong but accessible administration, and teachers who have positive attitudes toward their students and are willing to discuss race issues and concerns. The school should have a multicultural curriculum focus and resources available for the student teacher.

Prospective teachers need to be taught explicitly about the importance of creating classroom environments in which there is mutual trust and respect. They should be taught the significance of body language, informal conversations, and risk taking. Videotapes can be used to contrast relational styles. Trusting classrooms do not naturally spring into existence. They must be constantly and consciously constructed by teachers and students. Although, as this study indicates, some students resist this construction, most seem eager for the teacher to be trusting enough to reach across cultural barriers. These student teachers accomplished that feat by working on personal relations through several routes: being interested in students' lives, sharing their own lives, accepting racial challenges, and creating a multicultural curriculum and classroom environment. These types of successes should be shared with prospective students. Absent trusting relations, new teachers will not be effective in cross-cultural settings, no matter how sound their subject matter and pedagogical knowledge.

COALITION BUILDING AS A MEANS FOR CHANGING TEACHERS' CULTURAL KNOWLEDGE ABOUT MULTICULTURAL EDUCATION

Marilynne Boyle-Baise
Judith Washburn

It is not unusual to despair about the possibility of change in schools. Sarason (1993) urges us to consider the complexities inherent in the nature of change: "Changing the personal-psychological life-style of a single individual is no easy task. Effecting such a change in many individuals embedded in a complicated human system is galactically more difficult" (pp. 212–216). He argues that it is the "repairing, redirecting, and reorganizing" (p. 216) of systems that is difficult and often discouraging. Sarason proposes that there is more potential in preventing than repairing problems and challenges educators to create new settings to resolve old dilemmas. He cautions that "the process of creating a new system is not for the fainthearted or the light-headed or those with tunnel vision" (p.27), and the process must begin by answering the question: What do you want to prevent? (p.42).

The authors of this chapter, like most multicultural educators, want to prevent "monocultural" teaching that is biased toward one racial, ethnic, gender, social class, linguistic, or exceptionality group. This is a tall order, and review of the history of staff development for multicultural education shows that we are not sure how best to proceed.

REVIEWING MULTICULTURAL REFORM HISTORY

Although there are a number of proposals for training teachers to provide multicultural education (e.g., Gay, 1977; Grant & Melnick,1978; Nicolai-Mays & Davis, 1986), studies of actual staff development efforts are limited (Boyle, 1982; Grant & Grant, 1985; Hawley et al., 1983; King, 1980; Sleeter, 1992; Washington, 1981). Several of these studies describe staff development programs as voluntary, short term, lacking in long-range planning, and focused on attitudinal change (Hawley et al., 1983; King, 1980; Washington, 1981). Results of these efforts were mixed: some stimulated more positive attitudes (King, 1980), whereas others led to negative attitudes (Washington, 1981). Overall, findings were questionable because most were based primarily on teachers' self-evaluations of attitudinal change (Hawley et al., 1983).

We are more encouraged by studies of programs that responded to these shortcomings. In the following studies, development programs were extensive or intensive experiences centered around activities to develop awareness, acceptance, and affirmation of multicultural education (Boyle, 1982; Grant & Grant, 1985; Sleeter, 1992). Multicultural education was approached as a complex and visionary concept that required major changes in curriculum and instruction. Teachers (and a few principals) attended development programs voluntarily and accumulated fourteen to fifteen full days of training.

Following an intensive institute (Boyle, 1982) or a long-term training schedule (Sleeter, 1992), teachers were found to be at the awareness stage of learning, and little overall change was noted in classroom behavior. However, particular groups of teachers changed more than others and made attempts to include multicultural concepts in curriculum and instruction. Those making the most change included special education teachers, teachers of elective subjects (e.g., home economics, art, music), social studies teachers, and teachers of color.

After an intensive, "live-in" institute that fostered an esprit de corps among a select group of Teacher Corps candidates, Grant and Grant (1985) reported more positive results. According to a follow-up questionnaire, respondents seemed to be at the acceptance stage of learning but reported that they read more material and consulted with "institute buddies" (p.10) to continue to increase their awareness of multicultural education. Almost all respondents made some curricular modifications to include contributions of people of color and women.

Several additional studies showed that teachers willing to challenge monocultural teaching were already at work in schools. Moll (1988) identified two language arts teachers who were particularly effective with Latino students. He found that they were "theoretically equipped" (p.470) to justify what they considered best for children, and politically prepared to "buck the system" (p. 470) for their students. These teachers relied upon a support group of like-minded colleagues from other schools and a nearby university.

Ladson-Billings (1989) studied eight female teachers, both black and white, identified by parents and principals as "best" teachers for African-American students. She found that these teachers taught in a "culturally relevant" (p.18) manner, in contrast to the "assimilationist" (p.18) practices of most teachers. These teachers perceived themselves as part of the community, considered success possible for black students, and realized the biased nature of school knowledge.

Sleeter (1992) described two teachers who stood apart from the rest of the participants in her study; they initiated major changes in their teaching prior to the staff development program and continued instituting changes after the program ended. She found these teachers undaunted about "rocking the boat" (p.207) to bring about change, and proposed that "boat-rockers" are part of the teaching corps and need only to be given a "push and support" (p.207).

According to these studies, some groups of teachers seemed more amenable to change than others. An intensive format, which included team building, appeared to aid further learning. Teachers were likely to be at the awareness stage of learning at the conclusion of staff development efforts. Culturally relevant teachers needed to be identified and supported. A firm commitment to a vision of success for all students seemed necessary for multicultural teaching. There was also some indication of need for collegial support groups.

This research suggests caveats and provides broad parameters for change efforts. We are honored to have been part of a change effort that was conceived with these considerations in mind, but which became a new genre of its own. The story of this effort is reported here and considered in light of this reform history.

INTRODUCING THE COALITION

The Coalition for Education That Is Multicultural (the Coalition) formed after an intensive experience in a two-week summer school course on multicultural education. At the completion of the course, some of the participants and the professor, Boyle-Baise, decided to stay together for further study and support. Although these participants identified various reasons for taking the course, as a group their interest was in learning more about multicultural education. They created the Coalition and then named it to signify advocacy for the multicultural transformation of schooling.

The Coalition is in its third year of existence and has survived the growing pains of defining and establishing itself. (For a complete description of the Coalition's development, see Boyle-Baise, in press.) Although it is a small group with a central core of about ten people who do most of the work and about thirty other recorded members, it has many supporters and is a recognized alternative voice, especially within the local school system and community.

The recognition of the Coalition is due largely to two vehicles developed during its second year. The newsletter, *The Multicultural Message*, is published semimonthly and owes its quality to the persistence of the editor in encouraging, cajoling, and teaching other members to write. The Speakers Bureau stands on the continual outreach efforts of its director. Both of these communication arms are supported by the school district, which means that the district prints and distributes the newsletter and provides some release time for teachers to serve on the Speakers' Bureau.

At the time of this writing, the Coalition is struggling to maintain its independence as the school district seeks to subsume it and declare the group the district's own invention. The Coalition perceives this as akin to a corporate take-over and has responded by drafting a collaborative work agreement with the district and applying for not-for-profit status.

This chapter is not what Sarason (1993) calls a "no-holds-barred, warts-and-all account that tells us what happens when visions power actions" (p.39). Rather the focus here is on the thoughts and perceptions of six key individuals within the Coalition in answer to the question "what is it about the Coalition that works for you?" This account does not begin to tell about the frustrations, heartaches, and triumphs of sustaining this change. We ask the reader to assume the existence of these difficulties and place the positive responses of individuals within such a climate and context. This is only part of their story.

STUDYING THE COALITION

In order to find out what worked about the Coalition, we studied a select group of its members. Through long-term association with the Coalition, we became "connoisseurs" (Eisner, 1977) of the membership, able to appreciate the qualities which marked those that were outstanding. Easily the most active members of the group, six members agreed that they shared "absolute resolve" to keep the Coalition going. We chose these six members as "success stories" to represent the best of what is possible in a grass-roots effort for change.

All six informants were women (as were most Coalition members), two were African-American, three were European-American, and one had Native American ancestry. Four informants were experienced elementary educators: a fifth-grade teacher, a counselor, a teacher of the learning disabled (LD), and a librarian. One member worked in a community-oriented position as a child care specialist. Another member was a recent teacher education graduate working as assistant coordinator for an adult literacy center. The entire group worked with culturally diverse populations within urban settings.

This study was an ethnographic description of one case, focused on the cultural knowledge of participants, and written from an emic, or insider's, point of view. According to cognitive anthropologists, cultural knowledge is "the knowledge people use to generate and interpret social behavior" (Spradley & McCurdy, 1972, p. 8). Cultural knowledge is idiosyncratic, but there are domains of shared understandings within groups. Explanations of cultural knowledge usually illustrate these shared meanings. For this reason, such explanations were criticized for deemphasizing intracultural variation (Pelto & Pelto, 1978).

The principles of cognitive anthropology were used to describe teachers' thinking about the way the Coalition worked and affected them. A description of shared understandings was completed through a process of mapping the major categories or domains and subcategories used by respondents. Common and peripheral cultural meanings identified intragroup differences.

Data for this particular study were gathered over a six-month period. Interviewing was the primary source of information, with participant observation serving to document responses. The authors interviewed informants four times: three times individually and once as a group.

Nonscheduled standardized interviews were used to probe similar topics, yet allowed wide-ranging responses (Denzin, 1978). These interviews were organized around grand tour questions (Spradley & McCurdy, 1972), such as "What do you recall as memorable about the Coalition that happened at the beginning of this school year?" Structured interviews (Denzin, 1978) were used to gather more information about trends that emerged from the general interviews. These interviews included questions such as "Many of you referred to 'sharing' as an important aspect of the Coalition. Can you tell us more about what that means to you?"

The interviews were read independently many times by both researchers and examined for emerging patterns. Washburn analyzed the data from the perspective of "observer as participant" (Glesne & Peshkin, 1992, p.10): one who maintains a degree of marginality by remaining in the background. Boyle-Baise, on the other hand, approached the data from the perspective of "participant as observer" (Glesne & Peshkin, 1992, p. 10): one who interacts extensively with those studied. This provided a counterbalance of perspective with varying degrees of congruity and different patterns of intersubjectivity. Those patterns that emerged in common were considered salient.

The salient patterns were mapped as a taxonomy. A *domain* referred to a category mentioned by all informants. *Trends* were subcategories of domains and were salient to most informants. *Common meanings* referred to trends noted by three or more informants. *Peripheral meanings* were mentioned by one or two informants and often represented a dissenting opinion.

DESCRIBING THE FINDINGS

We found that five primary categories, or domains, of thought emerged. The description that follows refers to the cognitive map in Figure 12.1 The five domains were strong leader, vision, self-enhancement, support, and activism. Of these domains, two were overarching; they were constant and continual threads that ran through the fabric of cultural knowledge about the Coalition.

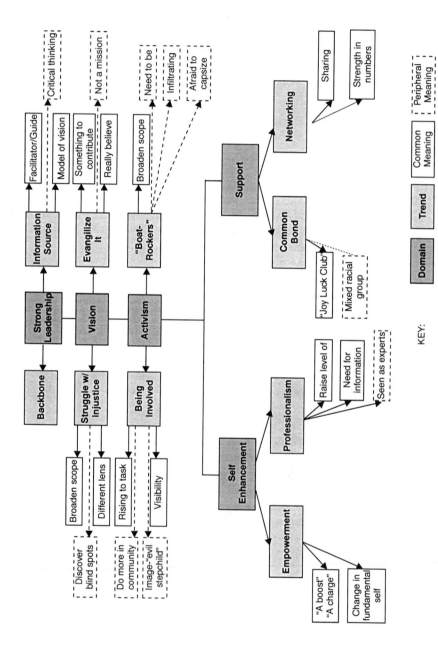

Figure 12.1 COGNITIVE MAP: "What about the Coalition works for you?"

These overarching domains were strong leadership and the vision of an education that is multicultural.

Strong Leader

The respondents strongly felt that the Coalition founder's leadership role was tantamount to the very essence of the Coalition. During interviews members described Boyle-Baise as the "backbone" (BW, 5/26/93) of the Coalition. Her influence took the shape of "heart" (BW, 3/11/93) of the Coalition and "mother figure" (KT, 3/11/93) to its members. Members saw her constantly modeling the vision in word and deed. "The other thing, too, is that this is the philosophy that we see you living and doing. And you are a great model for that" (GM, 4/23/93).

Informants looked to Boyle-Baise as a source of information. Terms like *guide* (MA, 3/17/93), *facilitator* (KT, 5/24/93), and *mentor* (KT, 3/11/93) were often used. Many members felt that Boyle-Baise taught them to examine their thinking and place it into a critical mode, thus expanding their perspectives. "Lynne pushed me to think more critically, because I would read anything a person said, right off the bat. If they wrote it, it was gospel truth . . . she fought with us . . . to ask questions about what was written" (BS, 3/18/93).

Vision

In addition, Boyle-Baise figured prominently in the second overarching domain: vision. "We are only here because of the vision you had" (GM, 4/23/93). Visionary commitment echoed throughout interviews, as illustrated in the following statement: "I think our vision works, I think that what we intend to do works. It will improve the schools in Springfield . . . it has to be seen that this is not a black and white issue, that it is much more encompassing than that" (BW, 3/11/93). One of the two general trends in regard to vision was "spreading the word" (BW, 5/26/93). In general, informants wanted to tell others about the multicultural message. "I'm spreading the word. I tell anybody who will listen about my philosophy on this" (BW, 5/26/93). Many informants likened spreading the word to evangelism: "I think you need to evangelize it, that's the only term I can think of . . . to get more people involved" (GM, 3/9/93). One informant disagreed with the notion of evangelism. She noted that "we are not a mission. We are a change agent" (MA, 5/26/93).

A common meaning expressed about spreading the word was "really believing" (BS, 3/18/93) in the potential and viability of the group. Another common meaning referred to the feeling of informants that the vision had "something to contribute" (BW, 3/11/93) to the improvement of schools.

The second major trend in regard to "vision" was struggling with "injustice." Coalition members struggled with new ideas about justice and fairness. "I had frustrations on the injustices of the world . . . I did realize that some of my ways of looking at things, even though they were good intentions, were . . . not adequate" (BW, 3/11/93). Two core meanings depicted the growth of new perspectives: members viewed education through a "broadened scope" (GM, 5/26/93) or "different lens" (KT, 5/24/93). "Being in the Coalition has helped me remember my roots . . . it has helped me know that education is for everyone . . . it has also given me some opportunities to broaden my scope" (GM, 5/26/93). One member noted that the Coalition helped her see "blind spots" (KT. 5/24/93) that she had overlooked.

> I discovered through the Coalition that I have some blind spots that are so deeply rooted that it's like digging out a real deep splinter, and there's some pain there. To do that in the Coalition, it's wonderful to do it in a real supportive environment. (KT, 5/24/93)

The remaining three domains that emerged contained an element of timing not present in the other two. When asked to recall their thinking about the Coalition, informants described the domains of *support* and *self-enhancement* as ongoing and historical. The domain of *activism* represented the salient concern of informants at the time of the study. Therefore, we chose to describe this domain first.

Activism

Our respondents viewed the Coalition as a vehicle for active participation.

> As teachers, I think we must be more proactive; we are the ones dealing with students in the classroom. So, therefore, if we are taking a proactive stance as a coalition, then I think I am fulfilling more than just a teach-

ing role. I am also becoming an educational activist, and this is a way for me to do this. (KT, 3/11/93)

A major trend indicated the desire on everyone's part to "be involved" (JT, 3/11/93). Core meanings related to this trend included the need for more "visibility" (BS, 5/27/93) and a sense of "rising to the task" (BS, 5/27/93).

> I guess the most significant thing for me was probably . . . I had to write . . . [articles for the newsletter], I had to get it done so I just did it. It was kind of fulfilling to me that people said, 'I read that,' . . . I think that that would be the most memorable thing for me . . . rising to the task. (BS, 5/27/93)

A few informants realized that "more community" (JT, 5/26/93) outreach needed to be done. One respondent looked on the negative side of this issue and expressed a concern about the image of the Coalition in the district. "I think we're kind of the evil stepchild. . . . They [the school administration] understand that we are necessary, and . . . that we can do good things. But it's one more thing pulling at them . . . for credibility, for attention, and for resources" (KT, 5/26/93).

Another major trend emerged as a strong response to a quote from Sleeter (1992) about people who "rock the boat" to effect change. When asked what they thought of this metaphor, five of the six respondents embraced it.

> I think boat-rockers could be our nickname because that is exactly what we are . . . the school system exists in our town in a certain way and has existed over time in the same way, but none of us are willing to accept that as its final form. (KT, 3/11/93)

Phrases like "I've always been a boat-rocker or someone who marches to a different drummer" (BW, 3/11/93) and "Oh, I definitely am a boat-rocker, I'm brassy, I've always been" (MA, 4/10/93) permeated the interviews. One respondent wanted "to be more of a 'boat-rocker' in relation to myself" (GM, 3/9/93). Another viewed it as a way of "infiltrating" (KT, 3/11/93). Yet another was afraid "that the boat may capsize" (BW, 3/18/93).

Support

One of the key aspects of the Coalition was the support of members for each other. "It is critical that I have, not only the sources and resources that the Coalition has to offer, but also, the support group part of the Coalition" (KT, 5/11/93). The group represented a bonding experience for members. "I think that . . . we are very close with one another. We don't always agree, but we find that common bond where we can solve our differences" (JT, 4/23/93).

One of the respondents considered the group one of her first successful mixed racial experiences. Prior to joining the group, she found "common ground" primarily within her own racial group. "I think that it is important to me because for so long, we haven't been able to express ourselves in a mixed group. We have relied on our group, our racial groups . . . I think now, with the Coalition, we are moving out more from that" (JT, 4/23/93). This same respondent described the group as her "Joy Luck Club" (JT, 4/23/93), referring to a similar group in Amy Tan's novel, *Joy Luck Club* (1989).

Another trend related to support was "networking." "I like the networking that we do. I like the feeling of camaraderie that we have . . . I don't see that a lot among teachers" (KT, 3/11/93). Networking was commonly defined as "sharing." "We come together, we share, and that's really important . . . to keep us going. Because if we don't share, we become burned-out. I think the Coalition has helped fight the burnout I was feeling in education" (GM, 4/23/93). Networking was also described as having "strength in numbers." "It works this way, because there is strength in numbers . . . one mind has a lot of potential, but the more you add minds to that, I think that your potential expands exponentially" (BW, 4/23/93).

Self-Enhancement

Last, but certainly not least, our informants referred to the domain of self-enhancement. They spoke of having gained a "sense of professionalism" (KT, 3/11/93) through working with the Coalition. Several saw a need for more information—"I still feel that I don't know enough" (GM, 4/23/93)—and looked to the Coalition as an information source. Through the learning process, many experienced a "raise" (GM, 4/23/93) in their professional status, and two noted that they were now seen as "experts" (BW, 4/23/93) in multicultural education.

> With knowledge came confidence and a feeling of em-
> powerment. The Coalition has made me a little more
> assertive . . . now I'm not just empowering certain kids
> who really have a need . . . I am providing information
> for my whole classroom and beyond my classroom.
> And most of all, it has come basically from knowing
> that the Coalition is there to pick me up if I fall over.
> (MA, 4/10/93)

This personal empowerment meant "a boost" and "a charge," as well as "a reminder of what I am really about" (GM, 3/9/93). One respondent summed it up this way: "I think the Coalition has been personally empowering for most of us. I think it has been validating and empowering, and it has caused changes in our very fundamental selves" (KT, 3/11/93).

DISCUSSING AND ANALYZING THE FINDINGS

The findings are considered in relation to the five domains of members' cultural knowledge. Information learned from this study is related to findings within the literature about staff development for multicultural education.

Strong Leadership

Leadership was not discussed explicitly in previous studies. Our findings indicated that strong, continual leadership, guided by the vision of an education that is multicultural, influenced informants. They considered this type of leadership essential to development of the Coalition and their personal growth.

This domain emerged from discussions about what worked for the Coalition, and was not the result of direct questioning. The candor with which informants described Boyle-Baise's leadership surprised us. We wondered about the impact of Boyle-Baise as an individual leader, compared to the impact of general leadership qualities. Along this line, we also wondered about the extent to which Boyle-Baise's race and gender, as a white female, may have influenced leadership credibility.

On the other hand, we found several descriptions of visionary leadership qualities in the literature that seemed congruent with our findings. According to Kouzes and Posner (1987), and interpreted from a multicultural perspective by Banks (1992), successful leadership is a dynamic process centered around five practices: challenging the monocultural nature of the status quo, inspiring commitment to multicultural education, empowering a diverse population to act, modeling congruence between multicultural values and actions, and encouraging the heart of the group through collective support. Similar factors were reported by Sergiovanni (1992). He found that successful leaders combined professional and moral authority to lead through ideas; the leader is the first follower for the idea. Consideration of these kinds of factors is unusual in leadership literature.

The Vision

Although Boyle (1982) and Grant and Grant (1985) worked with volunteers or selected candidates who presumably had some positive disposition toward cultural diversity, they did not explore teachers' perspectives in terms of visionary commitment. This type of commitment was an important consideration for the boatrockers in studies by Moll (1988), Ladson-Billings (1989), and Sleeter (1992).

It should be remembered that our informants joined the Coalition voluntarily to seek more information about and support for multicultural efforts. In doing so, they acted as new recruits to the idea of multicultural education. Our findings indicated that coalition activities supported and extended members' initial commitments. Also, the vision of total school reform represented by multicultural education served as a beacon for members and motivated them to rock the boat.

The trend to spread the word emerged strongly in our study. Members were anxious to tell others about multicultural education and did so through the newsletter and Speaker's Bureau. This trend was found in two other studies. Sleeter (1992) reported that teachers shared "tidbits" (p.131) about training with coworkers, but were hesitant to do much more. All of the participants in Grant and Grant's (1985) study placed multicultural materials in faculty lounges, and about half did some inservice training. Although a tendency to communicate with others was evident in these studies, there seemed to be some fervor to do so among our informants.

Self-Enhancement

According to the literature, teachers were at the awareness stage of learning following training sessions. For our informants, learning to be more multicultural took an extended period of study. It was important that this study was framed by a well-informed leader and centered around collegial interaction. The desire for more information was continual, but additional knowledge engendered feelings of increased personal and professional esteem and a sense of empowerment.

For the most part, empowerment has been discussed without a strong connection to a particular vision or philosophy (e.g., Lieberman & Miller, 1990; Rosenholtz, 1989). Conversations about multicultural education are noticeably missing.

Support

There was reference to the need for supportive, collegial groups or partnerships in several studies (Grant & Grant, 1985; Moll, 1988; Sleeter, 1992). This study showed strongly the power of support for professional growth. The strength of common bonding among people of like minds to create a "Joy Luck Club" cannot be overstated. It was joyful for members to break their previous isolation as self-sustaining professionals.

Also, the Coalition served as a vehicle for expanding members' knowledge and experience through sharing and networking. The supportive nature of the group helped members work through the stages of learning about multicultural education.

Both findings raise serious questions about the efficacy of short-term training sessions in which participants rarely form supportive networks that challenge the isolation of teaching. Teachers seem to need a safe and enduring place to explore new expressions of multicultural thinking.

Activism

Sleeter (1992) raises the question about the potential for supporting boat-rockers. This study added more information about boat-rockers in schools and social agencies. There were indications that boat-rockers may be pushed and supported through the coalescing of people of like minds.

The Coalition served as a vehicle for activism through the promotion and accomplishment of tasks, like developing the newsletter. Members rose to the task, sometimes before they were quite sure of themselves. In this way, activism built upon support for learning and motivation for self-enhancement. Although it was difficult to pinpoint where one stage of learning began and another left off, this study provided evidence of staged learning. Members discussed their growth through stages as stories of self-realization. Many stories could not be expressed fully within the confines of the taxonomic type of description provided here.

CONSIDERING IMPLICATIONS

To what extent did coalition building change teacher thinking in relation to multicultural education? Although these results relate to one particular coalition, our findings point toward new ways of perceiving multicultural staff development.

Strong, continual, visionary leadership is essential for coalition building. Creating a common bond around the multicultural vision needs to take place. Membership should be voluntary, but recruitment of boat-rockers may be fruitful. Provisions need to be made for small group interaction, long-term learning, collegial support, and task-oriented efforts.

There was a synergy created from the interaction of self-enhancement, support, and activism that should not be overlooked. Members developed deep collegial and personal bonds through interaction within the Coalition. This intensity of professional and personal growth has not been reported elsewhere. Such a response cannot occur within the "quick fix" staff development formats typically used for multicultural education.

Based on this study, several questions are raised for further research:

- What qualities of leadership are relevant to developing and maintaining a multicultural advocacy group?
- Should staff development programs be redesigned to include a visionary approach?
- Should staff development programs differentiate between introductory sessions for most teachers and follow-up sessions for those willing to expand their multicultural learning?
- Is there a link between discussions of empowerment and multicultural education that needs to be explored?

- What information could be gleaned by studying the integral workings of successful support groups?
- In what ways could investigation of kernels of activism inform theoretical proposals to politicize teachers?
- In what ways could research centered around story illuminate studies of personal growth?

SUMMARIZING AND CONCLUDING

This study was an effort to describe the Coalition for Education That Is Multicultural, a grass-roots, support group of individuals committed to multicultural education. In interviewing six "success stories" from this group, information was revealed about their cultural knowledge and the changes that took place in their thinking from the inception of the Coalition to the time this study took place.

We went into the field with the question "What is it about the Coalition that works for you?" From responses to this question and other probes, five domains emerged: the need for strong leadership, the focus of a guiding vision, the desire to be actively involved, the benefits of a strong supportive environment, and the rewards of a sense of self-enhancement. As these domains emerged, it became evident that the respondents had progressed along the continuum of stages of multicultural knowledge during their involvement with the Coalition. They had passed from awareness and acceptance into affirmation by the time this study was completed.

Through analysis, we were able to draw some definite conclusions. Primarily, we discovered that coalition building does work. With strong leadership and commitment to a vision, a group can form a common bond, develop a network of like-minded people, and work toward multicultural goals.

Also, we identified the need our respondents felt for coalescing with a broad range of individuals—not just teachers. Through coalescing across groups, informants were able to build a network of support and garner strength from a number of individuals with varied backgrounds.

In addition, we determined that most respondents felt they belonged in the category of boat-rockers. The idea developed that there may be an inherent factor that makes boat-rockers best prepared to challenge the status quo and embrace the notion of diversity.

"What works about the Coalition?" Our respondents spoke of leadership, a vision, support, self-enhancement, and a vehicle through which to put words and ideas into action. In attempting to answer this question, we also discovered strong evidence for why a traditional workshop orientation doesn't work. The supporting factors for personal growth discovered here may serve as a foundation for the creation of new settings for professional learning, rather than the reuse and repair of old formats.

We would like to see the formation, promotion, and evaluation of other coalitions. The ultimate goal is to bring about a change in teacher thinking in regard to multicultural education; our objective is finding the appropriate vehicle to do so.

Conclusion

NEW DIRECTIONS IN TEACHER THINKING
Linking Theory to Practice

David Whitehorse

The contributors to this volume have provided diverse perspectives and conclusions about teacher thinking in multicultural contexts. Yet embedded in these discussions are common themes and lessons learned that inform ways to think about teaching and learning in general, and teacher cognition in particular. Similarly, the contributors have directed attention to the overarching significance of external influences on teacher thinking and behaviors which have been widely articulated in the discipline of multicultural education (e.g., Banks, 1992; Banks & Banks, 1993; Davidman & Davidman, 1994; Grant, 1994; Locke, 1992; Sleeter & Grant, 1988), but which have been given cursory mention in the cognitive and educational psychology arenas.

Throughout, the contributors reinforce the argument that teacher thinking cannot be fully understood without examining the cultural context that informs teaching practice. To aid in achieving that understanding, this chapter merges ideas from cognitive and educational psychology with insights from multicultural education, cultural and ethnic studies, and cognitive and cultural anthropology. In doing so, it provides broader insight into the interactive nature of these fields of study.

These disciplinary foci, however, do not paint the entire picture of teacher thinking in cultural contexts. Therefore, this chapter revisits the model of factors influencing teachers' instruction as conceptualized by Porter and Brophy (1988; p. 76), and offers a more holistic interpretation of the interaction between teachers' personal experience and education, the characteristics of the class, and external factors, including the multicultural context.

Lastly, this chapter asserts that schools and classrooms are microcosms of a broader sociocultural context. Therefore, models that artificially and arbitrarily separate the school experience from the larger sociocultural context may be missing important implicit factors influencing both teacher cognition and teacher behavior. In this chapter, key elements of the Porter and Brophy (1988) model are contrasted with an adaptation of the social systems model initially advanced by Getzels and Guba (1957) in order to express, more adequately, dimensions of teacher thinking in multicultural contexts.

LESSONS LEARNED

The contributors advance a broad spectrum of lessons learned from their research that can be synthesized in the following general propositions. Although these are not all-inclusive, they form perhaps the most central and important lessons advanced by and shared among the majority of the contributors. The lessons are not specific to each chapter or section; rather, they surface at various levels throughout the volume. Further, a number of these general propositions also generate questions about both teacher thinking and multicultural education. These questions are included in the discussion of the contributions, since the former follow directly from the chapters; in the absence of providing direct answers, knowing some of the appropriate and/or central questions may be equally as informative. Similarly, questions generated might be pursued in further discussion of the effects of differing modes of teacher thinking.

The first lesson learned is, in reality, a validation of the necessity for and significance of the study of the recursive relationship between teacher cognition and teacher behavior. All the contributors reinforce the notion that teachers' theories about and behaviors regarding teaching in multicultural contexts are based on personal and educational experiences, and that these experiences are framed by the sociocultural context of the school, community, and student attributes. More importantly, they are significantly affected by the sociocultural contexts from which students and teachers come (and in which educational institutions exist). This may be a fundamental restatement of what this book is about, but is necessary since some might still question why further particularistic study of teacher thinking in cultural context is necessary. It is not only *appropriate* to investigate these factors, but it is *essential*, particularly if educators are to support the widest range of educational equity in a pluralistic society.

Second, the dichotomous representation of "theory and action" is at the very least problematic, and at the most, fundamentally flawed: teachers' behaviors are *always* guided by teachers' implicit theories and the values and beliefs from which they are generated. Montecinos and Tidwell couch this proposition in their subjects' different orientations toward instruction in the content areas as representing differing schemata. Likewise, Abt-Perkins details the influence of implicit theories and underlying assumptions in her subject's (Laura's) development of writing programs for ethnically diverse student populations. As Abt-Perkins and Hamilton in particular relate, one challenge is to determine the relationship between implicit theories, which are often difficult to bring to the surface, and those which are openly, usually verbally, supported. Implicit theories are critically linked to the individual's core values and are perceived to have considerably more effect on teaching practice and social behavior than those which are merely espoused. As with ideology, core beliefs organize behavior, though the extent to which that occurs varies and is affected by situational constraints and opportunities.

One common example which persists in contemporary education is that if one fundamentally believes that students of color are academically (if not racially or ethnically) inferior, teaching practice will tend to be congruent with that theory, despite the espousal by that same person of a belief that "all children can learn to use their minds well." The implicit theory held then becomes the basis for covert differential teaching practice which undermines the overt and often well-intentioned teaching practice based on espoused concern for equitable teaching (Banks & Banks, 1993).

As another example, consider Hamilton's description of a teacher's use of anthropomorphized representations of animals. Their use might be interpreted in a number of ways. The representations documented in the study may have been used just because they were readily available. An alternative interpretation might be that using animals as proxies for humans allows one to skirt the issues associated with interethnic human relationships. In the instance of animals anthropomorphized in multiethnic images, ethnic diversity is trivialized and reduced to a simplistic set of symbols. Although one might assume that this was not intentional, the teachers' belief that such representations were appropriate (without setting an appropriate context with and for students) could reinforce the marginalization of ethnic students of color who see themselves inappropriately represented as animals or as having animal attributes.

A related lesson is that educators need to make *explicit* those theories, values, and beliefs which are normally *implicit*. One must first be aware that most people have both implicit and explicit frames of reference, and that the two may not necessarily be congruent. A question developed by New, Gillette and Ríos in chapters 3 through 5 is: "In what ways do my implicit theories *inhibit* equitable and effective teaching for *all* students?" Asking and responding to this question provides an opportunity to apply reflective thinking to problem resolution centered in one's own thinking and practice.

A compounding and sometimes confounding lesson emerging from the previous proposition (and described in contributors' articles) is that teachers generally have an external locus of control (e.g., Hamilton's discussion of the low level of "self-related elements") when dealing with the academic achievement of students from culturally diverse backgrounds. However, the contributions of Abt-Perkins, Hamilton, and Montecinos and Tidwell in part 2 deal with this concern most directly. This external locus of control becomes evident when teachers view state-mandated standards (Montecinos and Tidwell), curricular reform and individual relationship to the reform elements (Hamilton), and standardized strategies for teaching (Abt-Perkins) as being more prescriptive of student achievement than the actions of the teacher. According to these contributors, most teachers tend to look beyond themselves in explaining why children do not learn. Teachers often do not recognize how their own thoughts, values, and beliefs affect student achievement. Although it's true that teachers are not fully responsible for student achievement in the aggregate, it's also true that teachers should be critically reflect on how their thoughts, values, and beliefs form the basis for their teaching and ultimately student academic success.

Having learned that knowledge, attitudes, values, beliefs, teaching behaviors, principles of practice, and affect are interconnected, positivistic research attempts to disentangle them, analyze them separately, compartmentalize them in tight disciplinary contexts, and then reassemble them to make some generalizable statement about "reality." A lesson learned from the studies in part 3 of this volume is that such a process may not be very useful. Generally, it is difficult to see the strength of the connections between educational elements by analyzing the components separately. A more appropriate schema for analysis might attempt to uncover the complex relationships between teacher thinking and multicultural contexts, which reflect reality more clearly (e.g., Artiles's discussion, "Benefiting from Related Areas of Inquiry: Toward an Interdisciplinary Paradigm"). Part 3, importantly, *moves from theory to method,* as the authors propose specific strategies for professional preservice teacher preparation and continuing inservice teacher development.

The stages-of-concern approach employed by Marshall is useful in defining and understanding complex relationships, as well as in developing systemic innovations in the professional education of teachers working with culturally diverse student populations. Similarly, constructivist approaches, as articulated by Pohan and Aguilar, combine knowledge of the underlying attitudes and beliefs of teachers in preparation with transformational approaches to understanding both curricula and students. Valli describes the critical role of developing relationships between students and teachers, which Boyle-Baise and Washburn extend to more complex relationships involved in a coalition of individuals and groups supporting the development of multiculturally astute educators.

In their entirety, a universal lesson developed from these contributions is that there is a need to broaden the knowledge base in multicultural education in order to fully articulate teacher thinking and fully prepare teachers to function effectively within multicultural education contexts. Although multicultural education is emerging as a discipline in its own right, it has still not addressed many critical questions that overlap other educational fields of study. Since knowledge begets knowledge, the ability of multiculturalists to expand and refine their theoretical and pedagogical understanding is seen to potentially affect teacher thinking, as well as teaching policy and practice.

Explicit in a number of the chapters (Abt-Perkins; Boyle-Baise and Washburn; Valli, in particular) is the idea that affect plays a major role in this scenario. Teaching and learning involve the interaction of cognitive, behavioral, and affective domains, and values and beliefs organize and cohere behavior. Even though the enterprise of education involves an equivalent measure of affect, this domain is rarely studied or appropriately and consistently assessed in students unless it manifests itself in negative ways. Yet most educators would agree that how students feel about teachers, schools, peers, curricula, and teaching methodology has a great deal to do with how students think and behave vis-à-vis those dimensions of the education environment: bonding does precede learning to a great extent (Whitehorse, 1992). Similarly, how *teachers* feel has much to do with their thought and action.

A more robust interpretation and articulation of teacher cognition may be possible, as proposed by Hamilton and Artiles, by including knowledge borrowed from sociology, cognitive anthropology, and ethnic studies disciplines with knowledge of educational psychology and multicultural education. This integration speaks to at least two important issues.

The first issue is that much of what various contributors propose does not require the reinvention of the wheel: appropriate answers to many questions raised may be found through a more expansive multidisciplinary, problem-solving approach. For example, utilizing existing studies of comparative education (Mungazi, 1993) combined with models for the study and interpretation of interactional sociolinguistics in teacher knowledge and discourse (Elbaz, 1990) provides new multidisciplinary opportunities for in-class problem solving (and problem resolution) through cross-cultural context setting.

The second issue reinforces the notion that systemic problems require systemic solutions. One cannot understand teacher thinking without an understanding of systemic factors affecting that thinking. Similarly, the manipulation of a few variables within a system may not change the system itself. If one proposes to evoke more appropriate teacher thinking in cultural context, that objective must be evident in curricula, pedagogy, institutional structure, symbolic content and representations, and the relationships of these factors in an open system. As will be indicated later, reconceptualization of social system relationships helps make this seem a more managable task.

GENERAL THEMES

A number of themes are embedded in contributors' chapters that deserve recapitulation and articulation as a whole. The contributors' examples and teaching practice scenarios indicate that, for many, teaching is still about the business of "fixing" ethnic students of color (Abt-Perkins, Montero-Sieburth, New, in particular). This need to fit students into mainstream molds stems from a commonly held belief in, and use of, a deficit model of the experiences which students of color bring to the teaching and learning environment. Students from nonmainstream backgrounds are marginalized when they enter the classroom, and that marginalization is more often reinforced than mitigated in the educational experience.

A second recurring theme is that teacher thinking in multicultural contexts is often dependent on how teachers view the role of and participation in different sociocultural and multicultural education contexts. Implicit in this theme is that teachers' conceptions of multicultural education and their conceptions about ethnic students of color have much to do with how teachers will tend to think and act, since real-world experiences with populations of color both in and outside the classroom have much to do with the formation and reinforcement of teachers' values, attitudes, and beliefs about those populations. The contributors reinforce the notion that separating teacher thinking *in* multicultural contexts from teacher conceptions *about* multicultural contexts may be problematic, given the reflective nature of the two.

A third theme is that implicit, institutionalized attitudes overwhelmingly dictate the structure of the multicultural education environment and that teacher thinking responds to that environment. As indicated in the development of the first theme, numerous examples point to an *institutional* as well as *individual* focus on "fixing" students (i.e., having students "culturally" adapt to the educational environment, rather than having the educational environment respond to the students' cultural context). As articulated in this volume, especially by Gillette, Montecinos and Tidwell, and Montero-Sieburth, many of the educational situations encountered reflect institutional attitudes that are based on deficit modeling of children from other than mainstream sociocultural backgrounds. Paradoxically, these institutional characteristics tend to *implicitly* marginalize children of color while constructing multicultural contexts *explicitly* intended to better serve them.

Attempting to resolve this paradox is critical because there is a trend toward state-mandated curricular change. One might conclude that "contributions" and "ethnic additive" approaches to curricular reform, as defined by Banks (1992), continue to institutionally marginalize and maintain deficit model perceptions of ethnic students of color, whereas "transformational" and "social action" approaches more adequately serve the educational needs of students of color in particular and *all students* in general. A more provocative proposition is that teachers, as direct representatives of the education institution, must be cognitively and pedagogically committed to transformational or social action education approaches in order to effectively respond to both student need and state mandate. For the institution of public education as a whole to resolve this paradox, transformational or social action attitudes, values, and behaviors must be *systemically* dominant among administrators, support staff, *and* teachers.

The fourth and most trenchant theme is also the most complex. This theme posits that investigating, understanding, and reframing teacher thinking is a difficult but necessary set of processes if education is to be appropriately responsive to the increasingly diverse student population. The contributors (Artiles, in particular) advance the notion that the components that affect teacher thinking create seeming paradoxes (one of which is advanced in the two preceding paragraphs) which cannot be resolved by superficial, cursory, or narrowly focused analyses. Rather, as Hilliard (1991) has indicated, a need exists to deeply restructure the investigation of teacher thinking, reconceptualize the sociocultural interactions between schools and communities, and fundamentally rethink how teacher thinking is viewed. For this reason, centering this discussion strictly in the realm of cognitive or educational psychology, or any other narrow academic disciplinary framework, may artificially limit the ability to resolve dilemmas described in preceding chapters. Since no one can know all the sociocultural contexts that frame student experience, there is a need to develop both models and methods as well as multidisciplinary theoretical bases that might act as proxies or exemplars for a range of sociocultural experiences.

A final theme gleaned from the preceding chapters is that the focus of teacher thinking should always be on ways in which all students can be taught more effectively. Yet many questions beg to be answered. For example, how do teachers think about the promises and pitfalls associated with differential treatment for students from different backgrounds? Do teachers think that these differential strategies represent resegregation, and how do they relate to explicit attempts to create educational environments based on the appreciation for and affirmation of cultural pluralism? How sound is the theoretical base supporting either differential or universal education strategies and contexts?

Additional questions include: How do teachers think about African-American students being taught in cultural immersion contexts? Do teachers think that Native American tribes have sovereign rights to control the education of their children, both on and off their tribal land base? Do teachers feel that the optimal educational context is endogenously derived, as are other elements of culture? If so, how do they determine which endogenous framework shall be applied and under what circumstances? How do teachers' cognitions about these issues reinforce the status quo, or permit new ways of knowing about and operationalizing teaching practice and positive student outcomes?

Finally, as teachers become more committed to their students and the diverse communities they serve, their knowledge becomes more differentiated. What if that differentiation, stemming from both commitment and expansion of knowledge, leads to dissonance in thinking, or raises paradoxical circumstances in teaching and learning? How is the inclusion of new ideas negotiated when it challenges or calls into question previous assumptions, beliefs, and practices?

REFLECTION AND RECONCEPTUALIZATION: IMPLICATIONS FOR PROFESSIONAL PRACTICE

In applying the Porter and Brophy model (see p. 6), an emphasis should be on minimizing the constraints associated with teachers' knowledge and convictions regarding content, pedagogy, and student needs, in order to maximize the opportunities for appropriate, immediate responses from the student and for long-term student achievement.

The reconstruction of teacher thinking proposed by individual contributors generally focuses on discrete elements of the above model. In the aggregate, however, it can be concluded that the reconstruction of teacher thinking requires addressing all elements defined by Porter and Brophy, at a minimum, in order to meet the apparent needs of multicultural student populations. Further, if this is the minimum, what additional elements should be factored into the model to make it more responsive?

In thinking about how to reconceptualize teacher thinking in multicultural contexts brings to mind the following specific questions: Do the elements in the Porter and Brophy (1994) model

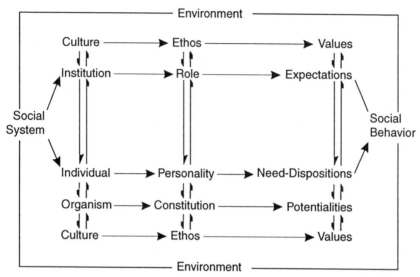

Getzels and Guba's Social System Model (from *School Review*, 65 (Winter), p. 429–433; copyright permission requested, January, 1995)

appropriately address the relationships between teacher thinking and its effects in multicultural contexts? If there are limitations to this model's utility, how might it be modified to meet the needs of all students? Whatever model is applied, how would a program be developed to change teacher thinking so that culturally sensitive and culturally appropriate pedagogy would result? By extension, how would this new model create positive, meaningful, direct personal experiences, and positive interpersonal relations with and for multicultural student populations?

One must recognize that there are a number of alternative paths to this end, including changing the fundamental structure of schooling as well as changing the composition of the teaching profession. However, should one possess a bias for systemic reform, then changing current teacher thinking is critical to reform and may present the most immediate need, given the protracted time requirements for the other two alternatives. With a focus on change in teacher thinking, could educational leaders deliver the essence of multiculturalism in the institutional mission and provide development and ongoing support for the teaching force, curricula, materials, and teaching methods?

The answer to the first question is that the model is limited in its discussion of teacher thinking and its effects in multicultural contexts. This is evident in the lack of a direct link between the "characteristics of the class" and "teacher knowledge and convictions." The most important interaction in classrooms occurs between student and teacher, and the thinking of both is affected by the dimensions of the relationship between the two. Further, it can be argued that more knowledge of the sociocultural context comes from (or through) students than comes from what Porter and Brophy refer to as "external factors." In addition, contributors believe that "teacher knowledge," "reflection," and "perceptions of the effects of their actions" (what is aggregated as "teacher thinking") are not only affected by feedback from "students' immediate feedback" and "long-term student outcomes" but are affected initially by the "characteristics of the class." Lastly, the "characteristics of the class" should form some subset of "teacher personal experience and professional (i.e., ongoing) education," whereas Porter and Brophy view them as discrete variables with only the latter affecting teacher cognition.

A major modification to this model might be its encapsulation within a framework labeled "sociocultural contexts," where the contexts are embedded within the "environment." Since both these variables affect all factors within, there is no need to define the effect with specific lines of influence or specific entry points. Further, the plural "sociocultural *contexts*" is important because they will not be exactly the same for every participant in the teaching and learning experience. The addition of these factors more appropriately reflects the relationships as being in an open, as opposed to a finite or closed, system. A more detailed definition of the sociocultural dimensions will be found in the ensuing discussion of the social systems model.

An additional modification to this model stems from the recognition that the interaction between teachers and students is more direct and reflexive than the model indicates. As an example, the only two-way interaction between teacher and student occurs indirectly through routines, planned actions, activities and instruction, and (possibly) directly, through interactive decision making.

The limitations of this volume do not allow us to address all of these questions. Nor should a model be produced that is universally generalizable. Rather, models which are adaptable are called for. As with most models and strategies, professional judgment and decision making appropriate to a particular situation probably hold more utility than adherence to any routine procedure.

DAVID WHITEHORSE

ANTHROPOLOGY AND COGNITION

The field of cognitive anthropology deals with the shared implicit knowledge held by cultural groups and how knowledge, belief, value system development, expectations, and cognitive patterns and decision processes shape culture (Tafoya, 1989). The argument might be made that all of human endeavor is endogenous: that it is particular to the culture from which it is derived. The structure of language, the construction of meaning, and the dimensions of social interaction are particular to individual cultures (Holland & Quinn, 1987). In order to more fully understand the underlying values and beliefs that affect all thinking, research from the field of cognitive anthropology might be incorporated into the multidisciplinary approach to understanding the interplay of teacher cognition and action. New has indicated that theoretical perspectives and research on teacher thinking continue to view "African-American culture as monolithic and one whose legacy produces flaws in the personality of its youth" (citing Washington, 1989). She does not state this as an artifact of Caucasian or Euro-American culture; however, within those groups, it is a commonly held perception. Is this perception ethnospecific, or derived from a particular belief system? A cognitive anthropological approach may help to define the bases for such perceptions as well as provide alternatives for modifying such perceptions to the benefit of the African-American as well as other ethnic (including Euro-American, Caucasian, or white) populations.

One approach, suggested by Hamilton, leads to the conclusion that symbol, ritualized interaction, visual and perceptual messages, and the manner in which learning environments are structured often represent what is implicitly thought, more so than what is explicitly stated. This study suggests that semiotic analysis, based in part in cognitive and cultural anthropology, may provide important understanding of underlying value orientation, cultural beliefs, and patterns of thought. The teaching environment is often rich with symbolic meaning, especially as teachers attempt to multiculturalize learning environments to match the multicultural aspects of the student population.

In these symbolically rich environments, researchers might expect to observe (and to compare) semiotica from both students and teachers. In this manner the degree of congruence of educational beliefs and values as represented by the disparate groups and individuals sharing the classroom can be determined. Rather than proposing this as a discrete field of study, semiotics and cultural anthropology provide important insights into the construction of meaning and the underlying cultural system through which knowledge is transmitted. Further, this approach supports a systems approach advocated in the next section.

A SYSTEMS APPROACH TO TEACHER THINKING

Several advantages of the Porter and Brophy (1988) model are that it is largely quantifiable, it contains a network of logical, procedural elements, and it addresses many of the relationships between teacher and student. However, its applicability to multicultural contexts is limited. This model does not fully account for or articulate the major external factors that provide the critical sociocultural elements which affect, if not determine, institutional and individual values, beliefs, assumptions, and cognition. In fact, those external factors are overwhelmingly determined by sociocultural contexts and the impact of the environment, as indicated earlier. As an alternative, consider the following model adapted from that proposed by Getzels and Guba (1957).

Getzels and Guba attempted to define the interaction of all social systems using a flexible model that was responsive to different environmental and cultural contexts. Importantly, they defined the role of values and beliefs in shaping behaviors, a factor which Porter and Brophy completely neglected. This model recognizes that culture and values are determining factors in the social behavior of both individuals and institutions. The model helps define the interplay between individuals and institutions; it could help define the interplay between teacher and students, teachers and schools, students and schools, and so on.

The definitions of culture, ethos, and values on the outer level of interaction form an underlying "belief system" affecting role, personality, expectations, and needs and dispositions of both the individual and the institution. These factors define the sociocultural context for both the individual (the student) and the institution (or its representative, the teachers) as well as the interactions which would frame both teacher and student behaviors in a sociocultural context. This model permits us to articulate those elements of shared implicit knowledge (the cultural belief system) that affect teacher thinking, especially as those elements are affected by the reflexive relationships between teachers, students, and the various sociocultural contexts.

Contributions to this volume support the use of a social systems model to articulate teacher thinking in cultural contexts, principally because the model deals with values and beliefs which shape both culture and cognition. Second, this conceptual model more appropriately responds to the need for flexibility in articulation, and is more holistic or systemic in its focus. The Porter and Brophy model does not adequately respond to the criteria which were indicated as important by the majority of contributors. That does not mean that one should reject the latter out of hand, since it provides a practical image for understanding teacher-student relationships in planning, delivering, and assessing instruction. Merging the two is not recommended because the models serve two different, but possibly compatible, purposes, with the social systems model having the greatest utility for conceptualizing, analyzing, and effecting change in teacher thinking.

EFFECTING AND MONITORING CHANGE

Throughout this volume, the contributors have pointed to the need for a process by which teachers and schools might implement and monitor change. They suggest that much of the change needed is contextually driven, deriving from the sociocultural contexts from which teachers and students come and the sociocultural context in which they interact. Therefore, any change model should be able to effectively use contextual frameworks rather than be limited by them. Hall and Hord (1987) indicate that, absent "needed systemic research and theory development around context," their Concerns-Based Adoption Model (CBAM) might be useful for this purpose (1987, pp. 346–347). Marshall's discussion of the multicultural dimension of teaching concerns is one application of CBAM principles which might be expanded upon, since it fits well with other professional practices and approaches which have been suggested.

The CBAM model is based on the idea that any innovation or proposed change will generate two components: stages of concern (SoC) and levels of use (LoU). Stages of concern correspond to teacher beliefs, attitudes, values, and assumptions, and levels of use correspond to the teaching behaviors and methods employed in the classroom. The model generally indicates that as stages of concern regarding change are reduced, the levels of use of the innovation or change will increase. If one is to modify the levels of use of appropriate teaching behaviors in multicultural contexts, then it is critically important to determine not only stages of concern, but the teacher's beliefs, values, and thinking which generate those concerns. The use of an instrument such as Marshall's Multicultural Teaching Concerns Survey (MCTS) in conjunction with the systemic analysis made possible by the Getzels and Guba models suggests a robust methodology for implementing and monitoring change. Further, this systemic approach is inherently reflective and constructivist in its conceptualization and supportive of focused schema developed from thinking about how to change thinking.

NEXT STEPS

Let us turn now to a further exploration of the questions raised by Ríos in the introduction to this volume. Many of these questions, placed initially on the back burner, now become important as (hopefully) readers have been led to a more holistic or systemic view of teacher thinking in broader contexts.

Although this volume has focused on culture, or more correctly ethnicity, as one of the principal determinants of the sociocultural context, it opened the door to considering other factors. Obviously, other indicators of diversity (gender, socioeconomic status, handicapping conditions, etc.) define values, beliefs, and thinking as much as do culture and ethnicity, and they evoke similar responses. Given a bias toward more systemic approaches, these factors must be considered when analyzing the effects of different patterns of teacher thinking. If research and implementation of change mechanisms exclusively deal with culture as evoking the need for change, then a risk exists of marginalizing particular cultures and developing unwarranted generalizations about them.

The second question asked if teacher thinking could be measured and/or modified. Whereas the first part of the question will continue to be a source of debate, the second is the more intriguing. There is general agreement (at least among the contributors) that changing core beliefs and values is a difficult task. If educational equity requires systemic change, then changing how educators think about their teaching and learning environments is an absolute necessity. If teacher thinking cannot be changed, then alternative strategies need to be considered. One of these is to replace "inappropriate" thinkers with "right" thinkers, including resolving the concomitant ethical and workability dilemmas associated with doing so. In either case, it is necessary to develop parallel systems which work toward educational equity if existing systems are unable to effect change from within. Again, this raises the dilemma of differential systems, and resurfaces old questions of "resegregation" and "separate but equal."

The degree to which cognition is translated into action lends itself to analysis from cognitive anthropological frameworks. Yet, investigating this area seems to be as problematic as quantifying or qualifying teacher thinking. Perhaps the most useful investigation of this question might center around the degree of correlation between thought and action, rather than the causal chain.

CONCLUSION

In the final analysis, these discussions of teacher thinking in cultural contexts represent starting points rather than end products for improving the educational environment for diverse student populations. There is utility in each of the approaches presented in this volume; however, the full measure of positive change can only come about through a more systemic analysis of factors which influence teacher thinking.

Don Locke's (1988) six-step model leading to an appreciation for and affirmation of cultural pluralism is particularly useful. He posits that the first step leading to teaching practice which operationalizes the goals of educational equity is to be aware of oneself. This awareness is only complete if the teacher reflectively, recursively, and consistently investigates his or her own belief and value systems. It is only through this process that the teacher is able to analyze his or her own sociocultural context which drives cognition and behavior. Locke's model continues with the stages of knowing one's own culture, the impacts of external factors of race, ethnicity, and socioeconomic status, and increasing one's knowledge base regarding other cultures. As one develops a greater understanding and appreciation for cultural similarities and differences and the sociocultural matrix in which they interact, one should be better prepared to implement changes leading to educational equity.

Much discussion has been devoted to notions of institutional and systemic change. It is important to explicitly restate the implicit understanding that institutions and systems are composed, first and foremost, of individuals. Educational institutions and systems will not be effective in multicultural contexts unless the individuals who work and learn there are effective. Individual and collective values, beliefs, cognition, and affect are the core elements in developing that sought-after goal: teaching effectiveness in *all* cultural contexts.

NOTES

INTRODUCTION

1. This term is used to identify those with European heritage living in the United States. It should not imply that all within this category are homogeneous.

2. This discussion is intended as a "working" conception of teacher cognition. So far no single conception of what constitutes teacher cognition has been accepted as definitive. Thus, each author may present her/his own understanding of the elements and processes associated with teacher cognition such as teachers' beliefs, knowledge, understandings, concerns, attributions, expectations, decision-making, interactive thoughts, perceptions, conceptions and/or theories. For my purpose and unless otherwise noted, teacher thinking is conceptualized as hierarchical with teachers' practical knowledge and beliefs comprising teachers' theories of professional action.

3. Like teacher cognition, each person has her or his own conception of what constitutes the "cultural context." Each author has been encouraged to describe his or her own conception of what he or she means by the cultural context. Although I acknowledge multiple cultural contexts (the family, the social group, the classroom, the school, etc.), for my purpose and unless otherwise noted, the cultural context describes either a school environment with a focus on multicultural education (Davidman & Davidman, 1994, for example, argue that multicultural education has less to do with who is in your classroom than it has to do with what and how you teach) or those classrooms and schools with a significant number of ethnic minority students.

4. As another example, consider Ogbu and Matute-Bianchi's (1986) work. Essentially they see minority student failure as the result of covert forms of self-defeating resistance to the power dynamics between differing minority groups and the dominant social group as they are recreated in schools (see also, New, Chapter 3, this volume).

CHAPTER 1. TEACHER THINKING IN URBAN SCHOOLS

1. I am grateful to Stanley Trent for his valuable comments on an earlier draft of this manuscript.

2. Because of the complex configuration of cultural forces present in urban settings, the term *urban* will be used as a synonym of *multicultural* throughout this chapter. Although I am aware that the construct *multicultural* is broader than the notion of *urbanicity,* I use them inter-

changeably to emphasize the rich cultural diversity found in urban settings.

3. Studies on teachers' recollections of student progress or difficulties have offered conflicting results (Artiles, 1994; Housner & Griffey, 1985), and thus further research is warranted.

4. Research on the instructional milieu of urban classrooms is one of the most prolific areas of inquiry in urban studies. Two main approaches have been used in this camp: microscopic and macroscopic models. The former refers to the efforts undertaken (a) to identify and test instructional practices that produce the highest rates of student academic achievement or (b) to examine specific instructional and social processes that have a bearing on academic outcomes. The research conducted from a macroscopic perspective involves the design and implementation of major intervention programs that generally include a multitude of specialists, intervention strategies, and assessment procedures that are implemented at a large scale. This literature will not be reviewed because of the focus of this volume, but readers can refer to numerous sources for a synthesis of these research programs (e.g., Carta 1991; Greenwood et al., 1992; Slavin, Karweit, & Madden, 1989; Winfield & Manning, 1992).

5. There is considerable debate about the use of the term *disadvantaged*. Unfortunately, space constraints do not allow me to elaborate on the ideological and philosophical underpinnings of this issue. Thus I use this term as applied in this particular literature (i.e., to refer to low-income students).

CHAPTER 2. TEACHERS', ADMINISTRATORS', AND STAFF'S IMPLICIT THINKING ABOUT "AT-RISK" URBAN HIGH SCHOOL LATINO STUDENTS

1. This research was undertaken with a grant awarded during 1989–1990 from the Inter-University program for Latino Research and the Social Research Council for a study entitled "The Interrelationship of Educational and Socio-Cultural Factors Affecting 'At Risk' Hispanic Students." David Whitenack, a doctoral candidate at Stanford University, and Dr. Carmen Ada Gonzalez, a practicing psychotherapist in Boston, are both acknowledged for their research assistantship.

2. The eight focal students from the major study were followed during 1989–1990, and return visits to the school made their outcomes known. During 1991 -1992, visits to the bilingual program teachers' classrooms were made to witness how different students were integrated through English as a Second Language courses.

3. The larger study is currently in press: see Montero-Sieburth (1993). "The Effects of Schooling Processes and Practices on Potential At-Risk Latino High School Students." In Ralph Rivera and Sonia Nieto (eds.). *Latinos in Massachusetts*. Amherst: University of Massachusetts Press.

4. Citywide dropout rates were estimated to be between 45 and 55 percent in Boston during 1989–1990. Latino dropout rates at this school numbered 44 in grades 9 to 12. Latino enrollments in grades 9 to 12 in June numbered 235, and the number of yearly dropouts per 100 Hispanic students was 15.8 (School Profile Tables for FY 90 High School Dropout Rates by Race, calculated by HS Zone Method).

5. By June of 1990, there were 149 Latinos in the bilingual program.

6. Bilingual classes are distinguished from regular classes throughout the school. The author makes this distinction sharper by using *bilingual* to mean "Spanish-bilingual" and *mainstream* to mean predominantly English-speaking classes.

7. The term *mainstream* is preferred instead of the term *regular teacher* to distinguish between teachers who teach traditional subjects, math, science, civics, and so on in English and bilingual teachers who use either Spanish or English as the medium of instruction.

8. By the end of the 1990 academic year, the Compact Venture administrator no longer had funding, the career counselor who specifically worked with at-risk students was leaving his position to go to graduate school, and the resource specialist's grant ran out. Thus this was the last year that students received any of these services.

9. The notion of assigning a group of ninth graders to the same teacher for all major subjects is known as clustering. Clusters are specifically directed for "at risk" students who have low reading scores. The purpose behind creating a smaller cohort of students is to develop a close-knit program of "hands on" help. Teachers are available for tutoring and guidance under this program.

10. The school's Bilingual Department appears to have a clearly defined method for identifying at-risk students. After each grading period, the Bilingual Department head checks the report card of each bilingual student and monitors any warning notices teachers have sent home to the parents of bilingual students. Students with two warnings are considered to be at risk and are then identified as such. The mainstream program does not have a comparable process. Identification of possible at-risk students is left entirely up to the teachers and counselors.

11. Twenty-two percent reported that the methods were basically the same. Twelve-and-a-half percent added that cultural factors should be considered; another 9 percent mentioned that students should get involved in school activities.

12. Some departments, aware of this problem, have developed pull-out "illiterate" classes to help these students. While this may be viewed as an attempt at remediation, it may also confound the problem if illiteracy is not viewed as a school-wide phenomenon.

13. The Special Education Department appears to have a clearly defined evaluation process for individual at-risk Latino students. Once a

student is referred to the Special Education Department, the department contacts the parents to obtain permission for evaluation and referral of the student. A bilingual teacher is assigned by the Special Education Department as the student's case manager, and this person gathers information from the student's parents and teachers to determine the nature of the problem. If necessary, the student is psychologically and medically tested as part of this diagnostic process. Once this is completed, the Special Education Department recommends a program designed to prevent the student from dropping out of school. This individualized education plan is followed closely by the Special Education Department, which contacts the parents and the teachers, as well as concerned parties, as they treat each Latino at-risk student on an individual basis.

14. In point of fact, for many of the immigrant Latino students, reading comic books is widely used throughout their countries of origin as a popular means to elicit reading of other materials as well as for developing high levels of "comprehensibility" of comic books.

15. Data from the Hispanic Policy Development Project (Vol. I, 1984) project that the proportion of Hispanic schoolchildren will rise from 10.5 to 33 percent by the year 2000 with ever-increasing numbers of dropouts.

16. According to the 1989–1990 census, there are 18 million Hispanics in the United States, yet this is considered a conservative figure given the unprecedented numbers of undocumented immigrants that have arrived in the last ten years and the census undercount. It is more likely that this figure is about 22 million.

CHAPTER 4. RESISTANCE AND RETHINKING

1. The school district where this study took place is besieged with requests for student teaching placements from seven different teacher preparation institutions in the local area. District officials do not allow "requests" and student teachers have no input in their school assignment. The students may refuse a placement and request another, but most do not because they are worried about how this may appear to potential employers.

2. The names of the school, the district, the college, and the students have been changed to ensure anonymity.

3. The researcher was the student teaching supervisor.

4. For more information about action research, see Kemmis & McTaggart (1988), *The Action Research Planner* (Victoria, Australia: Deakin University Press), or chapters by Noffke, Brennan, & Wood in B. R. Tabachnick, & K. Zeichner (eds.), *Issues and Practices in Inquiry-Oriented Teacher Education* (1991) (Bristol, PA: Falmer Press).

CHAPTER 5. TEACHERS' PRINCIPLES OF PRACTICE FOR TEACHING IN MULTICULTURAL CLASSROOMS

1. This paper is a partial summary of my dissertation conducted under the direction of R. Lehrer at the University of Wisconsin. For a complete description of any aspect of this study, see Ríos (1992). For a review of the qualitative component of this study, see Ríos (1993).

2. I take research on teachers' theorizing to be a variation of research on schema theory.

3. I see knowledge and beliefs as two essential elements that make up an individual's theories.

4. Briefly, to be assured that these scenes met the criteria specified by Fransella and Bannister (1977), I adapted the scenes from a book of teacher-generated descriptions of real classroom incidents (Kohut & Range, 1979). I modified the scenes so that the race and gender of the student were made explicit (three of the scenes did not specify a race). It should be noted that each scene did not portray an issue faced exclusively by students of a specific race or gender (i.e., though one race was specified, that type of issue might be presented by a student of another race or gender). I then gave the scenes to all eleven counselors at the target research school. The goal was to assure myself that the scenes were realistic at the local site. I received seven responses. Briefly, the results showed that all but one of the scenes were appropriate. Half of the scenes needed a word, phrase, or sentence modified. Four scenes needed two or three sentences modified. All scenes contained average ratings (on a scale of 1 = no relevance to 5 = very relevant) of between 3 and 4.5. Based on these responses, I reconstructed the scenes one final time.

5. As an example of a scene, consider the following: Stacy is a black tenth grader who gets straight U's on his report card because he makes no effort to cooperate in any of his classes. A bright young man, he is completely turned off by school, lacks desire, and frequently misses school. He would like to take a course in black history but no such class is offered this semester. His parents are aware of the situation but do little more than encourage him to take more "academic" courses.

CHAPTER 6. TEACHING WRITING IN A MULTICULTURAL CLASSROOM: STUDENTS AND TEACHERS AS STORYTELLERS

1. The basic features of writing workshop approaches are based on a functional perspective on language use wherein (1) the student decides on the purposes, form, and audience for her or his text; (2) feedback during the construction of the text is given by the teacher in one-on-one conferences, in minilessons, and by peers; and (3) evaluation of student writing is based on a portfolio system that the student puts together to represent her or his growth as a writer. The role of the teacher is to act from

an interpretivist position as a facilitator of response (Nystrand, 1990) and to work in "dialogic" relationship with writers (Dyson, 1992a) by following student purposes for writing acts. A primary instructional goal of the approach is to create a context in which students find value in school writing through their interactions within the social context of a community of writers.

2. All names of persons and places have been changed to protect anonymity.

3. The term *white* is used to denote all members of the dominant Euro-American culture.

CHAPTER 7. TACIT MESSAGES

1. The term *messages* represents the information, usually cultural, that is communicated implicitly or explicitly from one person to another. In this case, the messages are sent between teacher and student. These cultural messages may convey information about environment, symbols, and behavior as well as information about the placement of the individual in that context.

2. In this chapter *self* depicts the student and how that student might see himself or herself in relation to the classroom and school. I wanted to know whether a student might find artifacts, symbols, or people with whom he or she identified in the classroom, or not. For instance, were there pictures of African-American people, or not, in a class with predominantly African-American students?

3. I am compelled here to note that the teachers of Bradley Renaissance School have worked long, hard, and tirelessly to produce the best education possible for their students. Without a doubt, they always made choices with the best interest of their students in mind. Unfortunately, they are bound by a system that lacks tangible checkpoints regarding issues of culture, class, race, and gender and where they could not stop doing what they did not know existed.

CHAPTER 10. USING A CONSTRUCTIVIST APPROACH TO CHALLENGE PRESERVICE TEACHERS' THINKING ABOUT DIVERSITY IN EDUCATION

1. The activities suggested in this section are provided by the first author and are based on her experiences in teaching on racism in an introductory multicultural education course for preservice teachers.

2. A program of study designed specifically to learn about various ethnic groups is referred to as a "multiethnic education." This type of program or emphasis is not, however, to be interpreted as being synonymous with multicultural education.

3. The summer program was offered at the local elementary school for youth five to fifteen years of age. The local and regional artists served

as master teachers for their particular art or craft forms, and the university students served at teaching assistants. However, it should be noted that the university team was primarily responsible for daily preparation of materials, supplies, and space needs. Among the art forms in the program were traditional Mexican dances, creative writing, pottery and ceramics, jewelry making, visual arts (drawing, sketching, painting), pinatas, crafts, games, and drama. Only one of the ten students was an art education major. Most students had limited knowledge about art in general, and less about Mexican arts and crafts.

CHAPTER 11. LEARNING TO TEACH IN CROSS-CULTURAL SETTINGS

1. As is common practice, pseudonyms are used throughout the chapter.

2. As my graduate assistant, Darlene Bell, rightly noted, teachers have to be careful with carrying. If used inappropriately, students can be hurt, insulted, and embarrassed in front of their peers. They can, in fact, be carried too far. It is possible that Matt's student was trying to tell him that.

REFERENCES

INTRODUCTION

Anderson-Levitt, K. M. (1984). Teacher interpretation of student behavior: Cognitive and social processes. *The Elementary School Journal, 84*(3), 315–337.

Argyis, C., & Schon, D. (1975). *Theory in practice.* San Francisco: Jossey-Bass.

Banks, J. A. (1993). The canon debate, knowledge construction, and multicultural education. *Educational Researcher, 22*(5), 4–14.

Borko, H., Cone, R., Russo, N. A., & Shavelson, R. J. (1979). Teachers' decision-making. In P. L. Peterson and H. J. Walberg (Eds.), *Research on teaching.* Berkeley: McCutchan.

Brophy, J. E., & Good, T. L. (1974). *Teacher-student relationships: Causes and consequences.* New York: Holt, Rinehart & Winston.

Calderhead, J. (1983, April). *Research into teachers' and student-teachers' cognitions: Exploring the nature of classroom practice.* Paper presented at the annual meeting of the American Educational Research Association, Montreal, Canada.

Cazden, C. B. (1986). Classroom discourse. In M. C. Wittrock (Ed.), *Handbook of research on teaching* (3rd ed.). New York: Macmillan Publishing Co.

Chi, M. T. H., Glaser, R., & Rees, E. (1982). Expertise in problem solving. In R. J. Sternberg (Ed.), *Advances in the psychology of human intelligence* (pp. 7–75). Hillsdale, NJ: Erlbaum.

Clark, C. (1988). Teacher preparation: Contributions of research on teacher thinking. *Educational Researcher,* March, 5–11.

Clark, C. M., & Peterson, P. L. (1986). Teachers' thought processes. In M. C. Wittrock (Ed.), *Handbook of research on teaching* (3rd ed.). New York: Macmillan.

Clark, C. (1985, May). *Ten years of conceptual development in research on teacher thinking.* Paper presented at the ISATT's Conference, Tilburg, The Netherlands.

Cochran-Smith, M. (1993, May). *Color blindness and basket making are not the answers.* Paper presented at the Southwest Regional Laboratory METRO Center Seminar on Teachers for the 1990's and Beyond, Los Alamitos, CA.

Copa, P. M. (1984, April). *Making theory in the first year of teaching.* Paper presented at the annual meeting of the American Educational Research Association, New Orleans.

REFERENCES

Cummins, J. (1986). Empowering minority students: A framework for intervention. *Harvard Educational Review, 56,* 18–36.

Davidman, L., & Davidman, P. T. (1994). *Teaching with a multicultural perspective.* White Plains, NY: Longman.

Duffy, G. (1977). *A study of teacher conception of reading.* Paper presented at the National Reading Conference, New Orleans.

Eisner, E. W. (1985). *The educational imagination: On the design and evaluation of school programs* (2nd ed.). New York: Macmillan.

Elbaz, F. (1981). The teacher's "practical knowledge": Report of a case study. *Curriculum Inquiry, 11,* 43–71.

Erickson, F. (1986). Qualitative methods in research on teaching. In M. C. Wittrock (Ed.), *Handbook of research on teaching* (3rd ed.). New York: Macmillan.

Feiman-Nemser, S., & Floden, R. E. (1986). The cultures of teaching. In M. C. Wittrock (Ed.), *Handbook of research on teaching* (3rd. ed.) (pp. 505–526). New York: Macmillan Publishing Co.

Freire, P. (1968). *Pedagogy of the oppressed.* New York: Herder & Herder.

Freire, P. (1994). *The pedagogy of hope.* New York: Continuum Publishing.

Garcia, E. (1994). *Understanding and meeting the challenge of student cultural diversity.* Boston: Houghton Mifflin.

Good, T. L., & Brophy, J. E. (1986). Teacher behavior and student achievement. In M. C. Wittrock (Ed.), *Handbook of research on teaching* (3rd ed.). New York: Macmillan.

Grant, C. A., & Secada, W. G. (1990). Preparing teachers for diversity. In W. R. Houston (Ed.), *Handbook of research on teacher education.* New York: Macmillan. (pp. 403–422).

Haberman, M. (1991). The rationale for training adults as teachers. In C. Sleeter (Ed.), *Empowerment through multicultural education* (pp. 275–286). Albany, NY: SUNY Press.

Jackson, G., & Corsca, C. (1974). The inequality of educational opportunity in the Southwest: An observational study of ethnically mixed classrooms. *American Educational Research Journal, 11,* 219–229.

Jackson, P. W. (1968). *Life in classrooms.* New York: Holt, Rinehart & Winston.

Kaplan, A. (1964). *The conduct of inquiry: Methodology for behavioral science.* San Francisco: Chadler.

Kelly, G. A. (1955). *The psychology of personal constructs* (2 Vols.). New York: W. W. Norton.

Ladson-Billings, G. (1992). Culturally relevant teaching: The key to making multicultural education work. In C. Grant (Ed.), *Research and Multicultural Education* (pp. 106–121). London: Falmer Press.

Larkin, J. H., McDermott, J., Simon, D. P., & Simon, H. A. (1980). Models of competence in solving physics problems. *Cognitive Science, 4,* 317–345.

Lavely, C., Berger, N., Bullock, D., Follman, J., Kromrey, J., & Sawilowsky, S. (1986, November). *Expertise in teaching: Expert pedagogues*. Paper presented at the Institute for Instrumental Research and Practice, University of Florida, Tampa.

Leinhardt, G. (1990). Capturing craft knowledge in teaching. *Educational Researcher, 19,* 18–25.

Leinhardt, G., & Greeno, J. G. (1986). The cognitive skill of teaching. *Journal of Educational Psychology, 78*(2), 75–95.

Lortie, D. (1975). *Schoolteacher.* Chicago: University of Chicago Press.

Macmillan, C. J. B., & Garrison, J. W. (1984). Using the "new philosophy of science" in criticizing current research traditions in education. *Educational Researcher, 13,* 15–21.

Mandl, H., & Huber, G. (1982). *On teachers subjective theories.* Paper presented at the annual meeting of the American Educational Research Association, New York.

McCutcheon, G., & Jung, B. (1990). Alternative perspectives in action research. *Theory Into Practice,* (29)3, 144–151.

McDaniel, C. O., McDaniel, N. C., & McDaniel, A. K. (1988). Transferability of multicultural education from training to practice. *International Journal of Intercultural Relations, 12*(1), 19–33.

McDiarmid, W. (1991). What teachers need to know about cultural diversity: Restoring subject matter to the picture. In M. M. Kennedy (Ed.), *Teaching academic subjects to diverse learners.* New York: Teachers College Press.

Montero-Sieburth, M. (1989). Restructuring teachers' knowledge in urban settings. *Journal of Negro Education, 58*(3), 332–344.

Morine-Dershimer, G. (1979). *Teacher plan and classroom reality: The South Bay study.* Michigan State University: Institute for Research.

Morine-Dershimer, G. (1985). *Talking, listening and learning in elementary classrooms.* New York: Longman.

Munby, H. (1984). A qualitative approach to the study of a teacher's beliefs. *Journal of Research in Science Teaching, 21*(1), 27–38.

Neisser, U. (1967). *Cognitive psychology.* New York: Appleton-Century-Crofts.

Ogbu, J. U., & Matute-Bianchi, M. E. (1986). Understanding sociocultural factors: Knowledge, identity, and school adjustment. In Bilingual Education Office, California Department of Education (Ed.), *Beyond language: Social and cultural factors in schooling language minority students.* Los Angeles, Evaluation, Dissemination, and Assessment Center, California State University.

Pajares, M. F. (1992). Teachers' beliefs and educational research: Cleaning up a messy construct. *Review of Educational Research, 62*(3), 307–332.

Pearson, J. (1985). Are teachers' beliefs incongruent with their observed classroom behavior? *The Urban Review, 17*(2), 128–146.

REFERENCES

Peterson, P. L. (1988). Teachers' and students' cognitional knowledge for classroom teaching and learning. *Educational Researcher, 17*(5), 5–14.

Porter, A. C., & Brophy, J. (1988). Synthesis of research on good teaching: Insights from the work of the Institute for Research on Teaching. *Educational Leadership, 45*(8), 74–85.

Resnick, L. B. (1989). Introduction. In L. B. Resnick (Ed.), *Knowing, learning and instruction: Essays in honor of Robert Glaser* (pp. 1–24). Hillsdale, NJ: L. Erlbaum.

Sadker, M. P., & Sadker, D. M. (1985). Sexism in the classroom: From grade school to graduate school. *Phi Delta Kappan, 67*(7), 512–515.

Schon, D. A. (1983). *The reflective practitioner.* New York: Basic Books.

Shulman, L. S. (1986). Paradigms and research programs in the study of teaching: A contemporary perspective. In M. C. Wittrock (Ed.), *Handbook of research on teaching* (3rd ed.). New York: Macmillan.

Shulman, L. S. (1987). Knowledge and teaching: Foundations of the new reform. *Harvard Educational Review, 57,* 1–22.

Solas J. (1992). Investigating teacher and student thinking about the process of teaching and learning using autobiography and repertory grid. *Review of Educational Research, 62*(2), 205–225.

Stephens, J. (1967). *The process of schooling.* New York: Holt, Rinehart & Winston.

Sue, S., & Padilla, A. (1986). Ethnic minority issues in the United States: Challenges for the educational system. In Bilingual Education Office, California Department of Education (Ed.), *Beyond language: Social and cultural factors in schooling language minority students.* Los Angeles, Evaluation, Dissemination, and Assessment Center, California State University.

Tabachnick, R. B., & Zeichner, K. M. (1986). Teacher beliefs and classroom behaviors: Some teacher responses to inconsistency. In M. Ben-Peretz, R. Bromme, and R. Halkes (Eds.), *Advances of research on teacher thinking* (pp. 84–96). Lisse: Swets and Zeitlinger.

U.S. Department of Education, National Center for Educational Statistics (1993a). *The condition of education.* Washington, DC, 1993.

U.S. Department of Education, National Center for Educational Statistics (1993b). *Digest of education statistics.* Washington, DC, 1993.

Voss, J. F., Greene, T. R., Post, T. A., & Penner, B. C. (1983). Problem solving skill in the social sciences. In G. H. Bower (Ed.), *The psychology of learning and motivation* (vol. 17, pp. 165–213). New York: Academic Press.

Wittrock, M. (1987). Teaching and student thinking. *Journal of Teacher Education, 38,* 30–33.

Wright, B. C., & Tuska, S. A. (1968). From dream to life in the psychology of becoming a teacher. *School Review, 76,* 253–293.

Zeichner, K. M., & Gore, J. M. (1990). Teacher socialization. In W. R. Houston (Ed.), *Handbook of research on teacher education* (pp. 329–348). New York: Macmillan.

CHAPTER 1. TEACHER THINKING IN URBAN SCHOOLS

Ames, C. (1992). Classrooms: Goals, structures, and student motivation. *Journal of Educational Psychology, 84*, 261–271.

Armour-Thomas, E. (1989). The application of teacher cognition in the classroom: A new teaching competency. *Journal of Research and Development in Education, 22* (30), 29–37.

Artiles, A.J. (1992). *Teacher thinking and teacher effectiveness during second-grade reading instruction in inner city schools in Guatemala City: An exploratory study.* Unpublished doctoral dissertation. University of Virginia, Charlottesville, VA

Artiles, A.J. (1994, March). *Assessing teacher cognitions in context: A case study in Guatemala's urban schools.* Paper presented at the annual meeting of the Comparative and International Education Society, San Diego, CA.

Artiles, A.J. (1995, April). *Learning to teach in multicultural contexts: exploring preservice teachers' knowledge change* [Part 2]. Paper presented at the annual meeting of the Council for Exceptional Children, Indianapolis, IN.

Artiles, A.J., & Aguirre-Munoz, Z. (in press). Redefining classroom management for students with problem behaviors: The need for a contextualized research program on teaching. In F.E. Obiakor & B. Algozzine (Eds.), *Managing problem behaviors: Perspectives for special educators and other professionals.* Dubuque, IA: Kendall Hunt.

Artiles, A.J., Mostert, M.P., & Tankersley, M. (1994). Assessing the link between teacher cognitions, teacher behaviors, and pupil responses to lessons. *Teaching and Teacher Education, 10*, 465–481.

Artiles, A.J., & Trent, S.C. (1990). *Characteristics and constructs describing effective teachers.* ERIC Clearinghouse on Teacher Education. (ERIC Document Reproduction Service No. ED 340 691)

Artiles, A.J., & Trent, S.C. (1994). Overrepresentation of minority students in special education: A continuing debate. *The Journal of Special Education, 27*, 410–437.

Avery, P.G., & Walker, C. (1993). Prospective teachers' perceptions of ethnic and gender differences in academic achievement. *Journal of Teacher Education, 44*, 27–37.

Bandura, A. (1986). *Social foundations of thought and action: A social cognitive theory.* Englewood Cliffs, NJ: Prentice Hall.

Bandura, A. (1993). Perceived self-efficacy in cognitive development and functioning. *Educational Psychologist, 28*, 117–148.

REFERENCES

Banks, J.A. (1993). Multicultural education: Historical development, dimensions, and practice. *Review of Research in Education, 19*, 3–50.

Berliner, D. (1987). Ways of thinking about students and classrooms by more and less experienced teachers. In J. Calderhead (Ed.), *Exploring teachers' thinking* (pp. 60–83). London: Cassell.

Blumenfeld, P.C. (1992). Classroom learning and motivation: Clarifying and expanding goal theory. *Journal of Educational Psychology, 84*, 272–281.

Borko, H., Bellamy, M.L., Sanders, L. (1992). A cognitive analysis of patterns in science instruction by expert and novice teachers. In T. Russell & H. Munby (Eds.), *Teachers and teaching: From classroom to reflection* (pp. 49–70). London: Falmer.

Borko, H., & Livingston, C. (1989). Cognition and improvisation: Differences in mathematics instruction by expert and novice teachers. *American Educational Research Journal, 26*, 473–498.

Borko, H., & Shavelson, R.J. (1990). Teacher decision making. In B.F. Jones & L. Idol (Eds.), *Dimensions of thinking and cognitive instruction* (pp. 311–346). Hillsdale, NJ: Lawrence Erlbaum.

Bromme, R. (1987). Teachers' assessments of students' difficulties and progress in understanding in the classroom. In J. Calderhead (Ed.), *Exploring teachers' thinking* (pp. 125–146). London: Cassell.

Brophy, J., & Good, T.L. (1986). Teacher behavior and student achievement. In M.C. Wittrock (Ed.), *Handbook of research on teaching* (pp. 328–375). New York: Macmillan.

Carta, J.J. (1991). Education for young children in inner-city classrooms. *American Behavioral Scientist, 34*, 440–453.

Carter, K. (1990). Teachers' knowledge and learning to teach. In C.V. Houston (Ed.), *Handbook of research on teacher education* (pp. 291–310). New York: Macmillan.

Carter, K. (1993). The place of story in the study of teaching and teacher education. *Educational Researcher, 22* (1), 5–12.

Carter, K., Sabers, D., Cushing, K., Pinnegar, S., & Berliner, D.C. (1987). Processing and using information about students: A study of expert, novice, and postulant teachers. *Teaching and Teacher Education, 3*, 147–157.

Cazden, C.B. (1986). Classroom discourse. In M.C. Wittrock (Ed.), *Handbook of research on teaching* (pp.432–463). New York: Macmillan.

Chandler, S. (1992). Learning for what purpose? Questions when viewing classroom learning from a sociocultural curriculum perspective. In H.H. Marshall (Ed.), *Redefining student learning* (pp. 33–58). Norwood, NJ: Ablex.

Chow, V., & McClafferty, K. (1995, April). *Learning to teach in multicultural contexts: Exploring preservice teachers' knowledge change*

(Part 1). Paper presented at the annual meeting of the Council for Exceptional Children, Indianapolis, IN.

Clark, C. M., & Peterson, P.L. (1986). Teachers' thought processes. In M.C. Wittrock (Ed.), *Handbook of research on teaching* (pp. 255–296). New York: Macmillan.

Clark, M.D., & Artiles, A.J. (1994, July). *The impact of boys' learning disabilities on teachers' attributions for test failure: A cross-cultural comparison.* Paper presented at the 23rd International Congress of Applied Psychology, Madrid, Spain.

Cochran, K.F., DeRuiter, J.A., & King, R.A. (1993). Pedagogical content knowing: An integrative model for teacher preparation. *Journal of Teacher Education, 44,* 263–272.

Cochran-Smith, M., & Lytle, S.L. (1992). Interrogating cultural diversity: Inquiry and action. *Journal of Teacher Education, 43,* 104–115.

Colton, A.B., & Sparks-Langer, G.M. (1993). A conceptual framework to guide the development of teacher reflection and decision making. *Journal of Teacher Education, 44,* 45–54.

Condon, M.W.F., Clyde, J.A., Kyle, D.W., & Hovda, R.A. (1993). A constructivist basis for teaching and teacher education: A framework for program development and research on graduates. *Journal of Teacher Education, 44,* 273–278.

Cooper, H. M. (1985). Models of teacher expectation communication. In J.B. Dusek (Ed.), *Teacher expectancies* (pp. 135–158). Hillsdale, NJ: Erlbaum.

Cooper, H.M., & Tom, D.Y.H. (1984). Teacher expectation research: A review with implications for classroom instruction. *The Elementary School Journal, 85,* 77–89.

Cushner, K., McClelland, A., & Safford, P. (1992). *Human diversity in education: An integrative approach.* New York: McGraw-Hill.

Duranti, A., & Goodwin, C. (1992). Rethinking context: An introduction. In C. Goodwin & A. Duranti (Eds.), *Rethinking context: Language as an interactive phenomenon* (pp. 1–42). Cambridge: Cambridge University Press.

Dwyer, C.A. (1993). Teaching and diversity: Meeting the challenges for innovative teacher assessments. *Journal of Teacher Education, 44,* 119–129.

Farkas, G., Grobe, R.P., Sheehan, D., & Shuan, Y. (1990). Cultural resources and school success: Gender, ethnicity, and poverty groups within an urban school district. *American Sociological Review, 55,* 127–142.

Fennema, E., Peterson, P.L., Carpenter, T.P., & Lubinski, C.A. (1990). Teachers' atttributions and beliefs about girls, boys, and mathematics. *Educational Studies in Mathematics, 21,* 55–69.

Fenstermacher, G. (1994). The knower and the known: The nature of

REFERENCES

knowledge in research on teaching. *Review of Research in Education, 20,* 3–56.

Finn, J.D., & Voelkl, K.E. (1993). School characteristics related to student engagement. *Journal of Negro Education, 62,* 249–268.

Floden, R.E., & Klinzing, H.G. (1990). What can research on teacher thinking contribute to teacher preparation? A second opinion. *Educational Researcher, 19* (5), 15–20.

Garbarino, J., Dubrow, N., Kostelny, K., & Pardo, C. (1992). *Children in danger: Coping with the consequences of community violence.* San Francisco: Jossey-Bass.

Gordon, E.W., & Armour-Thomas, E. (1992). Urban education. In M. Alkin (Ed.), *Encyclopedia of educational research* (pp. 1459–1470). New York: Macmillan.

Graham, S. (1990). Communicating low ability in the classroom: Bad things good teachers sometimes do. In S. Graham & V.S. Folkes (Eds.), *Attribution theory: Applications to achievement, mental health, and interpersonal conflict* (pp. 17–36). Hillsdale, NJ: Erlbaum.

Greenfield, L. (1979). Engineering student problem solving. In J. Lockhead & J. Clement (Eds.), *Cognitive process instruction: Research on teaching thinking skills* (pp. 229–238). Philadelphia: The Franklin Institute Press.

Greenwood, C.R., Carta, J.J., Hart, B., Kamps, D., Terry, B., Arreaga-Mayer, C., Atwater, J., Walker, D., Risley, T., & Delquardi, J. (1992). Out of the laboratory and into the community: 26 years of applied behavior analysis at the Juniper Gardens Children's Project. *American Psychologist, 47,* 1464–1474.

Greenwood, C.R., Delquadri, J., Stanley, S.O., Sasso, G., Whorton, D., & Schulte, D. (1981, Summer). Allocating opportunity to learn as a basis for academic remediation: A developing model for teaching. *Monographs in Behavior Disorders* (pp. 21–33).

Gutierrez, K. (1993). How talk, context, and script shape contexts for learning: A cross-case comparison of journal sharing. *Linguistics and Education, 5,* 355–365.

Gutierrez, K., Kreuter, B., & Larson, J. (in press). James Brown vs Brown vs Board of Education: Scripts, counterscripts, and underlife in the classroom. *Harvard Educational Review.*

Haberman, M. (1984). Teacher education in 2000: Implications of demographic and societal trends. *Education and Urban Society, 16,* 497–509.

Haberman, M., & Rickards, W.H. (1990). Urban teachers who quit. *Urban Education, 25,* 297–303.

Hodapp, R.M., & Dykens, E.M. (1994). Mental retardation's two cultures of behavioral research. *American Journal of Mental Retardation, 98,* 675–687.

Housner, L., & Griffey, D. (1985). Teacher cognition: Differences in planning and interactive decision making between experienced and inexperienced teachers. *Research Quarterly for Exercise and Sport, 56,* 45–53.

Hunter, M., & Barker, G. (1987). "If at first . . . ": Attribution theory in the classroom. *Educational Leadership, 45* (2), 50–53.

Isenberg, J.P. (1990). Teachers' thinking and beliefs and classroom practice. *Childhood Education, 66,* 322–327.

Johnson, K.E. (1992). The relationship between teachers' beliefs and practices during literacy instruction for non-native speakers of English. *Journal of Reading Behavior, 24,* 83–108.

Kagan, D.M. (1990). Ways of evaluating teacher cognition: Inferences concerning the Goldilocks principle. *Review of Educational Research, 60,* 419–469.

Keogh, B.K. (1992). Risk and protective factors in school environments. In *School readiness: Scientific perspectives.* Washington, DC: National Center for Education in Maternal and Child Health.

Kincheloe, J.L., & Steinberg, S.R. (1993). A tentative description of post-formal thinking: The critical confrontation with cognitive theory. *Harvard Educational Review, 63,* 296–320.

Kozol, J. (1991). *Savage inequalities: Children in America's schools.* New York: Crown.

Lampert, M., & Clark, C.M. (1990). Expert knowledge and expert thinking in teaching: A response to Floden and Klinzing. *Educational Researcher, 19* (5), 21–23.

Lee, V.E., Winfield, L.F., & Wilson, T.C. (1991). Academic behaviors among high-achieving African-American students. *Education and Urban Society, 24,* 65–86.

Leinhardt, G., & Putnam, R.T. (1987). The skill of learning from classroom lessons. *American Educational Research Journal, 24,* 557–587.

Leinhardt, G., & Putnam, R.T., Stein, M.K., & Baxter, J. (1991). Where subject knowledge matters. *Advances in Research on Teaching, 2,* 87–113.

Levine, D.U., Levine, R.R., & Eubanks, E.E. (1985). Successful implementation of instruction at inner-city schools. *Journal of Negro Education, 54,* 313–332.

Levine, D.U., & Ornstein, A.C. (1989). Research on classroom and school effectiveness and its implications for improving big city schools. *The Urban Review, 21,* 81–94.

Luthar, S.S., & Zigler, E. (1991). Vulnerability and resilience: A review of research on resilience in childhood. *American Journal of Orthopsychiatry, 61,* 6–22.

Lytle, J.H. (1992). Prospects for reforming urban schools. *Urban Education, 27,* 109–131.

Manning, B.H., & Payne, B.D. (1993). A Vygotskyan-based theory of

REFERENCES

teacher cognition: Toward the acquisition of mental reflection and self-regulation. *Teaching and Teacher Education, 9,* 361–371.

Marshall, H.H. (1992). Seeing, redefining, and support student learning. In H.H. Marshall (Ed.), *Redefining student learning* (pp. 1–32). Norwood, NJ: Ablex.

Marshall, H.H., & Weinstein, R.S. (1986). Classroom context of student-perceived differential teacher treatment. *Journal of Educational Psychology, 78,* 441–453.

Maxwell, D.L. (1993). *A multivariate analysis of school features associated with urban teachers' sense of efficacy and propensity to stay in teaching.* Unpublished manuscript. UCLA Graduate School of Education, Los Angeles, CA.

McDiarmid, G.W. (1992). What to do about differences? A study of multicultural education for teacher trainees in the Los Angeles Unified School Dsitrict. *Journal of Teacher Education, 43,* 83–93.

McLaren, P. (1989). *Life in schools.* New York: Longman.

Meece, J.L. (in press). The role of motivation in self-regulated learning. In D.H. Schunk & B.J. Zimmerman (Eds.), *Self-regulation of learning and performance: Issues and educational applications.* Hillsdale, NJ: Erlbaum.

Montero-Sieburth, M. (1989). Restructuring teachers' knowledge for urban settings. *Journal of Negro Education, 58,* 332–344.

Morine-Dershimer. G. (1983). Instructional strategy and the "creation" of classroom status. *American Educational Research Journal, 20,* 645–661.

Morine-Dershimer, G. (1985). *Talking, listening, and learning in elementary classrooms.* New York: Longman.

Morine-Dershimer, G., Saunders, S., Artiles, A.J., Mostert. M.P., Tankersley, M., Trent, S.C., & Nuttycombe, D.G. (1992). Choosing among alternatives for tracing conceptual change. *Teaching and Teacher Education, 8,* 471–483.

Natriello, G., Pallas, E.L., & McDill, A.M. (1990). *Schooling disadvantaged children: Racing against catastrophe.* New York: Teachers College Press.

Needels, M.C. (1991). Comparison of student, first-year, and experienced teachers' interpretations of a first-grade lesson. *Teaching and Teacher Education, 7,* 269–278.

Nespor, J. (1987). The role of beliefs in the practice of teaching. *Curriculum Studies, 19,* 317–328.

Oakes, J. (1992). Can tracking research inform practice? Technical, normative, and political considerations. *Educational Researcher, 21* (4), 12–21.

Ornstein, A.C. (1984). Urban demographics for the 1980s: Educational implications. *Education and Urban Society, 16,* 477–496.

Ornstein, A.C., & Levine, D.U. (1989). Social class, race, and school achievement: Problems and prospects. *The Journal of Teacher Education, 40* (5), 17–23.

Pajares, M.F. (1992). Teachers' beliefs and educational research: Cleaning up a messy construct. *Review of Educational Research, 62,* 307–332.

Peterson, P.L., & Barger, S.A. (1985). Attribution theory and teacher expectancy. In J.B. Dusek (Ed.), *Teacher expectancies* (pp. 159–184). Hillsdale, NJ: Lawrence Erlbaum.

Peterson, P.L., & Clark, C.M. (1978). Teachers' reports of their cognitive process during teaching. *American Educational Research Journal, 15,* 555–565.

Peterson, P.L., Fennema, E., & Carpenter, T.P. (1991). Teachers' knowledge of students' mathematics problem-solving knowledge. *Advances in Research on Teaching, 2,* 49–86.

Pflaum, S.W., & Abramson, T. (1990). Teacher assignment, hiring, and preparation: Minority teachers in New York City. *The Urban Review, 22,* 17–31.

Pianta, R.C. (1990). Widening the debate on educational reform: Prevention as a viable alternative. *Exceptional Children, 56,* 306–313.

Pintrich, P.R., & De Groot, E.V. (1990). Motivational and self-regulated learning components of classroom academic performance. *Journal of Educational Psychology, 82,* 33–40.

Pintrich, P.R., Marx, R.W., & Boyle, R.A. (1993). Beyond cold conceptual change: The role of motivational beliefs and classroom contextual factors in the process of conceptual change. *Review of Educational Research, 63,* 167–199.

Pokay, P., & Blumenfeld, P.C. (1990). Predicting achievement early and late in the semester: The role of motivation and use of learning strategies. *Journal of Educational Psychology, 82,* 41–50.

Porter, A.C., & Brophy, J. (1988). Synthesis of research on good teaching and learning. *Educational Leadership, 45* (8), 74–85.

Prawat, R.S. (1992). Teachers' beliefs about teaching and learning: A constructivist perspective. *American Journal of Education,* 354–395.

Richardson, V., Anders, P., Tidwell, D., & Lloyd, C. (1991). The relationship between teachers' beliefs and practices in reading comprehension instruction. *American Educational Research Journal, 28,* 559–586.

Ríos, F.A. (1993). Thinking in urban, multicultural classrooms. *Urban Education, 28,* 245–266.

Rodríguez, R., & Tollefson, N. (1987). Consequences of Costa Rican teachers' attributions for students' failure. *Instructional Science, 16,* 381–387.

REFERENCES

Rolison, M.A., & Medway, F.J. (1985). Teachers' expectations and attributions for student achievement effects of label, performance pattern, and special education intervention. *American Educational Research Journal, 22,* 561–573.

Ross, D.D., & Smith, W. (1992). Understanding preservice teachers' perspectives on diversity. *Journal of Teacher Education, 43,* 94–103.

Rueda, R., & Moll, L.C. (in press). A sociocultural perspective on motivation. In H.F. O'Neil & M. Drillings (Eds.), *Motivation: Research and theory.* Englewood Cliffs, NJ: Erlbaum.

Schultz, G.F. (1993). Socioeconomic advantage and achievement motivation: Important mediators of academic performance in minority children in urban schools. *The Urban Review, 25,* 221–232.

Shavelson, R.J., & Stern, P. (1981). Research on teachers' pedagogical thoughts, judgments, decisions, and behavior. *Review of Educational Research, 51,* 455–498.

Shuell, T.J. (1993). Toward an integrated theory of teaching and learning. *Educational Psychologist, 28,* 291–311.

Shulman, L.S. (1986). Paradigms and research programs in the study of teaching: A contemporary perspective. In M.C. Wittrock (Ed.), *Handbook of research on teaching* (pp. 3–36). New York: Macmillan.

Slavin, R.E., Karweit, N.L., & Madden, N.A. (Eds.) (1989). *Effective programs for students at risk.* Boston: Allyn & Bacon.

Solas, J. (1992). Investigating teacher and student thinking about the process of teaching and learning using autobiography and repertory grid. *Review of Educational Research, 62,* 205–225.

Stevens, F.I. (1993). Opportunity to learn and other social contextual issues: Addressing the low academic achievement of African American students. *Journal of Negro Education, 62,* 227–231.

Swanson, H.L., O'Connor, J.E., & Cooney, J.B. (1990). An information processing analysis of expert and novice teachers' problem solving. *American Educational Research Journal, 27,* 533–556.

Talbert, J.E., McLaughlin, M.W., & Rowan, B. (1993). Understanding context effects on secondary school teaching. *Teachers College Record, 95,* 45–68.

Tharp, R.G., & Gallimore, R. (1988). *Rousing minds to life.* New York: Cambridge University Press.

Trent, S.C. (1992). *Needed: Minorities in educational research and development.* Washington, DC: Council for Educational Development and Research.

Vygotsky, L.S. (1978). *Mind in society.* Cambridge, MA: Harvard University Press.

Weade, G. (1992). Locating learning in the times and spaces of teaching. In H.H. Marshall (Ed.), *Redefining student learning* (pp. 87–118). Norwood, NJ: Ablex.

Weiner, B. (1986). *An attributional theory of motivation and emotion.* New York: Springer-Verlag.

Weiner, B. (1992). Motivation. In M.Alkin (Ed.), *Encyclopedia of educational research* (pp. 860–865). New York: Macmillan.

Weinstein, R.S. (1983). Student perceptions of schooling. *The Elementary School Journal, 83,* 287–308.

Wiley, M.G., & Eskilson, A. (1978). Why did you learn in school today? Teachers' perceptions of causality. *Sociology of Education, 51,* 261–269.

Wilson, W.J. (1987). *The truly disadvantaged: The inner city, the underclass, and public policy.* Chicago: University of Chicago Press.

Winfield, L.F. (1991). Resilience, schooling, and development in African-American youth. *Education and Urban Society, 24,* 5–14.

Winfield, L.F., Johnson, R., & Manning, J.B. (1993). Managing instructional diversity. In P.B. Forsyth & M. Tallerico (Eds.), *City principals: The problems comprising urban school leadership* (pp. 97–130). Corwin Press.

Winfield, L.F. & Manning, J.B. (1992). Changing school culture to accomodate student diversity. In M.E. Dilworth (Ed.), *Diversity in teacher education: New expectations* (pp. 181–214). San Francisco: Jossey-Bass.

Wittrock, M. C. (1986). Students' thought processes. In M.C. Wittrock (Ed.), *Handbook of research on teaching* (pp. 297–314). New York: Macmillan.

Zimmerman, B.J., Bandura, A., & Martinez-Pons, M. (1992). Self-motivation for academic attainment: The role of self-efficacy beliefs and personal goal setting. *American Educational Research Journal, 29,* 663–676.

CHAPTER 2. TEACHERS', ADMINISTRATORS', AND STAFF'S IMPLICIT THINKING ABOUT "AT-RISK" URBAN HIGH SCHOOL LATINO STUDENTS

Anderson, R. (1984). Some reflections on the acquisition of knowledge. *Educational Researcher,* November, 5–10.

Montero-Sieburth, M. (1989). Restructuring teachers' knowledge for urban settings. *Journal of Negro Education, 58* (3), 332–344.

Montero-Sieburth, M. (in press). The effects of schooling processes and practices on potential at-risk latino high school students. In R. Rivera and S. Nieto (Eds.), *Latinos in Massachusetts.* Amherst: University of Massachusetts Press.

Pallas, A. M., Natriello, G., & McDill, E. L. (1989). The changing nature of the disadvantaged population: Current dimensions and future trends. *Educational Leadership, 18* (5), 16–22.

REFERENCES

Peterson, P. (1988). Teachers and students cognitional knowledge for classroom teaching and learning. *Educational Researcher,* No. 17, 5–14.

Ríos, F. (1993). Thinking in urban, multicultural classrooms. Four teachers' perspectives. *Urban Education, 28,* (3), 245–266.

Steinberg, L., Blinde, P. L., & Chan, K. S. (1984). Dropping out among language minority youth. *Review of Educational Research, 54* (1), 113–132.

Tye, B. Benham (1987, December). The deep structure of schooling. *Phi Delta Kappan, 69,* 281–284.

CHAPTER 3. TEACHER THINKING AND PERCEPTIONS OF AFRICAN-AMERICAN MALE ACHIEVEMENT IN THE CLASSROOM

Alexander, K. L., Entwisle, D. R., & Thompson, M. S. (1987). School performance, status relations, and the structure of sentiment: Bring the teacher back in. *American Sociological Review, 52,* p. 665–682.

Allen, W. R. (1985). Black student, White campus: Structural interpersonal, and psychological correlates of success. *Journal of Negro Education, 54*(2), 134–147.

Anderson, M. (1989). Evaluating principals: Strategies to enhance their performance. *Oregon School Study Council Bulletin, 32,* 8.

Babad, E., Bernieri, F., & Rosenthal, R. (1991). Students as judges of teachers' verbal and nonverbal behavior. *American Educational Research Journal, 28* (1), 211–234.

Banks, J. A. (1989). Integrating the curriculum with ethnic content: Approaches and guidelines. In J.A. Banks and C.A. Banks (Eds.), *Multicultural education: Issues and perspectives* (pp. 189–207). Boston: Allyn & Bacon.

Banks, J. A. (1991). Curriculum for empowerment, action, and change. In C.E. Sleeter (Ed.), *Empowerment through multicultural education.* Albany: State University of New York Press.

Bell, C. C., Jr. (1985). Explaining the progressively decreasing scores on Comprehensive Tests of Basic Skills (CTBS) of the school children of the District of Columbia public schools as they progress from elementary school into high school. (ERIC #ED325539, 16 pp.)

Bennett, C. I. (1990). *Comprehensive multicultural education theory and practice* (2nd ed.). Boston: Allyn & Bacon.

Bennett, C., & Harris J. J., III. (1982). Suspensions and expulsions of male and black students. A study of the courses of disproportionality. *Urban Education, 16* (4), 399–423.

Bridges, R. E. (1986). *Black male child development: A broken model. A report on six years of formal observation and study.* Paper presented at the 16th Annual Conference of the National Black Child Development Institute, Miami, FL, October 8–10.

Eagle, E. (1989). *Socioeconomic status, family structure, and parental involvement: The correlates of achievement.* Paper presented at the annual meeting of the American Educational Research Association, San Francisco, CA, March 27–31.

Good, T.L., & Brophy, J.E. (1986). *Looking in classrooms* (1st ed.). New York: HarperCollins.

Good, T. L., & Brophy, J. E. (1991). *Looking in classrooms* (5th ed.). New York: HarperCollins.

Greathouse, B., & Sparling, S. (1993). African American male-only schools. Is that the solution? *Childhood Education,* Spring. 131–132.

Hale-Benson, J. E. (1982). *Black children: Their roots, culture and learning styles* (rev. ed.). Baltimore and London: John Hopkins University Press.

Hammond, R., & Howard, J. P. (1986). Doing what's expected of you: The roots and rise of the dropout culture. *Metropolitan Education, 2,* 53–71.

Hilliard, A. (1982). *Strengths: African-American children and families.* City College of New York: City College Workshop Center.

Hilliard, A. (1989). Teachers and cultural styles in a pluralistic society. *Today: Issues '89* [special edition], January, 5–69.

Johnson, W. R. (1990). Inviting conversations: The Holmes Group and tomorrow's schools. *American Educational Research Journal, 27,* (4), 581–588.

Koehler, V. R. (1988). *Teachers' beliefs about at-risk students.* Paper presented at the Annual Meeting at the American Education Research Association, New Orleans, LA, April.

Kraft, C. L. (1991). What makes a successful black student on a predominantly white campus? *American Educational Research Journal, 28,* (2), 423–443.

Leake, D., & Leake, B. (1992). Islands of hope: Milwaukee's African American immersion schools. *Journal of Negro Education, 61*(1), 24.

Marrett, C. B. (1985). Teacher goals and race/sex equity in mathematics and science education: Final Report. Program Report 85–18. Wisconsin Center for Education Research, Madison. 164 pp.

Ogbu, J. U. (1990). Minority education in comparative perspective. *Journal of Negro Education, 59* (1), 45–55.

Ornstein, A. C., & Levine, D. U. (1989). Social class, race, and school achievement: Problems and prospects. *Journal of Teacher Education, 40* (5), 17–23.

Parlardy, J. (1969). What teachers believe: What children achieve. *Elementary School Journal, 69,* 370–374.

REFERENCES

Rist, R. (1970). Student social class and teacher expectations: The self-fulfilling prophecy in ghetto education. *Harvard Review, 40* (August).

Shade, B. J. (Ed). (1991). *Culture and the educative process.* Springfield, IL: Charles C. Thomas.

Sizemore, B. (1987). *Developing effective instructional programs.* Office of Educational Research and Improvement. Washington, DC. 26 pp.

Sleeter, C.E. (Ed.). (1991). *Empowerment through multicultural education.* Albany: State University of New York Press.

Sleeter, C. E., & Grant, C. A. (1988). *Making choices for multicultural education.* Columbus: Merrill.

Smith, K. L. (1989). *Teacher expectations and minority achievement: A study of Black students in Fairfax County, Fairfax County Schools, Virginia.* Paper presented at the Eastern Educational Research Conference, Savannah, GA, February.

Steward, R. J., & Jackson, J. (1989). Academic persistence and Black university students' perceived personal competencies. (ERIC #ED304512, 16 pp.)

Tempes, F. (1987). *Effective instructional approaches to bilingual education.* Office of Educational Research and Improvement, Washington, DC.

Tracey, T. J., & Sedlacek, W. E. (1985). The relationship of noncognitive variables to academic success: A longitudinal study by race. *Journal of College Student Personnel, 26* (5), 405–410.

Washington, E. D. (1989). A componential theory of culture and its implications for African-American identity. *Equity & Excellence, 24,* (2), 24–30.

Williams, J. (1990). Reducing the disproportionately high frequency of disciplinary actions against minority students. An assessment-based policy approach. *Equity & Excellence, 24* (2), 31–37.

CHAPTER 4. RESISTANCE AND RETHINKING

Bennett, C., Okinaka, A., & Xiao-yang, W. (1988, April). *The effects of a multicultural education course on preservice teacher attitudes, knowledge, and behavior.* Paper presented at the annual conference of the American Educational Research Association, New Orleans, LA.

Clark, C. & Peterson, P. L. (1986). Teachers' thought processes. In M. C. Wittrock (Ed.), *Handbook of research on teaching* (3rd ed.). New York: Macmillan.

Comer, J. (1988). Educating poor minority children. *Scientific American, 259,* 42–48.

Goodlad, J. (1984). *A place called school.* New York: McGraw-Hill.

Grant, C. (in press). The multicultural preparation of U. S. teachers: Some hard truths. To appear in G. K. Verma (Ed.) *Inequality and teacher education: An international perspective.* Bristol, PA: Falmer Press.

Grant, C. A., & Koskela, R. (1986). Education that is multicultural and the relationship between pre-service campus learning and field experiences. *Journal of Educational Research, 79*(4), 197–203.

Grant, C., & Secada, W. (1990). Preparing teachers for diversity. In W. R. Houston (Ed.), *Handbook of research on teacher education* (pp. 403–422). New York: MacMillan.

Grant, C. A., & Sleeter, C. (1986). *After the school bell rings.* Bristol, PA: Falmer Press.

Haberman, M. (1987). *Recruiting and selecting teachers for urban schools.* New York: ERIC Clearinghouse on Urban Education, Institute for Urban & Minority Education.

Hilliard, A. (1991). Do we have the will to educate all children? *Educational Leadership,* 31–36.

Irvine, J. J. (1992). *Black students and school failure.* New York: Praeger.

King, J. (1991). Dysconscious racism: Ideology, identity, and the miseducation of teachers. *Journal of Negro Education, 60*(2), 133–146.

Ladson-Billings, G. (1991). Culturally relevant teaching: The key to making multicultural education work. In C. A. Grant (Ed.), *Research and multicultural education: From the margins to the mainstream.* Bristol, PA: Falmer Press.

Montero-Sieberth, M. (1989). Restructuring teachers' knowledge in urban settings. *Journal of Negro Education, 58*(3), 332–344.

Paine, L. (1988, April). *Orientations towards diversity: What do prospective teachers bring?* Paper presented at the annual meeting of the American Educational Research Association, New Orleans, LA.

Tamayo-Lott, J. (1993, January). Do United States racial/ethnic categories still fit? *Population Today.*

Weinstein, C. S. (1989). Teacher education students' preconceptions of teaching. *Journal of Teacher Education,* 40 (2), 53–60.

Zeichner, K. (1989). Preparing teachers for democratic schools. *Action in Teacher Education,* 11(1), 5–10.

Zimpher, N., & Ashburn, E. (1992). Countering parochialism in teacher candidates. In M. Dilworth (Ed.), *Diversity in teacher education: New expectations.* San Francisco: Jossey-Bass.

CHAPTER 5. TEACHERS' PRINCIPLES OF PRACTICE FOR TEACHING IN MULTICULTURAL CLASSROOMS

Aldenderfer, M. S., & Blashfield, R. K. (1984). *Cluster analysis.* Newberry Park, CA: Sage.

REFERENCES

Anderson-Levitt, K. M. (1984). Teacher interpretation of student behavior: Cognitive and social processes. *The Elementary School Journal, 84*(3), 315–337.

Argyis, C., & Schon, D. (1975). *Theory in practice.* San Francisco: Jossey-Bass.

Bussis, A. M., Chittenden, F., & Amarel, M. (1976). *Beyond surface curriculum.* Boulder, CO: Westview Press.

Calderhead, J. (1983, April). *Research into teachers' and student-teachers' cognitions: Exploring the nature of classroom practice.* Paper presented at the annual meeting of the American Educational Research Association, Montreal, Canada.

Carter, K. (1990). Teachers' knowledge and learning to teach. In W. R. Houston (Ed.), *Handbook of research on teacher education* (pp. 291–310). New York: Macmillan.

Chi, M. T. H., Glaser, R., & Rees, E. (1982). Expertise in problem solving. In R. J. Sternberg (Ed.), *Advances in the psychology of human intelligence* (pp. 7–75). Hillsdale, NJ: Erlbaum.

Clark, C. (1985, May). *Ten years of conceptual development in research on teacher thinking.* Paper presented at the ISATT's Conference, Tilburg, The Netherlands.

Clark, C. M., & Peterson, P. L. (1986). Teachers' thought processes. In M. C. Wittrock (Ed.), *Handbook of research on teaching* (3rd ed.) (pp. 255–296). New York: Macmillan.

Conners, R. D. (1978). *An analysis of teacher thought processes, beliefs, and principles during instruction.* Unpublished doctoral dissertation, University of Alberta, Edmonton, Canada.

Cooper, H. M., Baron, R. M., & Lowe, C. A. (1975). The importance of race and social class information in the formation of expectancies about academic performance. *Journal of Educational Psychology, 67*, 312–319.

Copa, P. M. (1984, April). *Making theory in the first year of teaching.* Paper present at the annual meeting of the American Educational Research Association, New Orleans.

Cortes C. E. (1986). The education of language minority students: A contextual interaction model. In Bilingual Education Office, California Department of Education (Ed.), *Beyond language: Social and cultural factors in schooling language minority students* (pp. 3–34). Los Angeles: Evaluation, Dissemination and Assessment Center, California State University.

Darly, J. M., & Fazio, R. H. (1980). Expectancy confirmation processes arising in the social interaction sequence. *American Psychologist, 35*, 867–881.

Delpit, L. (1988). The silenced dialogue: Power and pedagogy in educating other people's children. *Harvard Educational Review, 58*(3), 280–298.

Duffy, G. (1977). *A study of teacher conceptions of reading.* Paper presented at the National Reading Conference, New Orleans.

Elbaz, F. (1981). The teacher's "practical knowledge": Report of a case study. *Curriculum Inquiry, 11,* 43–71.

Ewan, R. B. (1984). *An introduction to personality theories.* Orlando, FL: Academic Press.

Fransella, F., & Bannister, D. (1977). *A manual for repertory grid technique.* New York: Academic Press.

Garcia, E. (1987, April). *An ethnographic study of teachers implicit theories of evaluation.* Paper presented at the annual meeting of the American Educational Research Association, Washington, DC. (ERIC Document No. 282 853)

Grant, C. A., & Secada, W. G. (1990). Preparing teachers for diversity. In W. R. Houston (Ed.), *Handbook of research on teacher education* (pp. 403–422). New York: Macmillan.

Hernandez, H. (1989). *Multicultural education.* Columbus, OH: Merrill.

Hoy, W., & Rees, R. (1977). The bureaucratic socialization of student teachers. *Journal of Teacher Education, 28*(1), 23–26.

Humphreys, L. G. (1988). Trends in levels of academic achievement of blacks and other minorities. *Intelligence, 12,* 231–260.

Janesick, V. (1977). *An ethnographic study of a teacher's classroom perspective.* Unpublished doctoral dissertation, Michigan State University, East Lansing.

Kelly, G. A. (1955). *The psychology of personal constructs* (2 Vols.). New York: W. W. Norton.

Kohut, S., & Range, D. G. (1979). *Classroom discipline: Case studies and viewpoints.* Washington, DC: National Education Association.

Lortie, D. (1975). *Schoolteacher.* Chicago: University of Chicago Press.

Mancuso, J. C., & Shaw, M. L. G. (1988). *Cognition and personal structure.* New York: Praeger.

Marascuilo, L. A., & Serlin, R. C. (1988). *Statistical methods for the social and behavioral sciences.* New York: W. H. Freeman.

Marcelo, C. (1987, April). *The study of implicit theories and beliefs about teaching in an elementary school teacher.* Paper presented at the American Educational Research Association. Washington, D.C. (ERIC Document No. 281-835).

Marland, P. W. (1977). *A study of teachers interactive thoughts.* Unpublished doctoral dissertation, University of Alberta, Edmonton, Canada.

McNair, K. (1978–1979). Capturing inflight decisions. *Educational Researcher Quarterly, 3*(4), 26–42.

Montero-Sieburth, M. (1989). Restructuring teachers' knowledge in urban settings. *Journal of Negro Education, 58*(3), 332–344.

Munby, H. (1983, April). *A qualitative study of teachers beliefs and principles.* Paper presented at the Annual Meeting of the American Educational Research Association, Montreal. (ERIC Document No. 228-215).

Olson, J. K. (1981). Teacher influence in the classroom. *Instructional Science, 10,* 259–275.

Peterson, P. L., & Barger, S. A. (1984). Attribution theory and teacher expectancy. In J. B. Dusek (Ed.), *Teacher expectancies* (pp. 159–184). Hillsdale, NJ: Erlbaum.

Ríos, F. A. (1992). *Teachers' implicit theories of multicultural classrooms.* Unpublished doctoral dissertation, University of Wisconsin.

Ríos, F. A. (1993). Thinking in urban, multicultural classrooms: Four teachers' perspectives. *Urban Education, 28*(3), pp. 245–263.

Rist, R. C. (1970). Student social class and teacher expectations: The self-fulfilling prophecy in ghetto education. *Harvard Educational Review, 46*(3), 411–451.

Salmon, D., & Lehrer, R. (1989). School consultants implicit theories of action. *Professional School Psychology, 4,* 173–187.

Salmon, D., & Lehrer, R. (1991). Experience and representation of the consultant role: Exploring the implicit theories of school psychology trainers and students. *School Psychology Quarterly, 6*(2), 112–130.

Sattath, S., & Tversky, A. (1977). Additive similarity trees. *Psychometrika, 42,* 319–345.

Schon, D. A. (1983). *The reflective practitioner.* New York: Basic Books.

Schon, D. A. (1987). *Educating the reflective practitioner.* San Francisco: Jossey-Bass.

Semmel, D. S. (1977, April). *The effects of training on teacher decision making.* Paper presented at the annual meeting of the American Educational Research Association, New York City. (ERIC Document No. ED 138 558)

Sleeter, C. E. (1989). Doing multicultural education across the grade levels and subject areas: A case study of Wisconsin. *Teaching and Teacher Education, 5*(3), 189–203.

Sleeter, C. E., & Grant, C. A. (1988). *Making choices for multicultural education: 5 approaches to race, class and gender.* Columbus, OH: Merrill.

Solas, J. (1992). Investigating teacher and student thinking about the process of teaching and learning using autobiography and repertory grid. *Review of Educational Research, 62*(2), 205–225.

Stanic, G. M. A., & Reyes, L. H. (1986, April). *Gender and race differences in mathematics: A case study of a seventh grade classroom.* Paper presented at the annual meeting of the American Educational Research Association, San Francisco. (ERIC Document No. 269 261)

Sue, S., & Padilla, A. (1986). Ethnic minority issues in the United States: Challenges for the educational system. In Bilingual Education Office, California Department of Education (Ed.), *Beyond language:*

Social and cultural factors in schooling language minority students. Los Angeles: Evaluation, Dissemination, and Assessment Center, California State University.

Taylor, P. H. (1970). *How teachers plan their courses.* Slough, Berkshire, England: National Foundation for Educational Research.

U. S. Commission on Civil Rights (1973). *Teachers and students. Report V: Mexican-American education study.* Washington, DC: U. S. Government Printing Office.

Vallacher, R. R., & Wegner, D. M. (1985). *A theory of action identification.* Hillsdale, NJ: Erlbaum.

Wiley, M. G., & Eskilson, A. (1978). What did you learn in school today? Teacher perceptions of causality. *Sociology of Education, 51,* 261–269.

Zeichner, K. M., & Gore, J. M. (1990). Teacher socialization. In W. R. Houston (Ed.), *Handbook of research on teacher education,* (pp. 329–348). New York: Macmillan.

CHAPTER 6. TEACHING WRITING IN A MULTICULTURAL CLASSROOM

Atwell, N. (1987). *In the middle: Writing, reading, and learning with adolescents.* Portsmouth, NH: Heinemann.

Bakhtin, M. M. (1981). *Discourse in the novel. The dialogic imagination: Four essays by M.M. Bakhtin* (M. Holquist, Ed. C. Emerson & M. Holquist, Trans.). Austin, TX: University of Texas Press.

Britzman, D.P. (1992). *The terrible problem of knowing thyself: Towards a poststructuralist view of teacher identity.* Paper presented to the National Conference on Research in the Teaching of English, Chicago.

Delpit, L. (1988). The silenced dialogue: Power and pedagogy in educating other people's children. *Harvard Educational Review, 58* (3), 281–298.

Dyson, A .H. (1986). Staying free to dance with the children: The dangers of sanctifying activities in the language arts curriculum. *English Education, 18* (3), 135–146.

Dyson, A .H. (1991). Viewpoints: The word and the world: Reconceptualizing written language development or do rainbows mean a lot to little girls? *Research in the Teaching of English, 25* (1), 97–123.

Dyson, A. H. (1992a). The case of the singing scientist: A performance perspective on the stages of school literacy. *Written Communication, 9* (1), 3–47.

Dyson, A. H. (1992b). Children's place in the language arts curriculum: Victims, beneficiaries, and critics. *English Education, 24* (1), 3–19.

Elbaz, F. (1990). Knowledge and discourse: The evolution of research on teacher thinking. In C. Day, M. Pope, & F. Denicolo (Eds.), *Insights into teachers' thinking and practice* (pp.15–42). New York: Falmer.

REFERENCES

Ferdman, B. (1990). Literacy and cultural identity. *Harvard Educational Review, 60* (2), 181–204.

Gee, J. P. (1990). *Social linguistics and literacies: Ideology in discourses.* New York: Falmer.

Geertz, C. (1983). *Local Knowledge.* New York: Basic Books.

Hart, S. (1982). Analyzing the social organization for reading in one elementary school. In G. Spindler (Ed.), *Doing the ethnography of schooling* (pp. 411–438). Prospect Heights, IL: Waveland Press.

Irvine, J .J. (1988). *Teacher race as a factor in Black students' achievement.* Paper presented at the American Educational Research Association meeting, New Orleans.

Labov, W., & Fanshel, D. (1977). *Therapeutic discourse: Psychotherapy as conversation.* New York: Academic Press.

Mason City Metropolitan School District. (1990). *Secondary minority student achievement committee report.* Paper prepared for the Mason City Metropolitan Schools, May.

McIntyre, A. (1984). *After virtue.* Notre Dame, IN: University of Notre Dame Press.

Mead, G. H. (1934). *Mind, self and society from the standpoint of a social behaviorist.* Chicago: University of Chicago Press.

Nespor, J., & Barylske, J. (1991). Narrative discourse and teacher knowledge. *American Educational Research Journal, 28* (4), 805–823.

Nystrand, M. (1990). On teaching writing as a verb rather than a noun: Research on writing for high school English teachers. In G. E. Hawisher & A. O. Soter (Eds.), *On literacy and its teaching* (pp. 144–155). Albany: State University of New York Press.

Rose, M. (1989). *Lives on the boundary.* New York: Penguin Books.

Shulman, L. S. (1986). Paradigms and research programs in the study of teaching: A contemporary perspective. In M. Wittrock (Ed.), *Handbook of research on teaching* (3rd ed.) (pp. 3–36). New York: Macmillan.

Sleeter, C. E. (1992). *Keepers of the American dream: A study of staff development and multicultural education.* New York: Falmer Press.

Spradley, J. P. (1979). *The ethnographic interview.* Chicago: Holt, Rinehart & Winston.

Vygotsky, L.S. (1978). *Mind in society: The development of higher psychological processes.* Cambridge: Harvard University Press.

Walkerdine, V. (1990). *Schoolgirl fictions.* London: Verso.

Wertsch, J. V. (1991). *Voices of the mind: A sociocultural approach to mediated action.* Cambridge: Harvard University Press.

Zeichner, K. M., Tabachnick, R., & Densmore, K. (1987). Individual, institutional and cultural influences on the development of teachers' craft knowledge. In J. Calderhead (Ed.), *Exploring teachers' thinking* (pp. 21–59). London: Cassell.

CHAPTER 7. TACIT MESSAGES

Blau, Z. (1981). *Black children/white children: Competence, socialization, and social structure.* New York: Free Press.

Bowers, C., & Flinders, D. (1990). *Responsive teaching.* New York: Teachers College Press.

Clandinin, D. J., & Connelly, F. M. (1987). Teachers' personal knowledge: What counts as "personal" in studies of the personal. *Journal of Curriculum Studies, 19* (6), 487–500.

Clark, C., & Peterson, P. (1986). Teachers' thought processes. In M. Wittrock (Ed.), *Handbook of research on teaching* (3rd ed.) (pp. 255–296). New York: Macmillan.

Cummins, J. (1986). Empowering minority students: A framework for intervention. *Harvard Educational Review, 56,* 18–36.

D'Andrade, R. (1984). Cultural meaning systems. In R. Shweder, & R. LeVine, (Eds.), *Culture theory* (pp. 88–122). Cambridge: Cambridge University Press.

D'Andrade, R. (1985). Cultural meaning systems. In J. Dougherty (Ed.), *Directions in cognitive anthropology.* Urbana: University of Illinois Press.

D'Andrade, R. (1990). Some propositions about the relations between culture and human cognition. In J. Stigler, R. Shweder, & G. Herdt, (Eds.), *Cultural psychology* (pp. 65–129). Cambridge: Cambridge University Press.

Eisenhart, M. (1990). Learning to romance: Cultural acquisition in college. *Anthropology and Education Quarterly, 21*(1), 19–40.

Elbaz, F. (1981). The teacher's practical knowledge: Report of a case study. *Curriculum Inquiry, 11,* 43–71.

Feiman-Nemser, S. & Floden, R. (1986). The cultures of teaching. In M. Wittrock, (Ed.), *Handbook of research on teaching* (3rd ed.) (pp. 505–526). New York: Macmillan.

Gardner, H. (1984). The development of competence in culturally defined domains: A preliminary framework. In R. Shweder, & R. LeVine, (Eds.), *Culture Theory* (pp. 257- 275). Cambridge: Cambridge University Press.

Geertz, C. (1973) *The interpretation of cultures.* New York: Basic Books.

Hamilton, M. L. (1993). Think you can: The influence of culture on beliefs. In C. Day, J. Calderhead, & P. Denicolo (Eds.), *Research on teaching thinking: Understanding professional development.* London: Falmer Press.

Hamilton, M. L., & Fleck, D. (1994, April). *What students see: Reading the implicit and explicit text of the classroom.* Paper to be presented at the American Educational Research Association Conference, New Orleans.

REFERENCES

Heath, S. B. (1983). *Ways with words*. Cambridge: Cambridge University Press.

Heath, S. B. (1986). What no bedtime story means: Narrative skills at home and school. In B. Schieffelin & E. Ochs (Eds.), *Language socialization across cultures* (pp. 97–126). Cambridge: Cambridge University Press.

Holland, D., & Quinn, N. (1987). *Cultural models in language and thought*. Cambridge: Cambridge University Press.

Holland, D., & Skinner, D. (1987). Prestige and intimacy: The cultural models behind Americans' talk about gender types. In D. Holland & N. Quinn (Eds.), *Cultural models in thought and language* (pp. 78–111). Cambridge: Cambridge University Press.

Kay, P. (1987). Linguistic competence and folk theories of language. In D. Holland & N. Quinn, (Eds.), *Cultural models in language and thought* (pp. 67–77). Cambridge: Cambridge University Press.

LeVine, R. (1984). Properties of culture: An ethnographic view. In R. Shweder & R. LeVine (Eds.), *Culture theory* (pp. 67–87). Cambridge: Cambridge University Press.

Lortie, D. (1975). *School teacher*. Chicago: University of Chicago Press.

McLaren, P. (1986). *Schooling as ritual performance*. London: Routledge & Kegan Paul.

Metz, M. (1983). Sources of constructive social relationships in an urban magnet school. *American Journal of Education, 91*, 202–245.

Metz, M. (1986). *Different by design: Politics, purpose and practice in three magnet schools*. London: Routledge & Kegan Paul.

Miller, P. (1986). Teaching as language socialization and verbal play in a white working-class community. In B. Schieffelin & E. Ochs (Eds.), *Language socialization across cultures* (pp. 199–212). Cambridge: Cambridge University Press.

Munby, H. (1983, April). *A qualitative study of teachers' beliefs and principles*. Paper presented at the American Educational Research Association Conference, Montreal, Canada.

Nespor, J. (1987). The role of beliefs in the practice of teaching. *Curriculum Inquiry, 19*(4), 317–328.

Ochs, E., & Schieffelin, B. (1984). Language acquisition and socialization: Three developmental stories and their implications. In R. Shweder & R. LeVine (Eds.), *Culture theory* (pp. 276–322). Cambridge: Cambridge University Press.

Ogbu, J. (1978). *Minority education and caste: The American system in cross-cultural perspective*. New York: Academic Press.

Ogbu, J. (1990). Cultural models, identity, and literacy. In J. Stigler, R. Shweder, & G. Herdt (Eds.), *Cultural psychology* (pp. 520–541). Cambridge: Cambridge University Press.

Ogbu, J. (1991). Low school performance as an adaptation. In M. Gibson & J. Ogbu (Eds.), *Minority status and schooling* (pp. 249–285). New York: Garland Press.

Olson, J.K. (1988). Making sense of teaching: Cognition v. culture. *Journal of Curriculum Studies, 20*(2), 167–169.

Page, R. (1988). Teachers' perceptions of students: A link between classrooms, school cultures, and the social order. *Anthropology and Education Quarterly, 87*(18), 77–99.

Philips, S. (1983). *Invisible culture.* New York: Longman.

Placier, P. (1993). Personal communication.

Price, L. (1987). Ecuadorian illness stories: Cultural knowledge in natural discourse. In D. Holland & N. Quinn (Eds.), *Cultural models in thought and language* (pp. 313–342). Cambridge: Cambridge University Press.

Proposal. (1990). Prepared for submission for private source funding by district central office people for Bradley Renaissance School.

Quinn, N., & Holland, D. (1987). Culture and cognition. In D. Holland & N. Quinn (Eds.), *Cultural models in language and thought* (pp. 3–42). Cambridge: Cambridge University Press.

Russell, T. (1987, April). *Learning the professional knowledge of teaching: Views of the relationship between theory and practice.* Paper presented at American Educational Research Association Conference, Washington, D.C.

Rutter, M., Maughan, B., Mortimore, B., & Oston, J. (1979). *Fifteen thousand hours: Secondary schools and their effects on children.* Cambridge: Harvard University Press.

Sarason, S. (1982). *The culture of the school and the problem of change.* Boston: Allyn & Bacon.

Schieffelin, B., & Ochs, E. (1986). *Language socialization across cultures.* Cambridge: Cambridge University Press.

Shor, I. & Freire, P. (1987). *A pedagogy for liberation.* South Hadley, Massachusetts: Bergin & Garvey.

Shweder, R. (1982). Beyond self-constructed knowledge: The study of culture and morality. *Merrill-Palmer Quarterly, 28,* 41–69.

Sleeter, C. (1992). *Keepers of the American dream.* London: Falmer Press.

Sleeter, C., & Grant, C. (1987). An analysis of multicultural education in the United States. *Harvard Educational Review, 57*(4), 421–444.

Sleeter, C., & Grant, C. (1988). *Making choices for multicultural education.* Columbus, OH: Merrill.

Sleeter, C., & Grant, C. (1991). Mapping terrains of power: Student cultural knowledge versus classroom knowledge. In C. Sleeter (Ed.), *Empowerment through multicultural education* (pp. 49–67). Albany: State University of New York Press.

Tobin, K. (1990, April). *Constructivist perspectives on teacher change.* Paper presented at the annual meeting of American Educational Research Association, Boston.

Tyler, R. (1987). Education reform. *Kappan, 69*(4), 277–281.

REFERENCES

Williams, S. (1987). A comparative study of black dropouts and black high school graduates in an urban public school system. *Education and Urban Society, 19*(3), 311–319.

CHAPTER 8. TEACHERS' CHOICES FOR INFUSING MULTICULTURAL CONTENT

Anderson, R. (1984). Role of the reader's schema in comprehension, learning, and memory. In R. Anderson, J. Osborn, & R. Tierney (Eds.), *Learning to read in American schools: Basal readers and content texts* (pp. 243–252). Hillside, NJ: Erlbaum.

Banks, J. A. (1989). Integrating the curriculum with ethnic content: Approaches and guidelines. In J. A. Banks & C. A. McGee Banks (Eds.), *Multicultural education: Issues and perspectives* (pp. 198–207). Needham Heights, MA: Allyn & Bacon.

Bartlett, F. (1932). *Remembering.* Cambridge: Cambridge University Press.

Bleich, D. (1975). *Reading and feelings: An introduction to subjective criticism.* Urbana, IL: National Council of Teachers of English.

Borland, H. (1963). *When legends never die.* Philadelphia: Lippincott.

Chatman, S. (1978). *Story and discourse.* Ithaca: Cornell University Press.

Darling-Hammond, L. (1990). Instructional policy into practice: "The power of the bottom over the top." *Educational and Evaluation Policy Analysis, 12,* 339–348.

Fenstermacher, G. D. (1986). A philosophy of research on teaching: Three aspects. In M. C. Wittrock (Ed.), *Handbook of research on teaching* (3rd ed.) (pp. 37–49). New York: Macmillan.

Gay, G. (1989). Ethnic minorities and educational equity. In J. A. Banks & C. A. McGee Banks (Eds.), *Multicultural education: Issues and perspectives* (pp. 167–197). Needham Heights, MA: Allyn & Bacon.

Gibson, W. (1960). *The miracle worker.* New York: Bantam.

Good, T. L., & Brophy, J. E. (1990). *Educational psychology: A realistic approach* (4th ed.). New York: Longman.

Good, T. L., & Grouws, D. (1979). The Missouri mathematics effectiveness project: An experimental study in fourth-grade classrooms. *Journal of Educational Psychology, 71,* 335–362.

Goodman, K. S. (1985). Unity in reading. In H. Singer & R. B. Ruddell (Eds.), *Theoretical models and processes of reading* (3rd ed.) (pp. 813–840). Newark, DE: International Reading Association.

Hayden, R. E. (1968). Middle passage. In A. Adoff (Ed.), *I am the darker brother: An anthology of modern poems by Negro Americans.* New York: Macmillan.

Iowa Department of Education (1989). *A guide to developing multicultural, nonsexist education across the curriculum.* Des Moines, IA: Author

Iowa Department of Education (1991). *Multicultural, nonsexist education: Business education.* Des Moines, IA: Author

Iser, W. (1978). *The act of reading: A theory of aesthetic response.* Baltimore: John Hopkins University Press.

LaBerge, D., & Samuels, S. J. (1985). Toward a theory of automatic information processing in reading. In H. Singer & R. B. Ruddell (Eds.), *Theoretical models and processes of reading* (3rd ed.)(pp. 689–718). Newark, DE: International Reading Association.

Martin, R. J. (1991). The power to empower: Multicultural education for student-teachers. In C. E. Sleeter (Ed.), *Empowerment through multicultural education* (pp. 287–297). Albany: State University of New York Press.

Mohlman, G. G., Coladarci, T., & Gage, N. L. (1982). Comprehension and attitude as predictors of implementation of teacher training. *Journal of Teacher Education, 33,* 31–36.

Richardson, V., & Anders, P. (1990). *The role of theory in descriptions of classroom practices.* Paper presented at the annual meeting of the American Educational Research Association, Boston, MA.

Richardson, V., Anders, P., Tidwell, D., & Lloyd, C. (1991). The relationship between teachers' beliefs and practices in reading comprehension instruction. *American Educational Research Journal, 28,* 559–586.

Rosenblatt, L. M. (1991). Literary theory. In J. Floyd, J. M. Jensen, D. Lapp, & J. R. Squire (Eds.), *Handbook of research on teaching the English language arts* (pp. 57–84), New York: Macmillan.

Rumelhart, D. E. (1985). Toward an interactive model of reading. In H. Singer & R. B. Ruddell (Eds.), *Theoretical models and processes of reading* (3rd ed.) (pp. 722–750). Newark, DE: International Reading Association.

Sleeter, C. E., & Grant, C. A. (1993) *Making choices for multicultural education* (2nd ed.). New York: Merrill.

Stallings, J. A., Needels, M., & Stayrook, N. (1979). *The teaching of basic reading skills in secondary schools, phase II and phase III.* Menlo Park, CA: SRI International.

Tidwell D., & Montecinos C. (December, 1993). *Negotiating a mandate: Secondary teachers' understandings and implementations of multicultural education in the language arts.* Paper presented at the annual meeting of the National Reading Conference, Charleston, North Carolina.

Yin, R. K. (1989). *Case study research: Design and methods.* Newbury Park: Sage.

Zeichner, K. M. (1993). *Educating teachers for cultural diversity.* Unpublished manuscript.

CHAPTER 9. TEACHING CONCERNS REVISITED

Anderson, J. A. (1988). Cognitive styles and multicultural education. *Journal of Teacher Education, 39*(2), 2–9.

REFERENCES

Banks, J. A. (1993). Multicultural education: Historical development, dimensions, and practice. In L. Darling-Hammond (Ed.), *Review of research in education* (pp. 3–49). Washington, DC: American Educational Research Association.

Bennett, C., Niggle, T., & Stage, F. (1989). Preservice multicultural teacher education: Predictors of student readiness. (ERIC Document Reproduction Service No. ED 308 161)

Boccia, J. A. (1989). Beginning teachers speak out: A study of professional concerns in the first three years of teaching. (ERIC Document Reproduction Service No. ED 316 555)

Brophy, J. & Evertson, C. M. (1981). *Student characteristics and teaching.* New York: Longman Press.

Brophy, J. and Good, T. (1974). *Teacher-student relationships: Causes and consequences.* New York: Holt, Rinehart and Winston.

Cicchelli, T., & Baecher, R. E. (1987). The use of concerns theory in inservice training for computer education. *Computer Education, 11*(2), 85–93.

Clark, C. M., & Peterson, P. L. (1985). Teachers' thought processes. In Wittrock M.C. (Ed.), *Handbook of research on teaching* (3rd ed.). New York: Macmillan.

Cornbleth, C., and Korth, W. (1980). Teacher perceptions and teacher-student interaction in integrated classrooms. *Journal of Experimental Education 48* 259–263.

Dusek, J. B., & Joseph, G. (1985). The bases of teacher expectancies. In J. B. Dusek (Ed.), *Teacher expectancies.* Hillsdale, NJ: Erlbaum.

Feiman, S., & Floden, R. E. (1980). What's all this talk about teacher development? (ERIC Document Reproduction Service No. ED 189 088)

Feiman, S., & Floden, R. E. (1981). A consumer's guide to teacher education development. (ERIC Document Reproduction Service No. ED 207 970)

Friedman, P. (1976). Comparisons of teacher reinforcement schedules for students with different social class backgrounds. *Journal of Educational Psychology, 68,* 286–292.

Fuller, F. F. (1969). Concerns of teachers: A developmental conceptualization. *American Educational Research Journal, 6*(2), 207–226.

Fuller, F. F., & Bown, O. (1975). Becoming a teacher. In K. Ryan (Ed.), *Teacher education* (pp. 25–52). Chicago: National Society for the Study of Education.

Fuller, F. F., & Case, C. (1972). A manual for scoring the teacher concerns statement. (ERIC Document Reproduction Service No. ED 079 361)

Fuller, F. F., & Parsons, J. S. (1972). Current research on the concerns of teachers. (ERIC Document Reproduction Service No. ED 063 257)

Fuller, F. F., Parsons, J. S., & Watkins, J. E. (1974). Concerns of teachers: Research and reconceptualization. (ERIC Document Reproduction Service No. ED 091 439)

Gay, G. (1994). *At the essence of learning: Multicultural education.* West Lafayette, IN: Kappa Delta Pi.

George, A. A. (1978). *Measuring self, task, and impact concerns: A manual for use of the teacher concerns questionnaire.* Austin: University of Texas Research and Development Center for Teacher Education.

Gunstone, R. F., Slattery, M., Baird, J. R., & Northfield, J. R. (1993). A case study exploration of development in preservice science teachers. *Science Education, 77*(1), 47–73.

Hall, G. E., & Loucks, S. (1978). Teacher concerns as a basis for facilitating and personalizing staff development. *Teacher College Record, 80*(1), 36–53.

Irvine, J. J. (1986). Teacher-student interactions: Effects of student race, sex, and grade level. *Journal of Educational Psychology, 78,* 14–21.

Irvine, J. J. (1990). *Black students and school failure.* New York: Praeger.

Katz, L. G. (1972). Developmental stages of preschool teachers. *Elementary School Journal, 73*(1), 50–54.

Kazelskis, R., & Reeves, C. K. (1987). Concern dimensions of preservice teachers. *Educational Research Quarterly, 11*(4), 45–52.

King, J. E. (1991). Dysconscious racism: Ideology, identity, and the miseducation of teachers. *Journal of Negro Education, 60*(2), 133–146.

Kochman, T. (1981). *Black and white styles in conflict.* Chicago: University of Chicago Press.

Kozol, J. (1992). *Savage inequalities.* New York: Crown.

Ladson-Billings, G. (1991). Beyond multicultural illiteracy. *Journal of Negro Education, 60*(2), 147–157.

Ladson-Billings, G. (1992). I don't see color, I just see children. *Social Studies and the Young Learner, 5*(2), 9–12.

Locke, D. C. (1988). Teaching culturally-different students: Growing pine trees or bonsai trees. *Contemporary Education, 59*(3), 130–133.

Marshall P. L. (1993). Concerns about teaching culturally diverse students. *Kappa Delta Pi Record, 29*(3), 73–75.

Marshall, P. L. (in press). Multicultural teaching concerns: A new dimensions in teacher concerns research? *Journal of Educational Research.*

Marshall, P. L. (1994a). Four misconceptions about multicultural education that impede understanding. *Action in Teacher Education, 16*(3), 10–27.

Marshall, P.L. (1994b). *Toward critical pedagogy in a multicultural education course: A case for the issues exchange.* Manuscript submitted for publication.

McBride, R.E. (1985). The concerns of inservice physical education teachers as compared with Fuller's concern model. (ERIC Document Reproduction Service No. ED 265 122)

REFERENCES

Parsons, J. S., & Fuller, F. F. (1974). Concerns of teachers: Recent research on two assessment instruments. (ERIC Document Reproduction Service No. ED 093 987)

Phillips, M. (1932). Some problems of adjustment in the early years of a teacher's life. *British Journal of Educational Psychology, 2*, 237–256.

Reeves, C., & Kazelskis, R. (1985). Concerns of preservice and inservice teachers. *Journal of Educational Research, 78*(5), 267–271.

Rist, R. C. (1970). Student social class and teacher expectations: The self-fulfilling prophecy in ghetto education. *Harvard Educational Review, 21*(3), 411–450.

Sleeter, C. E., & Grant, C. A. (1994). *Making choices for multicultural education: Race, class, and gender* (2nd ed.). Columbus: Merrill.

Sprinthall, N.A., & Thies-Sprinthall, L. (1983a). The need for theoretical frameworks in educating teachers: a cognitive-developmental perspective. In K. Howey & W. Gardner (Eds.), *The education of teachers: A look ahead.* New York: Longman.

Tanner, D. E. (1982). The early field experience and the preservice teacher's concerns. (ERIC Document Reproduction Service No. ED 234 036)

Thies-Sprinthall, L., & Sprinthall, N.A. (1987). Experienced teachers: Agents for revitalization and renewal as mentors and teacher educators. *Journal of Education, 169*(1), 65–79.

Vasquez, J. A. (1990). Teaching to the distinctive traits of minority students. *The Clearing House, 63*(7), 299–304.

Weinstein, R. & Middlestadt, S. (1979). Student perceptions of teacher interactions with male high and low achievers. *Journal of Educational Psychology, 71*, 421–431.

Washington, V. (1980). Teachers in integrated classrooms: Profiles of attitudes, perceptions and behavior. *The Elementary School Journal, 80*, 193–201.

CHAPTER 10. USING A CONSTRUCTIVIST APPROACH TO CHALLENGE PRESERVICE TEACHERS' THINKING ABOUT DIVERSITY

Aguilar, T. E. (1995). *The development of the multicultural knowledge test.* Unpublished manuscript, University of Nebraska-Lincoln, Lincoln.

Alkove, L., & McCarty, B. (1992). Plaintalk: Recognizing positivism and constructivism in practice. *Action in Teacher Education, 14*(2), 16–22.

Baldwin, J. (1988). A talk to teachers. In R. Simonson & S. Walker (Eds.), *Multicultural literacy: Opening the American mind.* St. Paul: Graywolf.

Banks, J. A. (1993). The canon debate, knowledge construction, and multicultural education. *Educational Researcher, 22*(5), 4–14.

Banks, J. A., & Banks, C. M. (1993). *Multicultural education: Issues and perspectives* (2nd ed.). Boston: Allyn & Bacon.

Baron, R., Tom, D., & Cooper, H. (1985). Social class, race, and teacher expectations. In J. B. Dusek, V. C. Hall, & W. J. Meyer (Eds.), *Teacher expectancies* (pp. 251–270). Hillsdale, NJ: Erlbaum.

Brooks, J. G. (1990, February). Teachers and students: Constructivists forging new connections. *Educational Leadership, 47*(5), 68–71.

Brophy, J. E., & Evertson, C. M. (1981). *Student characteristics and teaching.* New York: Longman.

Brophy, J., & Good, T. (1970). Teachers' communication of differential expectations for children's' classroom performance: Some behavioral data. *Journal of Educational Psychology, 61,* 365–374.

Byrnes, D., & Kiger, G. (1989). Racial attitudes and discrimination: University teacher education students compared to the general student population. *College Student Journal, 22,* 176–184.

Chesher, J. E. (1993). Begging the knowledge question. *Educational Researcher, 22*(9), 5–6.

Cooper, H. M., Baron, R. M., & Lowe, C. A. (1975). The importance of race and social class information in the formation of expectancies about academic performance. *Journal of Educational Psychology, 67*(2), 312–319.

Fosnot, C. (1989). *Enquiring teachers, enquiring learners.* New York: Teachers College Press.

Gay, G. (1983). Why multicultural education in teacher preparation programs. *Contemporary Education, 54*(2), 79–85.

Giroux, H. A. (1988). *Postmodernism, feminism, and cultural politics.* New York: State University of New York Press.

Grant, C.(1985). Race-gender status, classroom interaction and children's socialization in elementary school. In L. Wilkinson & C. Marrett (Eds.), *Influences in classroom interaction.* New York: Academic Press.

Grant, C.A., & Secada, W. G. (1990). Preparing teachers for diversity. In W. R. Houston (Ed.), *Handbook on research on teacher education* (pp. 403–422). New York: Macmillan.

Gudmundsdottir, S. (1991). Pedagogical models of subject matter. In J. Brophy (Ed.), *Advances in research on teaching* (Vol. 2) (pp. 265–304). Greenwich, CT: JAI Press.

Guttman, J., & Bar-Tal, D. (1982). Stereotypic perceptions of teachers. *American Educational Research Journal, 19*(4), 519–528.

Hale-Benson, J. (1982). *Black children: Their roots, culture, and learning styles.* Baltimore: Johns Hopkins University Press.

Hollon, R. E., Anderson, C. W., & Roth, K. J. (1991). Science teachers' conceptions of teaching and learning. In J. Brophy (Ed.), *Advances in research on teaching* (Vol. 2) (pp. 265–304). Greenwich, CT: JAI Press.

REFERENCES

Janesick, V. (1982). Of snakes and circles: Making sense of classroom group processes through a case study. *Curriculum Inquiry, 12,* 161–189.

Jonassen, D. (1991). Objectivism versus constructivism: Do we need a new philosophical paradigm? *Educational Technology, Research and Development, 39*(3), 5–14.

Kagan, D. (1992). Implications for research on teacher belief. *Educational Psychologist, 27*(1), 65–90.

McIntosh, P. (1989, July/August). White privilege: Unpacking the invisible knapsack. *Peace and Freedom, 49*(4), 10–12.

Morine-Dershimer, G. (1988). Premises in the practical arguments of preservice teachers. *Teaching and Teacher Education, 4,* 215–229.

Nieto, S. (1992). *Affirming diversity: The sociopolitical context of multicultural education.* New York: Longman.

Oakes, J. (1985). *Keeping track: How schools structure inequality.* New Haven, CT: Yale University Press.

Pajares, M. F. (1992). Teachers' beliefs and educational research: Cleaning up a messy construct. *Review of Educational Research, 62*(3), 307–332.

Palardy, J. (1969). What teachers believe—what children achieve. *Elementary School Journal, 69,* 370–374.

Prawat, R. S. (1992, May). Teachers' beliefs about teaching and learning: A constructivist perspective. *American Journal of Education, 100*(3), 354–395.

Rennie, L. J. (1989, March). *The relationship between teacher beliefs, management, and organizational processes, and student participation in individualized classrooms.* Paper presented at the annual meeting of the American Educational Research Association, San Francisco.

Rist, R. C. (1970). Student social class and teacher expectations: The self-fulfilling prophecy in ghetto education. *Challenging the myths: The schools, the Blacks, and the poor.* Reprint series #5. Cambridge: Harvard Educational Review.

Ross, D., & Smith, W. (1992). Understanding preservice teachers' perspectives on diversity. *Journal of Teacher Education, 43*(2), 94–103.

Sadker, M., Sadker, D., & Long, L. (1993). Gender and educational equity. In James A. Banks & Cherry A. McGee Banks (Eds.), *Multicultural education: Issues and perspectives* (2nd ed.) (pp. 111–128). Boston: Allyn & Bacon.

Salomon, G. (1979). *The interactions of media, cognition and learning.* San Francisco: Jossey-Bass.

Sleeter, C. (in press). Reflections on my use of multicultural and critical pedagogy when students are white. In C. Sleeter & P. McLaren (Eds.), *Multicultural education and critical pedagogy.* New York: State University of New York Press.

Sleeter, C. E., & Grant, C. A. (1988). *Making choices for multicultural education: Five approaches to race, class, and gender.* New York: Macmillan.

Triandis, H. (1971). *Attitude and attitude change.* New York: Wiley.

CHAPTER 11. LEARNING TO TEACH IN CROSS-CULTURAL SETTINGS

Banks, J., & Banks, C. (1989). *Multicultural education: Issues and perspectives.* Boston: Allyn & Bacon.

Erickson, F. (1987). Transformation and school success: The politics and culture of educational achievement. *Anthropology and Education Quarterly, 18* (4), 335–356.

Kleinfeld, J. (1972). *Effective teachers of Indian and Eskimo high school students.* Fairbanks: University of Alaska Institute of Social, Economic and Government Research, Center for Northern Educational Research.

Ladson-Billings, G., & Henry, A. (1990). Blurring the borders: Voices of African liberatory pedagogy in the United States and Canada. *Journal of Education, 172* (2), 72–88.

McDiarmid, G. W. (1992). What to do about differences? A study of multicultural education for teacher trainees in the Los Angeles Unified School District. *Journal of Teacher Education, 43* (2), 83–93.

Paine, L. (1990). *Orientation towards diversity: What do prospective teachers bring?* (Research Report 89–9). East Lansing, MI: National Center for Research on Teacher Education.

Ross, D., & Smith, W. (1992). Understanding preservice teachers' perspectives on diversity. *Journal of Teacher Education, 43* (2), 94–103.

Weinstein, C. (1989). Teacher education students' preconceptions of teaching. *Journal of Teacher Education, 40* (2), 53–60.

Zeichner, K. (1993). *Educating teachers for cultural diversity.* East Lansing, MI: National Center for Research on Teacher Education.

Zimpher, N. & Ashburn, E. (1992). Countering parochialism in teacher candidates. In M. Dilworth (Ed.), *Diversity in teacher education: New expectations* (pp. 40–62). San Francisco: Jossey-Bass.

CHAPTER 12. COALITION BUILDING AS A MEANS FOR CHANGING TEACHERS' CULTURAL KNOWLEDGE

Banks, C. M. (1992). The leadership challenge in multicultural education. In C. Diaz (Ed.), *Multicultural education for the 21st century* (pp. 204–213). Washington, DC: National Education Association.

Boyle, M. (1982). *Teaching in a desegregated and mainstreamed school: A study of the affirmation of human diversity.* Unpublished doctoral dissertation, University of Wisconsin-Madison.

REFERENCES

Boyle-Baise, M. (in press). The Coalition For Education That Is Multicultural: A network of advocates for educational equity. In R. Martin (Ed.), *On equal terms: Approaches to dealing with issues of race, class, and gender in the classroom.* New York: State University of New York Press.

Denzin, N. K. (1978). *Sociological methods: A source book.* New York: McGraw-Hill.

Eisner, E. W. (1977). On the uses of educational connoisseurship and criticism for evaluating classroom life. *Teachers College Record, 78*(3), 345–358.

Gay, G. (1977). Curriculum for multicultural teacher education. In F. J. Klassen and D. M. Gollnick (Eds.), *Pluralism and the American teacher: Issues and case studies* (pp. 31–62). Washington, DC: American Association of Colleges for Teacher Education.

Glesne, C., & Peshkin, A. (1992). *Becoming qualitative researchers: An introduction.* New York: Longman.

Grant, C. A., & Grant, G. W. (1985). Staff development and education that is multicultural: A study of an in-service institute for teachers and principals. *British Journal of In-service Education, 12*(1), 6–18.

Grant, C. A., & Melnick, S. L. (1978). Multicultural perspectives of curriculum development and their relationship to in-service education. In R. A. Edelfelt & E. B. Smith (Eds.), *Breakaway to multidimensional approaches: Integrating curriculum development and in-service education* (pp. 81–100). Washington, DC: American Association of Colleges for Teacher Education.

Hawley, W. D., Crain, R. L., Russell, C. H., Smylie, M. A., Fernandez, R. R., Schofield, J. W., Tompkins, R., Trent, W. T., & Zlotnik, M. S. (1983). *Strategies for effective desegregation: Lessons from research.* Lexington, MA: Lexington Books.

King, N. J. (1980). *Staff development programs in desegregated settings.* Santa Monica, CA: Rand.

Kouzes, J. M., & Posner, B. Z. (1987). *The leadership challenge: How to get extraordinary things done in organizations.* San Francisco: Jossey-Bass.

Ladson-Billings, G. (1989, February). *Like lightning in a bottle: Attempting to capture the pedagogical excellence of successful teachers of black students.* Paper presented at the Tenth Annual Ethnography in Education Research Forum, Philadelphia, PA.

Lieberman, A., & Miller, L. (1990). Teacher development in professional practice schools. *Teachers College Record, 92*(1), 107–122.

Moll, L. (1988). Some key issues in teaching Latino students. *Language Arts, 65*(5), 465–472.

Nickolai-Mays, S., & Davis, J. L. (1986). In-service training teachers in multicultural urban schools: A systematic model. *Urban Education, 21*(2), 169–179.

Pelto, J., & Pelto, G. H. (1978). *Anthropological research: The structure of inquiry.* London: Cambridge University Press.

Rosenholtz, S. (1989). *Teachers' workplace.* New York: Longman.

Sarason, S. B. (1993). *The case for change: Rethinking the preparation of educators.* San Francisco: Jossey-Bass.

Sergiovanni, T. J. (1992). *Moral leadership: Getting to the heart of school improvement.* San Francisco: Jossey-Bass.

Sleeter, C. E. (1992). *Keepers of the American dream: A study of staff development and multicultural education.* London: Falmer Press.

Spradley, J. P., & McCurdy, D. W. (1972). *The cultural experience.* Chicago: Science Research Associates.

Washington, V. (1981). Impact of antiracism/multicultural education training on elementary teachers' attitudes and classroom behavior. *Journal of Education, 81*(3), 186–192.

CONCLUSION. NEW DIRECTIONS IN TEACHER THINKING

Banks, J. A. (1992). *Teaching strategies for ethnic studies (5th ed.).* Boston: Allyn & Bacon.

Banks, J. A., & Banks, C. A. M. (1993). *Multicultural education: Issues and perspectives.* Boston: Allyn & Bacon.

Davidman, L., & Davidman, P. T. (1994). *Teaching with a multicultural perspective.* White Plains, NY: Longman Press.

Elbaz, F. (1990). Knowledge and discourse: The evolution of research on teacher thinking. In C. Day, M. Pope & F. Denicols (Eds.), *Insights into teacher's thinking and practice* (pp. 15–42). New York: Falmer Press.

Getzels, J. W., & Guba, E. G. (1957). Social behavior and the administrative process. *School Review, 65,* 429–433

Grant, C. A. (1994). *Multicultural education for the twenty-first century: Proceedings of the second annual meeting, National Association for Multicultural Education, February 13–16, 1992.* Morristown, NJ: Silver Burdett Ginn.

Hall, G. E. and Hord, S. M. (1987). *Change in schools: Facilitating the process.* Albany: State University of New York Press.

Hilliard, A. (1991). Do we have the will to educate all children? *Educational Leadership,* 31–36

Holland, D., & Quinn, N. (1987). *Cultural models in language and thought.* Cambridge: Cambridge University Press.

Locke, D. (1988). Teaching culturally different students: Growing pine trees or bonsai trees? *Contemporary Education, 59*(1), 130–133.

Locke, D. C. (1992). *Increasing multicultural understanding: A comprehensive model.* Newbury Park, CA: Sage.

Mungazi, D. (1993). *Educational policy and national character.* Westport, CT: Praeger Publishers.

REFERENCES

Porter, A. C., & Brophy, J. (1988). Synthesis of research on good teaching: Insights from the work of the Institute for Research on Teaching. *Educational Leadership, 45*(8), 74–85.

Sleeter, C. E., & C. A. Grant. (1988). *Making choices for multicultural education: Five approaches to race, class and gender.* Columbus, OH: Merrill.

Tafoya, T. (1989). "Coyote's eyes: Native cognition styles." *Journal of American Indian Education,* Special Issue, August, 29–42.

Whitehorse, D. (1992). *Cultural identification and institutional character: Retention factors for American Indian students in higher education.* Ann Arbor: Dissertation Abstracts International (UMI).

INDEX

INDEX

INDEX

urban schools (See also, students, minority)
and urbanicity, 33–34
causes of differential student outcomes, by ethnicity, 35
critique of research on, 38
described, 23, 35–36, 57
disconnected to teacher thinking, 24
questions to consider, 39
teacher thinking in, 37–38
teachers in, 36–37

V

Vallacher, R. R., 130, 137
Vasquez, J. A., 245
Voelkl, K. E., 36
Voss, J. F., 9
Vygotsky, L. S., 39, 152

W

Walker, C., 47
Walkerdine, V., 179–180
Walter, D., 47–48, 344
Washington, E. D., 87, 336
Washington, V., 245, 309
Watkins, J. E., 241
Weade, G., 45
Wegner, D. M., 130, 137
Weiner, B., 27, 28

Weinstein, C. S., 126, 283
Weinstein, R. S., 44, 239
Wertsch, J. V., 180
Whitehorse, D., 330
Whorton, D., 47, 47–48, 344
Wiley, M. G., 29, 133
Williams, J., 86
Williams, S., 187
Wilson, T. C., 48
Wilson, W. J., 23, 33, 34, 39
Winfield, L. F., 35, 38, 39, 43, 48, 344
Wittrock, M. C., 3, 344
Wright, B. C., 5

X

Xiao-yang, W., 104

Y

Yin, R. K., 234

Z

Zeichner, K. M., 4, 5, 104, 139, 152, 234, 236, 285
Zigler, E., 48
Zimmerman, B. J., 49
Zimpher, N., 105, 282
Zlotnik, M. S., 309